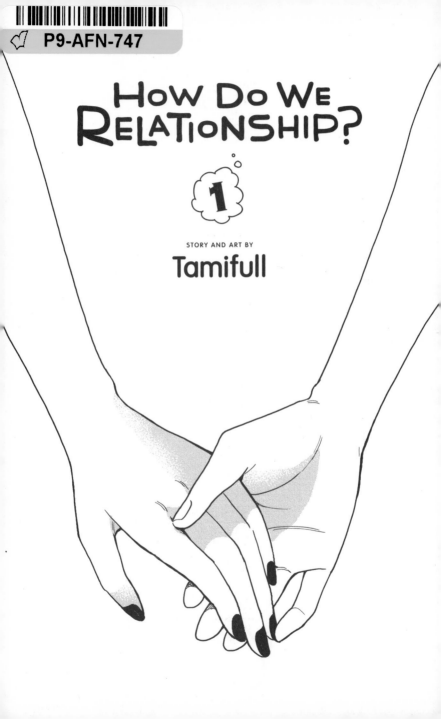

HOW DO WE RELATIONSHIP?

1

STORY AND ART BY

Tamifull

Contents.

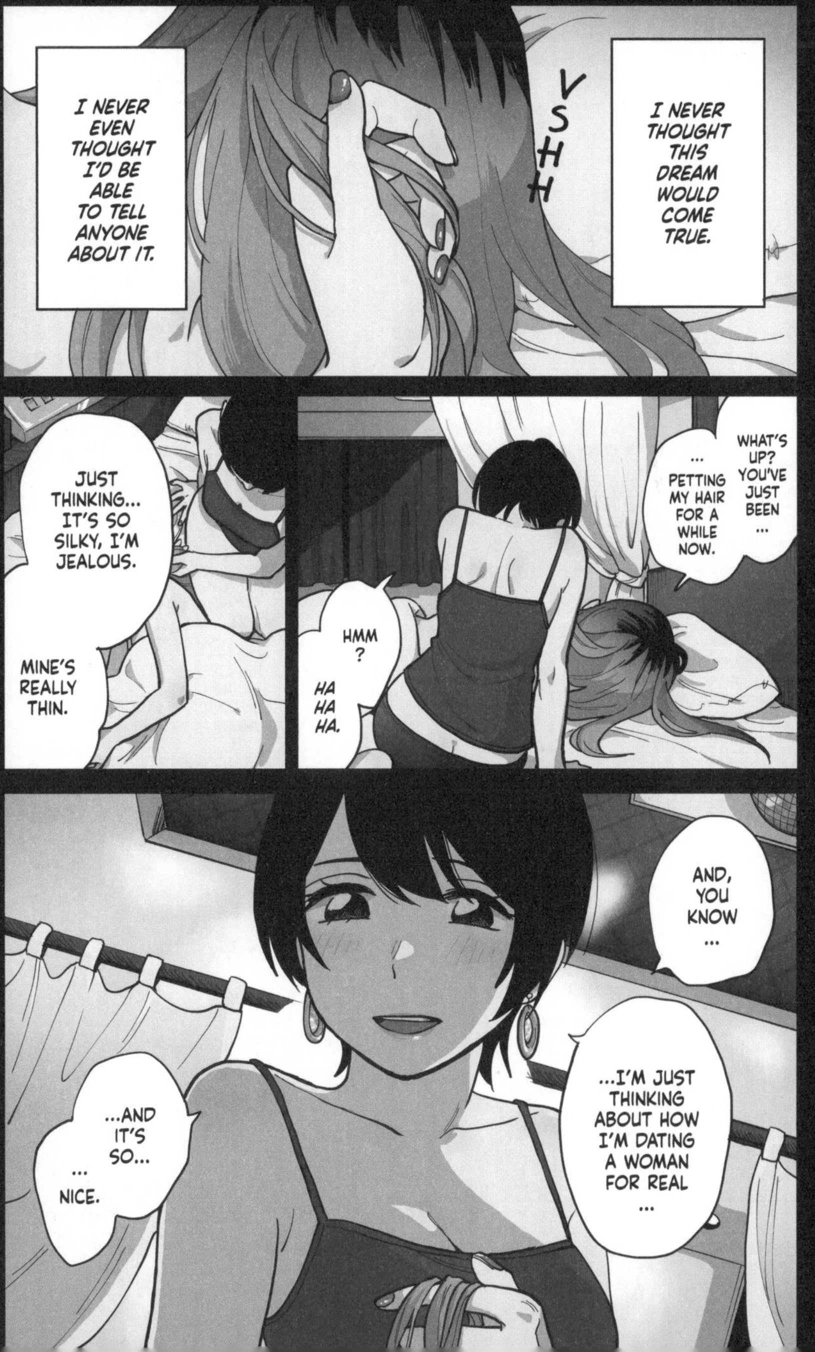
I NEVER THOUGHT THIS DREAM WOULD COME TRUE.
VSHH
I NEVER EVEN THOUGHT I'D BE ABLE TO TELL ANYONE ABOUT IT.
WHAT'S UP? YOU'VE JUST BEEN ...
... PETTING MY HAIR FOR A WHILE NOW.
HMM? HA HA HA.
JUST THINKING... IT'S SO SILKY, I'M JEALOUS.
MINE'S REALLY THIN.
AND, YOU KNOW ...
...I'M JUST THINKING ABOUT HOW I'M DATING A WOMAN FOR REAL ...
...AND IT'S SO... ... NICE.

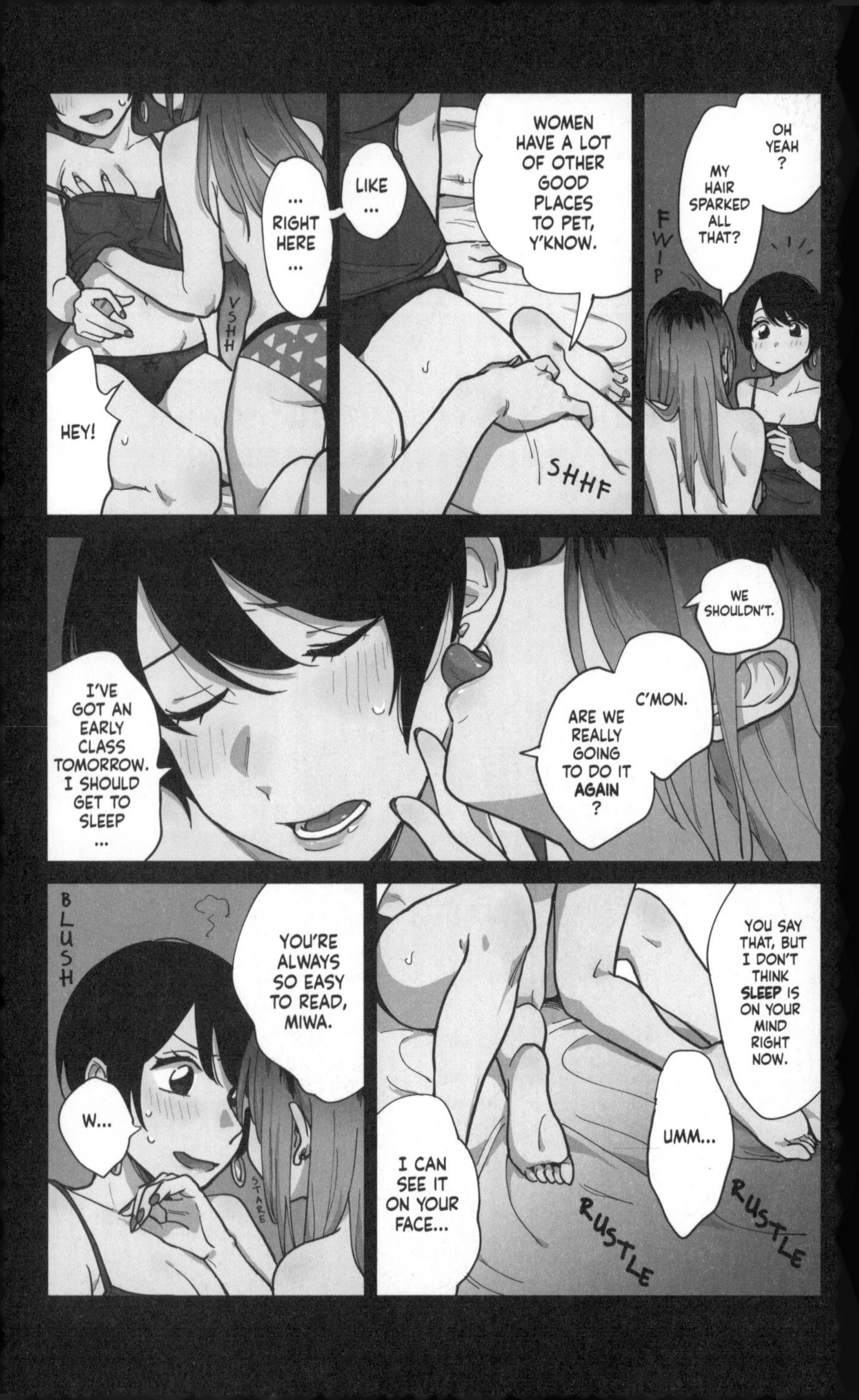
OH YEAH?
MY HAIR SPARKED ALL THAT?
FWIP
WOMEN HAVE A LOT OF OTHER GOOD PLACES TO PET, Y'KNOW.
LIKE ...
SHHF
... RIGHT HERE ...
VSHH
HEY!
WE SHOULDN'T.
C'MON.
ARE WE REALLY GOING TO DO IT **AGAIN**?
I'VE GOT AN EARLY CLASS TOMORROW. I SHOULD GET TO SLEEP ...
YOU SAY THAT, BUT I DON'T THINK **SLEEP** IS ON YOUR MIND RIGHT NOW.
UMM...
RUSTLE
RUSTLE
I CAN SEE IT ON YOUR FACE...
YOU'RE ALWAYS SO EASY TO READ, MIWA.
BLUSH
W...
STARE

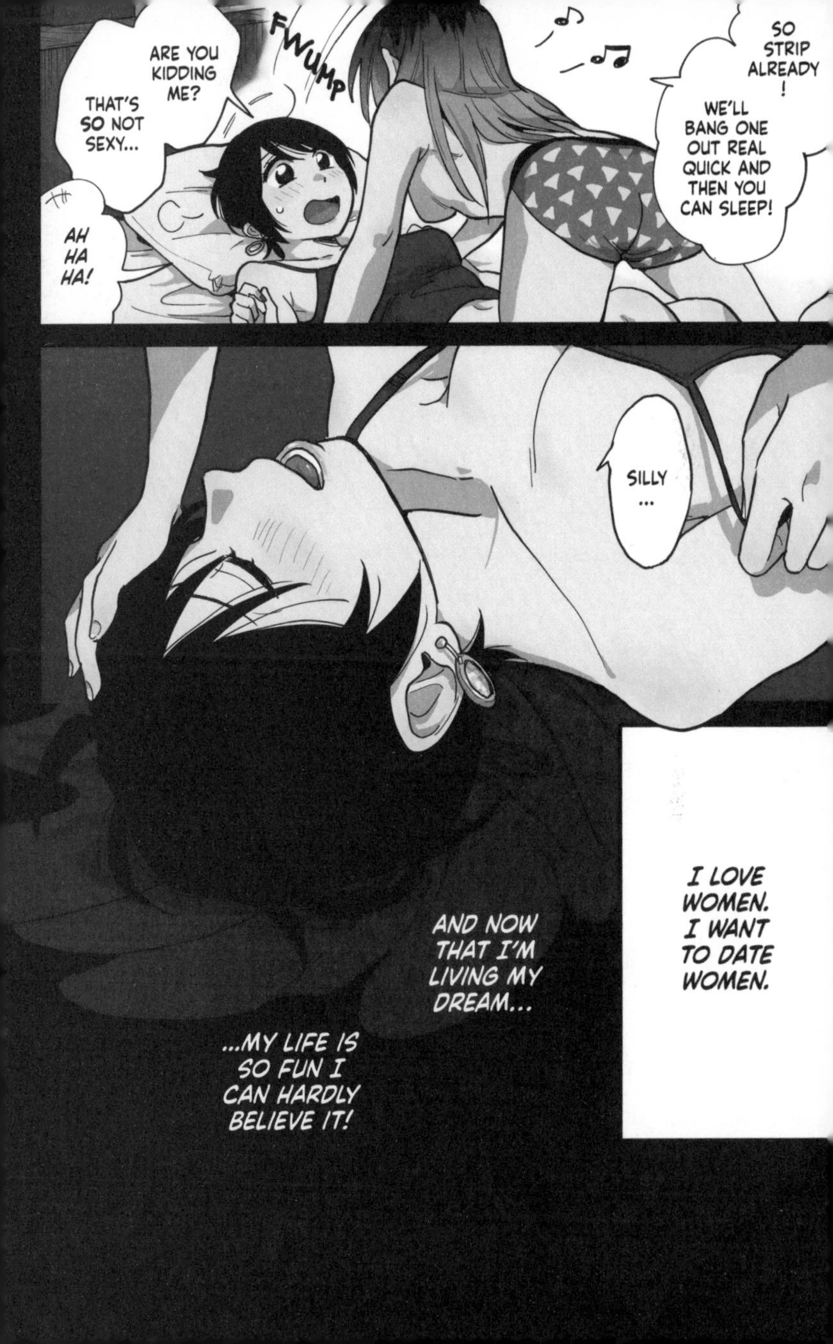
SO STRIP ALREADY!
WE'LL BANG ONE OUT REAL QUICK AND THEN YOU CAN SLEEP!
FWUMP
ARE YOU KIDDING ME?
THAT'S SO NOT SEXY...
AH HA HA!
SILLY ...
I LOVE WOMEN. I WANT TO DATE WOMEN.
AND NOW THAT I'M LIVING MY DREAM...
...MY LIFE IS SO FUN I CAN HARDLY BELIEVE IT!

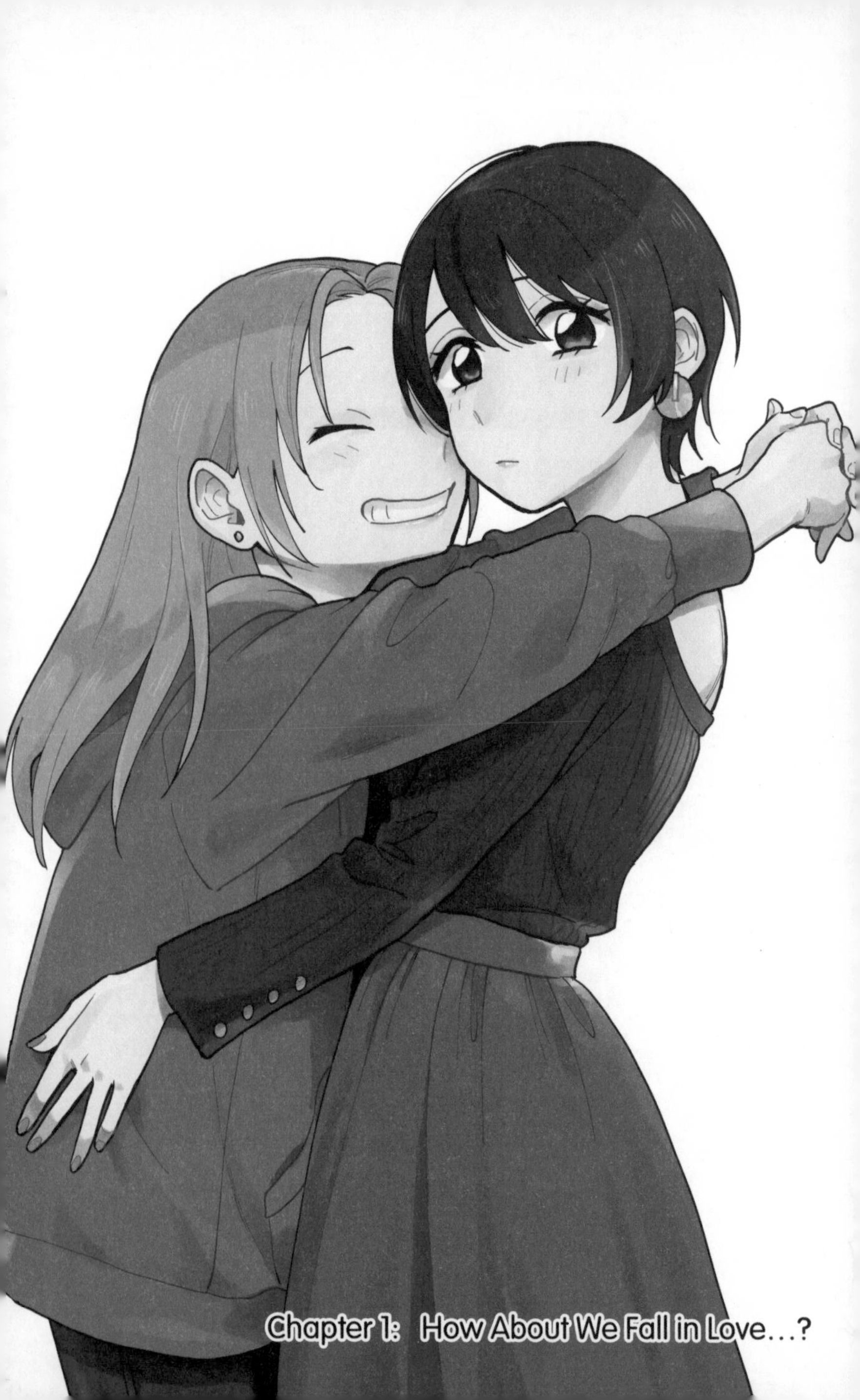

Chapter 1: How About We Fall in Love…?

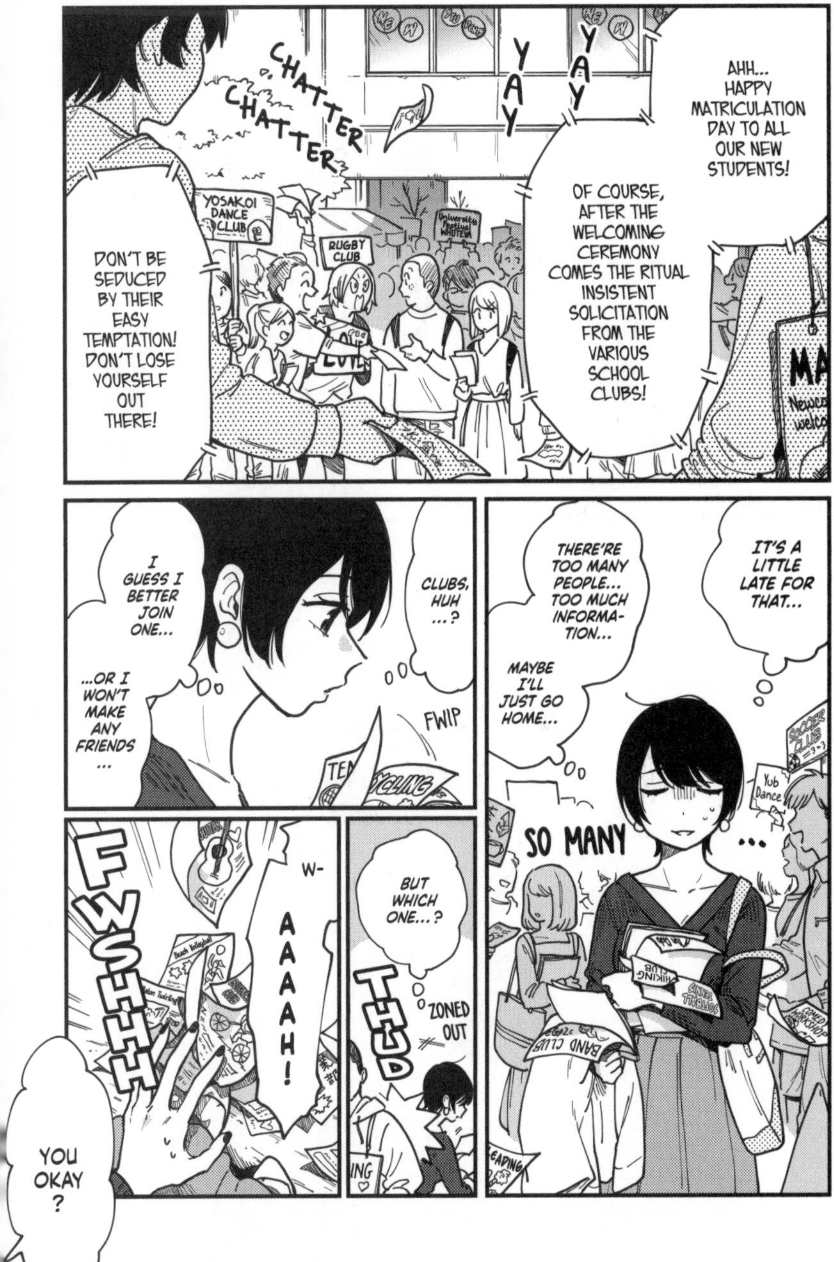
AHH... HAPPY MATRICULATION DAY TO ALL OUR NEW STUDENTS!
OF COURSE, AFTER THE WELCOMING CEREMONY COMES THE RITUAL INSISTENT SOLICITATION FROM THE VARIOUS SCHOOL CLUBS!
YAY
YAY
CHATTER
CHATTER
YOSAKOI DANCE CLUB
RUGBY CLUB
DON'T BE SEDUCED BY THEIR EASY TEMPTATION! DON'T LOSE YOURSELF OUT THERE!
IT'S A LITTLE LATE FOR THAT...
THERE'RE TOO MANY PEOPLE... TOO MUCH INFORMA-TION...
MAYBE I'LL JUST GO HOME...
SO MANY
...
SOCCER CLUB
Yub Dance
HIKING CLUB
SOFTBALL TENNIS
BAND CLUB
CLUBS, HUH ...?
I GUESS I BETTER JOIN ONE...
...OR I WON'T MAKE ANY FRIENDS ...
FWIP
BUT WHICH ONE...?
THUD
ZONED OUT
W-
AAAAAH!
FWSHHH
Beach Volleyball
Baton Twirling
YOU OKAY ?

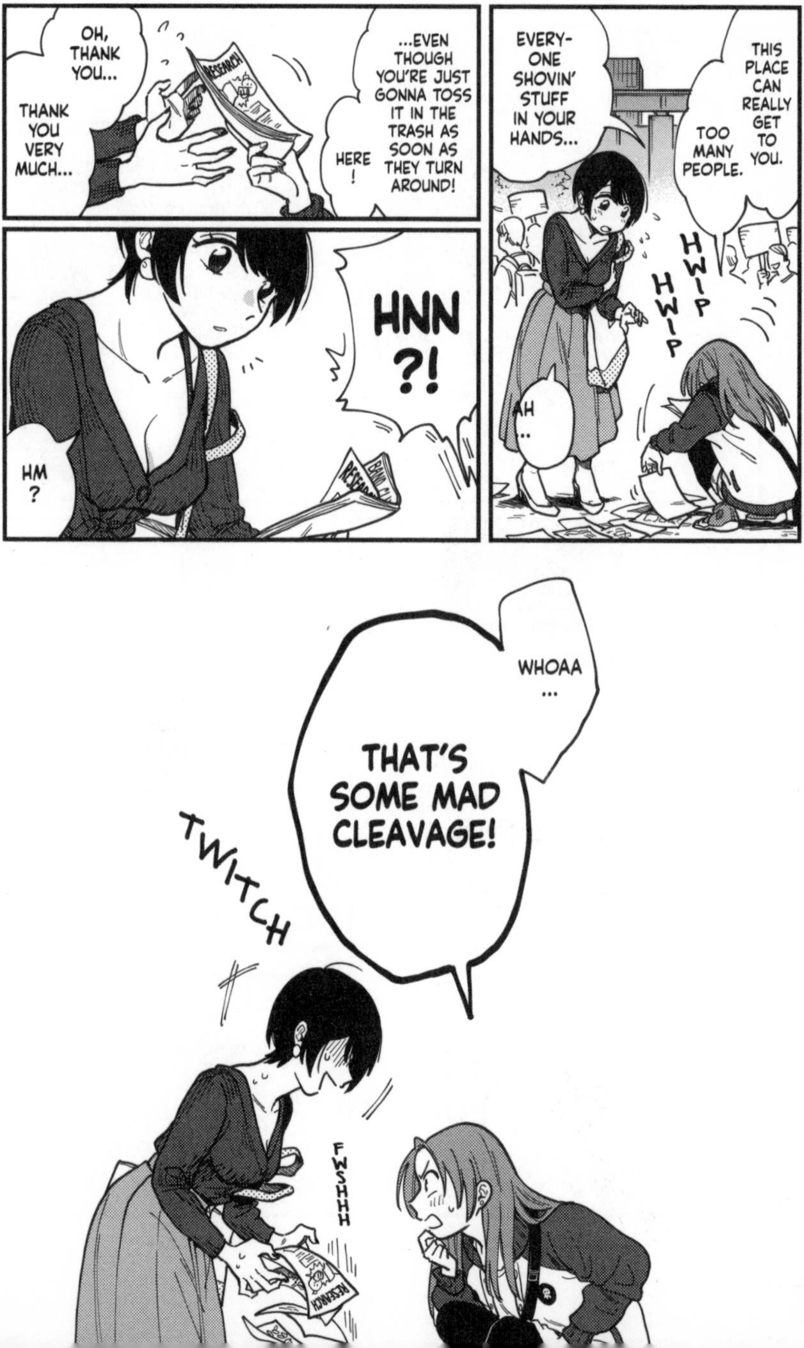
THIS PLACE CAN REALLY GET TO YOU.
TOO MANY PEOPLE.
EVERY-ONE SHOVIN' STUFF IN YOUR HANDS...
HWIP
HWIP
AH...
...EVEN THOUGH YOU'RE JUST GONNA TOSS IT IN THE TRASH AS SOON AS THEY TURN AROUND!
HERE!
OH, THANK YOU...
THANK YOU VERY MUCH...
RESEARCH
HNN?!
HM?
WHOAA...
THAT'S SOME MAD CLEAVAGE!
TWITCH
FWSHHH
RESEARCH

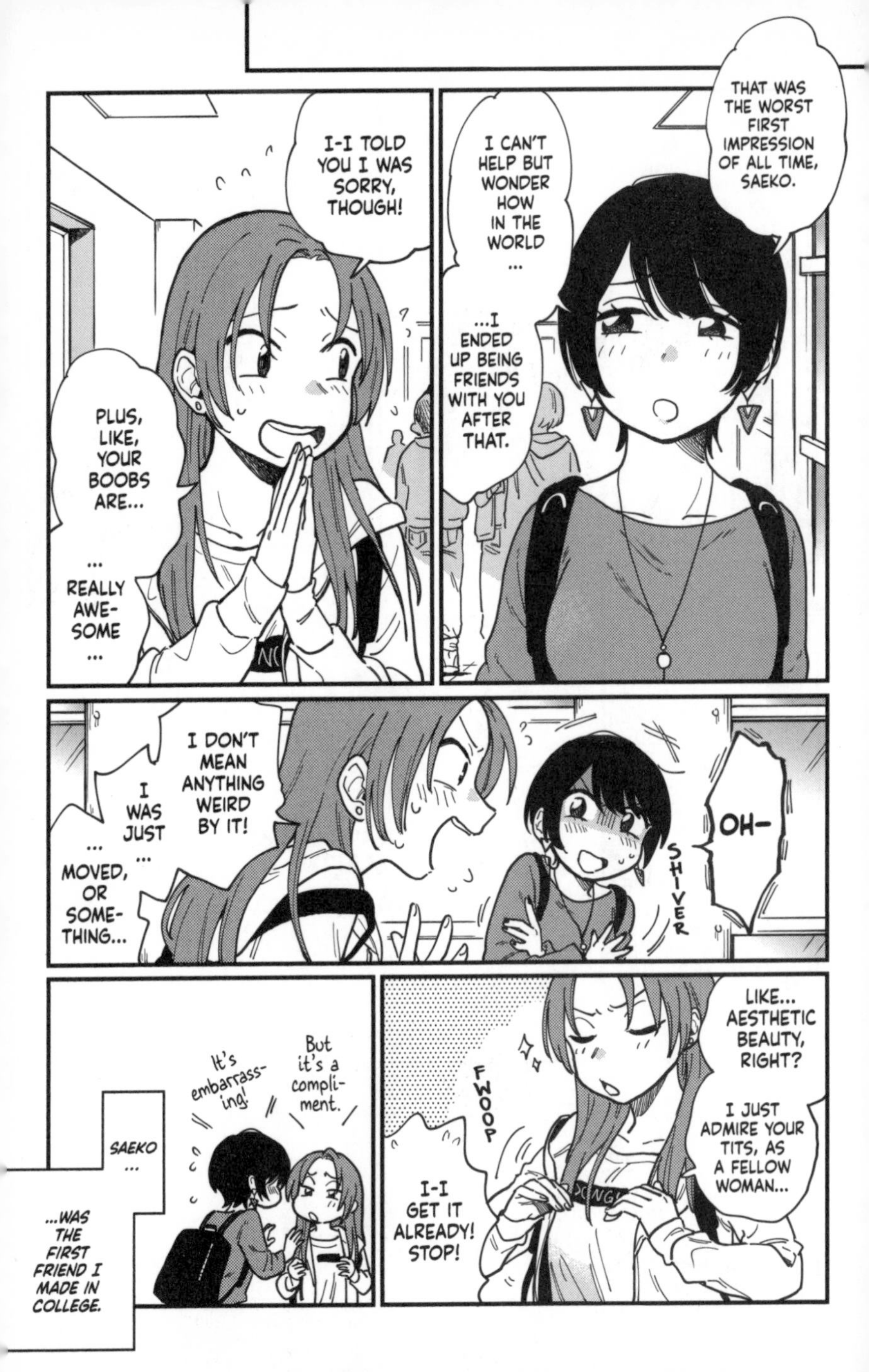
THAT WAS THE WORST FIRST IMPRESSION OF ALL TIME, SAEKO.
I CAN'T HELP BUT WONDER HOW IN THE WORLD ...
...I ENDED UP BEING FRIENDS WITH YOU AFTER THAT.
I-I TOLD YOU I WAS SORRY, THOUGH!
PLUS, LIKE, YOUR BOOBS ARE...
... REALLY AWE-SOME ...
OH–
SHIVER
I DON'T MEAN ANYTHING WEIRD BY IT!
I WAS JUST ... MOVED, OR SOME-THING...
LIKE... AESTHETIC BEAUTY, RIGHT?
I JUST ADMIRE YOUR TITS, AS A FELLOW WOMAN...
FWOOP
I-I GET IT ALREADY! STOP!
But it's a compli-ment.
It's embarrass-ing!
SAEKO ...
...WAS THE FIRST FRIEND I MADE IN COLLEGE.

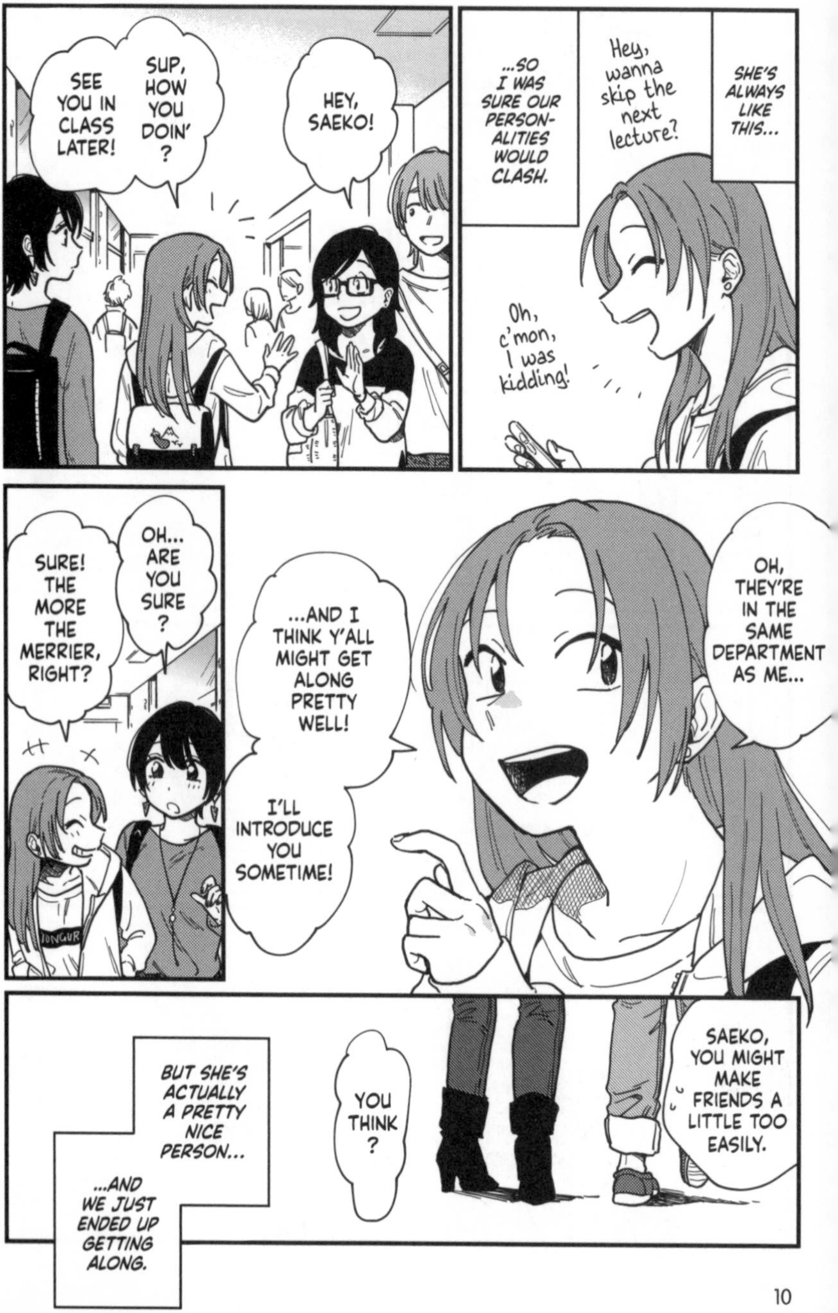
SHE'S ALWAYS LIKE THIS...
Hey, wanna skip the next lecture?
...SO I WAS SURE OUR PERSON-ALITIES WOULD CLASH.
Oh, c'mon, I was kidding!
HEY, SAEKO!
SUP, HOW YOU DOIN'?
SEE YOU IN CLASS LATER!
OH, THEY'RE IN THE SAME DEPARTMENT AS ME...
...AND I THINK Y'ALL MIGHT GET ALONG PRETTY WELL!
I'LL INTRODUCE YOU SOMETIME!
OH... ARE YOU SURE?
SURE! THE MORE THE MERRIER, RIGHT?
SAEKO, YOU MIGHT MAKE FRIENDS A LITTLE TOO EASILY.
YOU THINK?
BUT SHE'S ACTUALLY A PRETTY NICE PERSON...
...AND WE JUST ENDED UP GETTING ALONG.

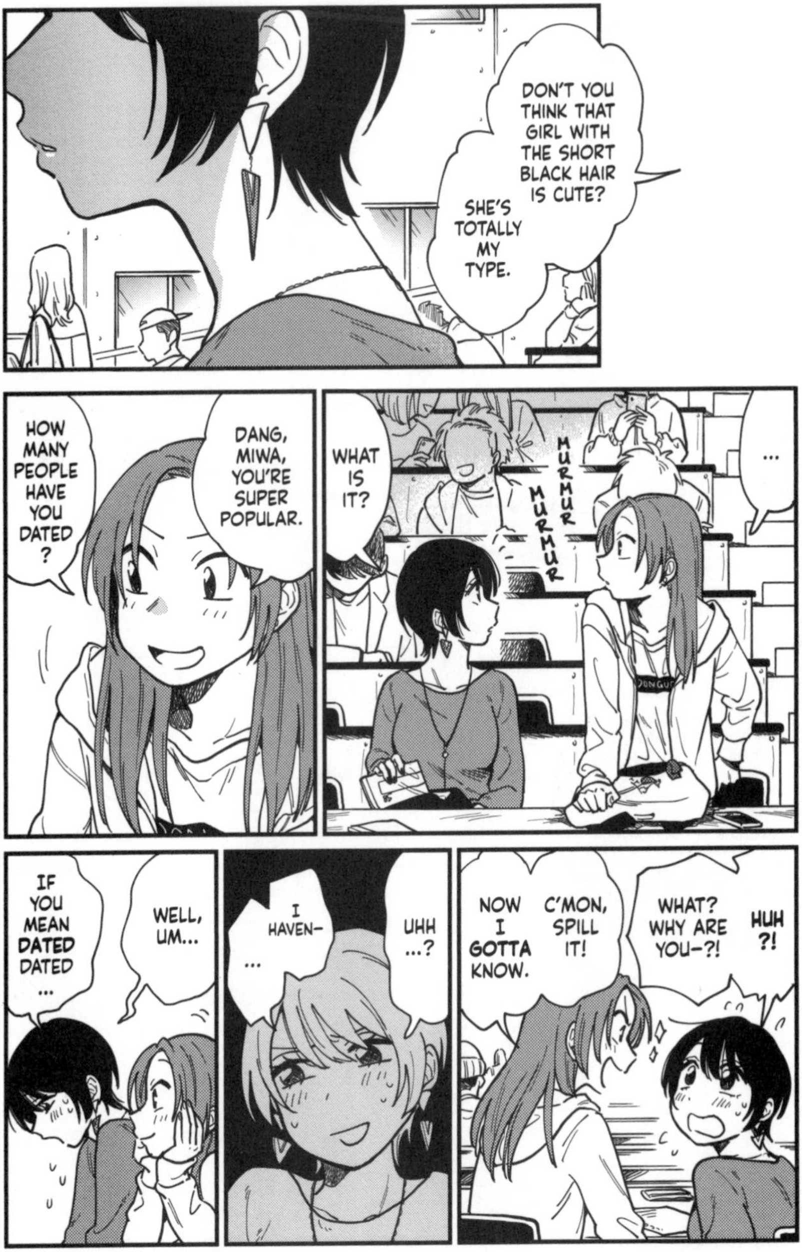
DON'T YOU THINK THAT GIRL WITH THE SHORT BLACK HAIR IS CUTE?
SHE'S TOTALLY MY TYPE.
...
WHAT IS IT?
MURMUR MURMUR
DANG, MIWA, YOU'RE SUPER POPULAR.
HOW MANY PEOPLE HAVE YOU DATED?
HUH ?!
WHAT? WHY ARE YOU-?!
C'MON, SPILL IT!
NOW I GOTTA KNOW.
UHH ...?
I HAVEN- ...
WELL, UM...
IF YOU MEAN DATED DATED ...

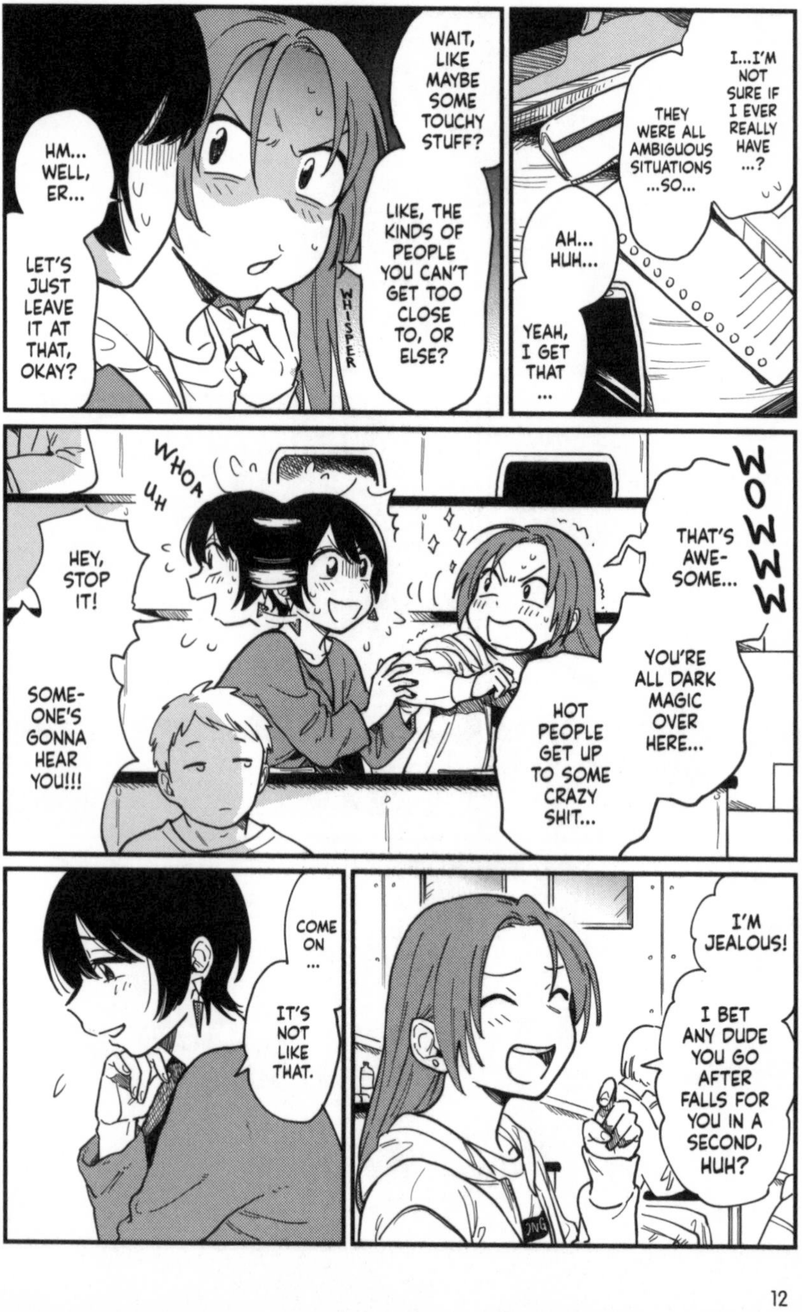
I...I'M NOT SURE IF I EVER REALLY HAVE ...?
THEY WERE ALL AMBIGUOUS SITUATIONS ...SO...
AH... HUH...
YEAH, I GET THAT ...
WAIT, LIKE MAYBE SOME TOUCHY STUFF?
LIKE, THE KINDS OF PEOPLE YOU CAN'T GET TOO CLOSE TO, OR ELSE?
WHISPER
HM... WELL, ER...
LET'S JUST LEAVE IT AT THAT, OKAY?
WOWWW
THAT'S AWE-SOME...
YOU'RE ALL DARK MAGIC OVER HERE...
HOT PEOPLE GET UP TO SOME CRAZY SHIT...
WHOA
UH
HEY, STOP IT!
SOME-ONE'S GONNA HEAR YOU!!!
I'M JEALOUS!
I BET ANY DUDE YOU GO AFTER FALLS FOR YOU IN A SECOND, HUH?
COME ON ...
IT'S NOT LIKE THAT.

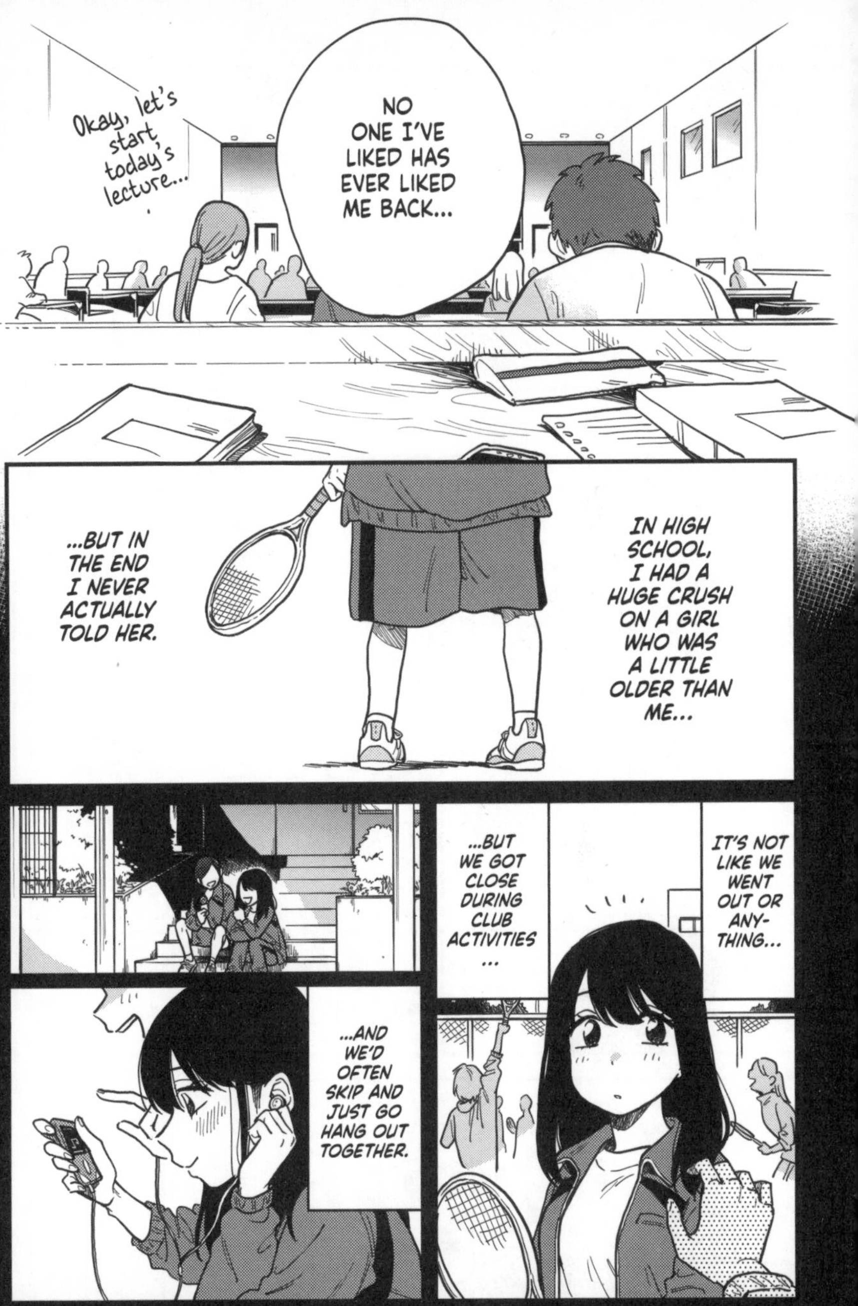
NO ONE I'VE LIKED HAS EVER LIKED ME BACK...
Okay, let's start today's lecture...
IN HIGH SCHOOL, I HAD A HUGE CRUSH ON A GIRL WHO WAS A LITTLE OLDER THAN ME...
...BUT IN THE END I NEVER ACTUALLY TOLD HER.
IT'S NOT LIKE WE WENT OUT OR ANY-THING...
...BUT WE GOT CLOSE DURING CLUB ACTIVITIES ...
...AND WE'D OFTEN SKIP AND JUST GO HANG OUT TOGETHER.

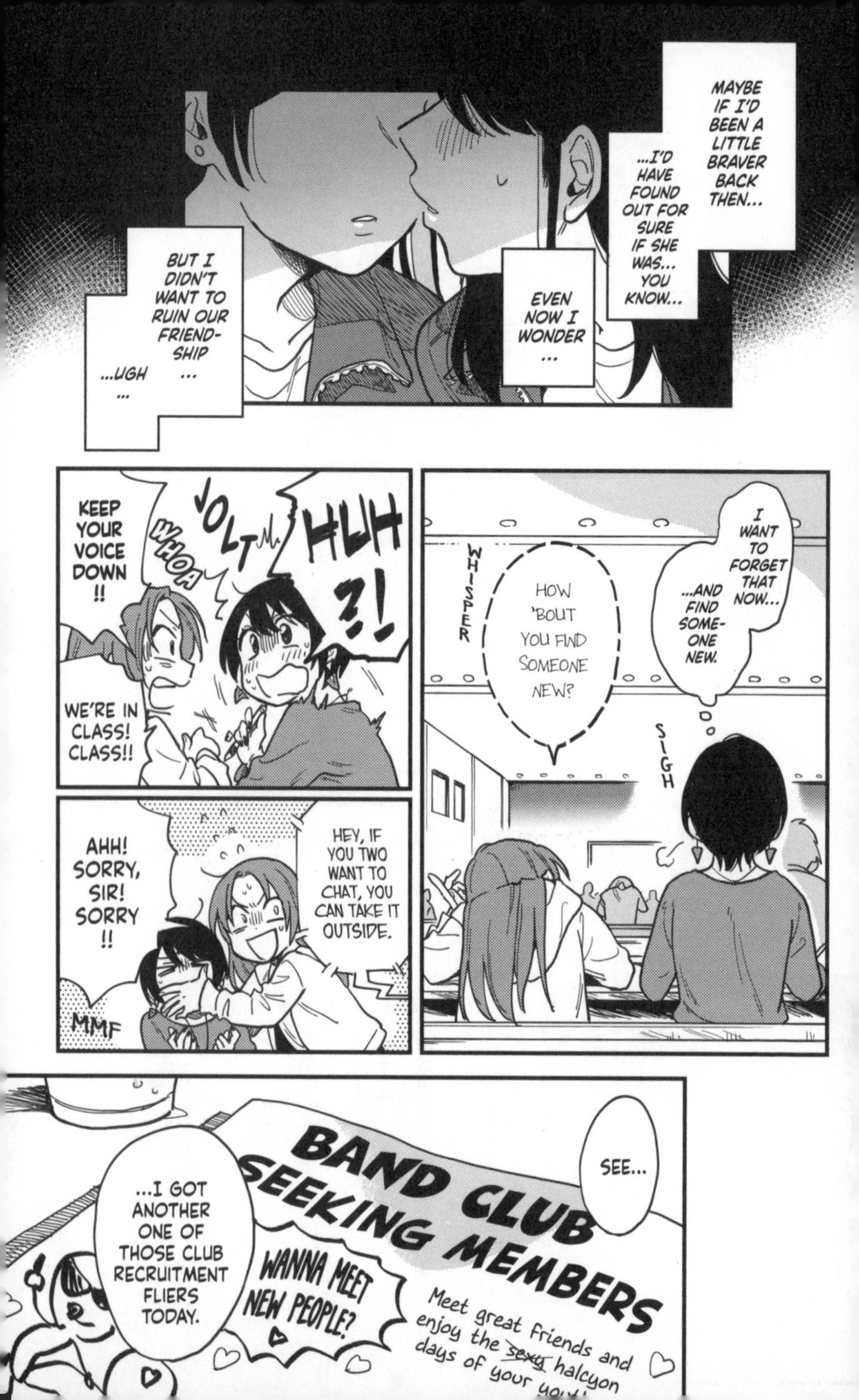
MAYBE IF I'D BEEN A LITTLE BRAVER BACK THEN...
...I'D HAVE FOUND OUT FOR SURE IF SHE WAS... YOU KNOW...
EVEN NOW I WONDER...
BUT I DIDN'T WANT TO RUIN OUR FRIENDSHIP...
...UGH...
I WANT TO FORGET THAT NOW...
...AND FIND SOMEONE NEW.
SIGH
HOW 'BOUT YOU FIND SOMEONE NEW?
WHISPER
HUH ?!
JOLT
WHOA
KEEP YOUR VOICE DOWN!!
WE'RE IN CLASS! CLASS!!
HEY, IF YOU TWO WANT TO CHAT, YOU CAN TAKE IT OUTSIDE.
AHH! SORRY, SIR! SORRY!!
MMF
SEE...
...I GOT ANOTHER ONE OF THOSE CLUB RECRUITMENT FLIERS TODAY.
BAND CLUB SEEKING MEMBERS
WANNA MEET NEW PEOPLE?
Meet great friends and enjoy the sexy halcyon days of your

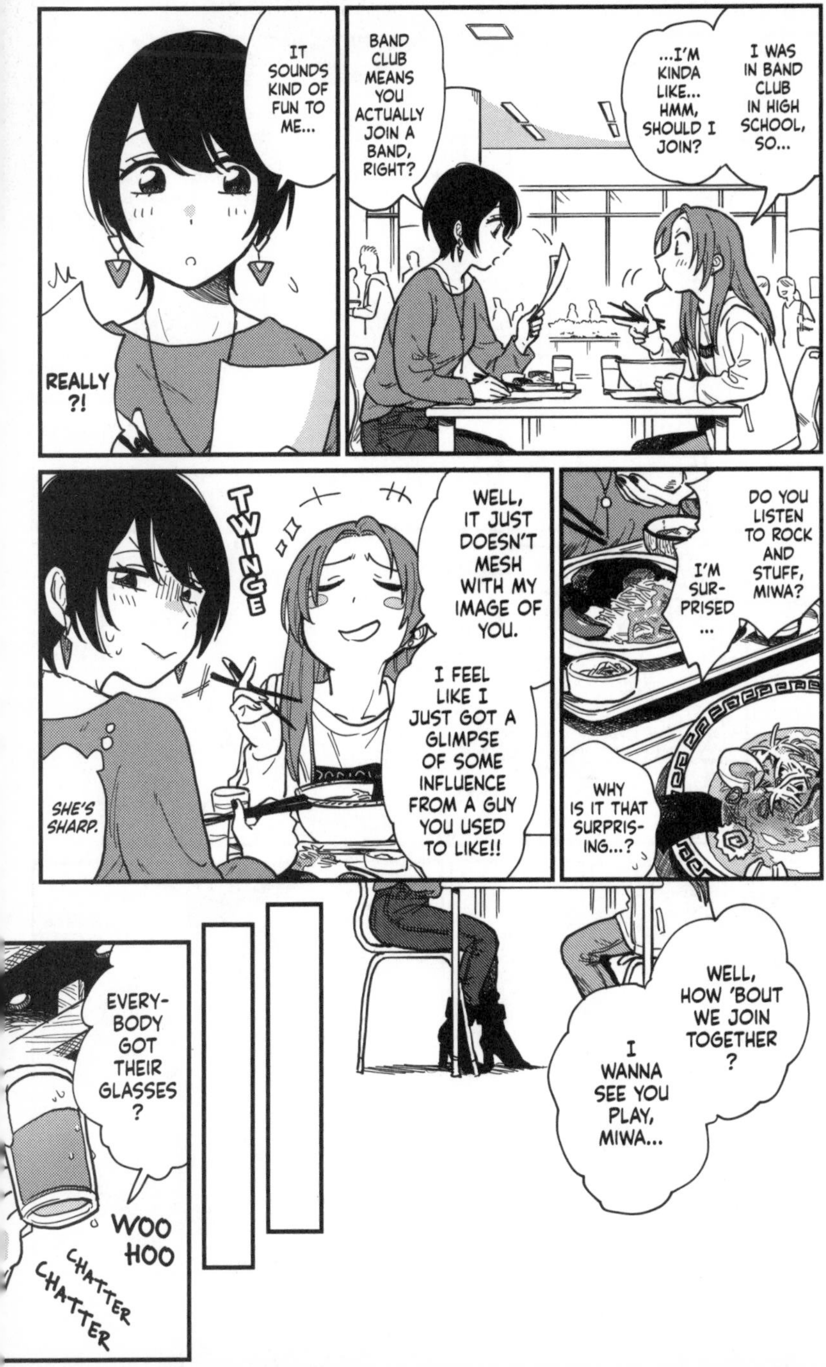
I WAS IN BAND CLUB IN HIGH SCHOOL, SO...
...I'M KINDA LIKE... HMM, SHOULD I JOIN?
BAND CLUB MEANS YOU ACTUALLY JOIN A BAND, RIGHT?
IT SOUNDS KIND OF FUN TO ME...
REALLY ?!
DO YOU LISTEN TO ROCK AND STUFF, MIWA?
I'M SUR-PRISED ...
WHY IS IT THAT SURPRIS-ING...?
WELL, IT JUST DOESN'T MESH WITH MY IMAGE OF YOU.
TWINGE
I FEEL LIKE I JUST GOT A GLIMPSE OF SOME INFLUENCE FROM A GUY YOU USED TO LIKE!!
SHE'S SHARP.
WELL, HOW 'BOUT WE JOIN TOGETHER ?
I WANNA SEE YOU PLAY, MIWA...
EVERY-BODY GOT THEIR GLASSES ?
WOO HOO
CHATTER CHATTER

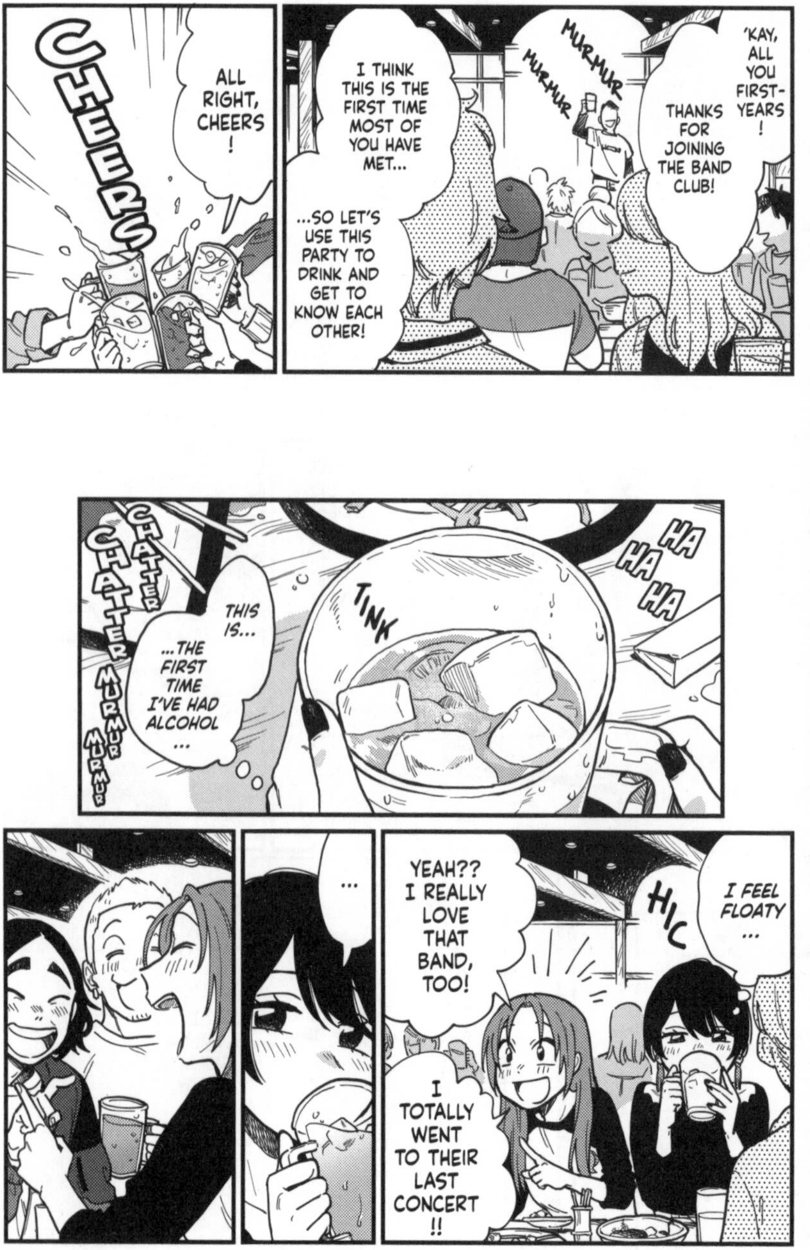
'KAY, ALL YOU FIRST-YEARS!
THANKS FOR JOINING THE BAND CLUB!
MURMUR MURMUR
I THINK THIS IS THE FIRST TIME MOST OF YOU HAVE MET...
...SO LET'S USE THIS PARTY TO DRINK AND GET TO KNOW EACH OTHER!
ALL RIGHT, CHEERS!
CHEERS
HA HA HA
TINK
THIS IS...
...THE FIRST TIME I'VE HAD ALCOHOL...
CHATTER CHATTER MURMUR MURMUR
I FEEL FLOATY...
HIC
YEAH?? I REALLY LOVE THAT BAND, TOO!
I TOTALLY WENT TO THEIR LAST CONCERT!!
...

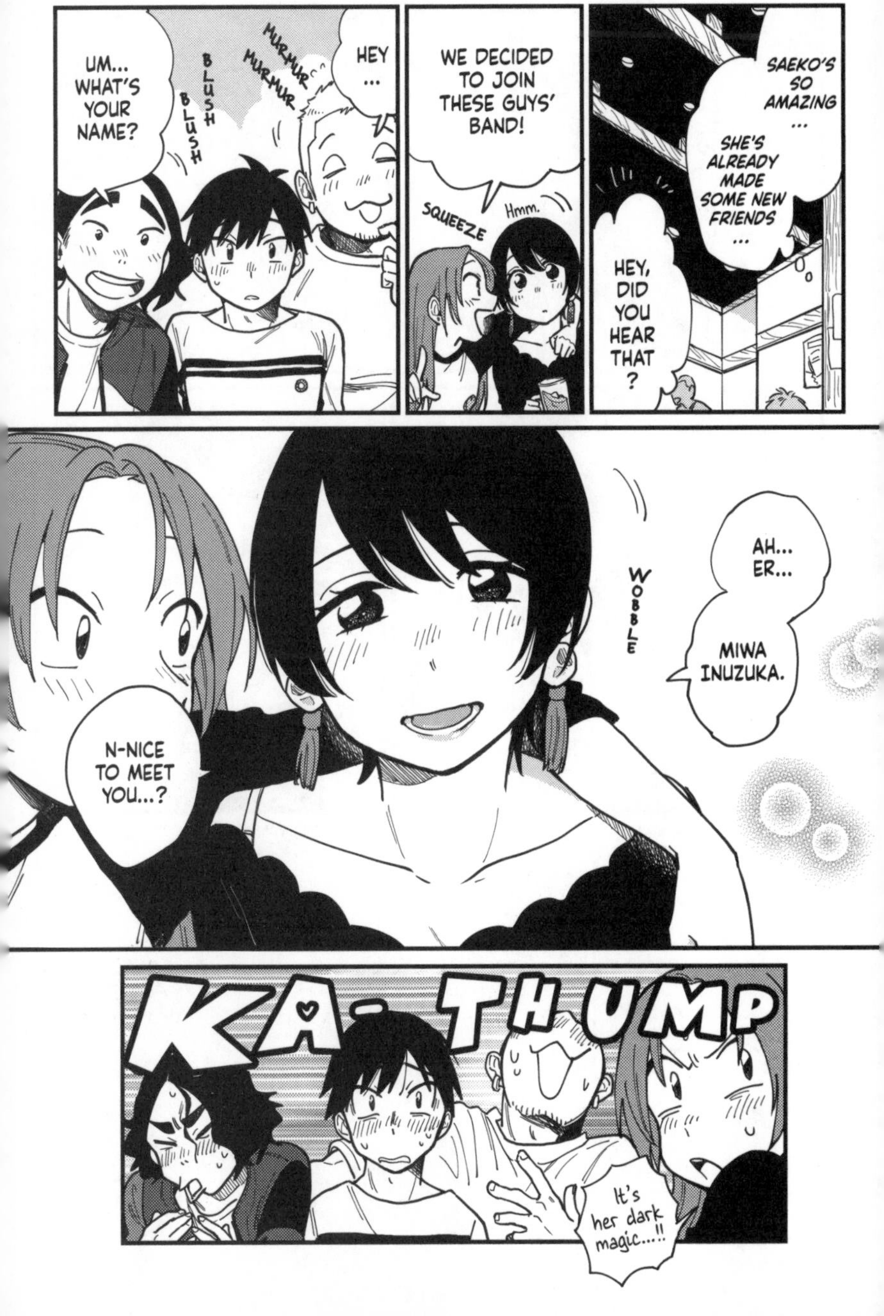
SAEKO'S SO AMAZING ...
SHE'S ALREADY MADE SOME NEW FRIENDS ...
HEY, DID YOU HEAR THAT ?
WE DECIDED TO JOIN THESE GUYS' BAND!
Hmm.
SQUEEZE
HEY ...
MURMUR
MURMUR
BLUSH
BLUSH
UM... WHAT'S YOUR NAME?
AH... ER...
MIWA INUZUKA.
WOBBLE
N-NICE TO MEET YOU...?
KA-THUMP
It's her dark magic...!!

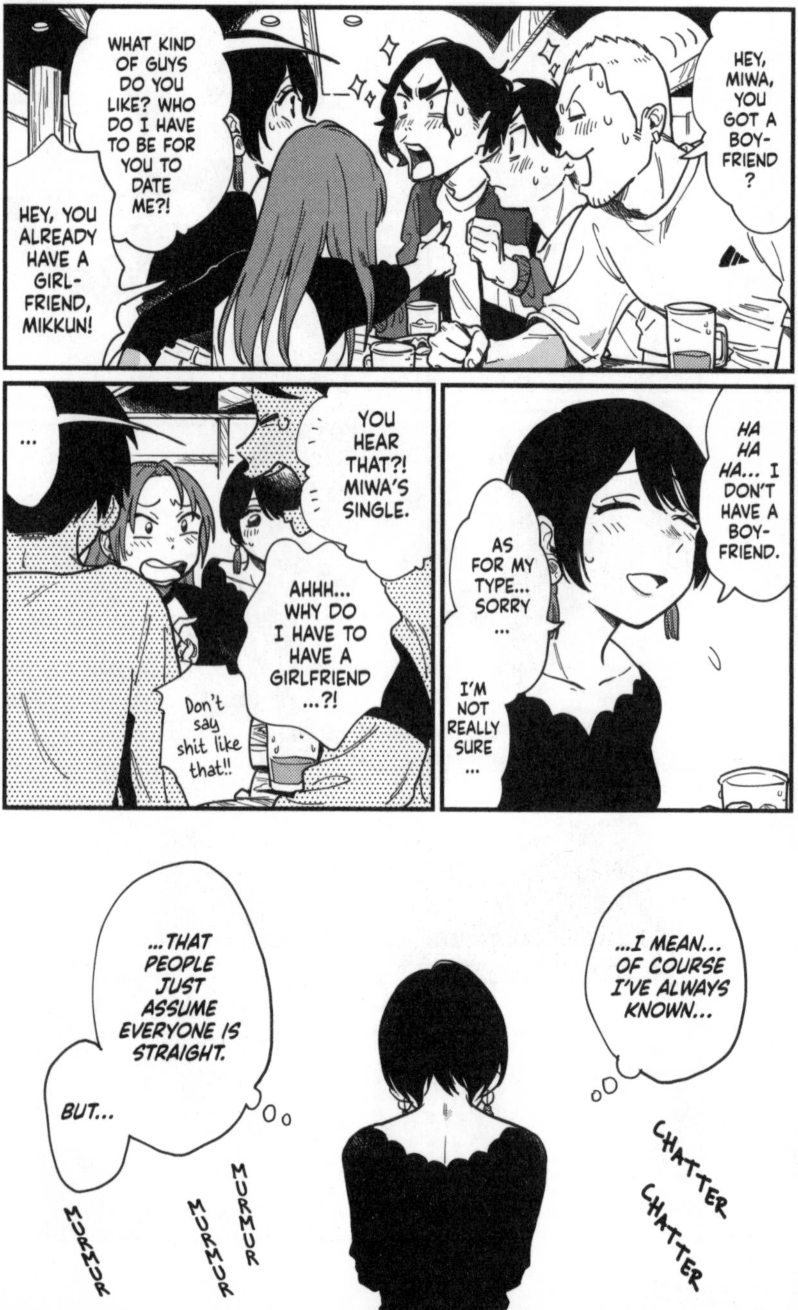
HEY, MIWA, YOU GOT A BOY-FRIEND?
WHAT KIND OF GUYS DO YOU LIKE? WHO DO I HAVE TO BE FOR YOU TO DATE ME?!
HEY, YOU ALREADY HAVE A GIRL-FRIEND, MIKKUN!
HA HA HA... I DON'T HAVE A BOY-FRIEND.
AS FOR MY TYPE... SORRY...
I'M NOT REALLY SURE...
YOU HEAR THAT?! MIWA'S SINGLE.
...
AHHH... WHY DO I HAVE TO HAVE A GIRLFRIEND...?!
Don't say shit like that!!
...I MEAN... OF COURSE I'VE ALWAYS KNOWN...
CHATTER CHATTER
...THAT PEOPLE JUST ASSUME EVERYONE IS STRAIGHT.
BUT...
MURMUR MURMUR MURMUR

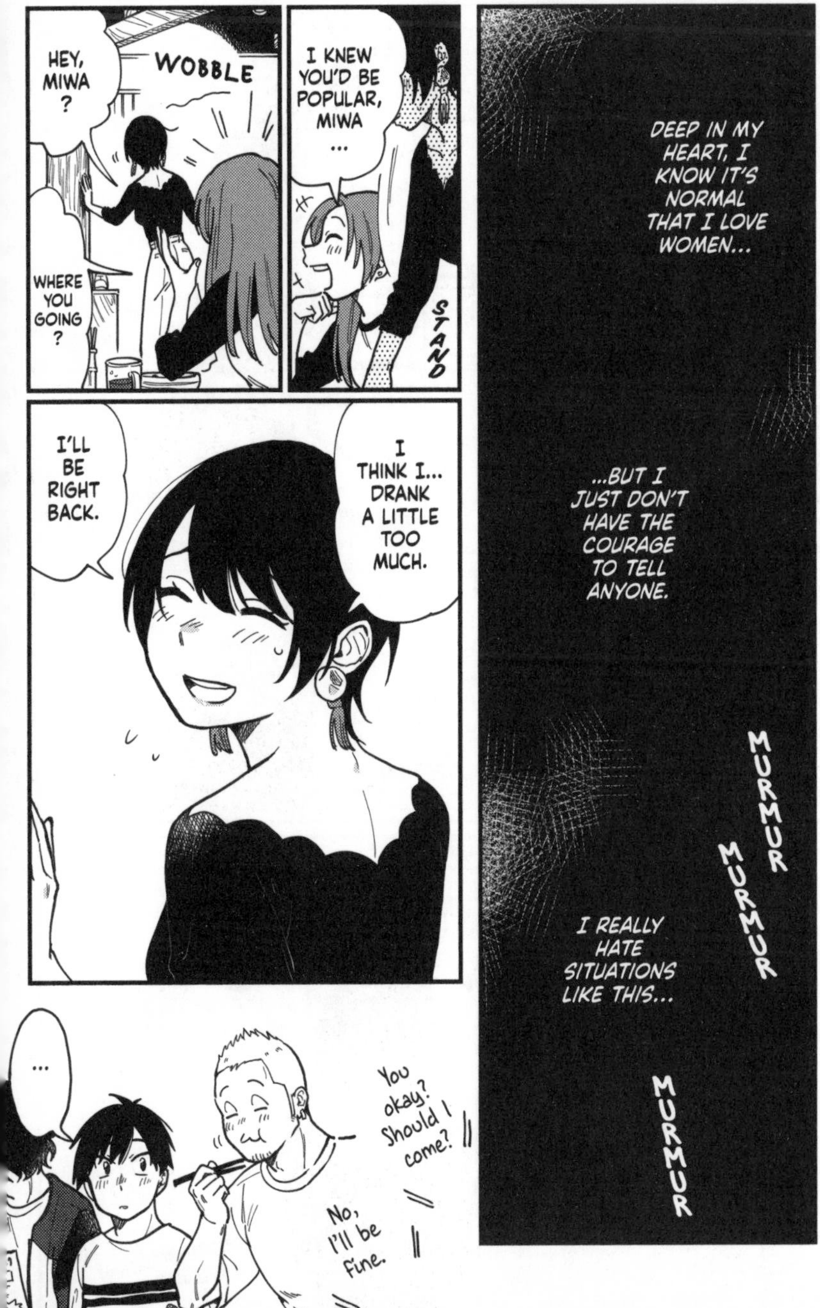
DEEP IN MY HEART, I KNOW IT'S NORMAL THAT I LOVE WOMEN...
...BUT I JUST DON'T HAVE THE COURAGE TO TELL ANYONE.
MURMUR
MURMUR
I REALLY HATE SITUATIONS LIKE THIS...
MURMUR
I KNEW YOU'D BE POPULAR, MIWA ...
STAND
WOBBLE
HEY, MIWA ?
WHERE YOU GOING ?
I THINK I... DRANK A LITTLE TOO MUCH.
I'LL BE RIGHT BACK.
You okay? Should I come?
...
No, I'll be fine.

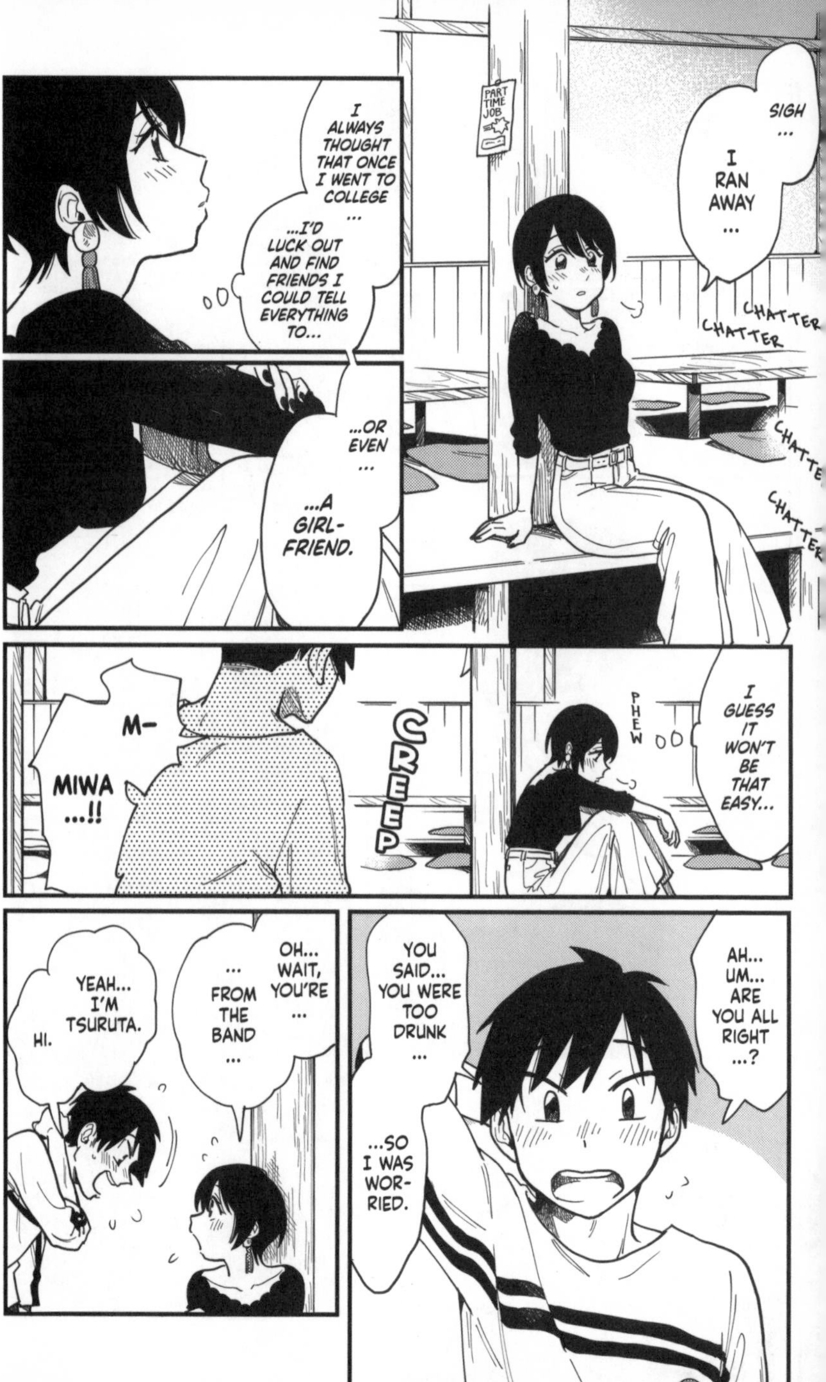
SIGH ...
I RAN AWAY ...
CHATTER CHATTER
CHATTER
CHATTER
PART TIME JOB
I ALWAYS THOUGHT THAT ONCE I WENT TO COLLEGE ...
...I'D LUCK OUT AND FIND FRIENDS I COULD TELL EVERYTHING TO...
...OR EVEN ...
...A GIRL-FRIEND.
PHEW
I GUESS IT WON'T BE THAT EASY...
CREEP
M-
MIWA ...!!
AH... UM... ARE YOU ALL RIGHT ...?
YOU SAID... YOU WERE TOO DRUNK ...
...SO I WAS WOR-RIED.
OH... WAIT, YOU'RE ...
... FROM THE BAND ...
YEAH... I'M TSURUTA.
HI.

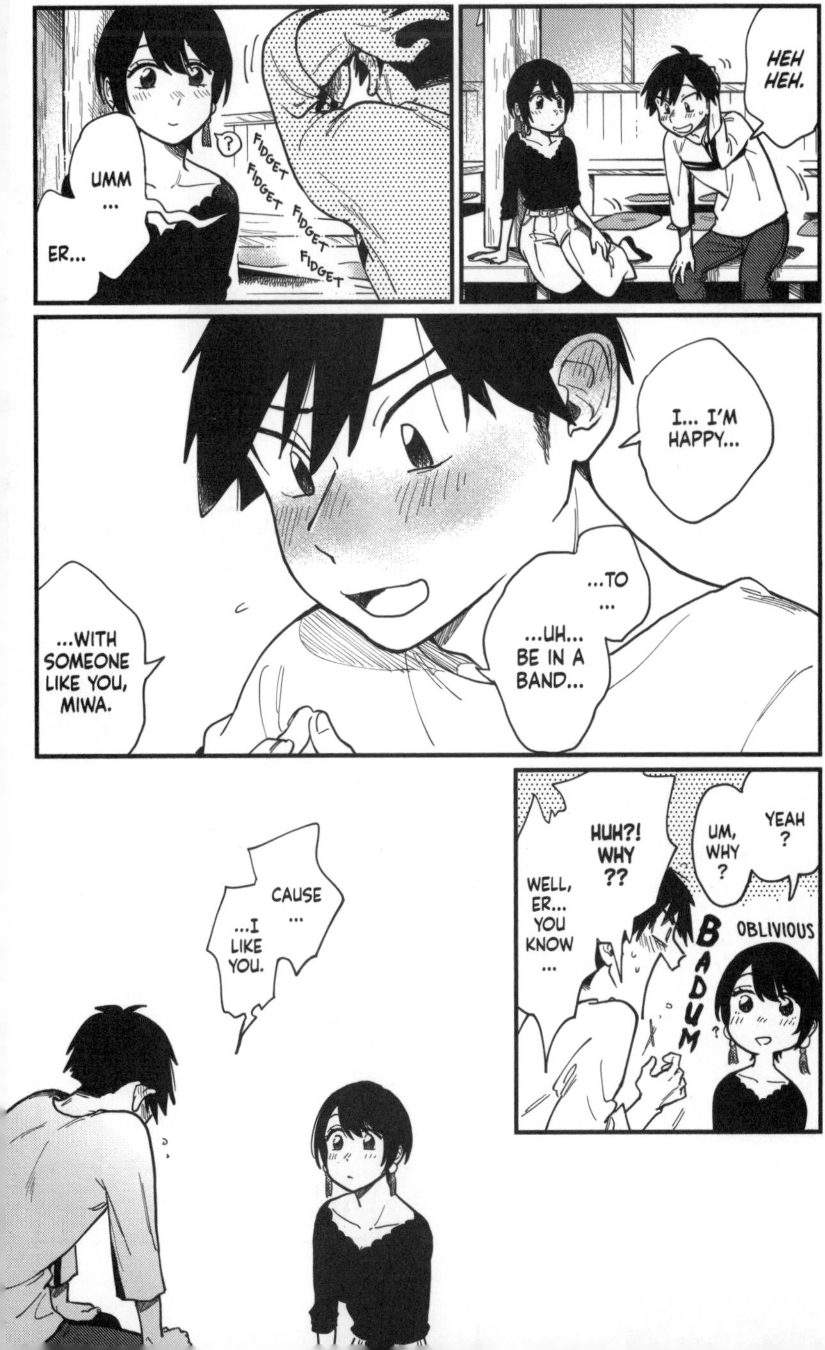
HEH HEH.
UMM ...
ER...
?
FIDGET FIDGET FIDGET FIDGET FIDGET
I... I'M HAPPY...
...TO ...
...UH... BE IN A BAND...
...WITH SOMEONE LIKE YOU, MIWA.
YEAH ?
UM, WHY ?
HUH?! WHY ??
OBLIVIOUS
BADUM
WELL, ER... YOU KNOW ...
CAUSE ...
...I LIKE YOU.

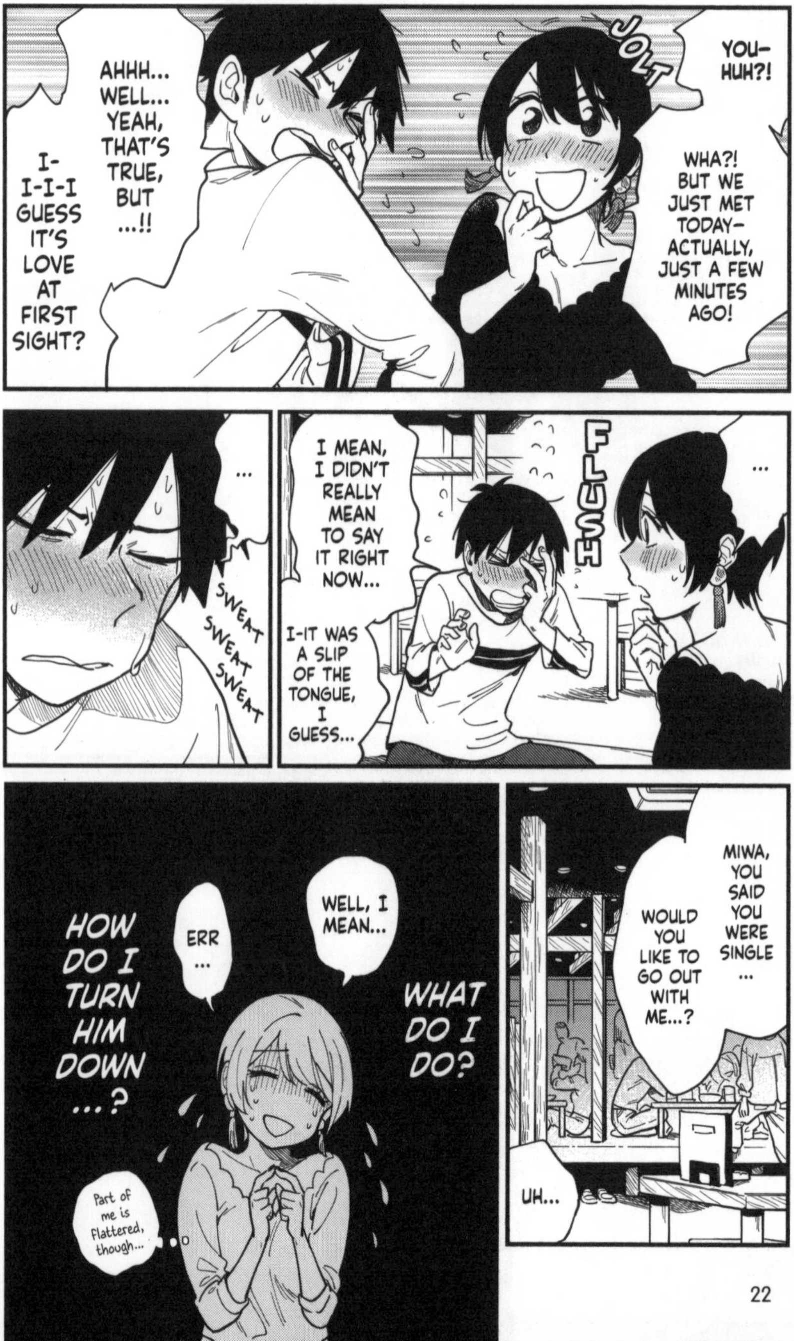
YOU— HUH?!
JOLT
WHA?! BUT WE JUST MET TODAY— ACTUALLY, JUST A FEW MINUTES AGO!
AHHH... WELL... YEAH, THAT'S TRUE, BUT ...!!
I- I-I-I GUESS IT'S LOVE AT FIRST SIGHT?
...
FLUSH
I MEAN, I DIDN'T REALLY MEAN TO SAY IT RIGHT NOW...
I-IT WAS A SLIP OF THE TONGUE, I GUESS...
...
SWEAT SWEAT SWEAT
MIWA, YOU SAID YOU WERE SINGLE ...
WOULD YOU LIKE TO GO OUT WITH ME...?
UH...
WHAT DO I DO?
WELL, I MEAN...
ERR ...
HOW DO I TURN HIM DOWN ...?
Part of me is flattered, though...

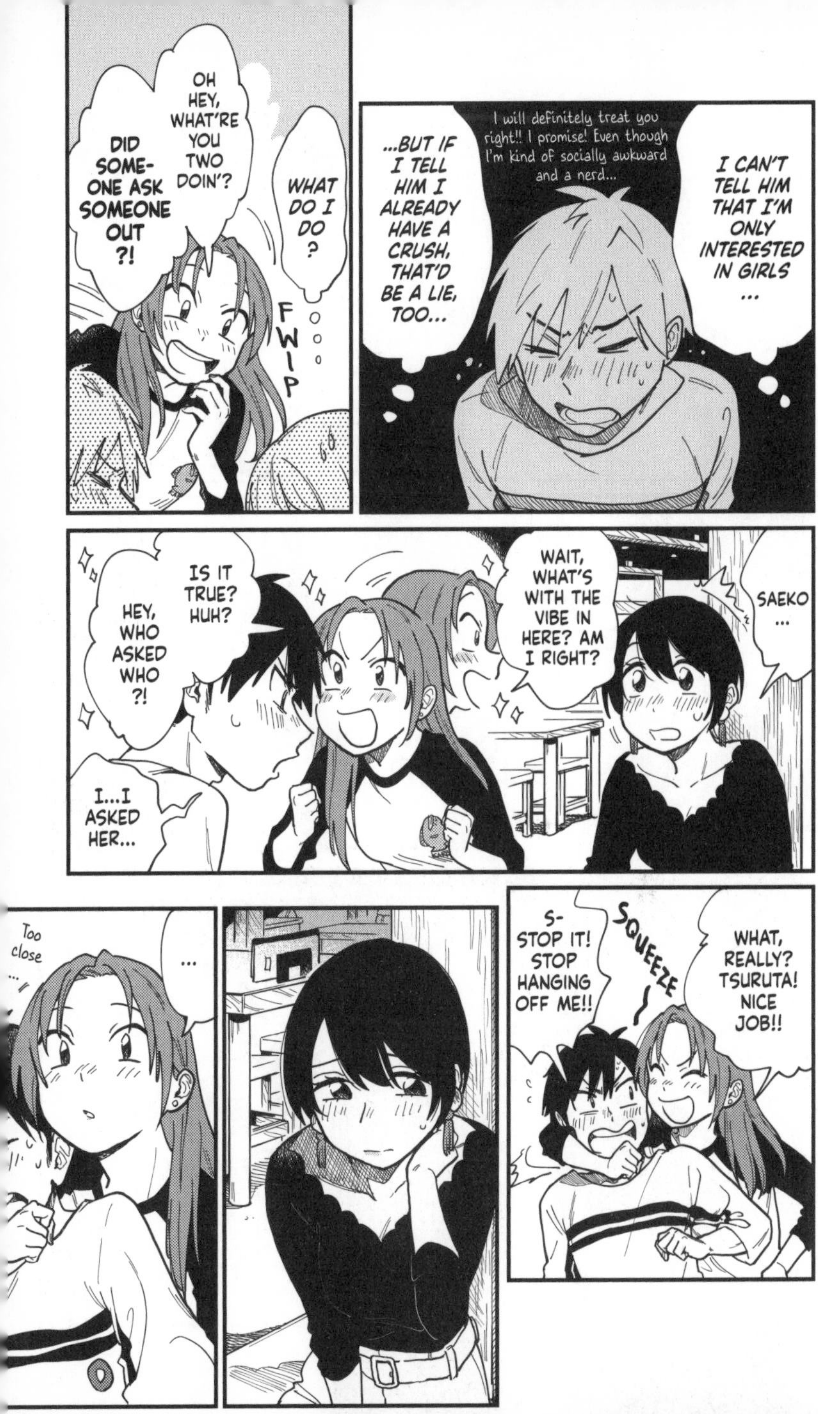
I CAN'T TELL HIM THAT I'M ONLY INTERESTED IN GIRLS...
I will definitely treat you right!! I promise! Even though I'm kind of socially awkward and a nerd...
...BUT IF I TELL HIM I ALREADY HAVE A CRUSH, THAT'D BE A LIE, TOO...
WHAT DO I DO?
OH HEY, WHAT'RE YOU TWO DOIN'?
DID SOME-ONE ASK SOMEONE OUT?!
FWIP
SAEKO...
WAIT, WHAT'S WITH THE VIBE IN HERE? AM I RIGHT?
IS IT TRUE? HUH?
HEY, WHO ASKED WHO?!
I...I ASKED HER...
WHAT, REALLY? TSURUTA! NICE JOB!!
SQUEEZE
S-STOP IT! STOP HANGING OFF ME!!
...
Too close...

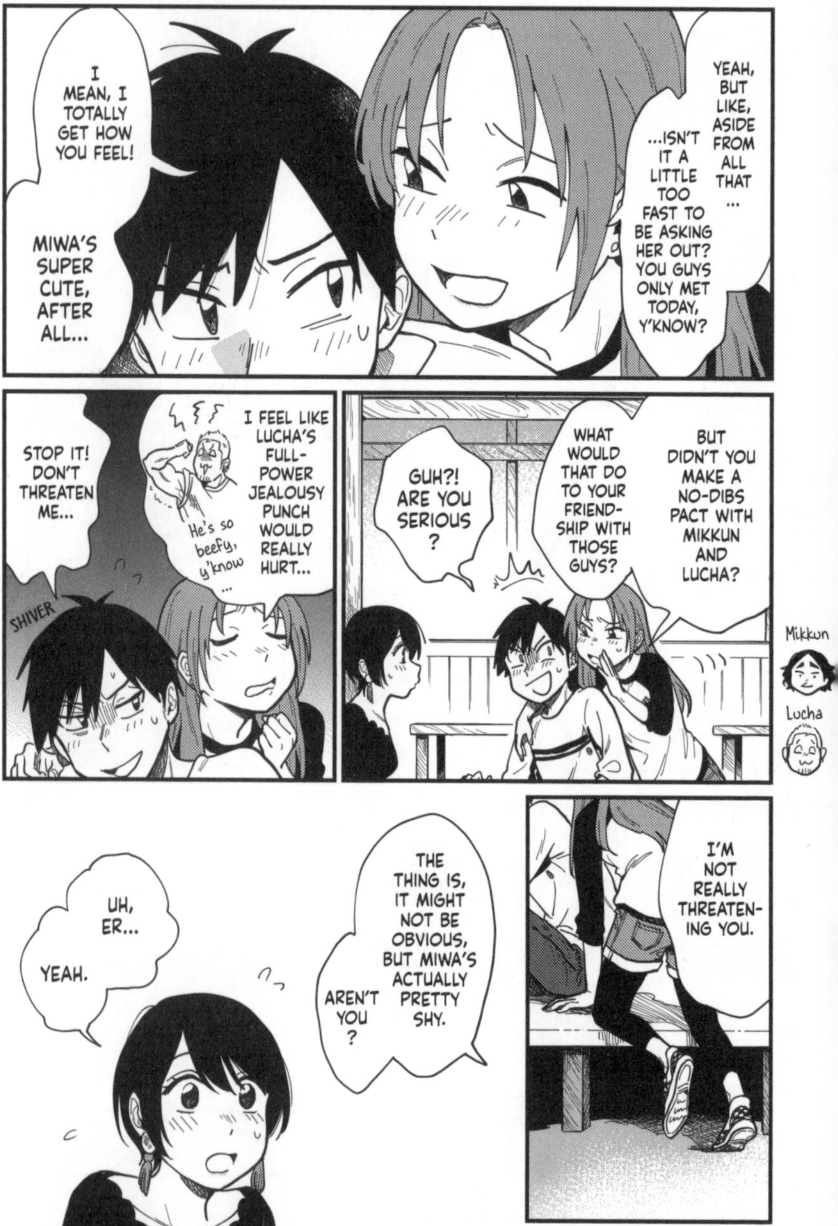
YEAH, BUT LIKE, ASIDE FROM ALL THAT ...
...ISN'T IT A LITTLE TOO FAST TO BE ASKING HER OUT? YOU GUYS ONLY MET TODAY, Y'KNOW?
I MEAN, I TOTALLY GET HOW YOU FEEL!
MIWA'S SUPER CUTE, AFTER ALL...
BUT DIDN'T YOU MAKE A NO-DIBS PACT WITH MIKKUN AND LUCHA?
WHAT WOULD THAT DO TO YOUR FRIEND-SHIP WITH THOSE GUYS?
GUH?! ARE YOU SERIOUS ?
Mikkun
Lucha
I FEEL LIKE LUCHA'S FULL-POWER JEALOUSY PUNCH WOULD REALLY HURT...
He's so beefy, y'know ...
STOP IT! DON'T THREATEN ME...
SHIVER
I'M NOT REALLY THREATEN-ING YOU.
THE THING IS, IT MIGHT NOT BE OBVIOUS, BUT MIWA'S ACTUALLY PRETTY SHY.
AREN'T YOU ?
UH, ER...
YEAH.

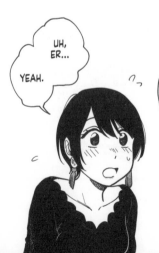

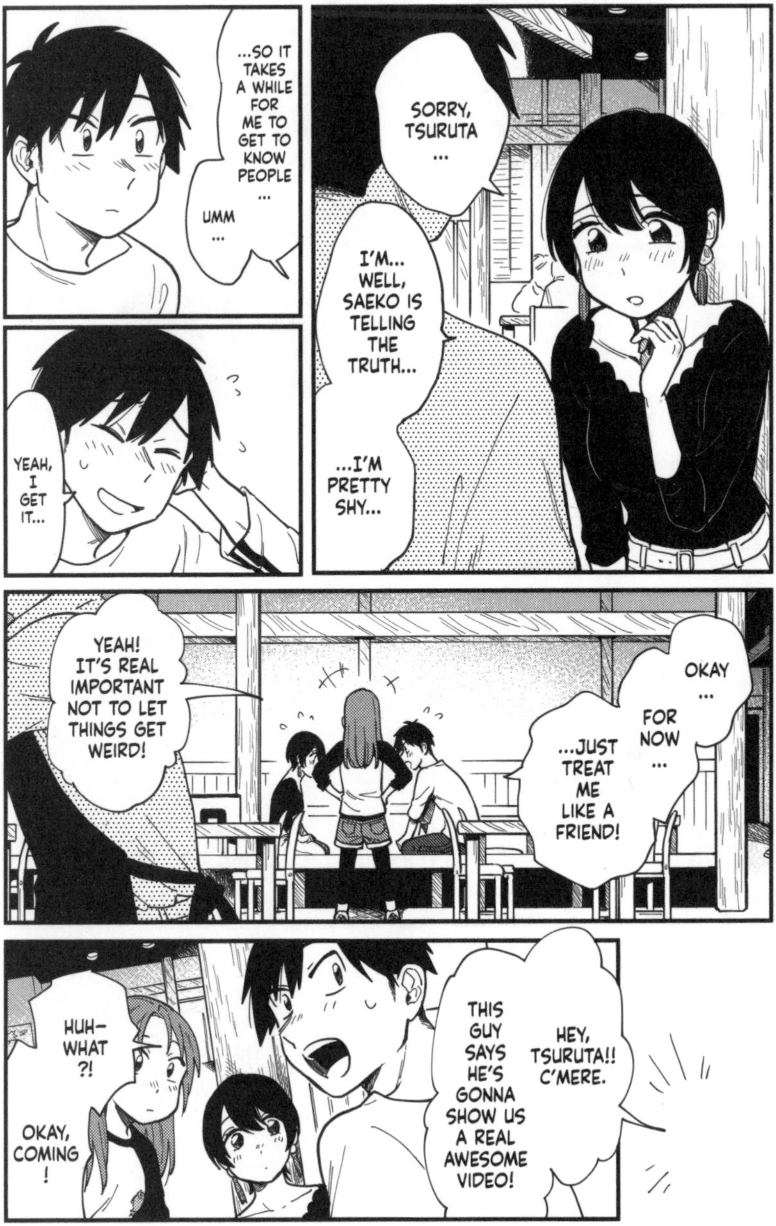
SORRY, TSURUTA ...
I'M... WELL, SAEKO IS TELLING THE TRUTH...
...I'M PRETTY SHY...
...SO IT TAKES A WHILE FOR ME TO GET TO KNOW PEOPLE ...
UMM ...
YEAH, I GET IT...
OKAY ...
FOR NOW ...
...JUST TREAT ME LIKE A FRIEND!
YEAH! IT'S REAL IMPORTANT NOT TO LET THINGS GET WEIRD!
HEY, TSURUTA!! C'MERE.
THIS GUY SAYS HE'S GONNA SHOW US A REAL AWESOME VIDEO!
HUH-WHAT ?!
OKAY, COMING !

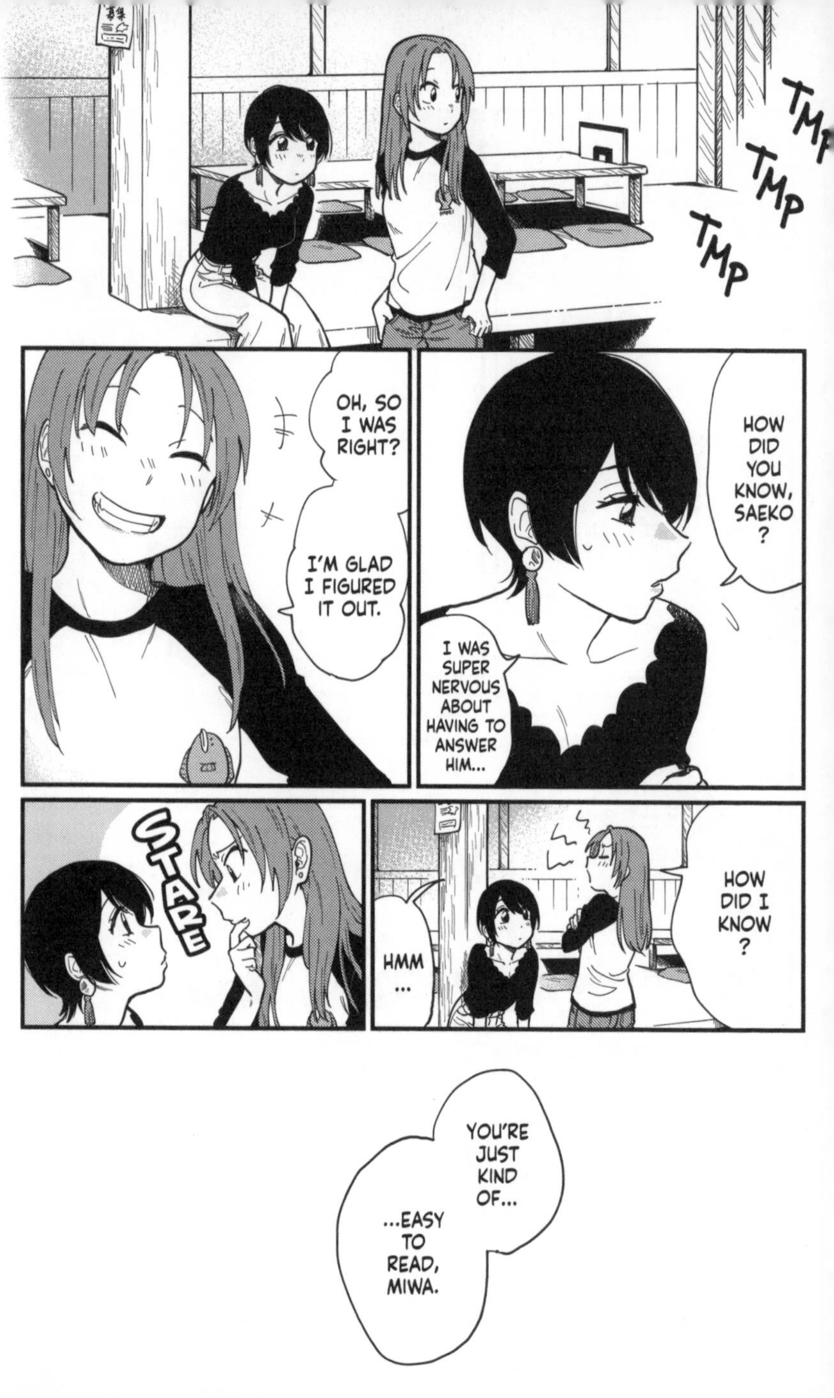
TMP
TMP
TMP
HOW DID YOU KNOW, SAEKO?
I WAS SUPER NERVOUS ABOUT HAVING TO ANSWER HIM...
OH, SO I WAS RIGHT?
I'M GLAD I FIGURED IT OUT.
HOW DID I KNOW?
HMM...
STARE
YOU'RE JUST KIND OF...
...EASY TO READ, MIWA.

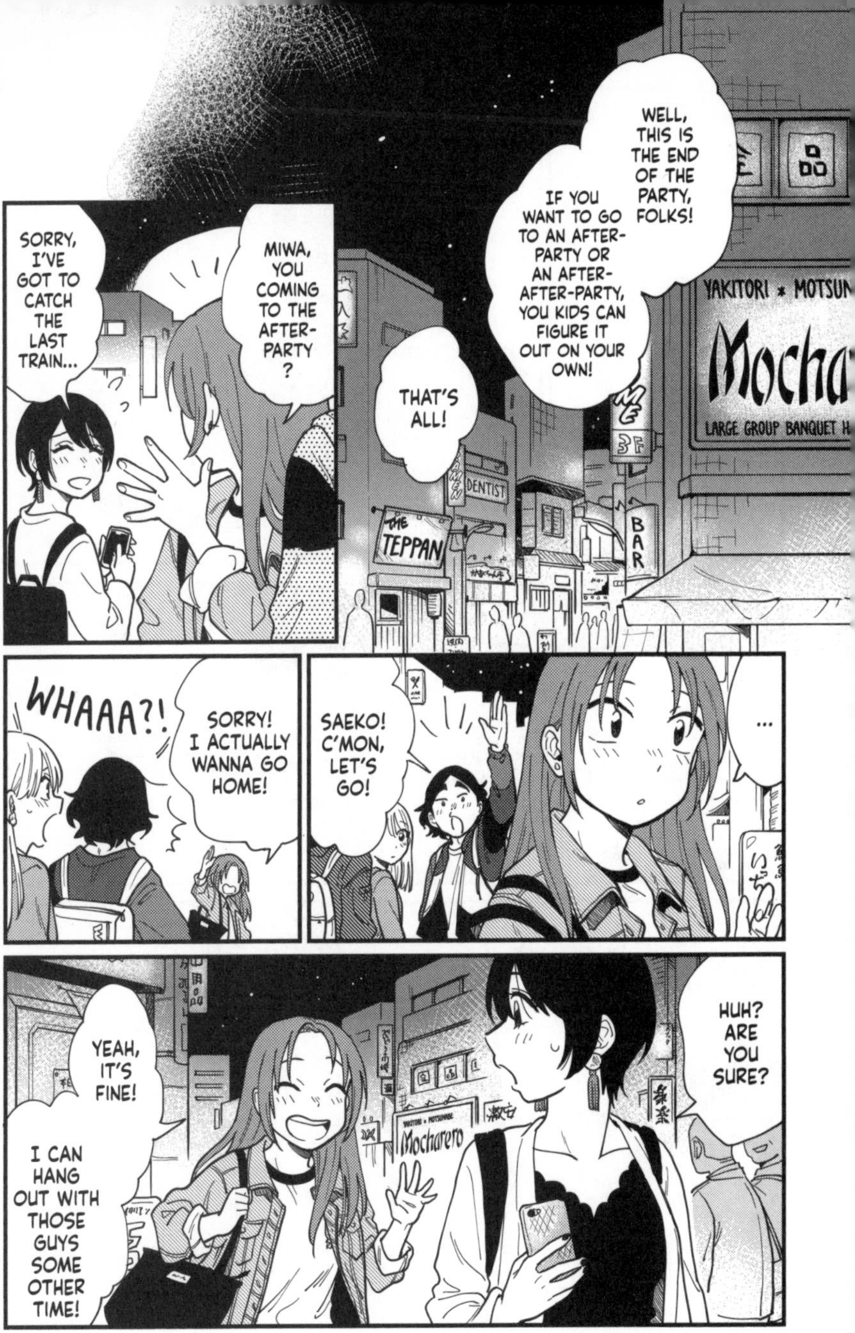
WELL, THIS IS THE END OF THE PARTY, FOLKS!
IF YOU WANT TO GO TO AN AFTER-PARTY OR AN AFTER-AFTER-PARTY, YOU KIDS CAN FIGURE IT OUT ON YOUR OWN!
THAT'S ALL!
DENTIST
THE TEPPAN
BAR
MIWA, YOU COMING TO THE AFTER-PARTY?
SORRY, I'VE GOT TO CATCH THE LAST TRAIN...
...
SAEKO! C'MON, LET'S GO!
SORRY! I ACTUALLY WANNA GO HOME!
WHAAA?!
HUH? ARE YOU SURE?
YEAH, IT'S FINE!
I CAN HANG OUT WITH THOSE GUYS SOME OTHER TIME!
Mocharero

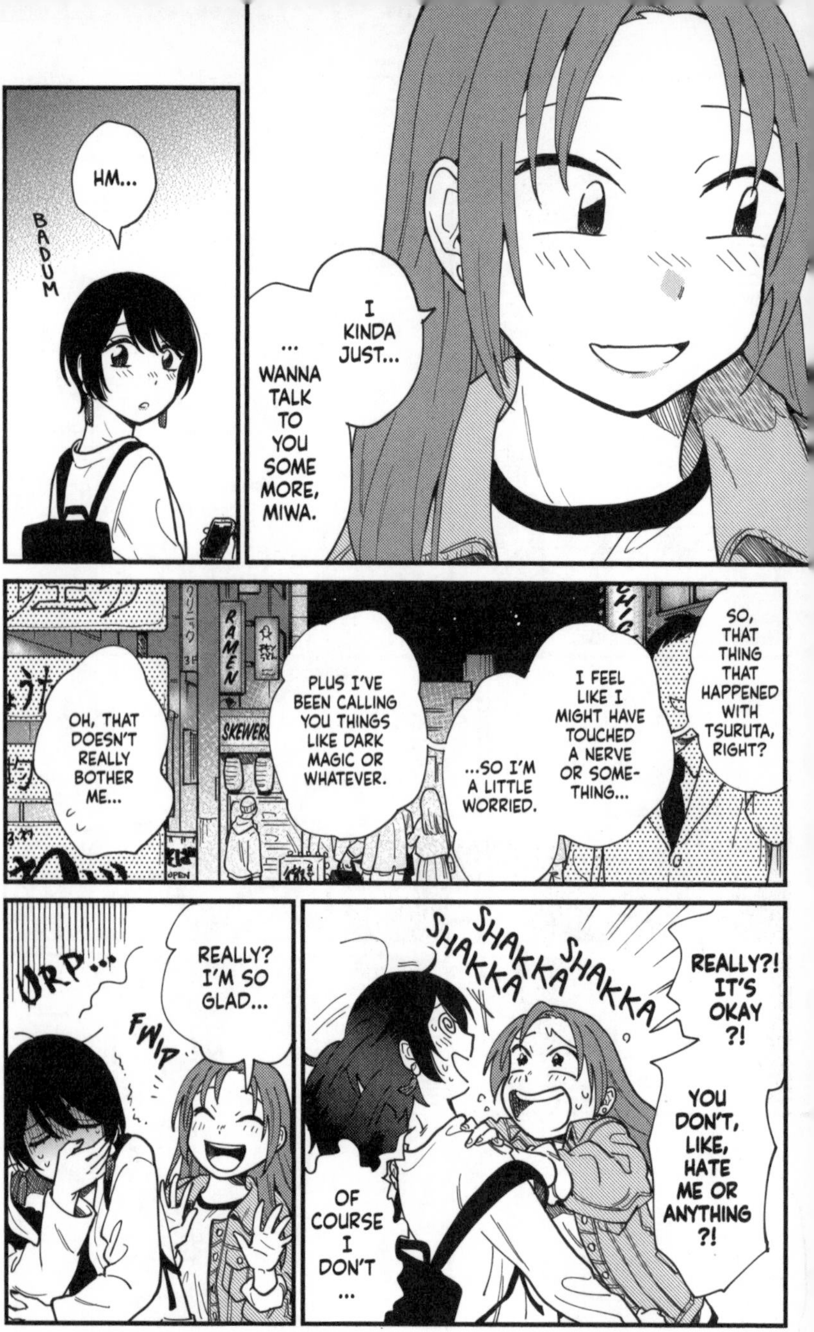
I KINDA JUST...
... WANNA TALK TO YOU SOME MORE, MIWA.
HM...
BADUM
SO, THAT THING THAT HAPPENED WITH TSURUTA, RIGHT?
I FEEL LIKE I MIGHT HAVE TOUCHED A NERVE OR SOME-THING...
...SO I'M A LITTLE WORRIED.
RAMEN
SKEWERS
PLUS I'VE BEEN CALLING YOU THINGS LIKE DARK MAGIC OR WHATEVER.
OH, THAT DOESN'T REALLY BOTHER ME...
OPEN
SHAKKA SHAKKA SHAKKA
REALLY?! IT'S OKAY?!
YOU DON'T, LIKE, HATE ME OR ANYTHING?!
OF COURSE I DON'T...
REALLY? I'M SO GLAD...
FWIP
URP...

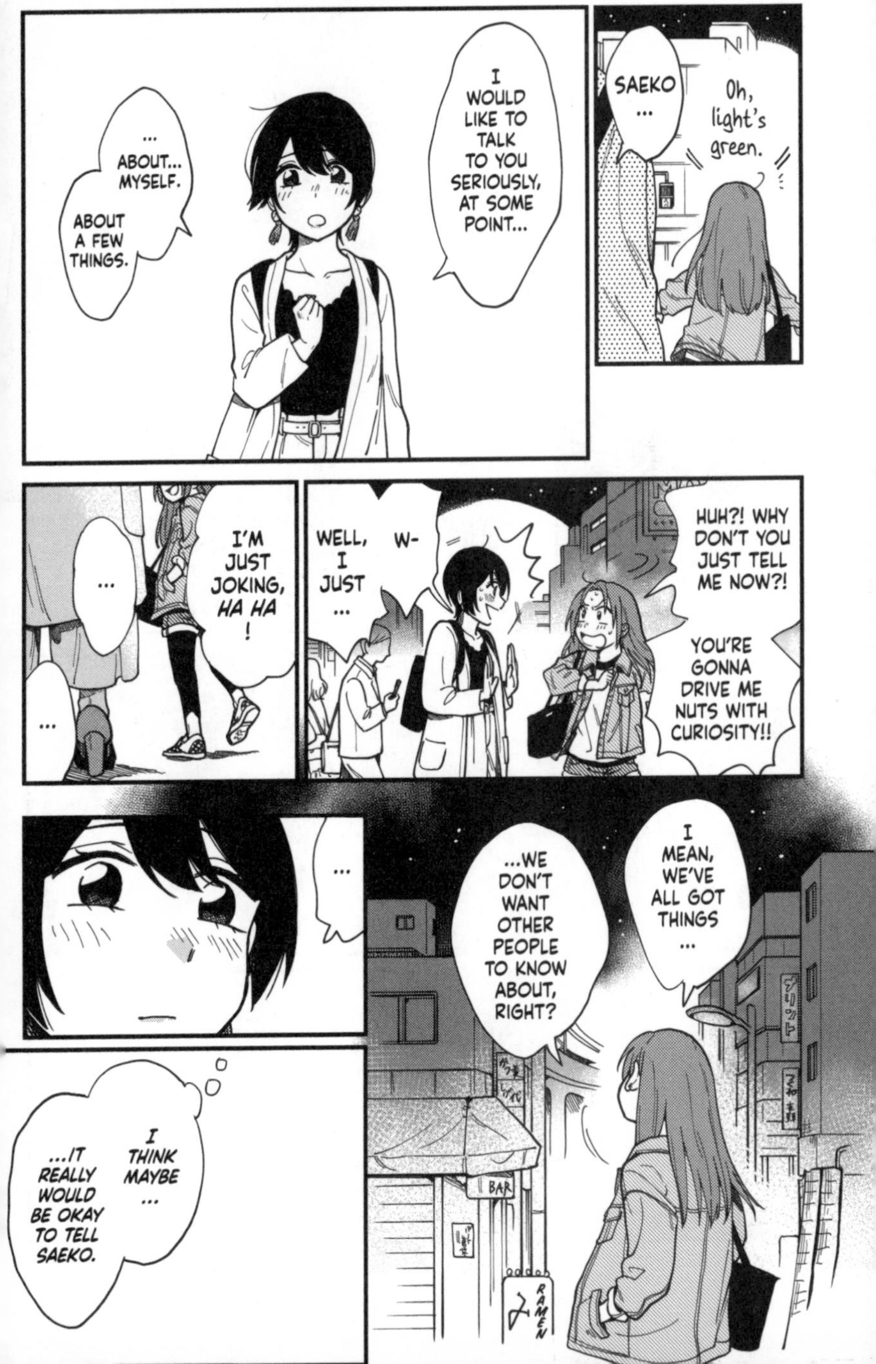
Oh, light's green.
SAEKO ...
I WOULD LIKE TO TALK TO YOU SERIOUSLY, AT SOME POINT...
... ABOUT... MYSELF.
ABOUT A FEW THINGS.
HUH?! WHY DON'T YOU JUST TELL ME NOW?!
YOU'RE GONNA DRIVE ME NUTS WITH CURIOSITY!!
W-
WELL, I JUST ...
I'M JUST JOKING, HA HA!
...
...
I MEAN, WE'VE ALL GOT THINGS ...
...WE DON'T WANT OTHER PEOPLE TO KNOW ABOUT, RIGHT?
BAR
RAMEN
...
I THINK MAYBE ...
...IT REALLY WOULD BE OKAY TO TELL SAEKO.

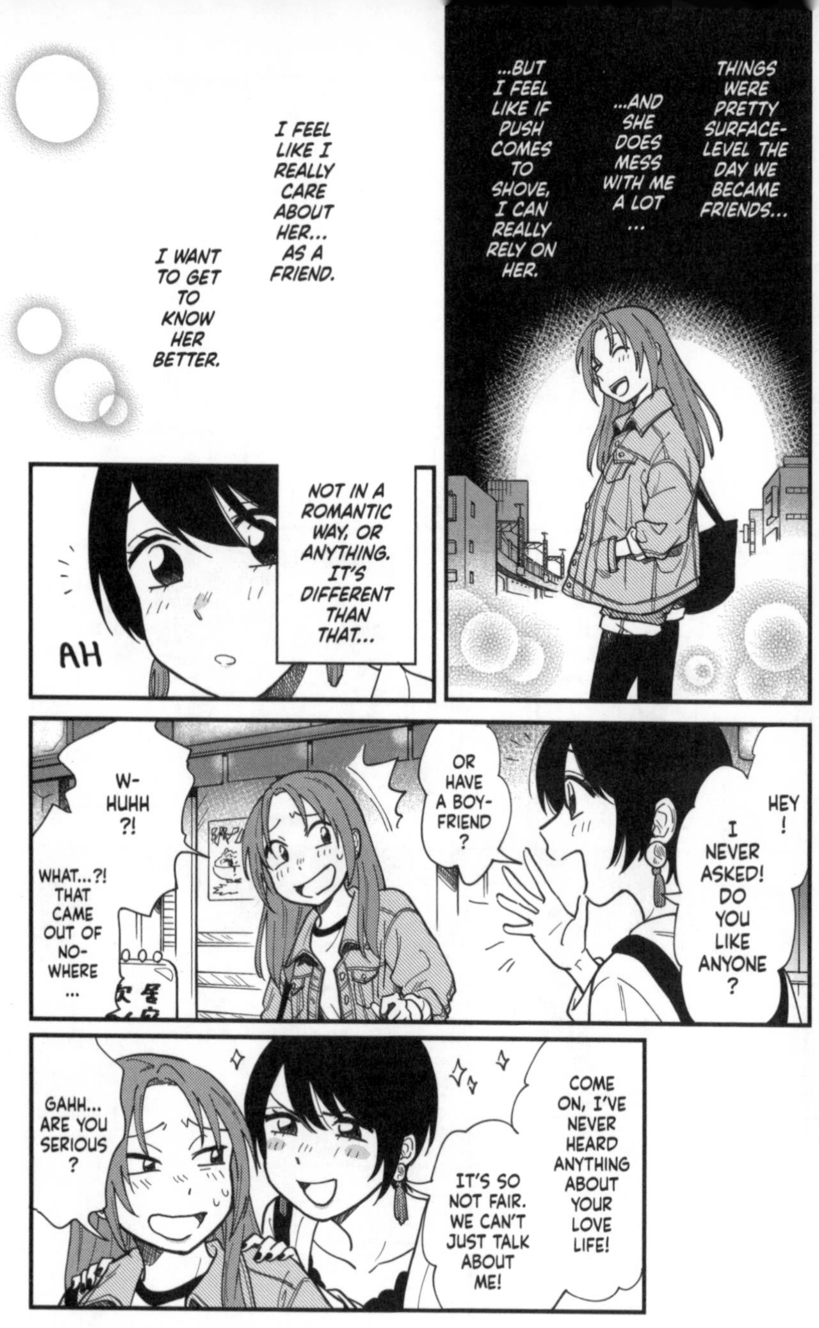
THINGS WERE PRETTY SURFACE-LEVEL THE DAY WE BECAME FRIENDS...
...AND SHE DOES MESS WITH ME A LOT...
...BUT I FEEL LIKE IF PUSH COMES TO SHOVE, I CAN REALLY RELY ON HER.
I FEEL LIKE I REALLY CARE ABOUT HER... AS A FRIEND.
I WANT TO GET TO KNOW HER BETTER.
NOT IN A ROMANTIC WAY, OR ANYTHING. IT'S DIFFERENT THAN THAT...
AH
HEY! I NEVER ASKED! DO YOU LIKE ANYONE?
OR HAVE A BOY-FRIEND?
W-HUHH?!
WHAT...?! THAT CAME OUT OF NO-WHERE...
COME ON, I'VE NEVER HEARD ANYTHING ABOUT YOUR LOVE LIFE!
IT'S SO NOT FAIR. WE CAN'T JUST TALK ABOUT ME!
GAHH... ARE YOU SERIOUS?

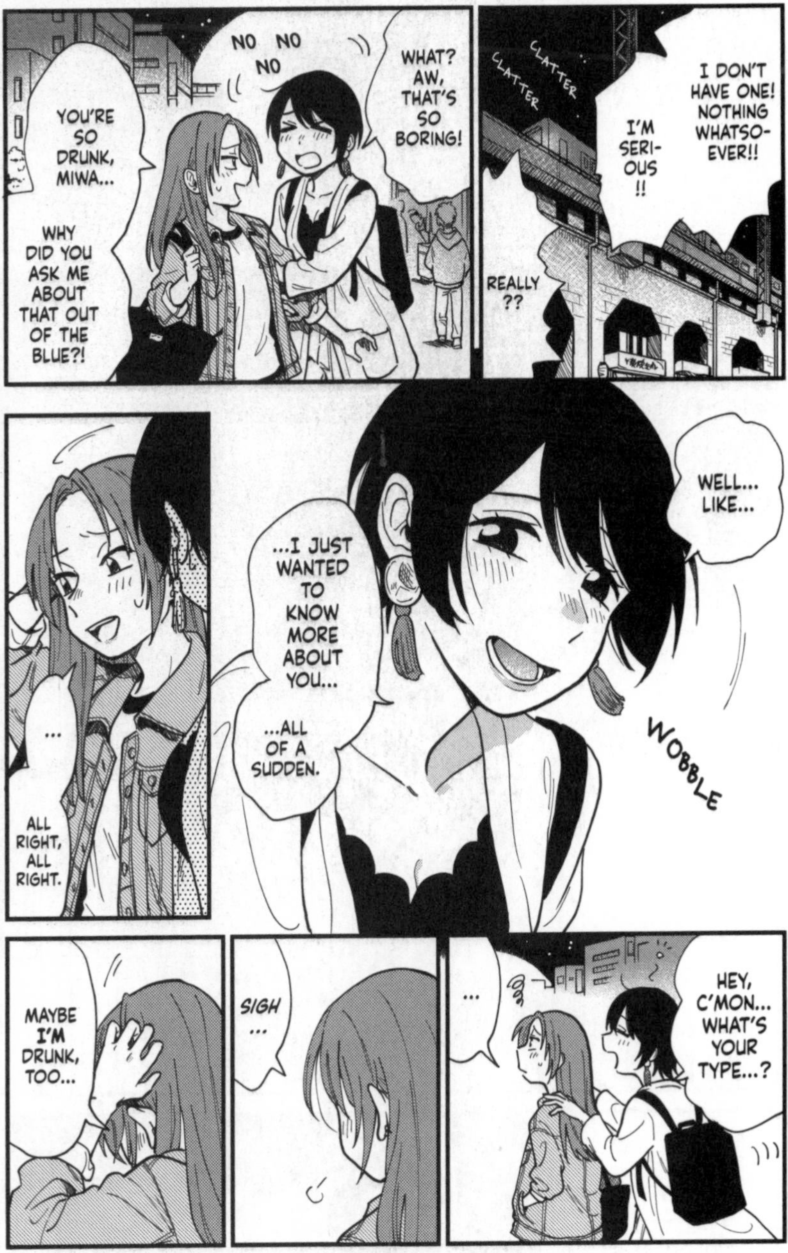
I DON'T HAVE ONE! NOTHING WHATSO-EVER!!
I'M SERI-OUS!!
CLATTER
CLATTER
REALLY??
WHAT? AW, THAT'S SO BORING!
NO NO NO
YOU'RE SO DRUNK, MIWA...
WHY DID YOU ASK ME ABOUT THAT OUT OF THE BLUE?!
WELL... LIKE...
WOBBLE
...I JUST WANTED TO KNOW MORE ABOUT YOU...
...ALL OF A SUDDEN.
...
ALL RIGHT, ALL RIGHT.
HEY, C'MON... WHAT'S YOUR TYPE...?
...
SIGH...
MAYBE I'M DRUNK, TOO...

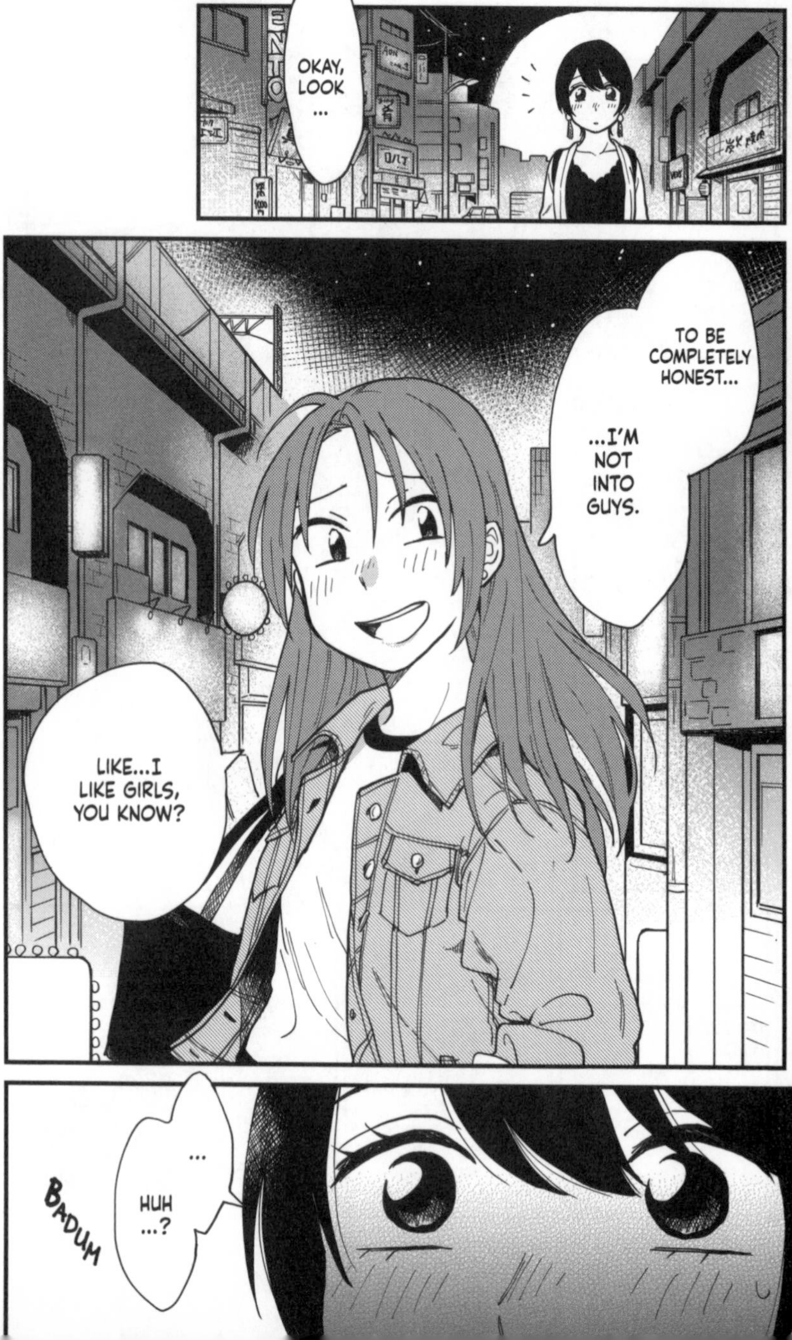
OKAY, LOOK ...
TO BE COMPLETELY HONEST...
...I'M NOT INTO GUYS.
LIKE...I LIKE GIRLS, YOU KNOW?
... HUH ...?
BADUM

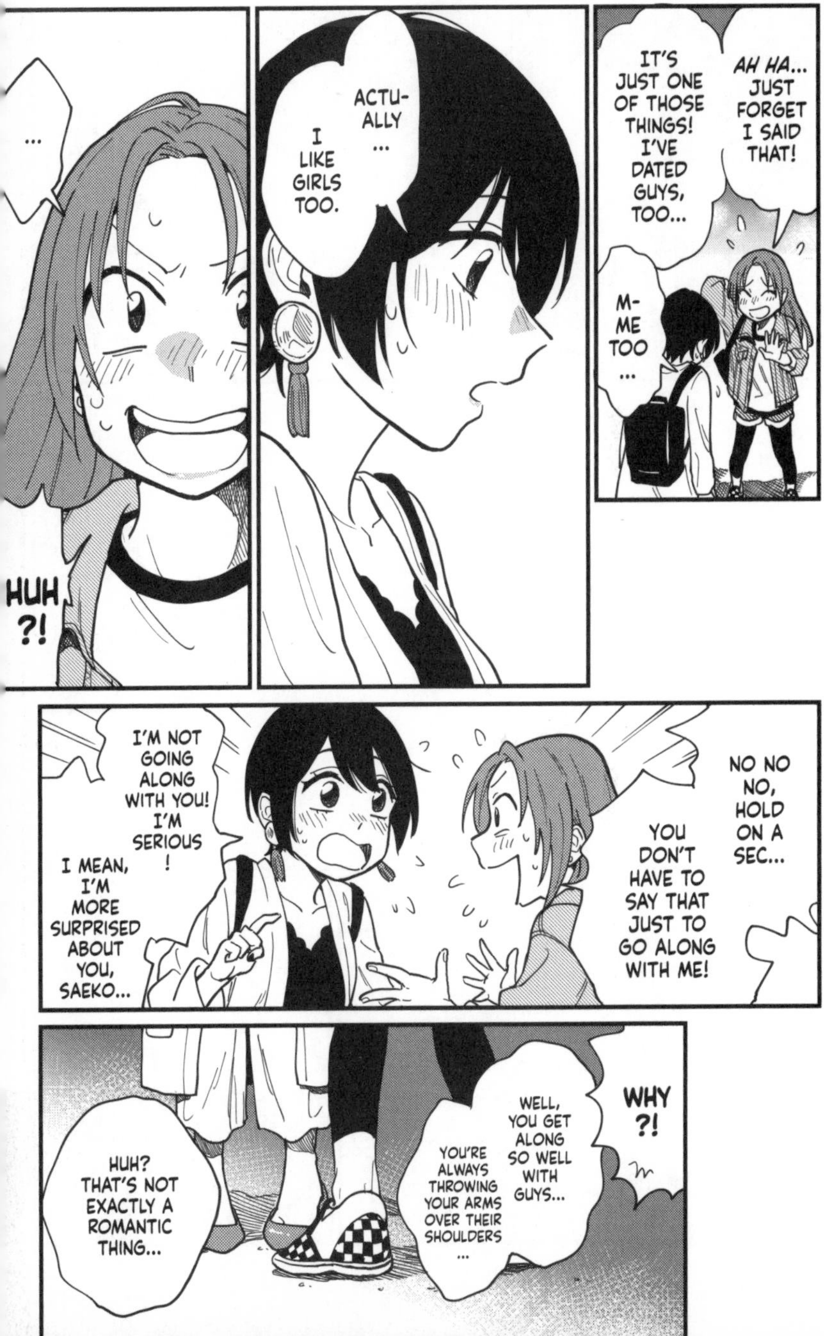
AH HA... JUST FORGET I SAID THAT!
IT'S JUST ONE OF THOSE THINGS! I'VE DATED GUYS, TOO...
M-ME TOO...
ACTU-ALLY...
I LIKE GIRLS TOO.
...
HUH?!
NO NO NO, HOLD ON A SEC...
YOU DON'T HAVE TO SAY THAT JUST TO GO ALONG WITH ME!
I'M NOT GOING ALONG WITH YOU! I'M SERIOUS!
I MEAN, I'M MORE SURPRISED ABOUT YOU, SAEKO...
WHY?!
WELL, YOU GET ALONG SO WELL WITH GUYS...
YOU'RE ALWAYS THROWING YOUR ARMS OVER THEIR SHOULDERS...
HUH? THAT'S NOT EXACTLY A ROMANTIC THING...

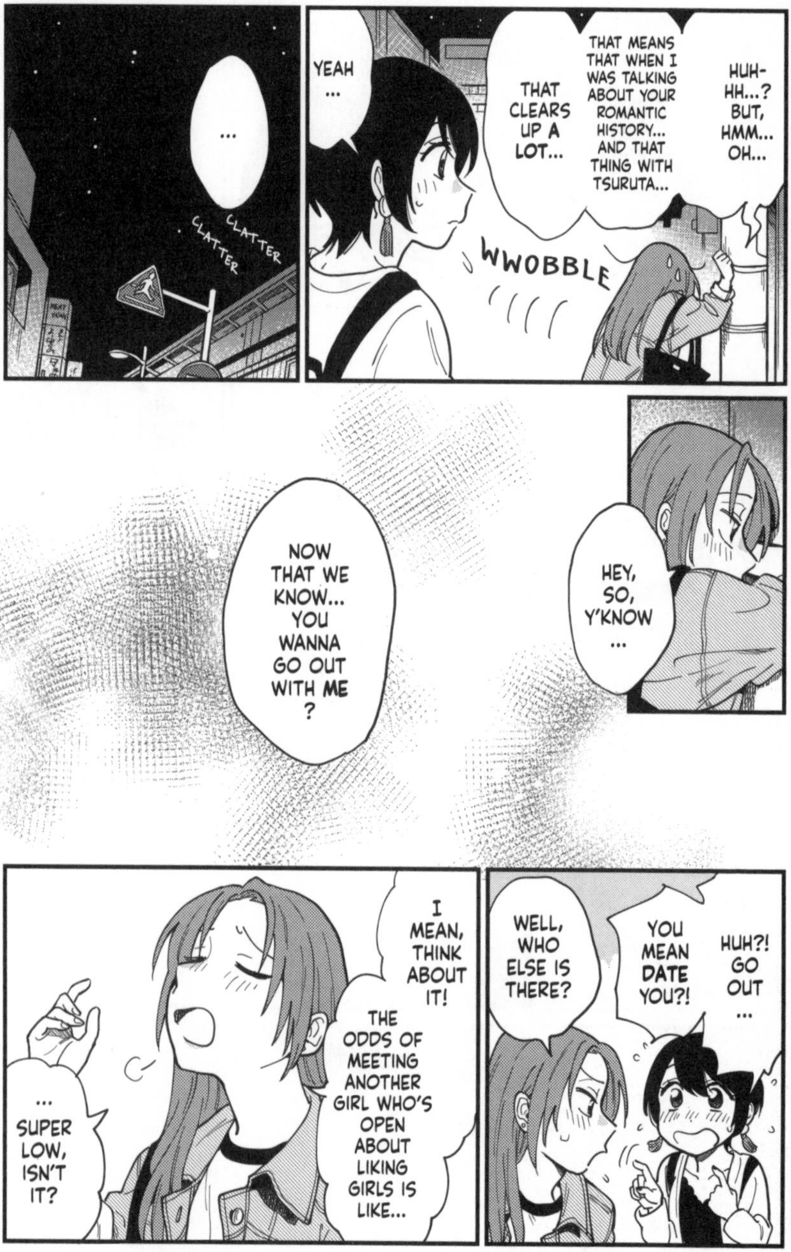
HUH-HH...? BUT, HMM... OH...
THAT MEANS THAT WHEN I WAS TALKING ABOUT YOUR ROMANTIC HISTORY... AND THAT THING WITH TSURUTA...
THAT CLEARS UP A LOT...
WWOBBLE
YEAH ...
...
CLATTER
CLATTER
HEY, SO, Y'KNOW ...
NOW THAT WE KNOW... YOU WANNA GO OUT WITH ME ?
HUH?! GO OUT ...
YOU MEAN DATE YOU?!
WELL, WHO ELSE IS THERE?
I MEAN, THINK ABOUT IT!
THE ODDS OF MEETING ANOTHER GIRL WHO'S OPEN ABOUT LIKING GIRLS IS LIKE...
... SUPER LOW, ISN'T IT?

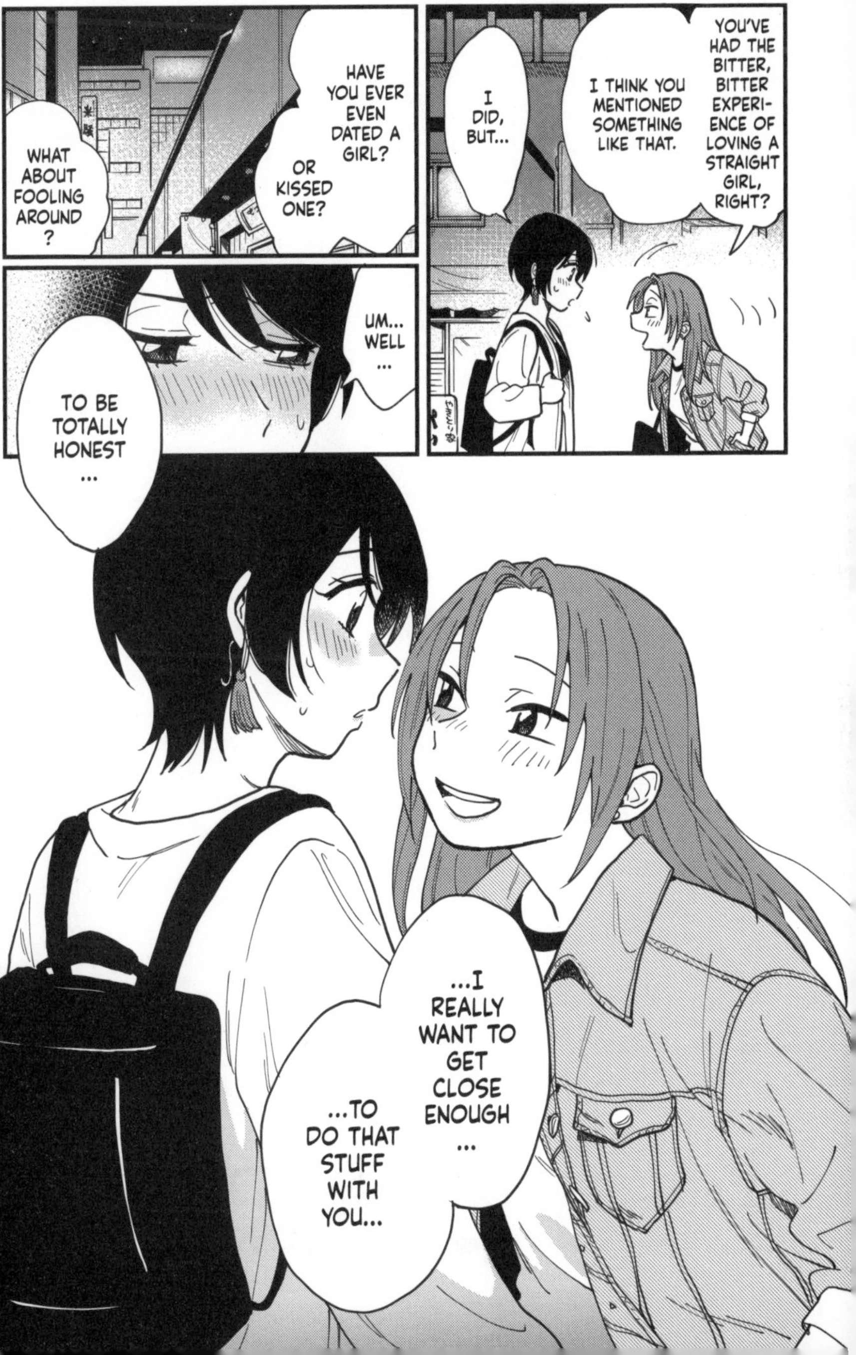
YOU'VE HAD THE BITTER, BITTER EXPERIENCE OF LOVING A STRAIGHT GIRL, RIGHT?
I THINK YOU MENTIONED SOMETHING LIKE THAT.
I DID, BUT...
HAVE YOU EVER EVEN DATED A GIRL?
OR KISSED ONE?
WHAT ABOUT FOOLING AROUND?
UM... WELL...
TO BE TOTALLY HONEST...
...I REALLY WANT TO GET CLOSE ENOUGH...
...TO DO THAT STUFF WITH YOU...

HOW DO WE RELATIONSHIP?

Chapter 2: I'll Go Out With You?

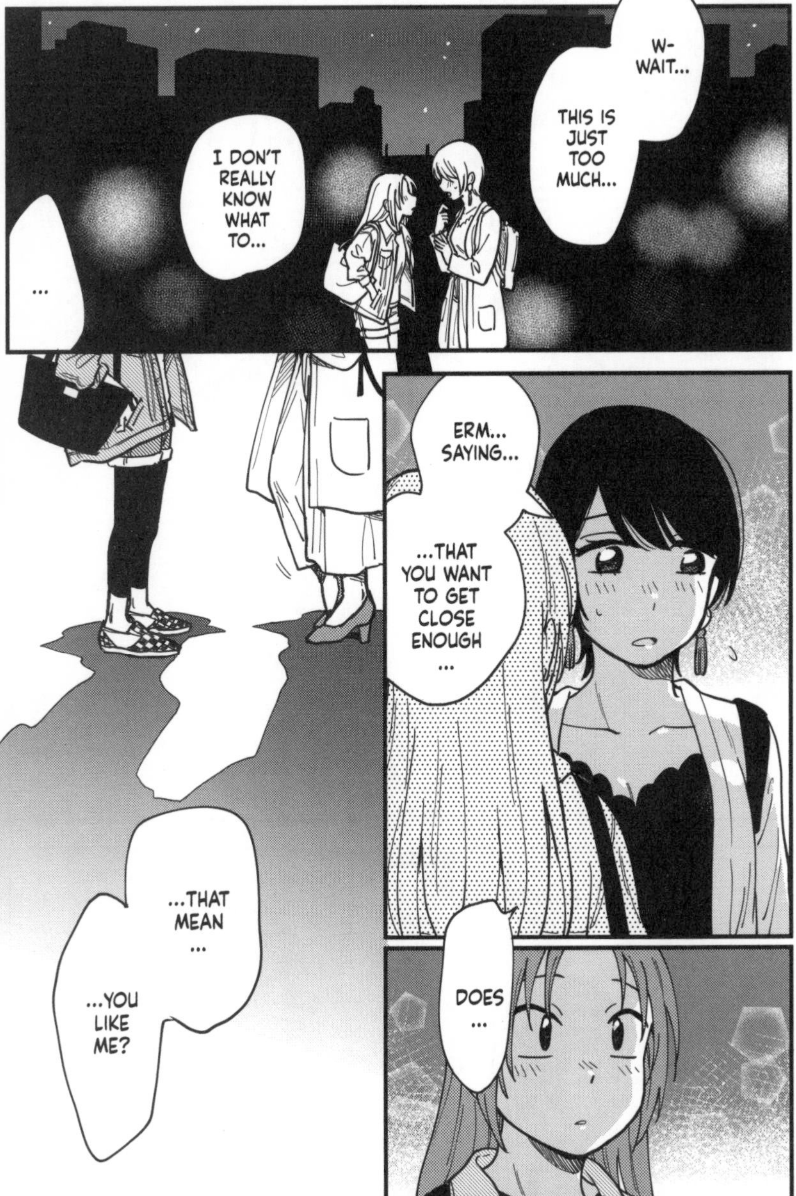
W- WAIT...
THIS IS JUST TOO MUCH...
I DON'T REALLY KNOW WHAT TO...
...
ERM... SAYING...
...THAT YOU WANT TO GET CLOSE ENOUGH ...
DOES ...
...THAT MEAN ...
...YOU LIKE ME?

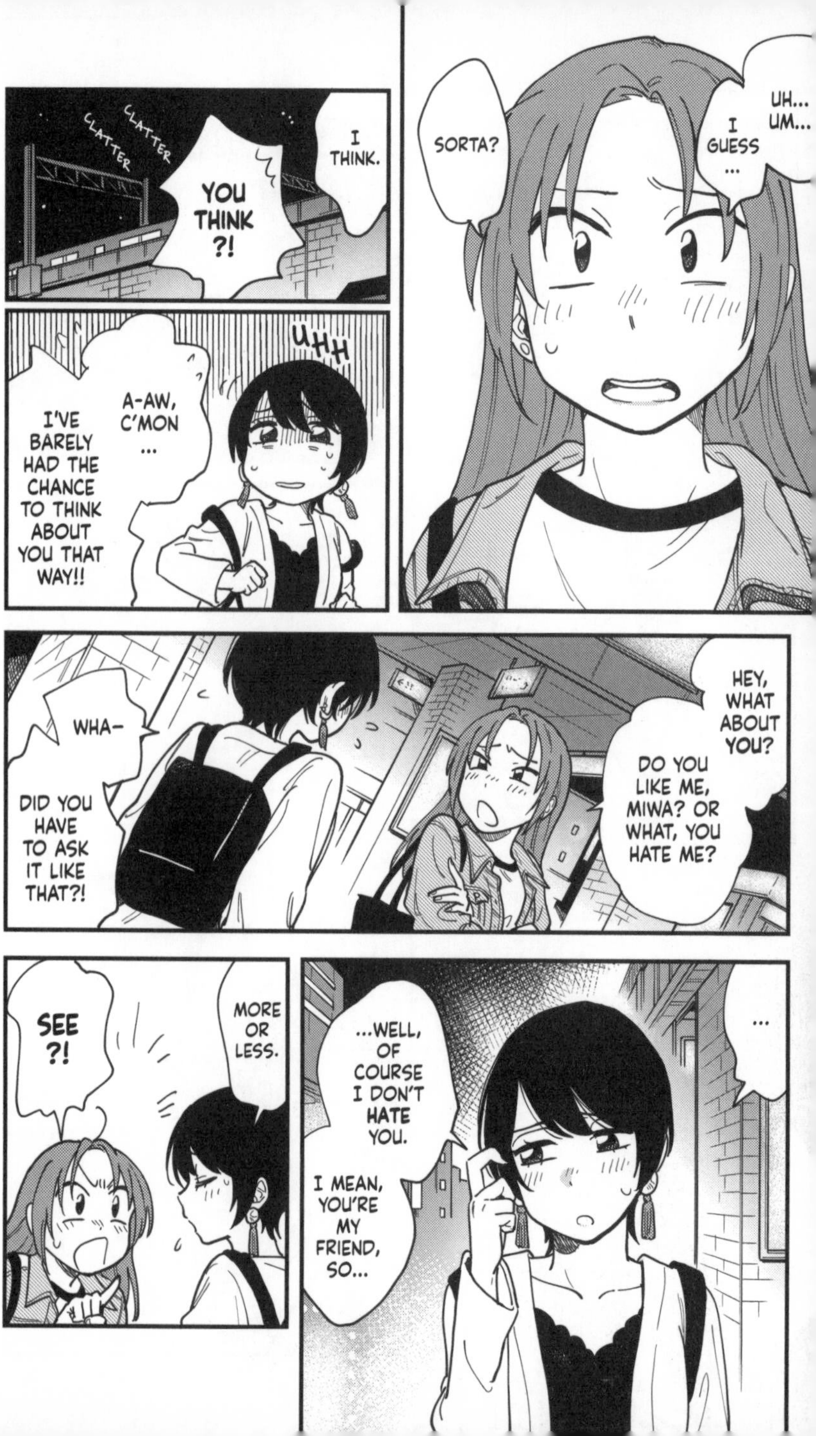
UH... UM...
I GUESS...
SORTA?
I THINK.
YOU THINK?!
CLATTER
CLATTER
UHH
A-AW, C'MON...
I'VE BARELY HAD THE CHANCE TO THINK ABOUT YOU THAT WAY!!
HEY, WHAT ABOUT YOU?
DO YOU LIKE ME, MIWA? OR WHAT, YOU HATE ME?
WHA-
DID YOU HAVE TO ASK IT LIKE THAT?!
...
...WELL, OF COURSE I DON'T HATE YOU.
I MEAN, YOU'RE MY FRIEND, SO...
MORE OR LESS.
SEE?!

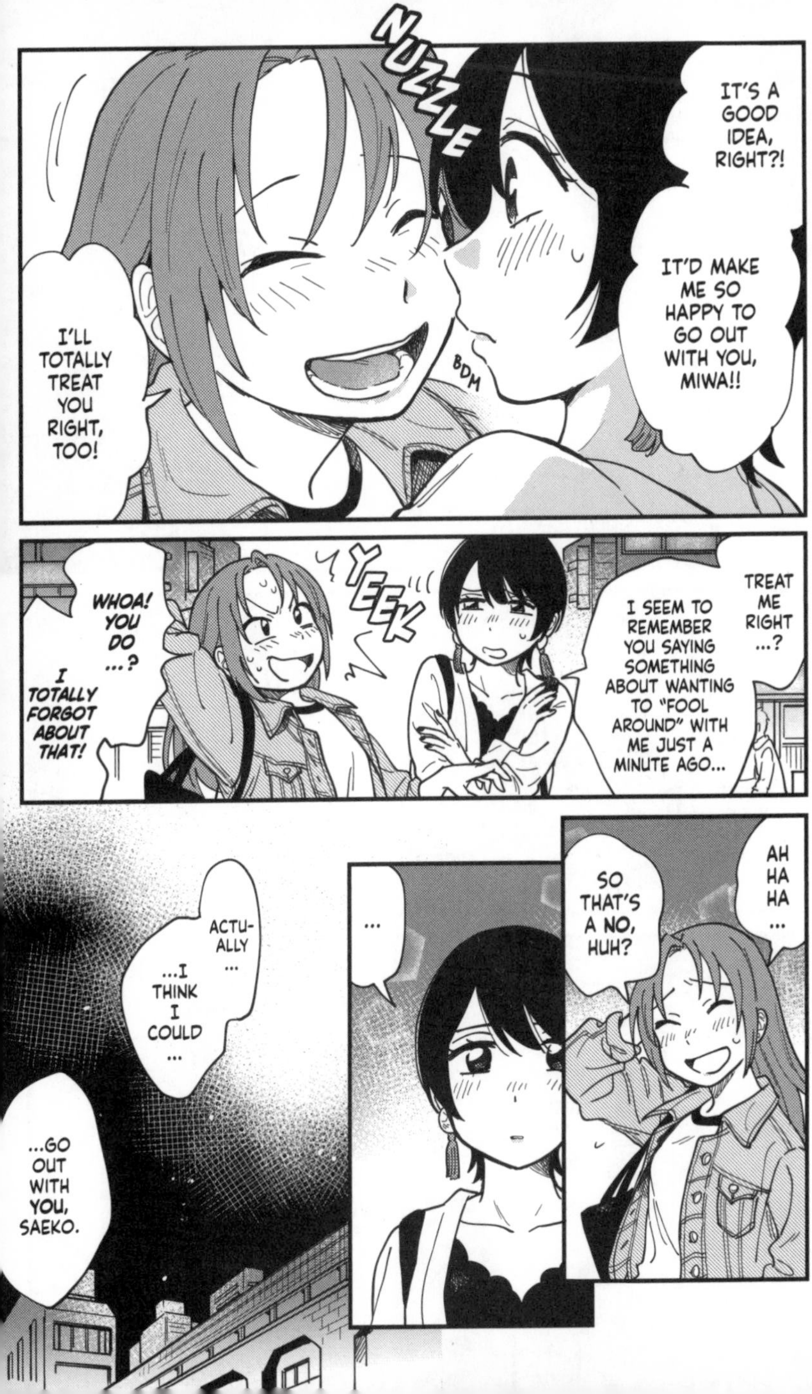
NUZZLE
IT'S A GOOD IDEA, RIGHT?!
IT'D MAKE ME SO HAPPY TO GO OUT WITH YOU, MIWA!!
BDM
I'LL TOTALLY TREAT YOU RIGHT, TOO!
TREAT ME RIGHT ...?
I SEEM TO REMEMBER YOU SAYING SOMETHING ABOUT WANTING TO "FOOL AROUND" WITH ME JUST A MINUTE AGO...
YEEK
WHOA! YOU DO ...?
I TOTALLY FORGOT ABOUT THAT!
AH HA HA ...
SO THAT'S A NO, HUH?
...
ACTUALLY ...
...I THINK I COULD ...
...GO OUT WITH YOU, SAEKO.

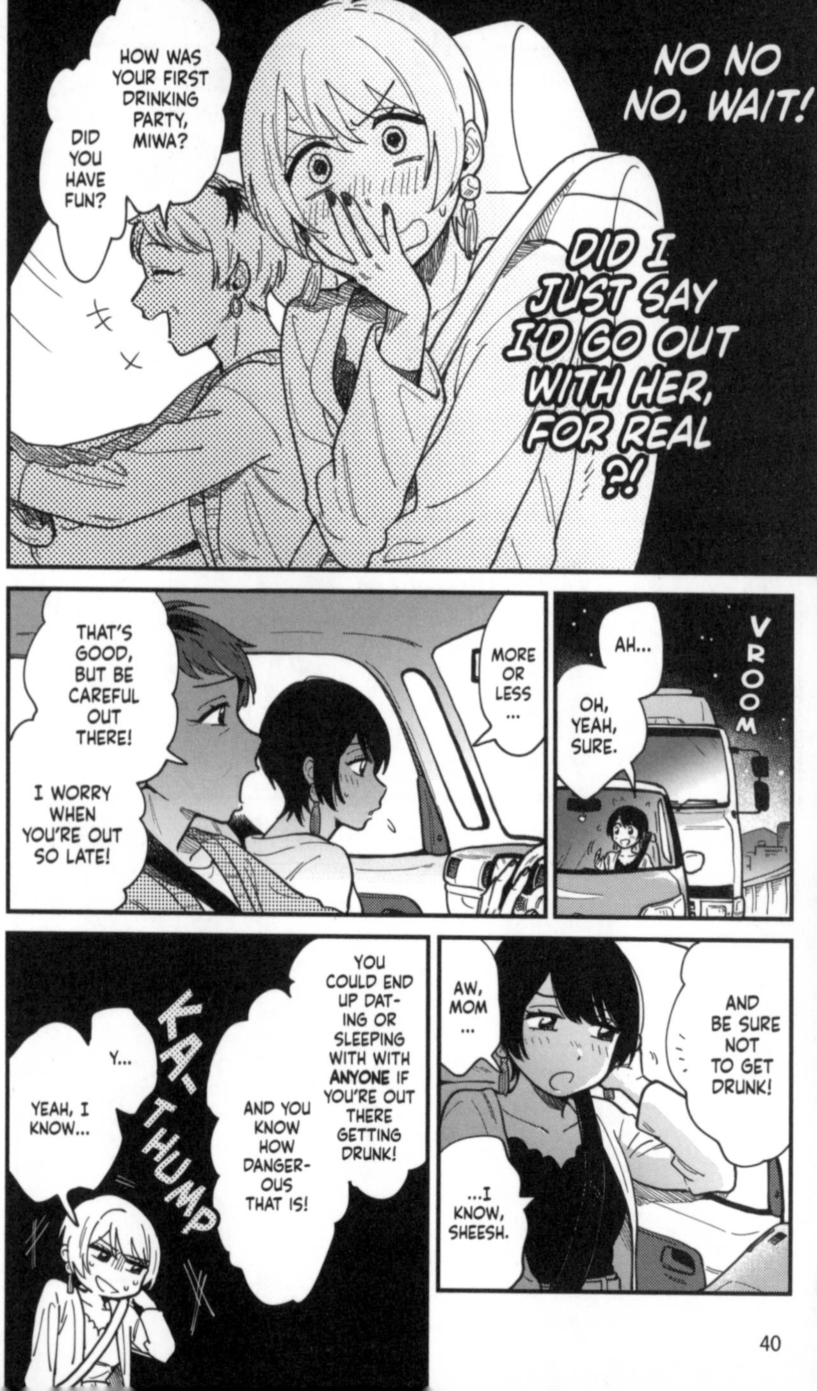
NO NO NO, WAIT!
HOW WAS YOUR FIRST DRINKING PARTY, MIWA?
DID YOU HAVE FUN?
DID I JUST SAY I'D GO OUT WITH HER, FOR REAL ?!
VROOM
AH...
OH, YEAH, SURE.
MORE OR LESS ...
THAT'S GOOD, BUT BE CAREFUL OUT THERE!
I WORRY WHEN YOU'RE OUT SO LATE!
AND BE SURE NOT TO GET DRUNK!
AW, MOM ...
...I KNOW, SHEESH.
YOU COULD END UP DAT-ING OR SLEEPING WITH WITH **ANYONE** IF YOU'RE OUT THERE GETTING DRUNK!
AND YOU KNOW HOW DANGER-OUS THAT IS!
KA-THUMP
Y...
YEAH, I KNOW...

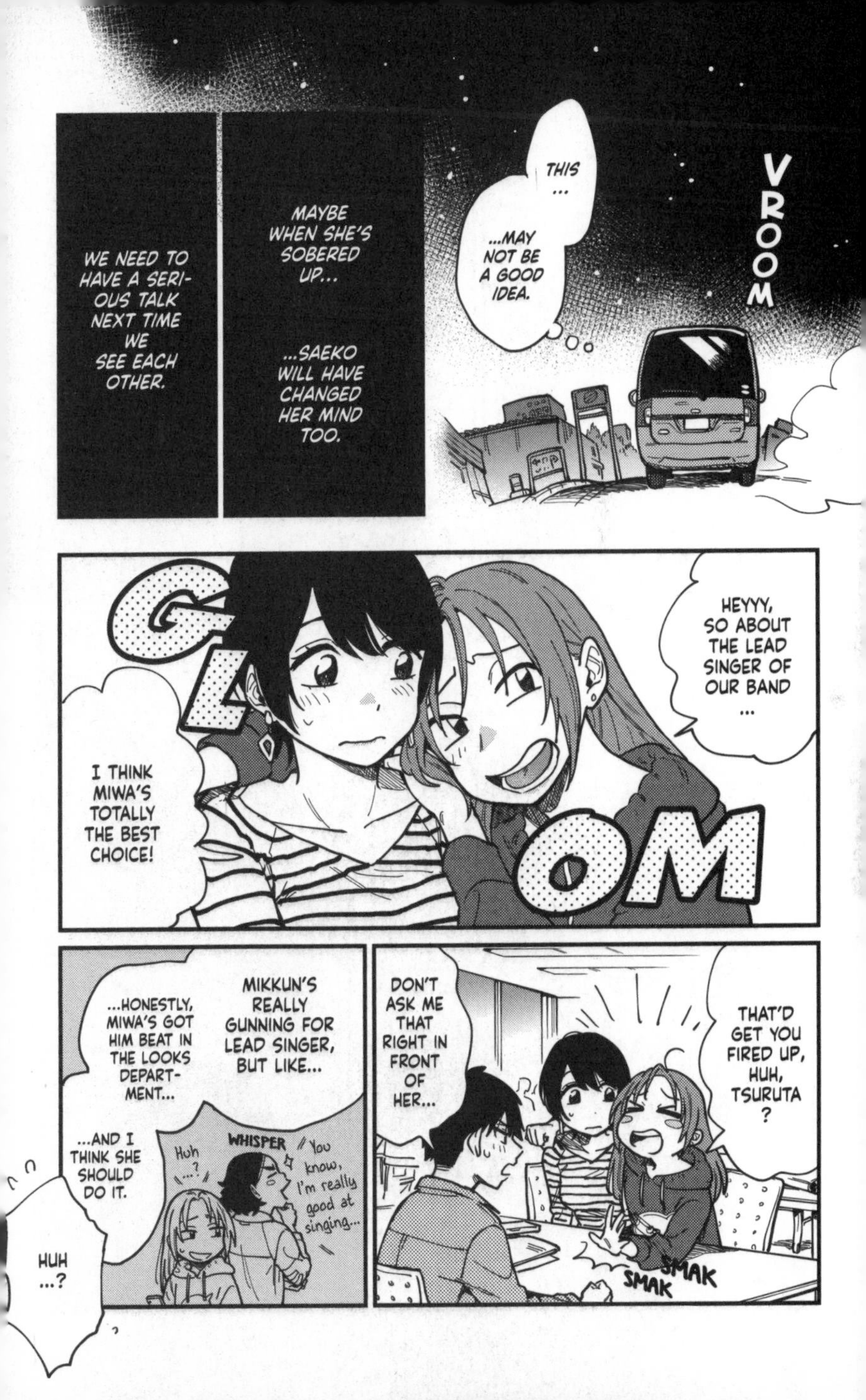
VROOM
THIS ...
...MAY NOT BE A GOOD IDEA.
MAYBE WHEN SHE'S SOBERED UP...
...SAEKO WILL HAVE CHANGED HER MIND TOO.
WE NEED TO HAVE A SERI-OUS TALK NEXT TIME WE SEE EACH OTHER.
GLOOM
HEYYY, SO ABOUT THE LEAD SINGER OF OUR BAND ...
I THINK MIWA'S TOTALLY THE BEST CHOICE!
THAT'D GET YOU FIRED UP, HUH, TSURUTA ?
DON'T ASK ME THAT RIGHT IN FRONT OF HER...
SMAK
SMAK
MIKKUN'S REALLY GUNNING FOR LEAD SINGER, BUT LIKE...
...HONESTLY, MIWA'S GOT HIM BEAT IN THE LOOKS DEPART-MENT...
WHISPER
You know, I'm really good at singing...
Huh ...?
...AND I THINK SHE SHOULD DO IT.
HUH ...?

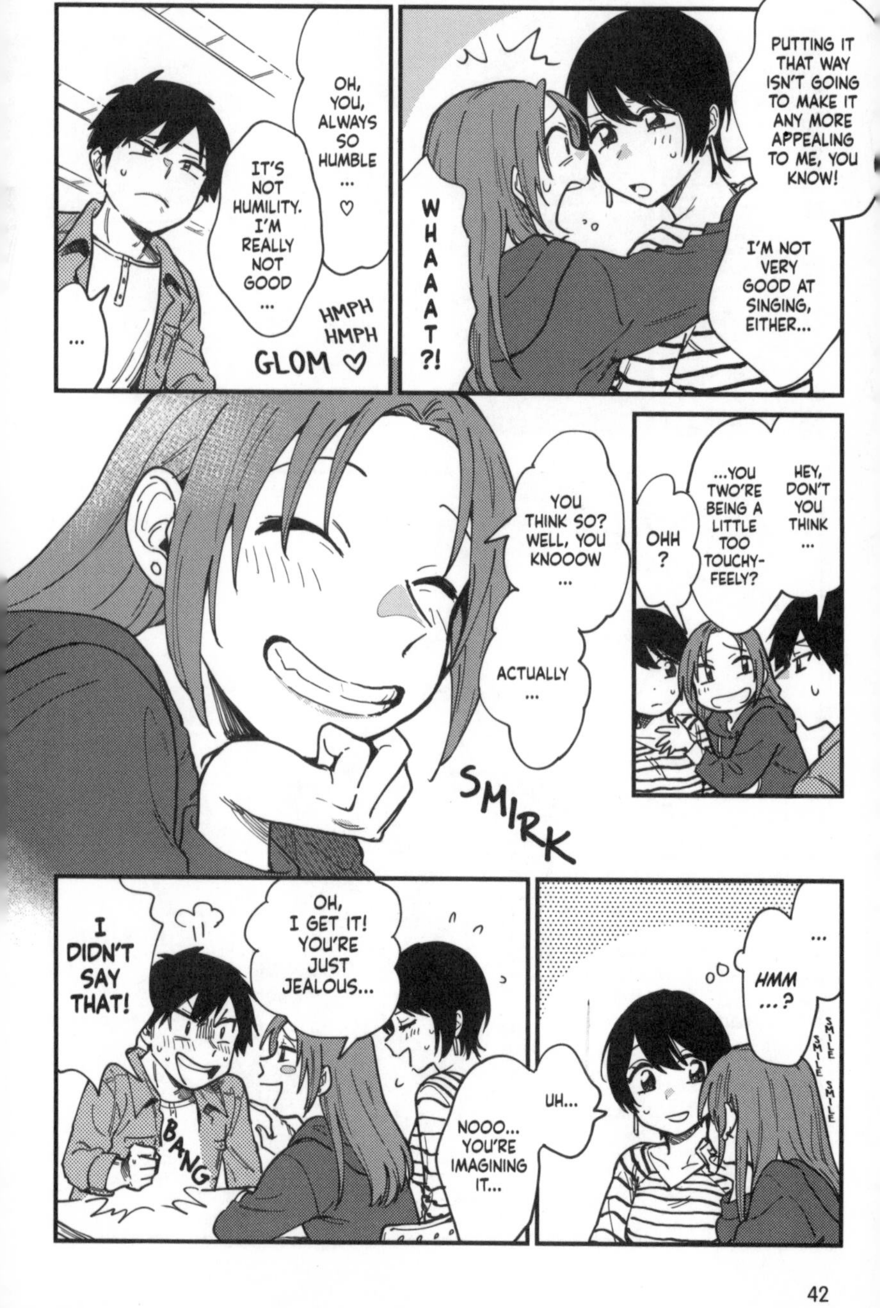
PUTTING IT THAT WAY ISN'T GOING TO MAKE IT ANY MORE APPEALING TO ME, YOU KNOW!
I'M NOT VERY GOOD AT SINGING, EITHER...
WHAAAAT?!
OH, YOU, ALWAYS SO HUMBLE... ♡
IT'S NOT HUMILITY. I'M REALLY NOT GOOD...
HMPH HMPH
GLOM ♡
...
HEY, DON'T YOU THINK...
...YOU TWO'RE BEING A LITTLE TOO TOUCHY-FEELY?
OHH?
YOU THINK SO? WELL, YOU KNOOOW...
ACTUALLY...
SMIRK
...
HMM...?
SMILE SMILE SMILE SMILE
UH...
NOOO... YOU'RE IMAGINING IT...
OH, I GET IT! YOU'RE JUST JEALOUS...
I DIDN'T SAY THAT!
BANG

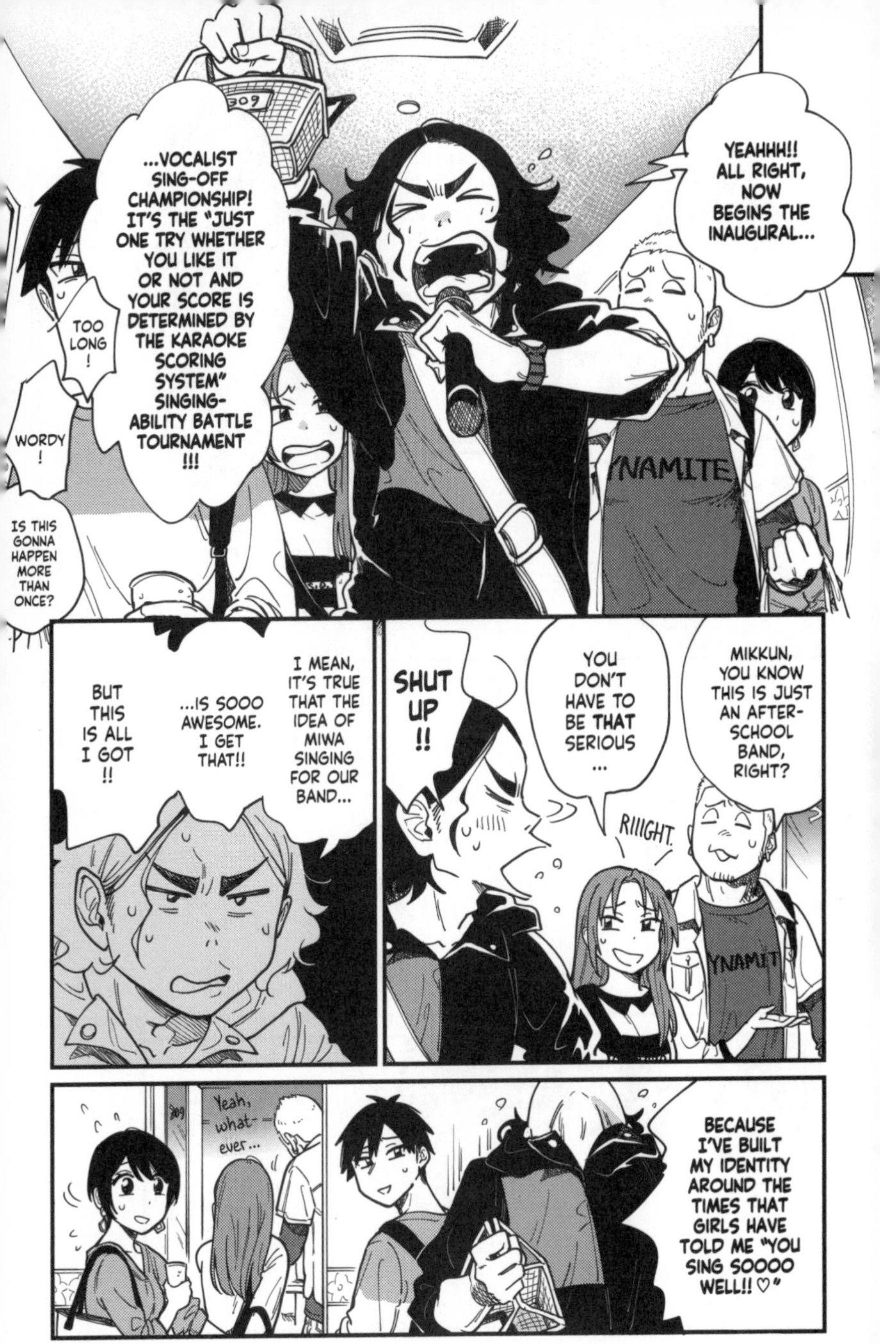

YEAHHH!! ALL RIGHT, NOW BEGINS THE INAUGURAL...
...VOCALIST SING-OFF CHAMPIONSHIP! IT'S THE "JUST ONE TRY WHETHER YOU LIKE IT OR NOT AND YOUR SCORE IS DETERMINED BY THE KARAOKE SCORING SYSTEM" SINGING-ABILITY BATTLE TOURNAMENT!!!
TOO LONG!
WORDY!
IS THIS GONNA HAPPEN MORE THAN ONCE?
MIKKUN, YOU KNOW THIS IS JUST AN AFTER-SCHOOL BAND, RIGHT?
YOU DON'T HAVE TO BE THAT SERIOUS...
RIIIGHT.
SHUT UP!!
I MEAN, IT'S TRUE THAT THE IDEA OF MIWA SINGING FOR OUR BAND...
...IS SOOO AWESOME. I GET THAT!!
BUT THIS IS ALL I GOT!!
BECAUSE I'VE BUILT MY IDENTITY AROUND THE TIMES THAT GIRLS HAVE TOLD ME "YOU SING SOOOO WELL!! ♡"
Yeah, whatever...

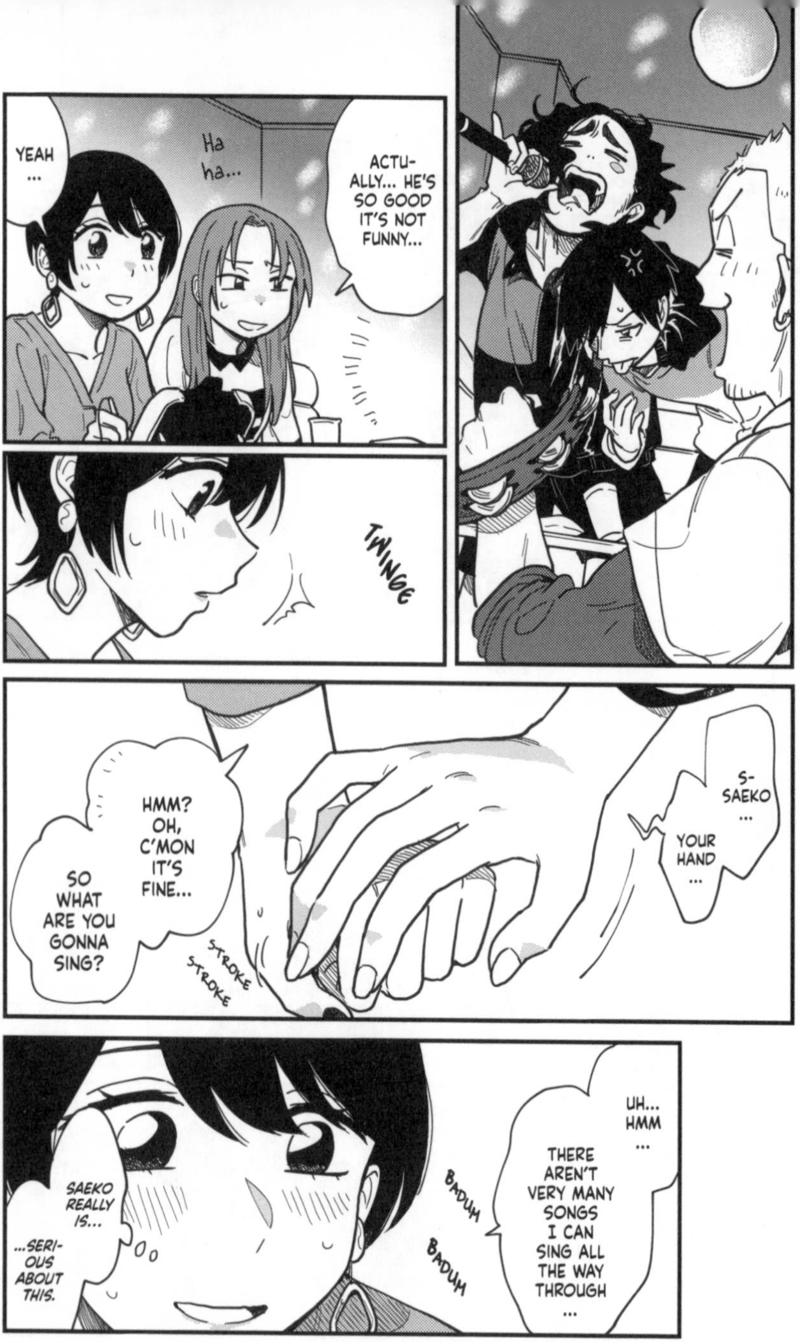
ACTUALLY... HE'S SO GOOD IT'S NOT FUNNY...
Ha ha...
YEAH ...
TWINGE
S-SAEKO ... YOUR HAND ...
HMM? OH, C'MON IT'S FINE...
SO WHAT ARE YOU GONNA SING?
STROKE STROKE
UH... HMM ...
THERE AREN'T VERY MANY SONGS I CAN SING ALL THE WAY THROUGH ...
BADUM BADUM
SAEKO REALLY IS...
...SERIOUS ABOUT THIS.

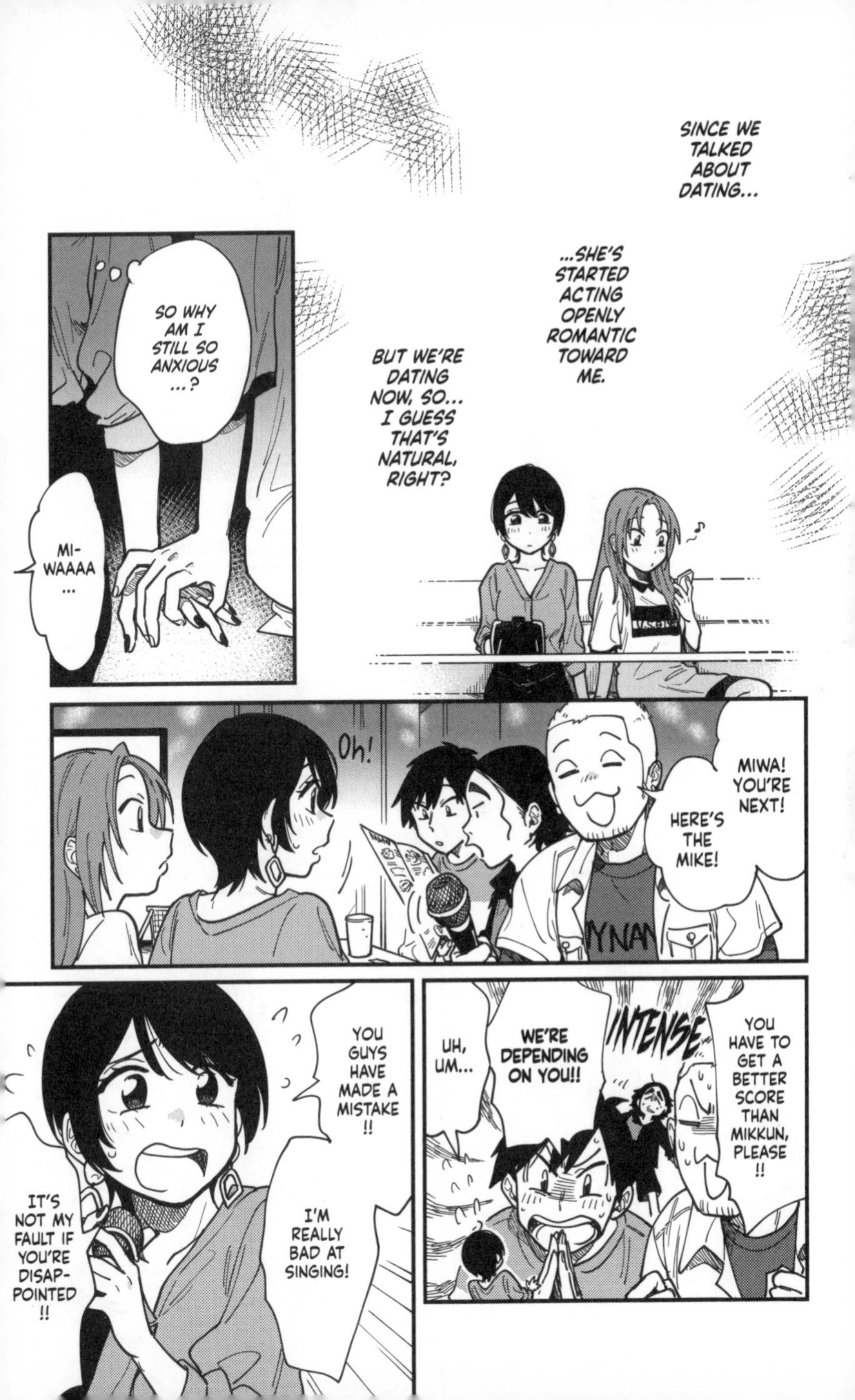
SINCE WE TALKED ABOUT DATING...
...SHE'S STARTED ACTING OPENLY ROMANTIC TOWARD ME.
BUT WE'RE DATING NOW, SO... I GUESS THAT'S NATURAL, RIGHT?
SO WHY AM I STILL SO ANXIOUS ...?
MI-WAAAA ...
MIWA! YOU'RE NEXT!
HERE'S THE MIKE!
Oh!
YOU HAVE TO GET A BETTER SCORE THAN MIKKUN, PLEASE !!
INTENSE
WE'RE DEPENDING ON YOU!!
UH, UM...
YOU GUYS HAVE MADE A MISTAKE !!
I'M REALLY BAD AT SINGING!
IT'S NOT MY FAULT IF YOU'RE DISAPPOINTED !!

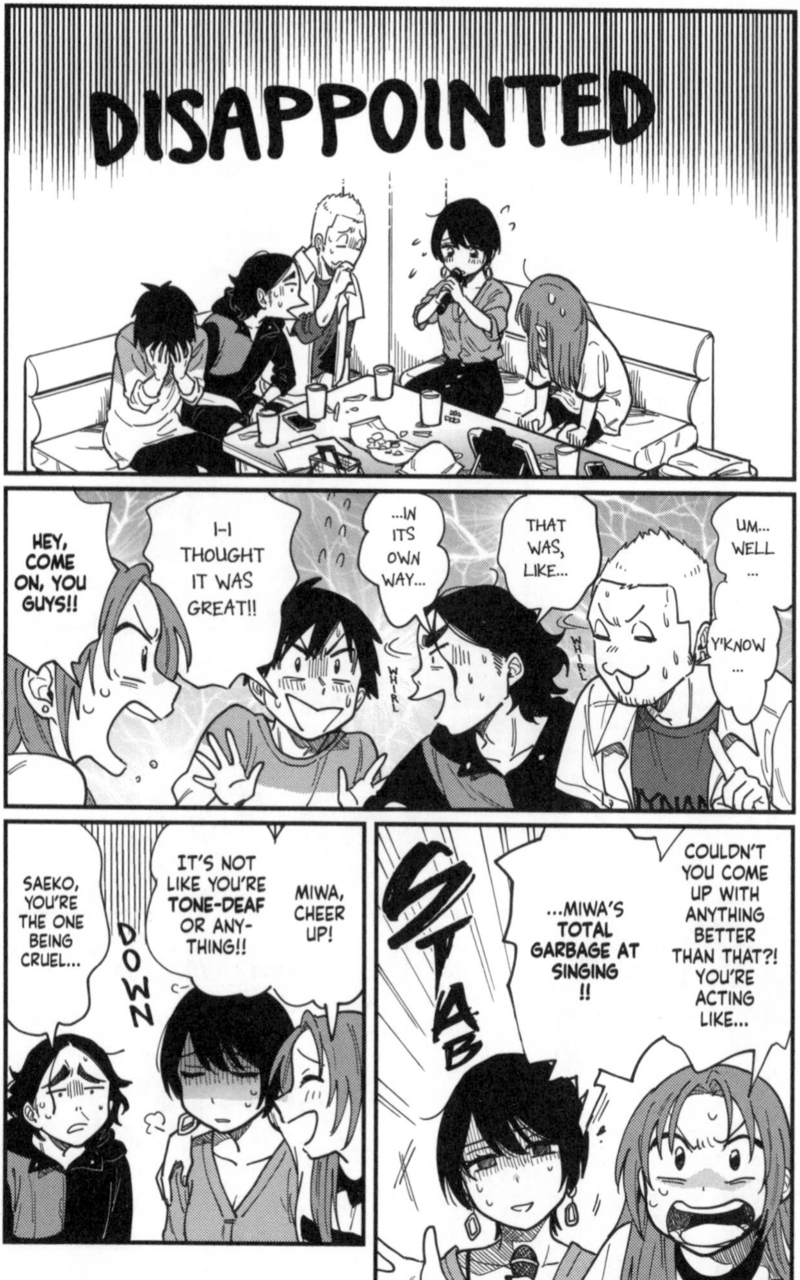
DISAPPOINTED
UM... WELL ...
Y'KNOW ...
THAT WAS, LIKE...
WHIRL
...IN ITS OWN WAY...
WHIRL
I-I THOUGHT IT WAS GREAT!!
HEY, COME ON, YOU GUYS!!
COULDN'T YOU COME UP WITH ANYTHING BETTER THAN THAT?! YOU'RE ACTING LIKE...
...MIWA'S TOTAL GARBAGE AT SINGING !!
STAB
MIWA, CHEER UP!
IT'S NOT LIKE YOU'RE TONE-DEAF OR ANY-THING!!
DOWN
SAEKO, YOU'RE THE ONE BEING CRUEL...

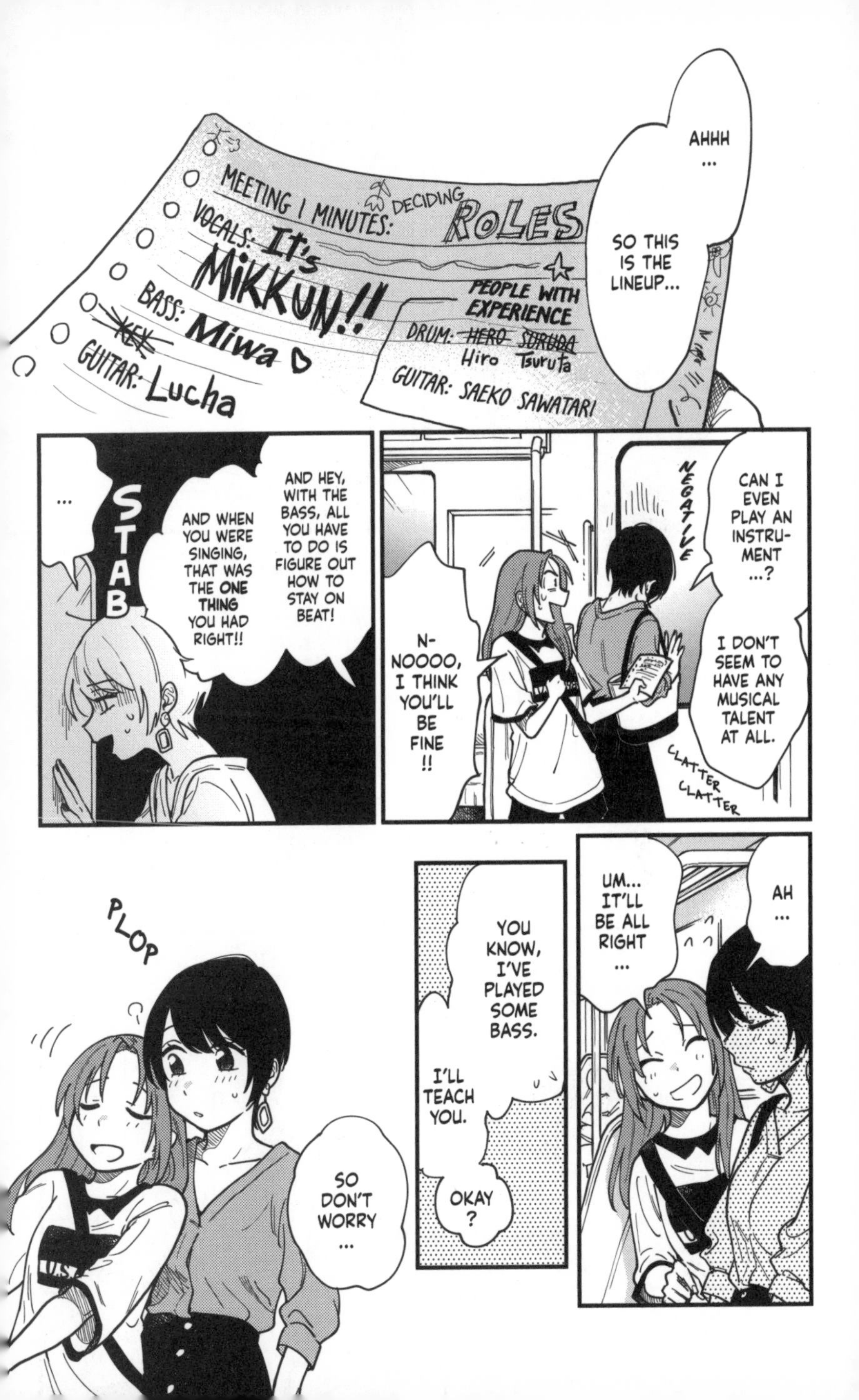
AHHH ...
SO THIS IS THE LINEUP...
MEETING 1 MINUTES: DECIDING ROLES
VOCALS: It's MIKKUN!!
BASS: ~~KEK~~ Miwa
GUITAR: Lucha
PEOPLE WITH EXPERIENCE
DRUM: ~~HERO SURUDA~~ Hiro Tsuruta
GUITAR: SAEKO SAWATARI
NEGATIVE
CAN I EVEN PLAY AN INSTRUMENT ...?
I DON'T SEEM TO HAVE ANY MUSICAL TALENT AT ALL.
CLATTER CLATTER
N- NOOOO, I THINK YOU'LL BE FINE !!
AND HEY, WITH THE BASS, ALL YOU HAVE TO DO IS FIGURE OUT HOW TO STAY ON BEAT!
AND WHEN YOU WERE SINGING, THAT WAS THE ONE THING YOU HAD RIGHT!!
STAB
...
AH ...
UM... IT'LL BE ALL RIGHT ...
YOU KNOW, I'VE PLAYED SOME BASS.
I'LL TEACH YOU.
OKAY ?
PLOP
SO DON'T WORRY ...

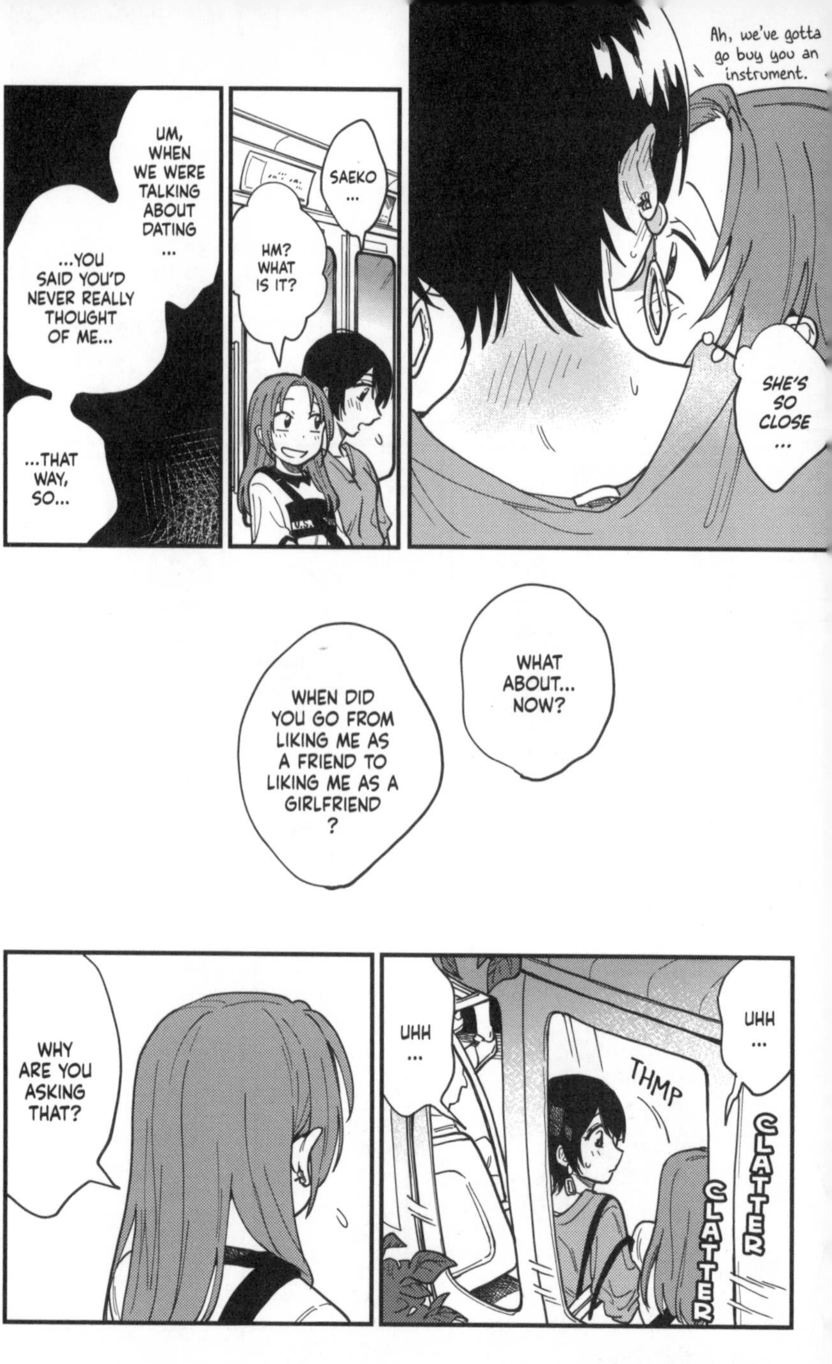
Ah, we've gotta go buy you an instrument.
SHE'S SO CLOSE...
SAEKO...
HM? WHAT IS IT?
UM, WHEN WE WERE TALKING ABOUT DATING...
...YOU SAID YOU'D NEVER REALLY THOUGHT OF ME...
...THAT WAY, SO...
WHAT ABOUT... NOW?
WHEN DID YOU GO FROM LIKING ME AS A FRIEND TO LIKING ME AS A GIRLFRIEND?
UHH...
CLATTER
CLATTER
THMP
UHH...
WHY ARE YOU ASKING THAT?

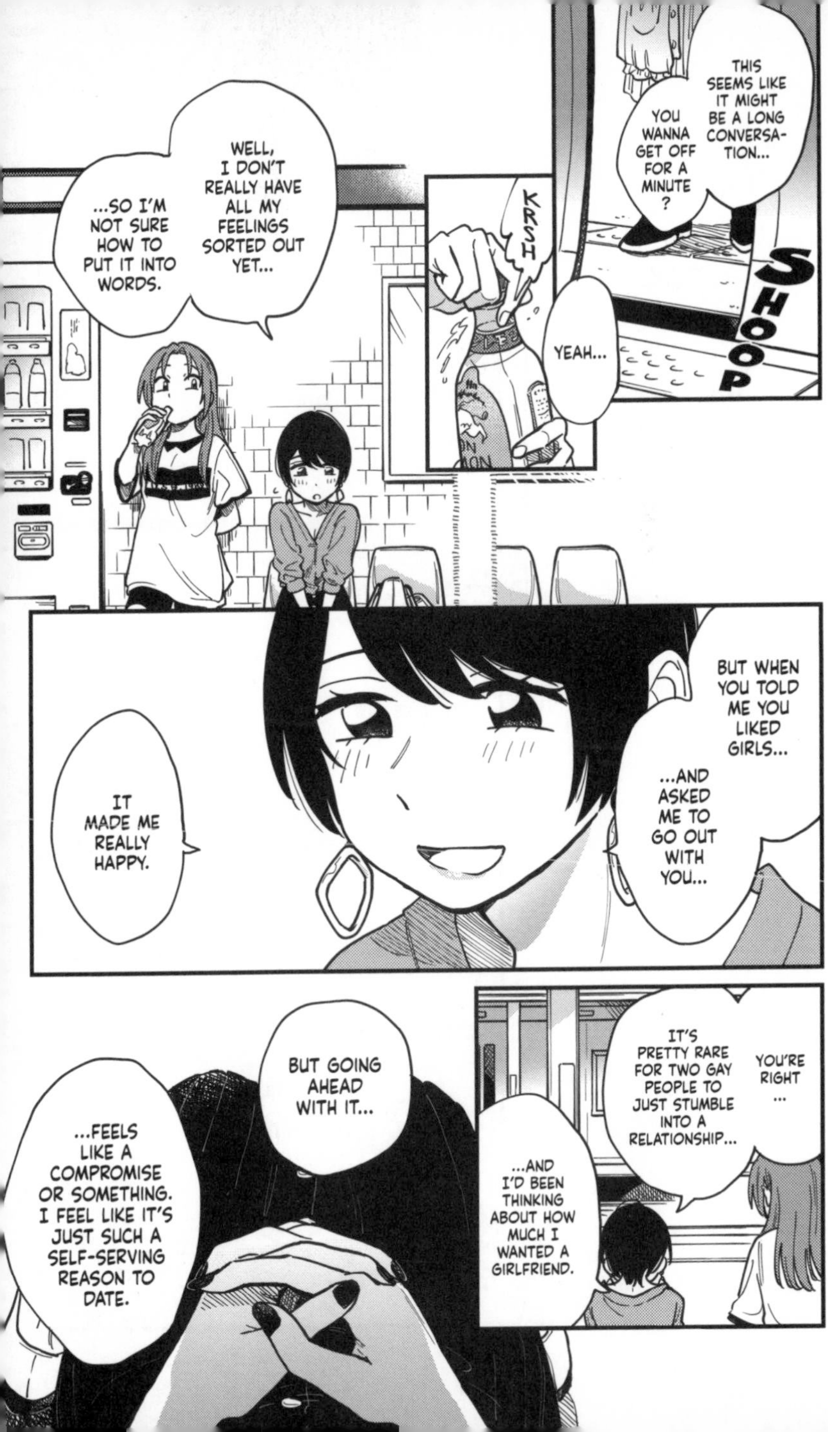
THIS SEEMS LIKE IT MIGHT BE A LONG CONVERSA-TION...
YOU WANNA GET OFF FOR A MINUTE?
SHOOP
KRSH
YEAH...
WELL, I DON'T REALLY HAVE ALL MY FEELINGS SORTED OUT YET...
...SO I'M NOT SURE HOW TO PUT IT INTO WORDS.
BUT WHEN YOU TOLD ME YOU LIKED GIRLS...
...AND ASKED ME TO GO OUT WITH YOU...
IT MADE ME REALLY HAPPY.
YOU'RE RIGHT...
IT'S PRETTY RARE FOR TWO GAY PEOPLE TO JUST STUMBLE INTO A RELATIONSHIP...
...AND I'D BEEN THINKING ABOUT HOW MUCH I WANTED A GIRLFRIEND.
BUT GOING AHEAD WITH IT...
...FEELS LIKE A COMPROMISE OR SOMETHING. I FEEL LIKE IT'S JUST SUCH A SELF-SERVING REASON TO DATE.

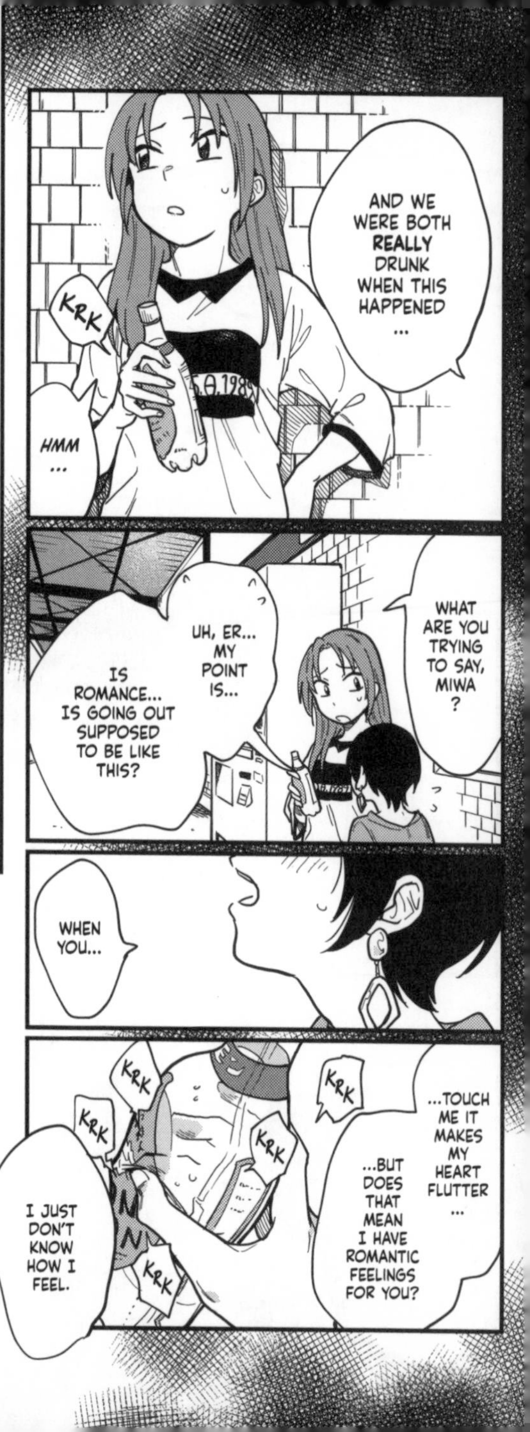
AND WE WERE BOTH REALLY DRUNK WHEN THIS HAPPENED...
KRK
HMM...
WHAT ARE YOU TRYING TO SAY, MIWA?
UH, ER... MY POINT IS...
IS ROMANCE... IS GOING OUT SUPPOSED TO BE LIKE THIS?
WHEN YOU...
...TOUCH ME IT MAKES MY HEART FLUTTER...
KRK
...BUT DOES THAT MEAN I HAVE ROMANTIC FEELINGS FOR YOU?
KRK
KRK
KRK
KRK
I JUST DON'T KNOW HOW I FEEL.

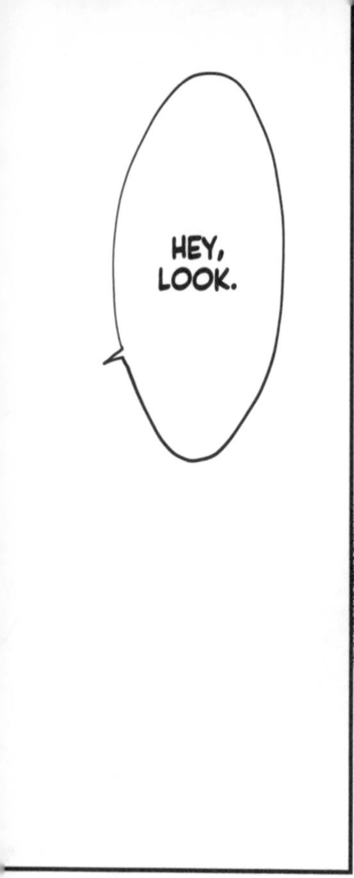
HEY, LOOK.

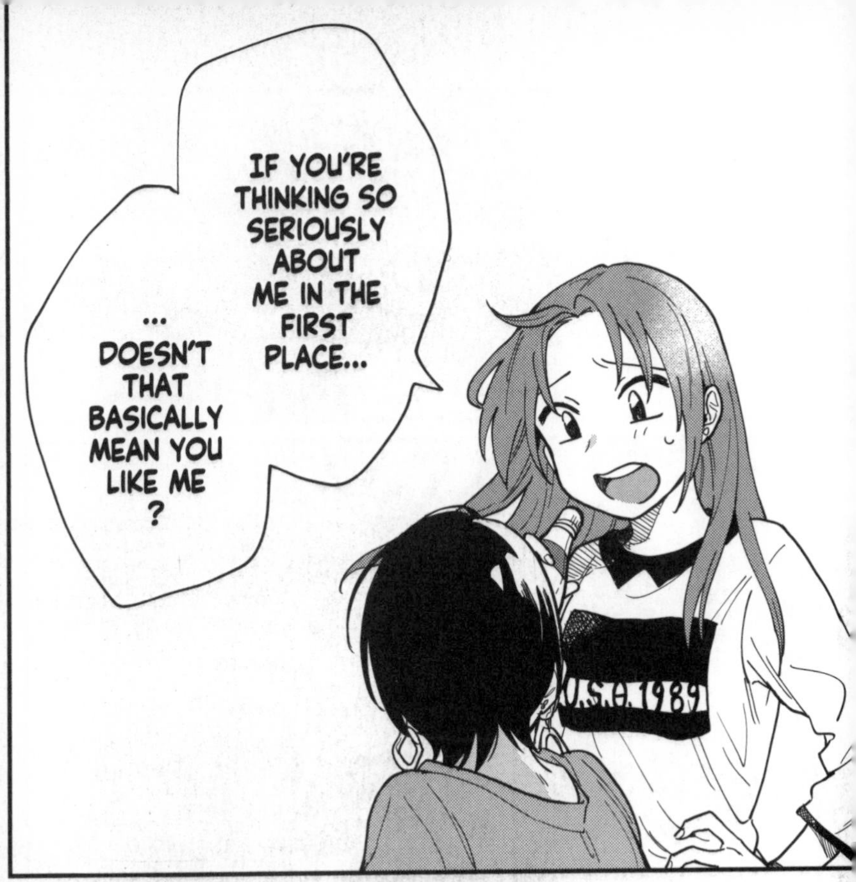
IF YOU'RE THINKING SO SERIOUSLY ABOUT ME IN THE FIRST PLACE...
... DOESN'T THAT BASICALLY MEAN YOU LIKE ME ?

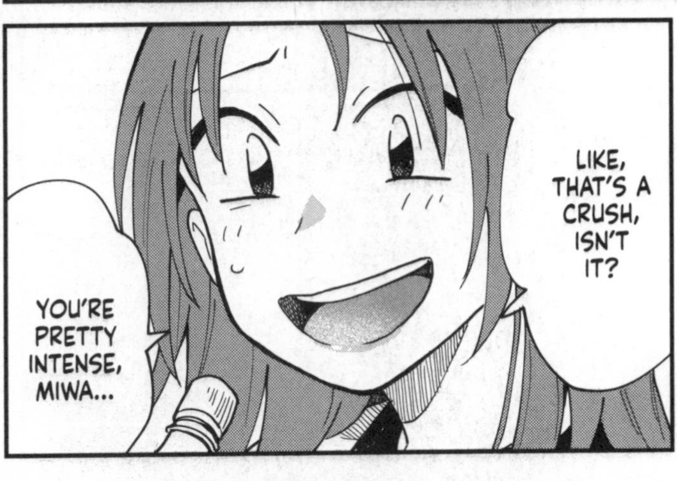
LIKE, THAT'S A CRUSH, ISN'T IT?
YOU'RE PRETTY INTENSE, MIWA...

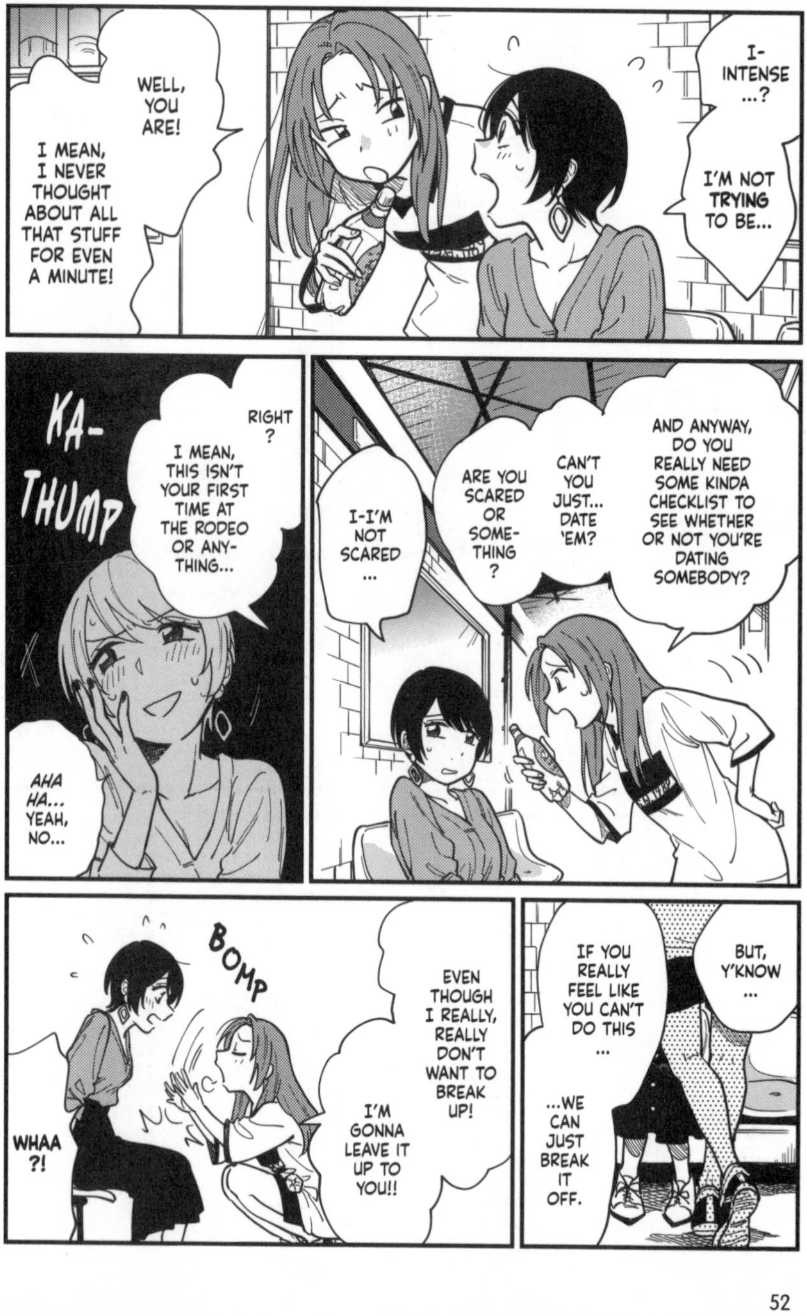
I-INTENSE...?
I'M NOT **TRYING** TO BE...
WELL, YOU ARE!
I MEAN, I NEVER THOUGHT ABOUT ALL THAT STUFF FOR EVEN A MINUTE!
AND ANYWAY, DO YOU REALLY NEED SOME KINDA CHECKLIST TO SEE WHETHER OR NOT YOU'RE DATING SOMEBODY?
CAN'T YOU JUST... DATE 'EM?
ARE YOU SCARED OR SOME-THING?
I-I'M NOT SCARED...
RIGHT?
I MEAN, THIS ISN'T YOUR FIRST TIME AT THE RODEO OR ANY-THING...
KA-THUMP
AHA HA... YEAH, NO...
BUT, Y'KNOW...
IF YOU REALLY FEEL LIKE YOU CAN'T DO THIS...
...WE CAN JUST BREAK IT OFF.
EVEN THOUGH I REALLY, REALLY DON'T WANT TO BREAK UP!
I'M GONNA LEAVE IT UP TO YOU!!
BOMP
WHAA?!

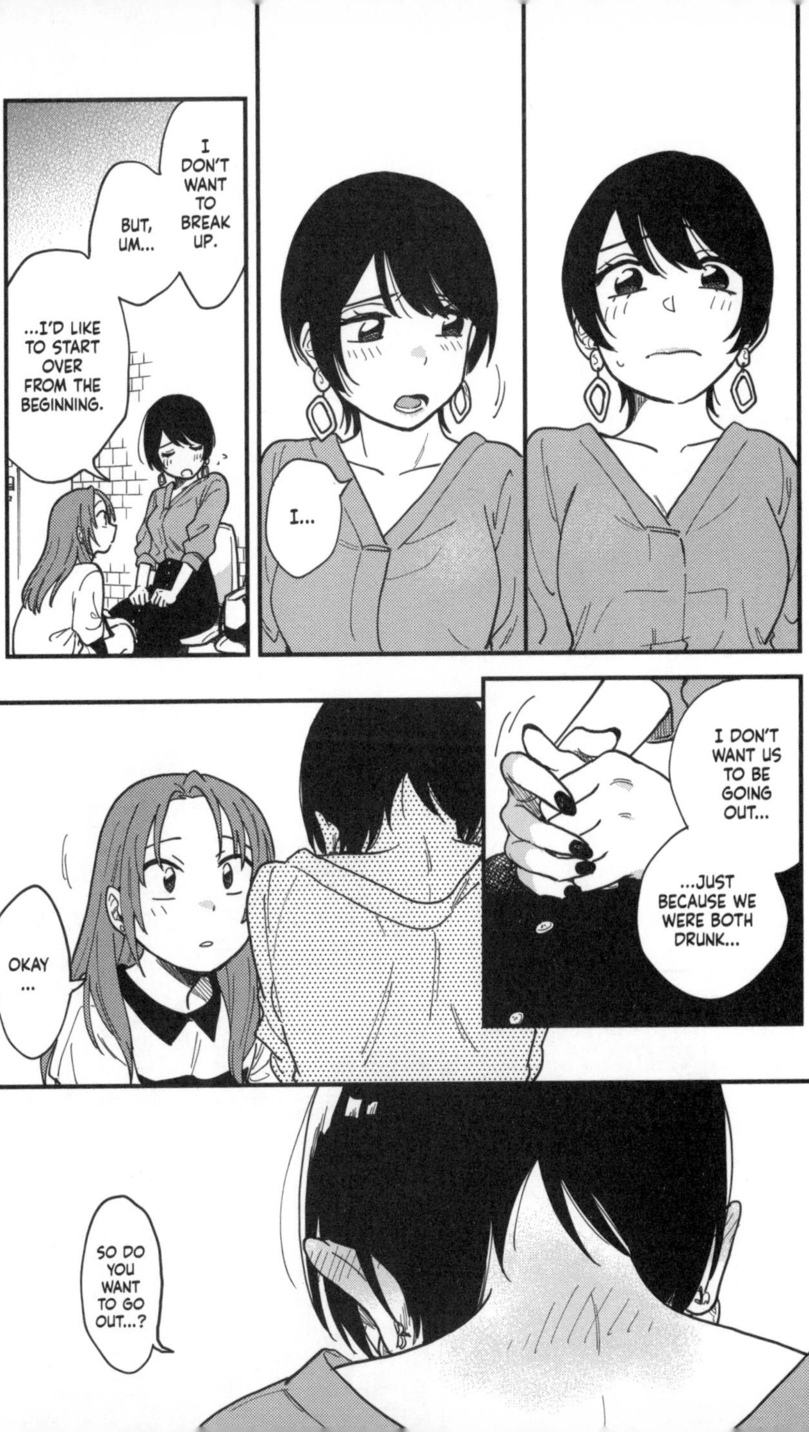
I...
I DON'T WANT TO BREAK UP.
BUT, UM...
...I'D LIKE TO START OVER FROM THE BEGINNING.
I DON'T WANT US TO BE GOING OUT...
...JUST BECAUSE WE WERE BOTH DRUNK...
OKAY ...
SO DO YOU WANT TO GO OUT...?

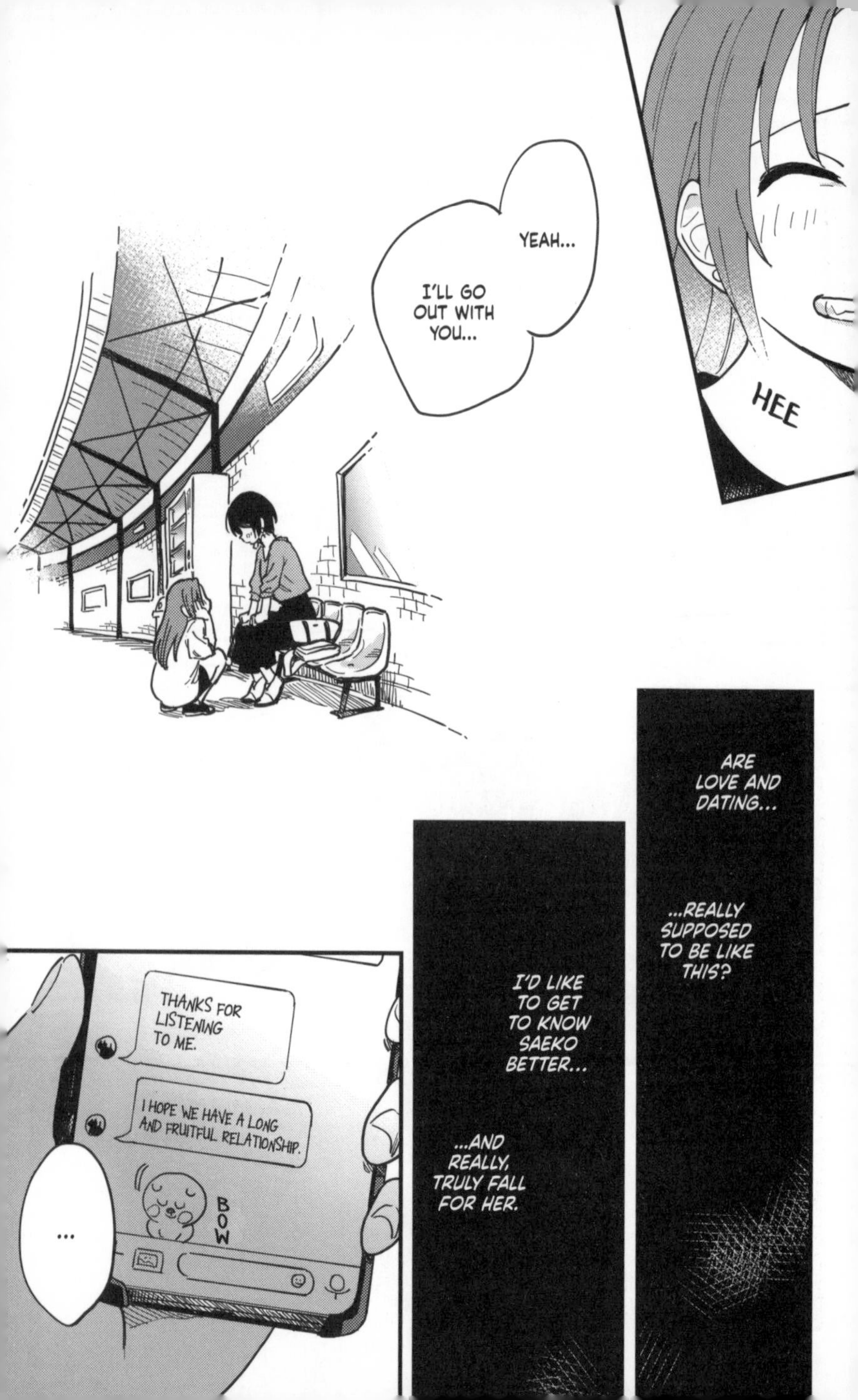
YEAH...
I'LL GO OUT WITH YOU...
HEE
ARE LOVE AND DATING...
...REALLY SUPPOSED TO BE LIKE THIS?
I'D LIKE TO GET TO KNOW SAEKO BETTER...
...AND REALLY, TRULY FALL FOR HER.
THANKS FOR LISTENING TO ME.
I HOPE WE HAVE A LONG AND FRUITFUL RELATIONSHIP.
BOW
...

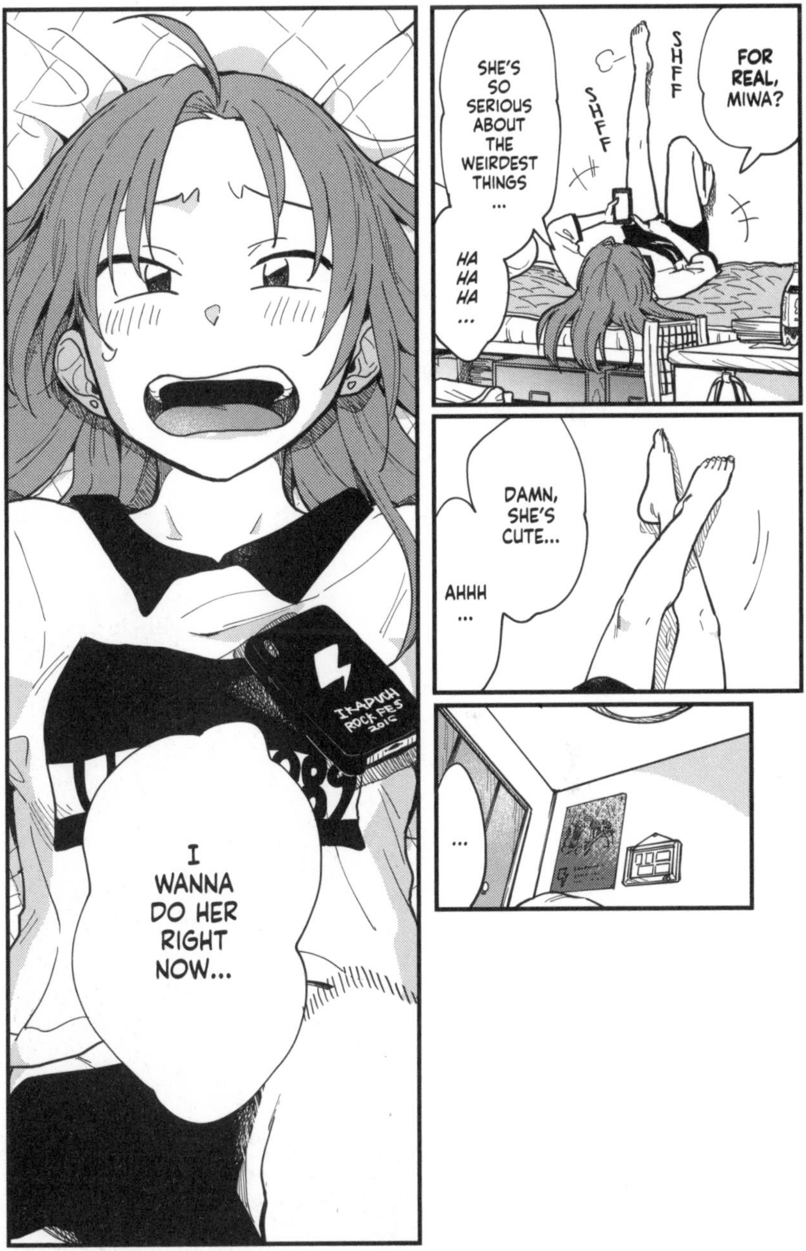
FOR REAL, MIWA?
SHFF
SHFF
SHE'S SO SERIOUS ABOUT THE WEIRDEST THINGS ...
HA HA HA ...
DAMN, SHE'S CUTE...
AHHH ...
...
IKADUCH ROCK FES
I WANNA DO HER RIGHT NOW...

How Do We
Relationship?

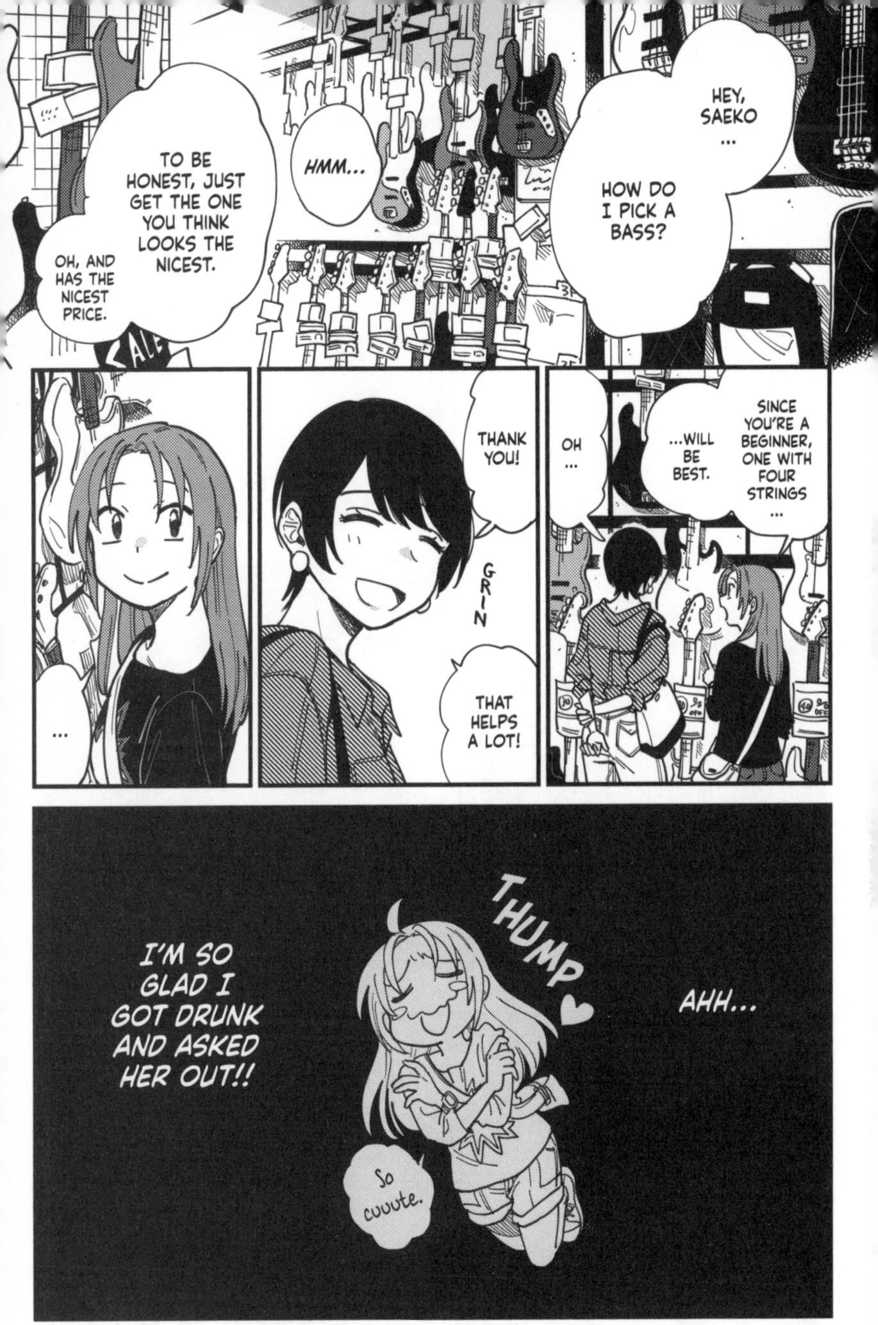
HEY, SAEKO ...
HOW DO I PICK A BASS?
HMM...
TO BE HONEST, JUST GET THE ONE YOU THINK LOOKS THE NICEST.
OH, AND HAS THE NICEST PRICE.
SALE
SINCE YOU'RE A BEGINNER, ONE WITH FOUR STRINGS ...
...WILL BE BEST.
OH ...
THANK YOU!
GRIN
THAT HELPS A LOT!
...
AHH...
THUMP
I'M SO GLAD I GOT DRUNK AND ASKED HER OUT!!
So cuuute.

Chapter 3: Embraceable You

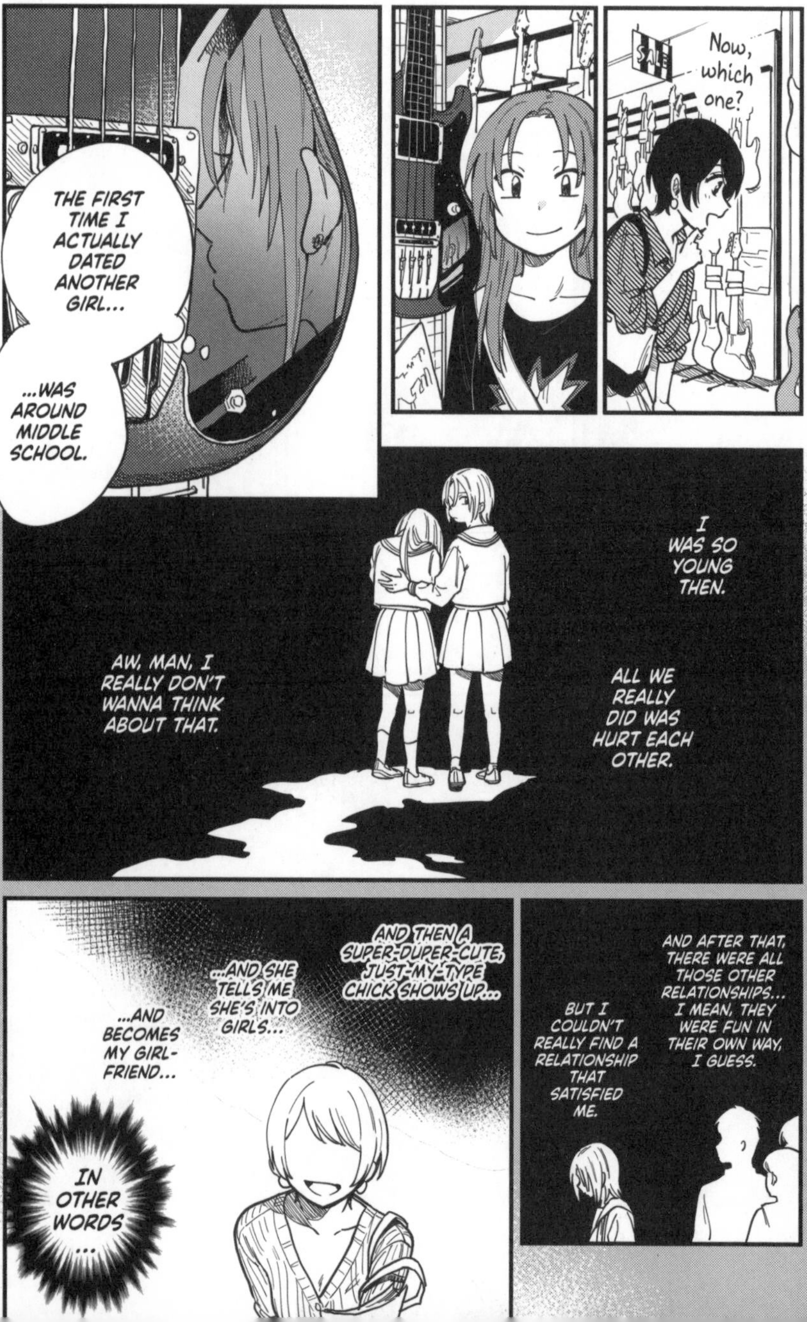
SALE
Now, which one?
THE FIRST TIME I ACTUALLY DATED ANOTHER GIRL...
...WAS AROUND MIDDLE SCHOOL.
I WAS SO YOUNG THEN.
ALL WE REALLY DID WAS HURT EACH OTHER.
AW, MAN, I REALLY DON'T WANNA THINK ABOUT THAT.
AND AFTER THAT, THERE WERE ALL THOSE OTHER RELATIONSHIPS... I MEAN, THEY WERE FUN IN THEIR OWN WAY, I GUESS.
BUT I COULDN'T REALLY FIND A RELATIONSHIP THAT SATISFIED ME.
AND THEN A SUPER-DUPER-CUTE, JUST-MY-TYPE CHICK SHOWS UP...
...AND SHE TELLS ME SHE'S INTO GIRLS...
...AND BECOMES MY GIRL-FRIEND...
IN OTHER WORDS...

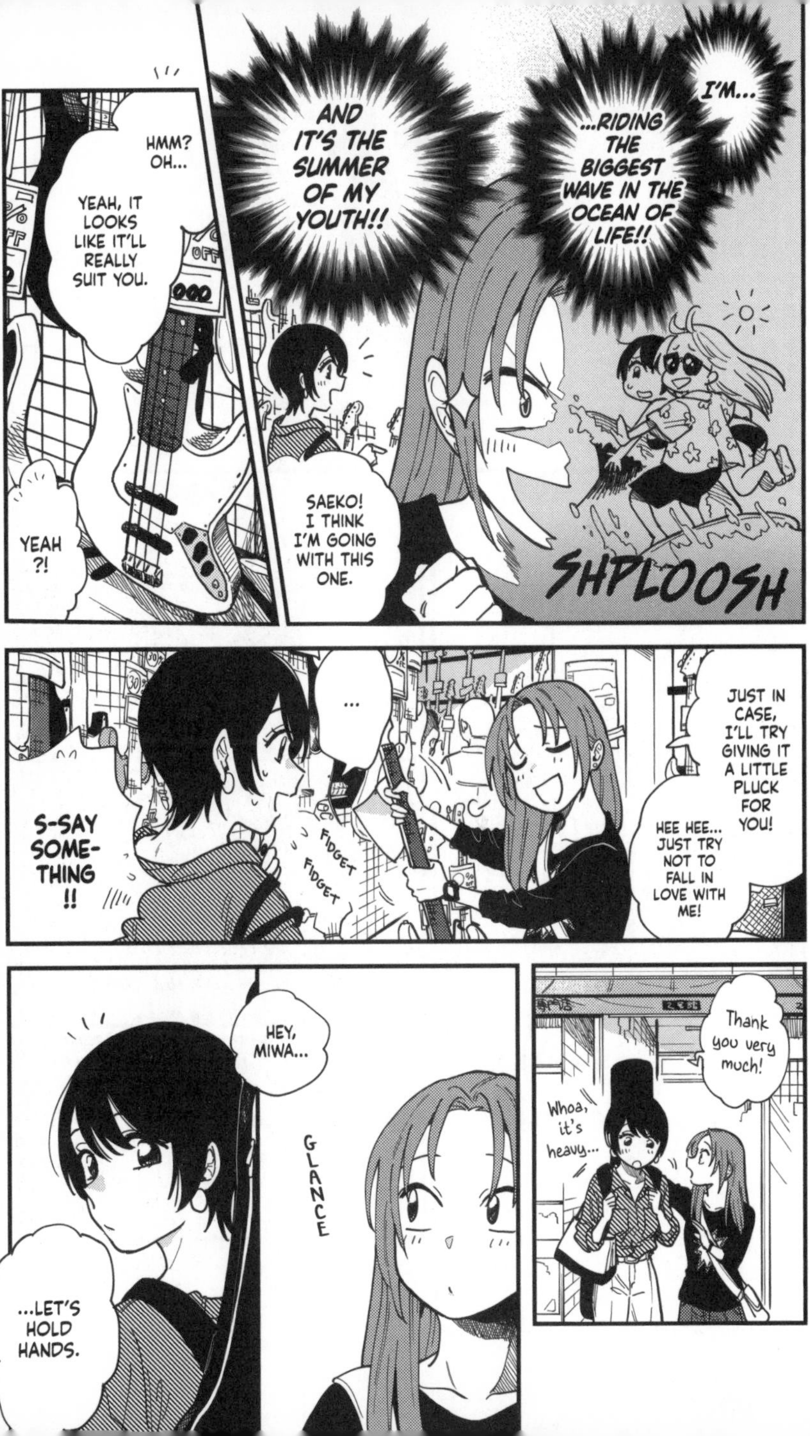
I'M...
...RIDING THE BIGGEST WAVE IN THE OCEAN OF LIFE!!
AND IT'S THE SUMMER OF MY YOUTH!!
SHPLOOSH
SAEKO! I THINK I'M GOING WITH THIS ONE.
HMM? OH...
YEAH, IT LOOKS LIKE IT'LL REALLY SUIT YOU.
YEAH ?!
JUST IN CASE, I'LL TRY GIVING IT A LITTLE PLUCK FOR YOU!
HEE HEE... JUST TRY NOT TO FALL IN LOVE WITH ME!
...
FIDGET FIDGET
S-SAY SOME-THING !!
Thank you very much!
Whoa, it's heavy...
HEY, MIWA...
GLANCE
...LET'S HOLD HANDS.

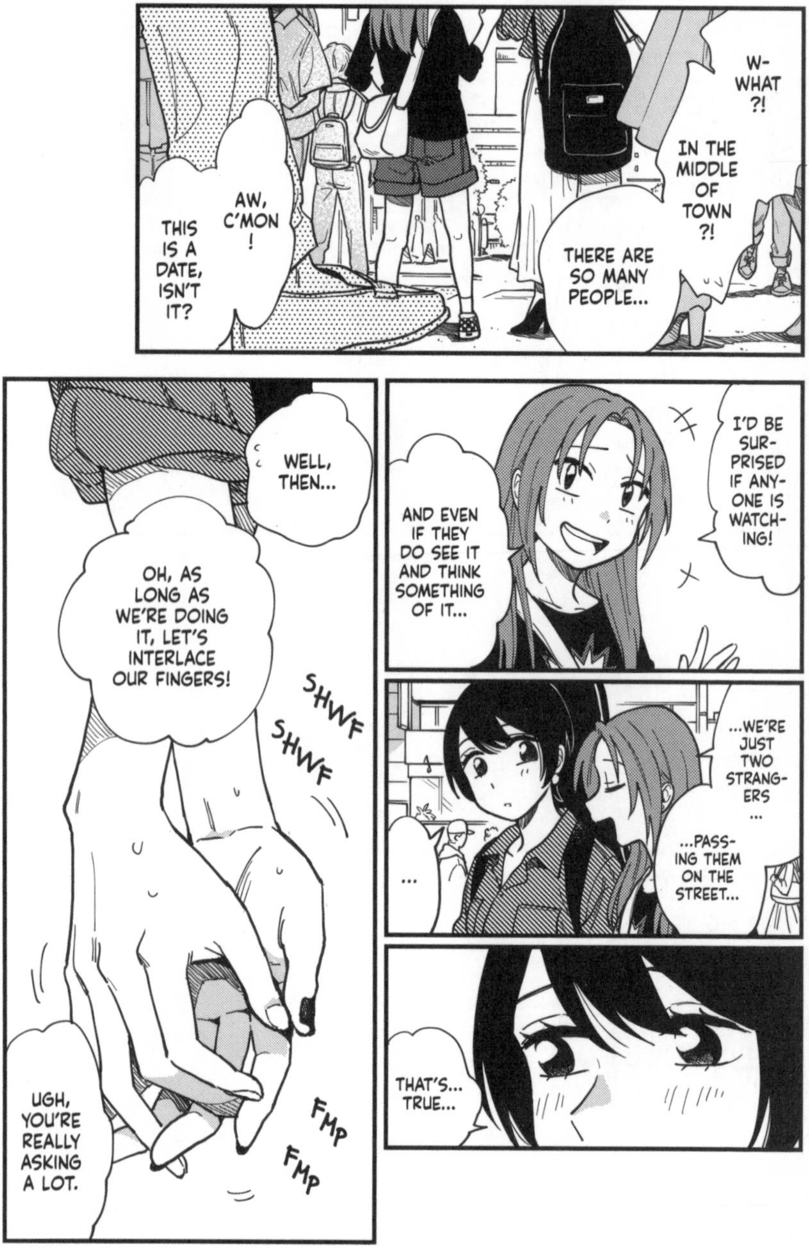
W-WHAT?!
IN THE MIDDLE OF TOWN?!
THERE ARE SO MANY PEOPLE...
AW, C'MON!
THIS IS A DATE, ISN'T IT?
I'D BE SURPRISED IF ANYONE IS WATCHING!
AND EVEN IF THEY DO SEE IT AND THINK SOMETHING OF IT...
...WE'RE JUST TWO STRANGERS...
...PASSING THEM ON THE STREET...
...
THAT'S... TRUE...
WELL, THEN...
OH, AS LONG AS WE'RE DOING IT, LET'S INTERLACE OUR FINGERS!
SHWF
SHWF
FMP
FMP
UGH, YOU'RE REALLY ASKING A LOT.

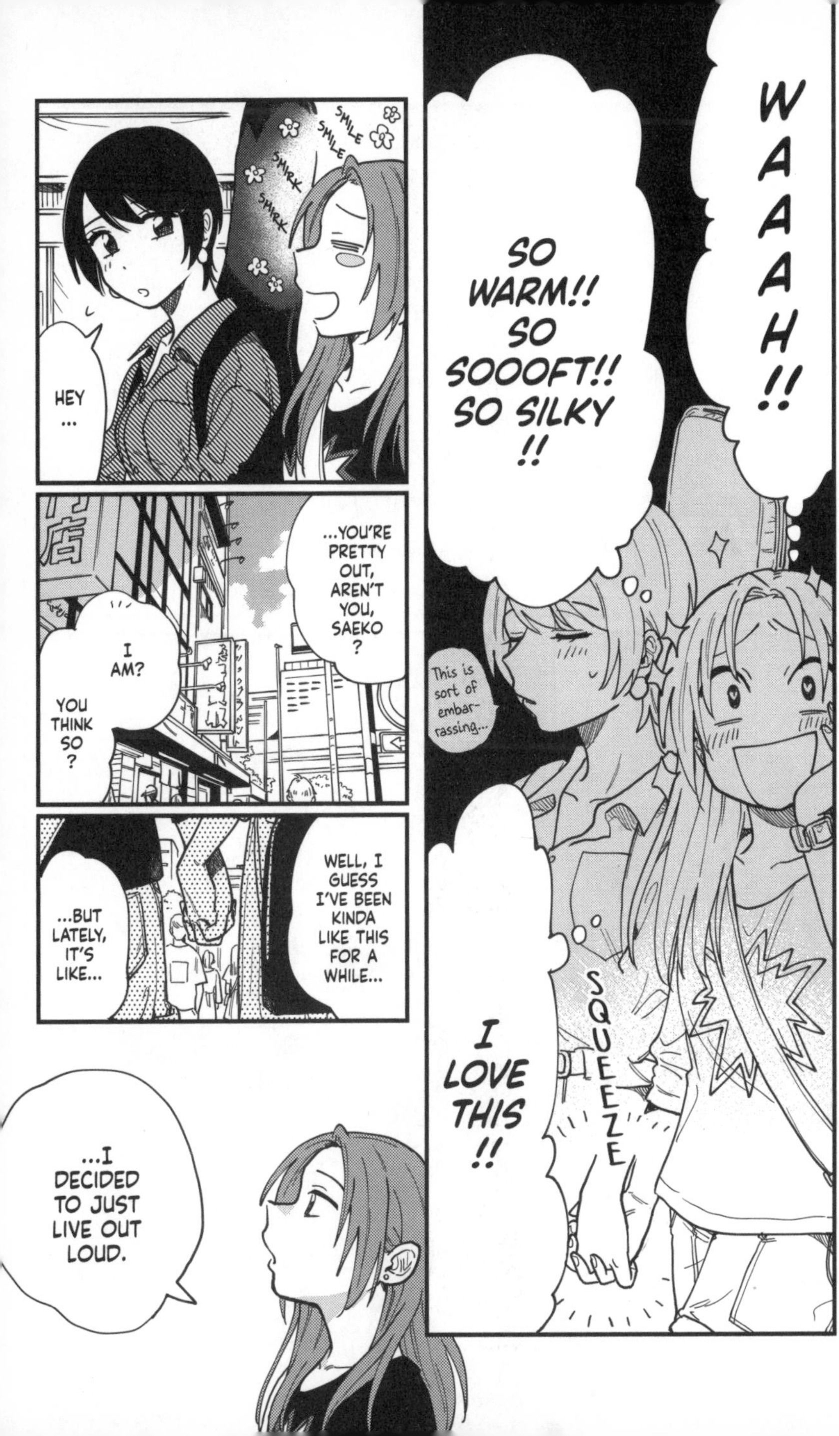
WAAAAH!!
SO WARM!! SO SOOOFT!! SO SILKY!!
This is sort of embarrassing...
I LOVE THIS!!
SQUEEZE
SMILE SMILE
SMIRK SMIRK
HEY ...
...YOU'RE PRETTY OUT, AREN'T YOU, SAEKO?
I AM?
YOU THINK SO?
WELL, I GUESS I'VE BEEN KINDA LIKE THIS FOR A WHILE...
...BUT LATELY, IT'S LIKE...
...I DECIDED TO JUST LIVE OUT LOUD.

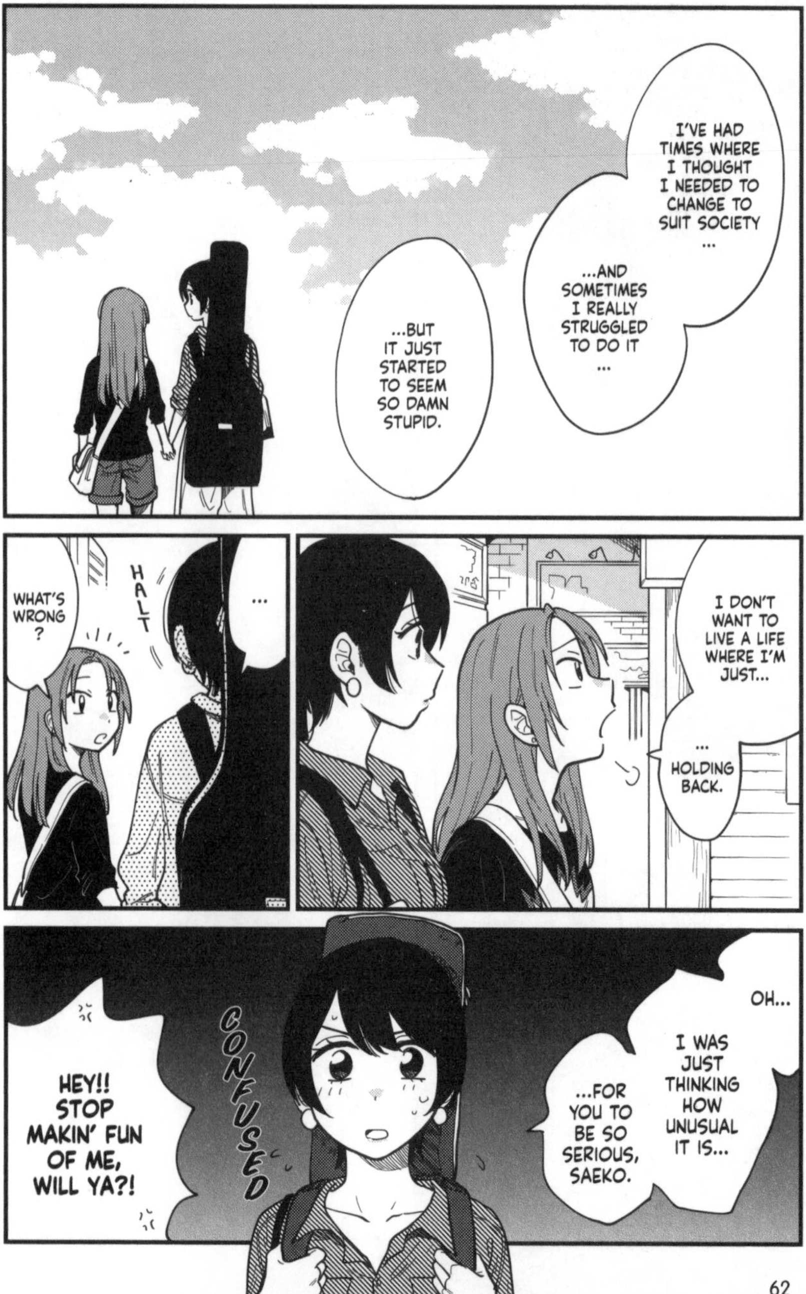
I'VE HAD TIMES WHERE I THOUGHT I NEEDED TO CHANGE TO SUIT SOCIETY ...
...AND SOMETIMES I REALLY STRUGGLED TO DO IT ...
...BUT IT JUST STARTED TO SEEM SO DAMN STUPID.
I DON'T WANT TO LIVE A LIFE WHERE I'M JUST...
... HOLDING BACK.
...
HALT
WHAT'S WRONG ?
OH...
I WAS JUST THINKING HOW UNUSUAL IT IS...
...FOR YOU TO BE SO SERIOUS, SAEKO.
CONFUSED
HEY!! STOP MAKIN' FUN OF ME, WILL YA?!

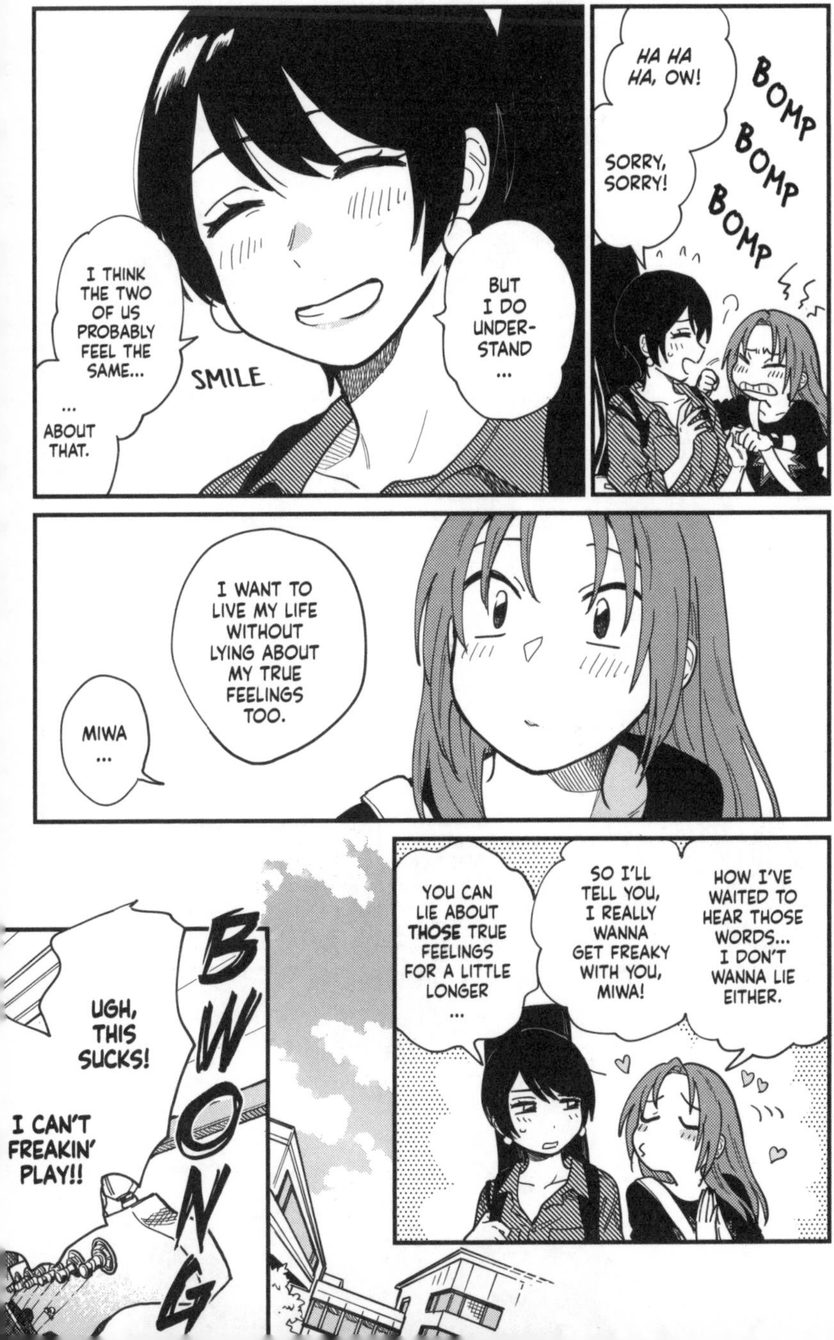
HA HA HA, OW!
BOMP
BOMP
BOMP
SORRY, SORRY!
BUT I DO UNDERSTAND ...
SMILE
I THINK THE TWO OF US PROBABLY FEEL THE SAME...
... ABOUT THAT.
I WANT TO LIVE MY LIFE WITHOUT LYING ABOUT MY TRUE FEELINGS TOO.
MIWA ...
HOW I'VE WAITED TO HEAR THOSE WORDS... I DON'T WANNA LIE EITHER.
SO I'LL TELL YOU, I REALLY WANNA GET FREAKY WITH YOU, MIWA!
YOU CAN LIE ABOUT **THOSE** TRUE FEELINGS FOR A LITTLE LONGER ...
BWONG
UGH, THIS SUCKS!
I CAN'T FREAKIN' PLAY!!

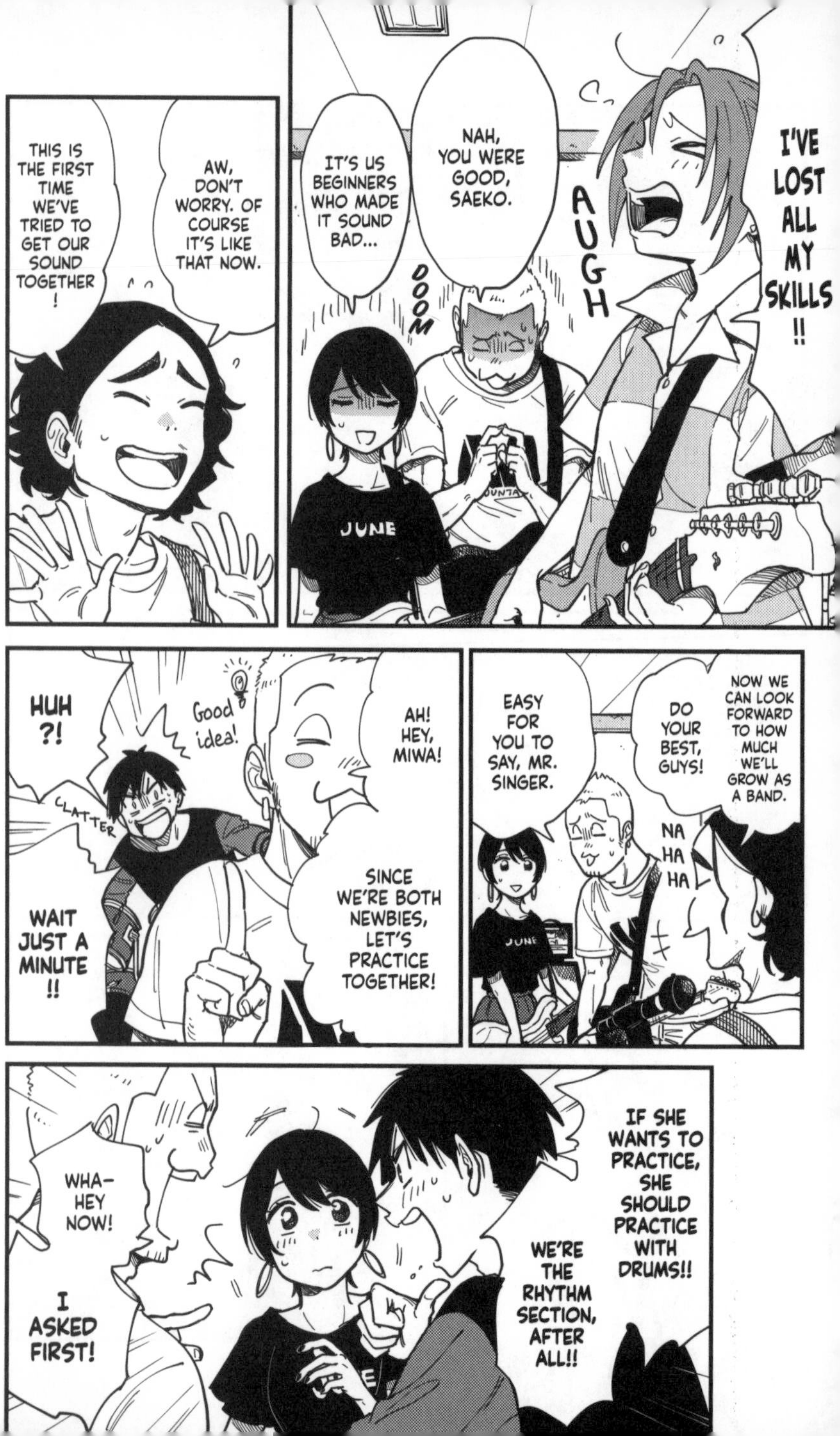
I'VE LOST ALL MY SKILLS!!
AUGH
NAH, YOU WERE GOOD, SAEKO.
IT'S US BEGINNERS WHO MADE IT SOUND BAD...
DOOOM
AW, DON'T WORRY. OF COURSE IT'S LIKE THAT NOW.
THIS IS THE FIRST TIME WE'VE TRIED TO GET OUR SOUND TOGETHER!
NOW WE CAN LOOK FORWARD TO HOW MUCH WE'LL GROW AS A BAND.
DO YOUR BEST, GUYS!
EASY FOR YOU TO SAY, MR. SINGER.
NA HA HA
AH! HEY, MIWA!
SINCE WE'RE BOTH NEWBIES, LET'S PRACTICE TOGETHER!
Good idea!
HUH?!
CLATTER
WAIT JUST A MINUTE!!
IF SHE WANTS TO PRACTICE, SHE SHOULD PRACTICE WITH DRUMS!!
WE'RE THE RHYTHM SECTION, AFTER ALL!!
WHA— HEY NOW!
I ASKED FIRST!

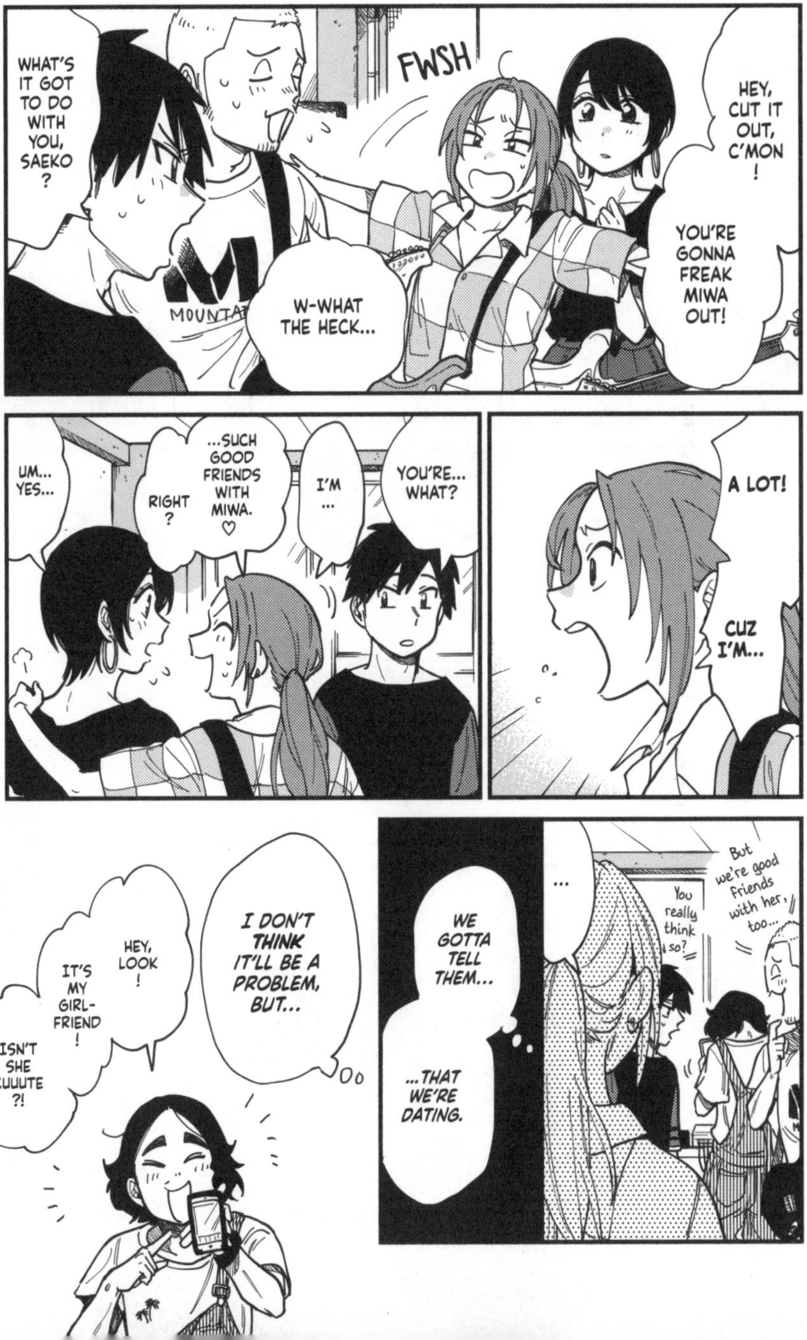
HEY, CUT IT OUT, C'MON!
YOU'RE GONNA FREAK MIWA OUT!
FWSH
WHAT'S IT GOT TO DO WITH YOU, SAEKO?
W-WHAT THE HECK...
A LOT!
CUZ I'M...
YOU'RE... WHAT?
I'M...
...SUCH GOOD FRIENDS WITH MIWA. ♡
RIGHT?
UM... YES...
But we're good friends with her, too...
You really think so?
...
WE GOTTA TELL THEM...
...THAT WE'RE DATING.
I DON'T THINK IT'LL BE A PROBLEM, BUT...
HEY, LOOK!
IT'S MY GIRLFRIEND!
ISN'T SHE CUUUTE?!

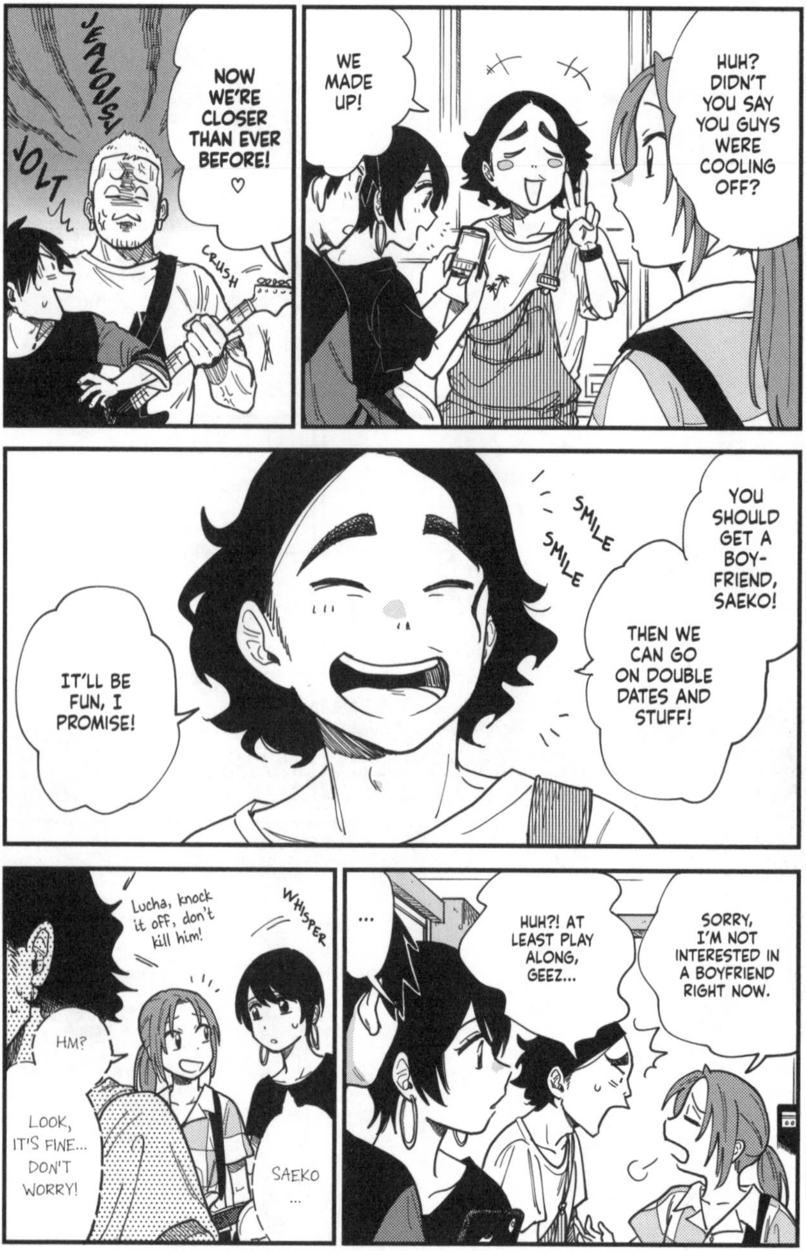
HUH? DIDN'T YOU SAY YOU GUYS WERE COOLING OFF?
WE MADE UP!
NOW WE'RE CLOSER THAN EVER BEFORE! ♡
JEALOUSY
JOLT
CRUSH
YOU SHOULD GET A BOY-FRIEND, SAEKO!
SMILE
SMILE
THEN WE CAN GO ON DOUBLE DATES AND STUFF!
IT'LL BE FUN, I PROMISE!
SORRY, I'M NOT INTERESTED IN A BOYFRIEND RIGHT NOW.
HUH?! AT LEAST PLAY ALONG, GEEZ...
...
WHISPER
Lucha, knock it off, don't kill him!
HM?
SAEKO ...
LOOK, IT'S FINE... DON'T WORRY!

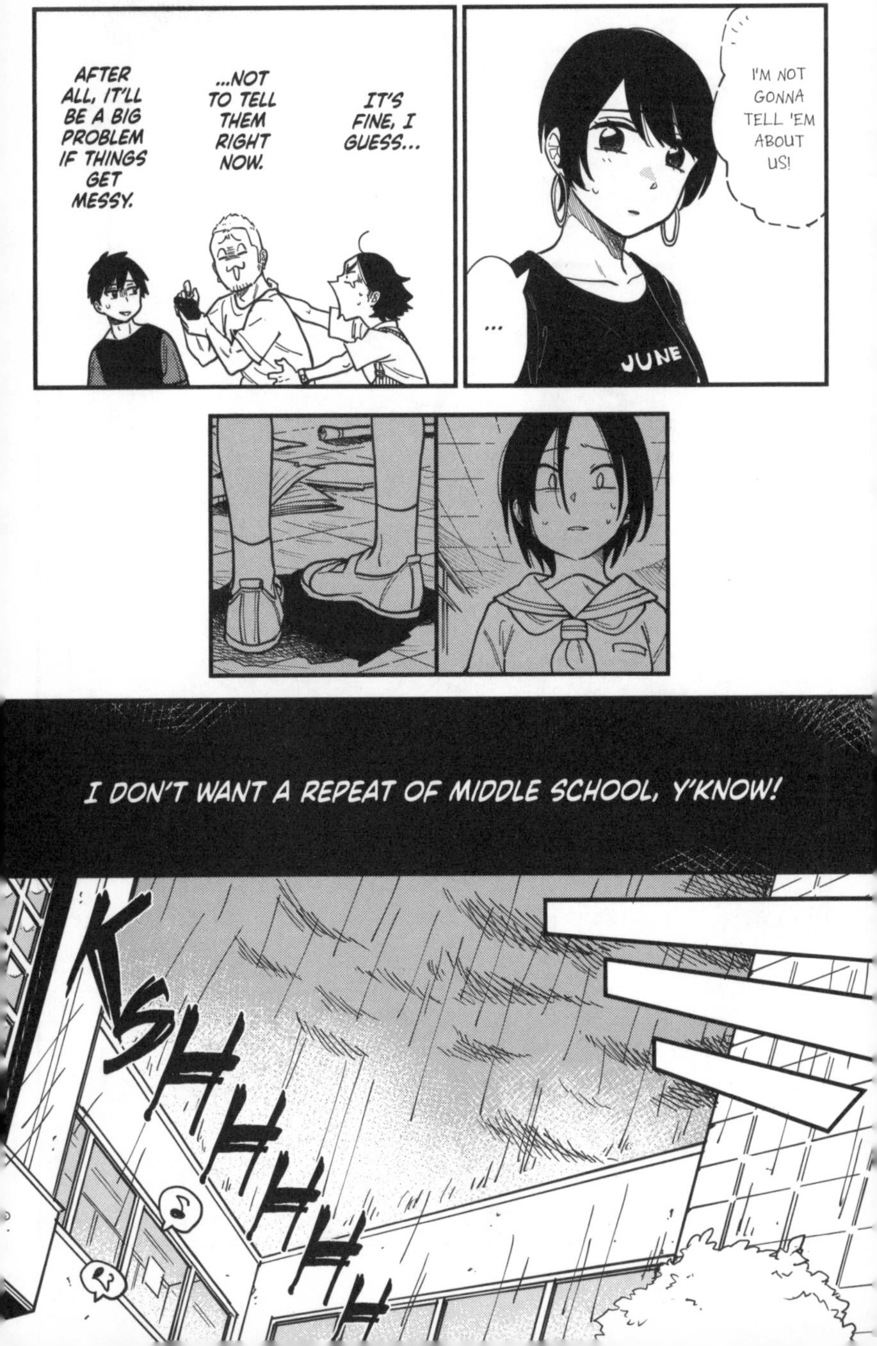
I'M NOT GONNA TELL 'EM ABOUT US!
...
IT'S FINE, I GUESS...
...NOT TO TELL THEM RIGHT NOW.
AFTER ALL, IT'LL BE A BIG PROBLEM IF THINGS GET MESSY.
I DON'T WANT A REPEAT OF MIDDLE SCHOOL, Y'KNOW!
KSHHHHHH

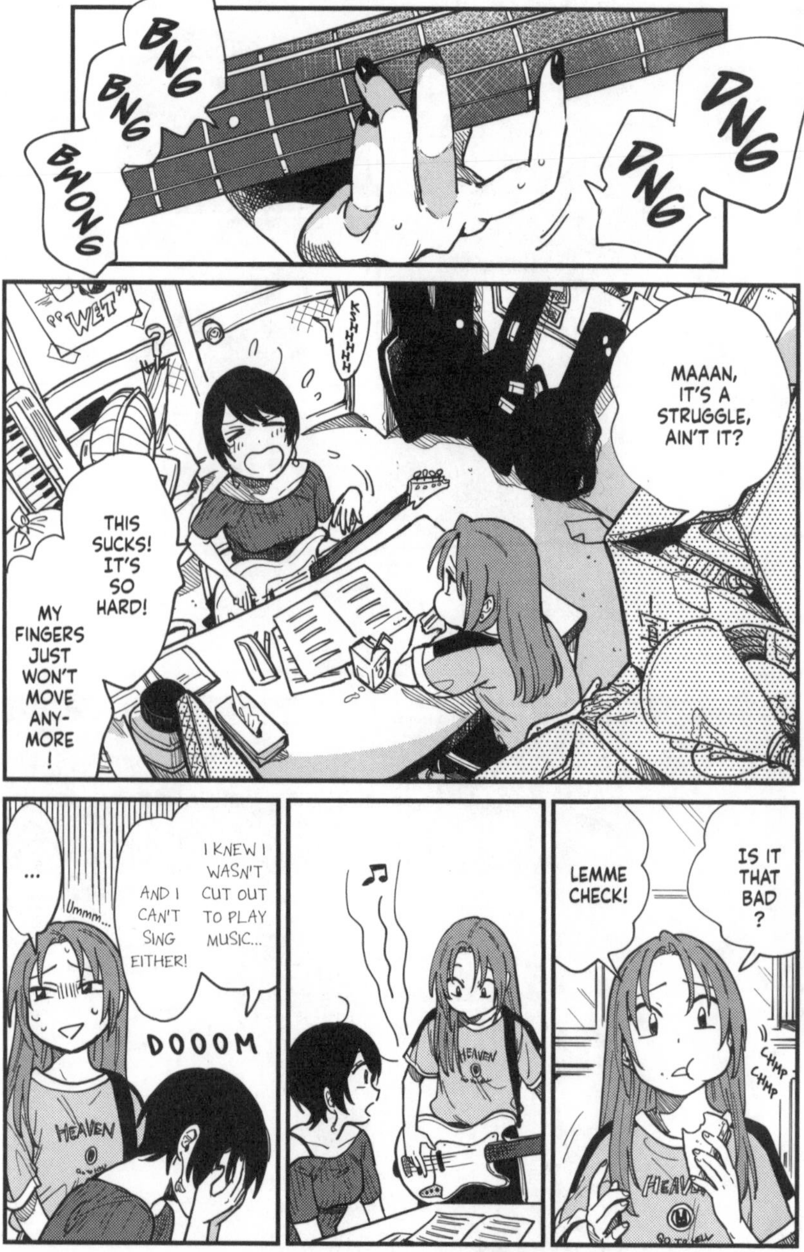

DNG DNG
BNG BNG BWONG
MAAAN, IT'S A STRUGGLE, AIN'T IT?
KSHHHHH
THIS SUCKS! IT'S SO HARD!
MY FINGERS JUST WON'T MOVE ANY-MORE!
IS IT THAT BAD?
LEMME CHECK!
CHMP CHMP
♫
I KNEW I WASN'T CUT OUT TO PLAY MUSIC...
AND I CAN'T SING EITHER!
...
Ummm...
DOOOM

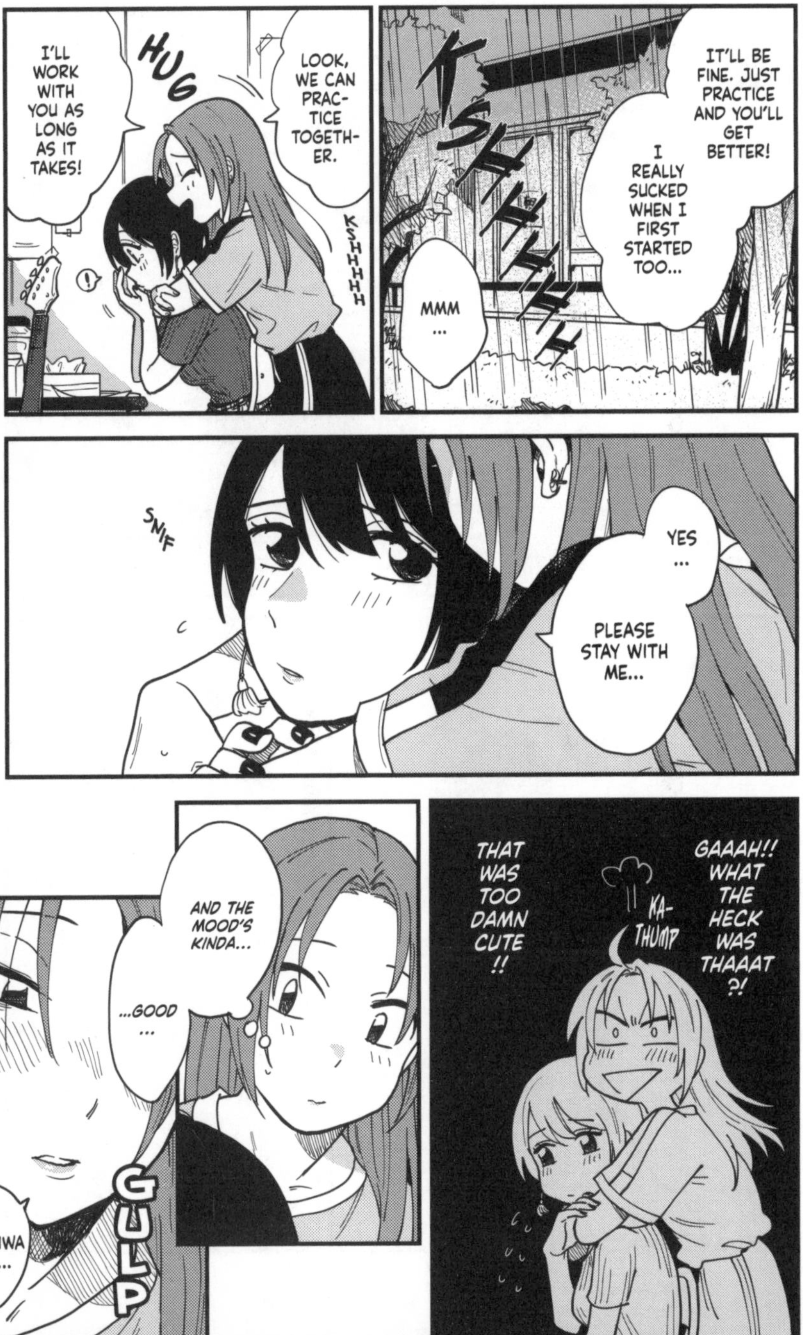
KSHHHHHHH
IT'LL BE FINE. JUST PRACTICE AND YOU'LL GET BETTER!
I REALLY SUCKED WHEN I FIRST STARTED TOO...
MMM...
LOOK, WE CAN PRAC-TICE TOGETH-ER.
HUG
I'LL WORK WITH YOU AS LONG AS IT TAKES!
KSHHHHHH
!
SNIF
YES...
PLEASE STAY WITH ME...
GAAAH!! WHAT THE HECK WAS THAAAT?!
KA-THUMP
THAT WAS TOO DAMN CUTE!!
AND THE MOOD'S KINDA...
...GOOD...
GULP
MIWA...

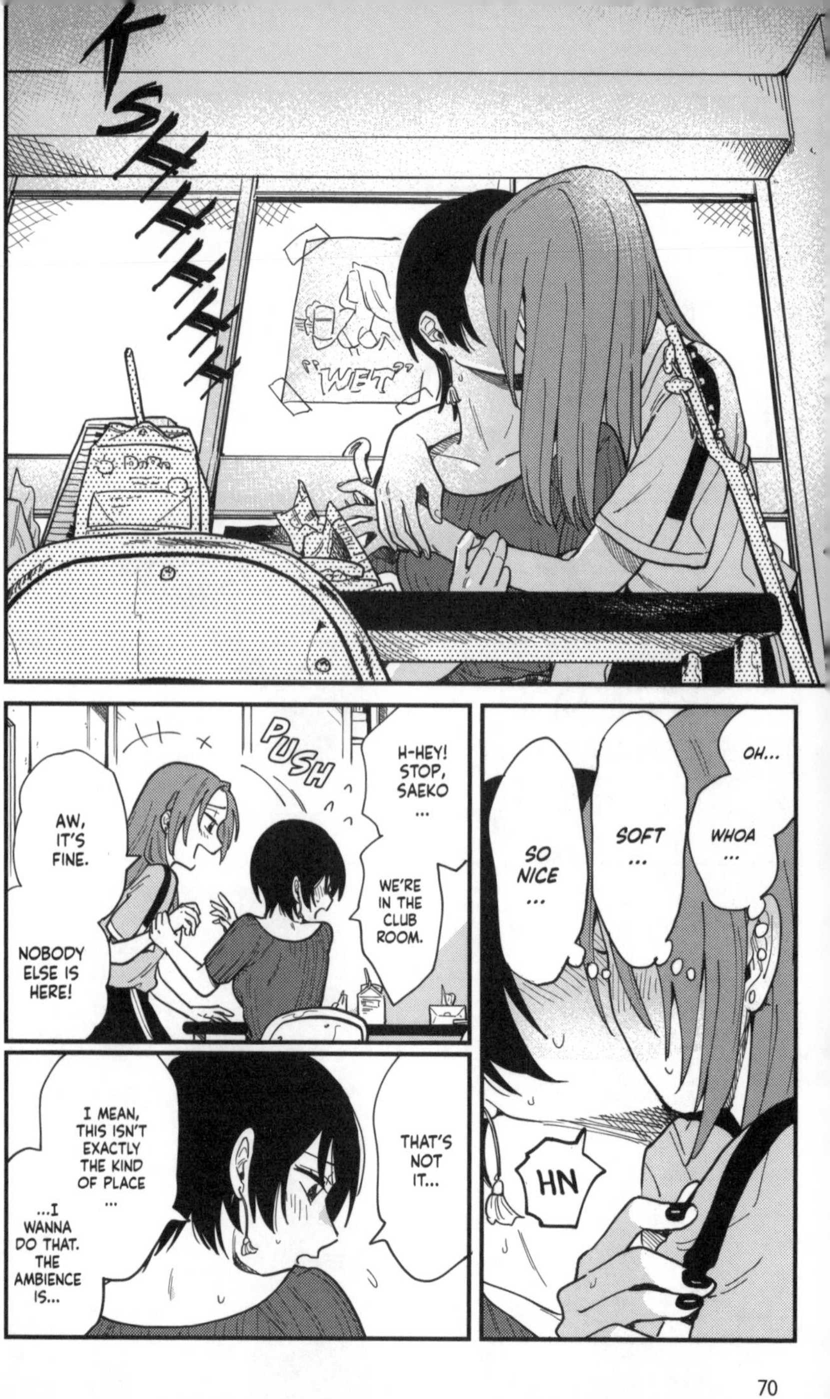
KSHHHHHH
"WET"
OH... WHOA...
SOFT...
SO NICE...
HN
PUSH
H-HEY! STOP, SAEKO...
WE'RE IN THE CLUB ROOM.
AW, IT'S FINE.
NOBODY ELSE IS HERE!
THAT'S NOT IT...
I MEAN, THIS ISN'T EXACTLY THE KIND OF PLACE...
...I WANNA DO THAT. THE AMBIENCE IS...

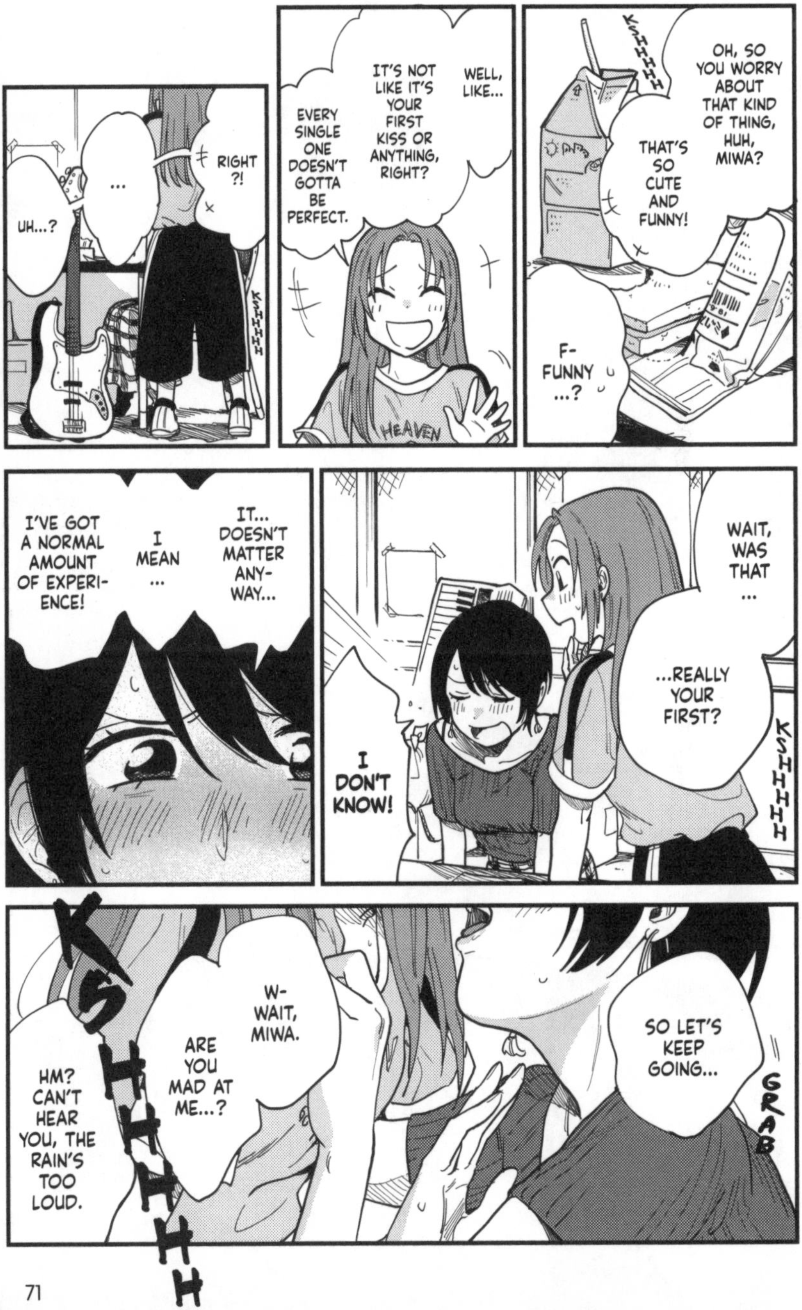
KSHHHHH
OH, SO YOU WORRY ABOUT THAT KIND OF THING, HUH, MIWA?
THAT'S SO CUTE AND FUNNY!
F- FUNNY ...?
WELL, LIKE...
IT'S NOT LIKE IT'S YOUR FIRST KISS OR ANYTHING, RIGHT?
EVERY SINGLE ONE DOESN'T GOTTA BE PERFECT.
HEAVEN
RIGHT ?!
...
UH...?
KSHHHHH
WAIT, WAS THAT ...
...REALLY YOUR FIRST?
KSHHHHH
I DON'T KNOW!
IT... DOESN'T MATTER ANY- WAY...
I MEAN ...
I'VE GOT A NORMAL AMOUNT OF EXPERI- ENCE!
GRAB
SO LET'S KEEP GOING...
W- WAIT, MIWA.
ARE YOU MAD AT ME...?
HM? CAN'T HEAR YOU, THE RAIN'S TOO LOUD.
KSHHHHHHH

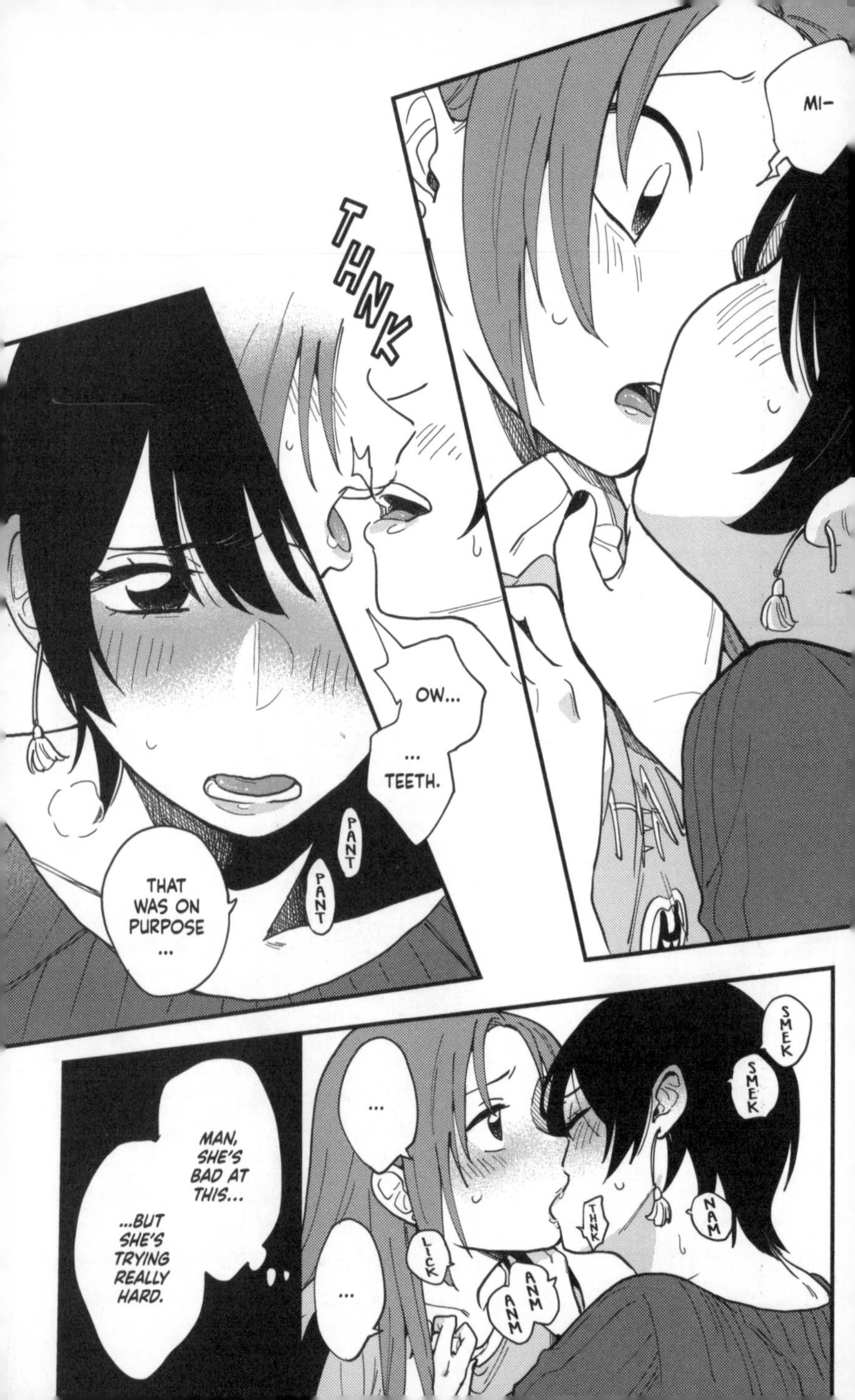
MI—
THNK
OW...
... TEETH.
PANT PANT
THAT WAS ON PURPOSE ...
SMEK SMEK
...
NAM
THNK
LICK
ANM ANM
...
MAN, SHE'S BAD AT THIS...
...BUT SHE'S TRYING REALLY HARD.

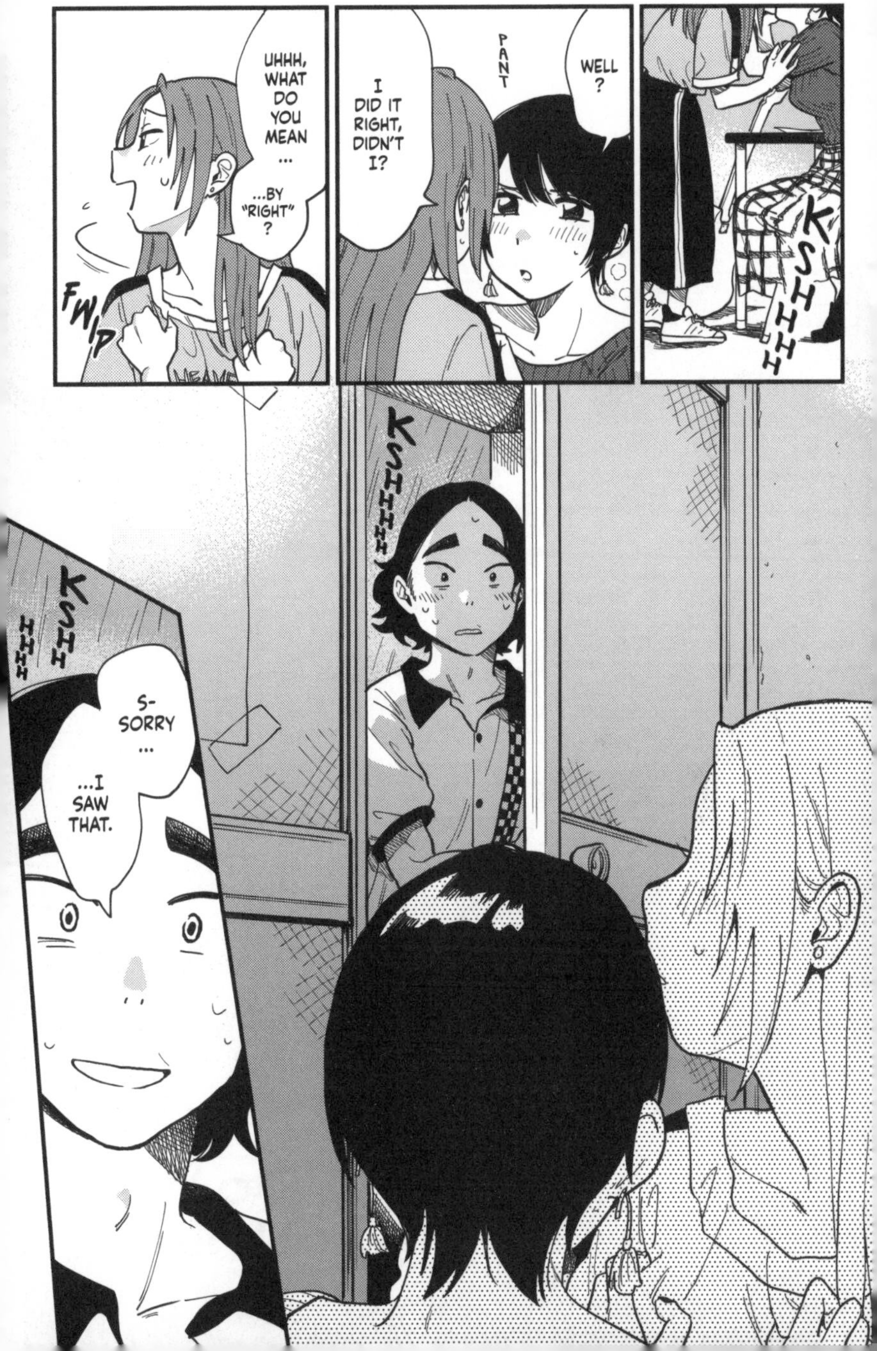

KSHHHHH
WELL?
PANT
I DID IT RIGHT, DIDN'T I?
UHHH, WHAT DO YOU MEAN...
...BY "RIGHT"?
FWIP
KSHHHHHH
KSHHHHHH
S-SORRY...
...I SAW THAT.

How Do We
Relationship?

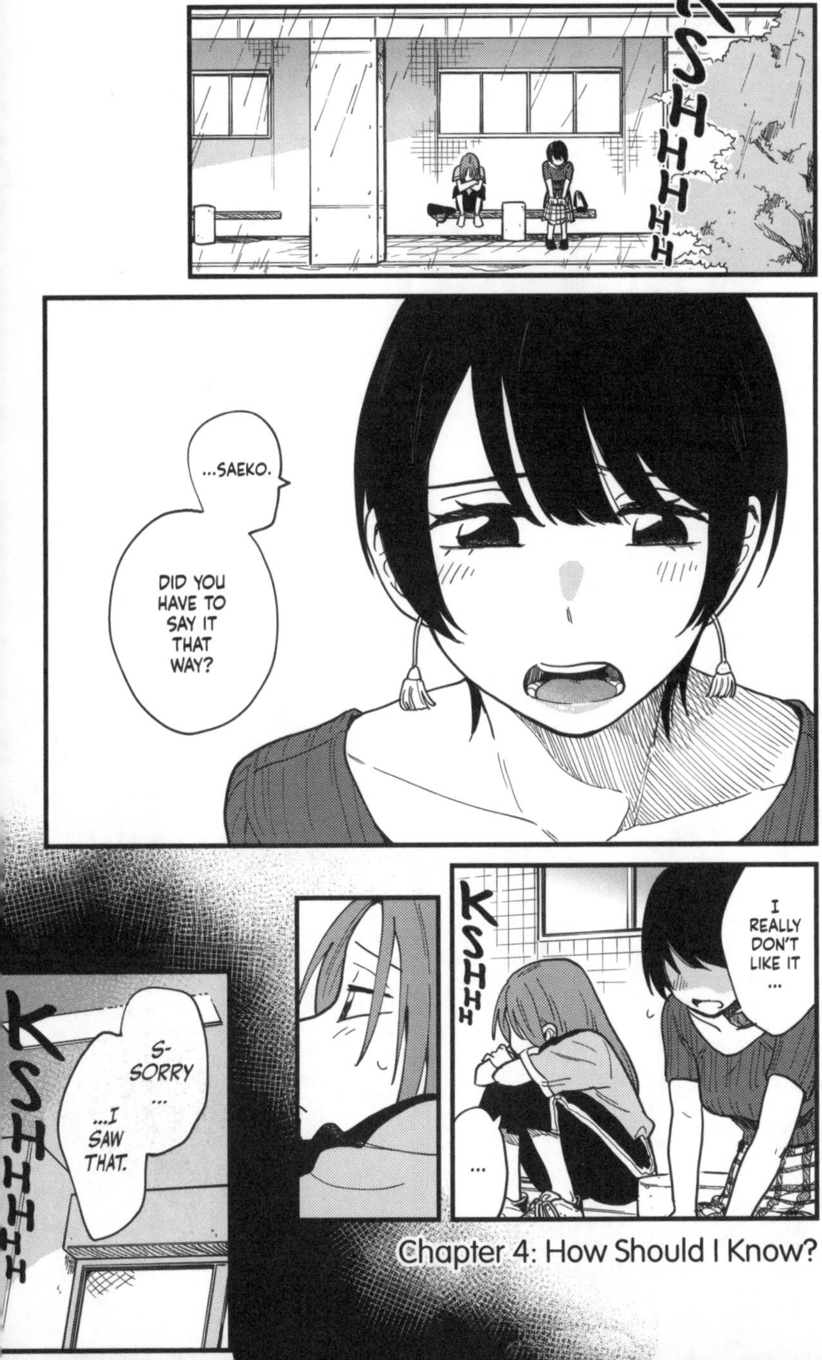
KSHHHHHH
...SAEKO.
DID YOU HAVE TO SAY IT THAT WAY?
KSHHH
I REALLY DON'T LIKE IT ...
...
KSHHHHH
S-SORRY ...
...I SAW THAT.

Chapter 4: How Should I Know?

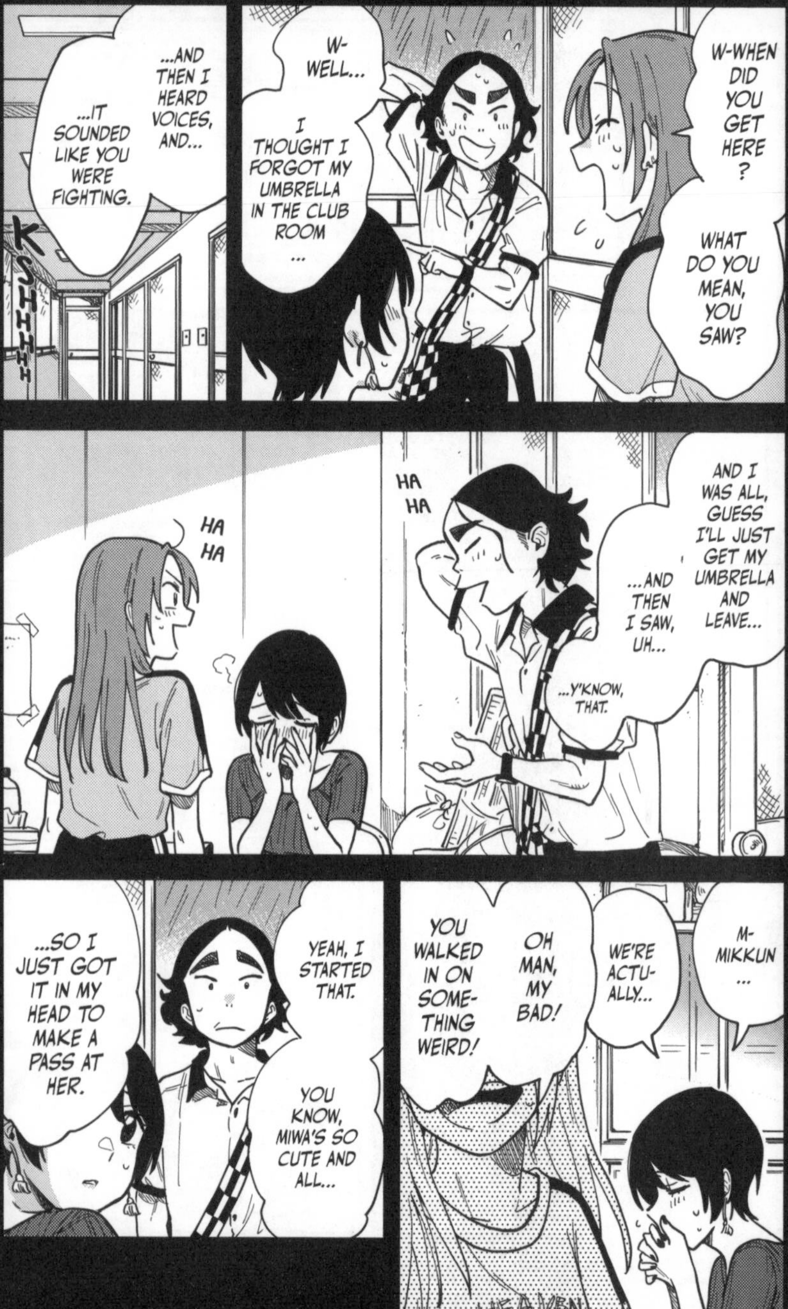
W-WHEN DID YOU GET HERE?
WHAT DO YOU MEAN, YOU SAW?
W-WELL...
I THOUGHT I FORGOT MY UMBRELLA IN THE CLUB ROOM...
...AND THEN I HEARD VOICES, AND...
...IT SOUNDED LIKE YOU WERE FIGHTING.
KSHHHHH
AND I WAS ALL, GUESS I'LL JUST GET MY UMBRELLA AND LEAVE...
...AND THEN I SAW, UH...
...Y'KNOW, THAT.
HA HA
HA HA
M-MIKKUN...
WE'RE ACTU-ALLY...
OH MAN, MY BAD!
YOU WALKED IN ON SOME-THING WEIRD!
HEAVEN
YEAH, I STARTED THAT.
YOU KNOW, MIWA'S SO CUTE AND ALL...
...SO I JUST GOT IT IN MY HEAD TO MAKE A PASS AT HER.

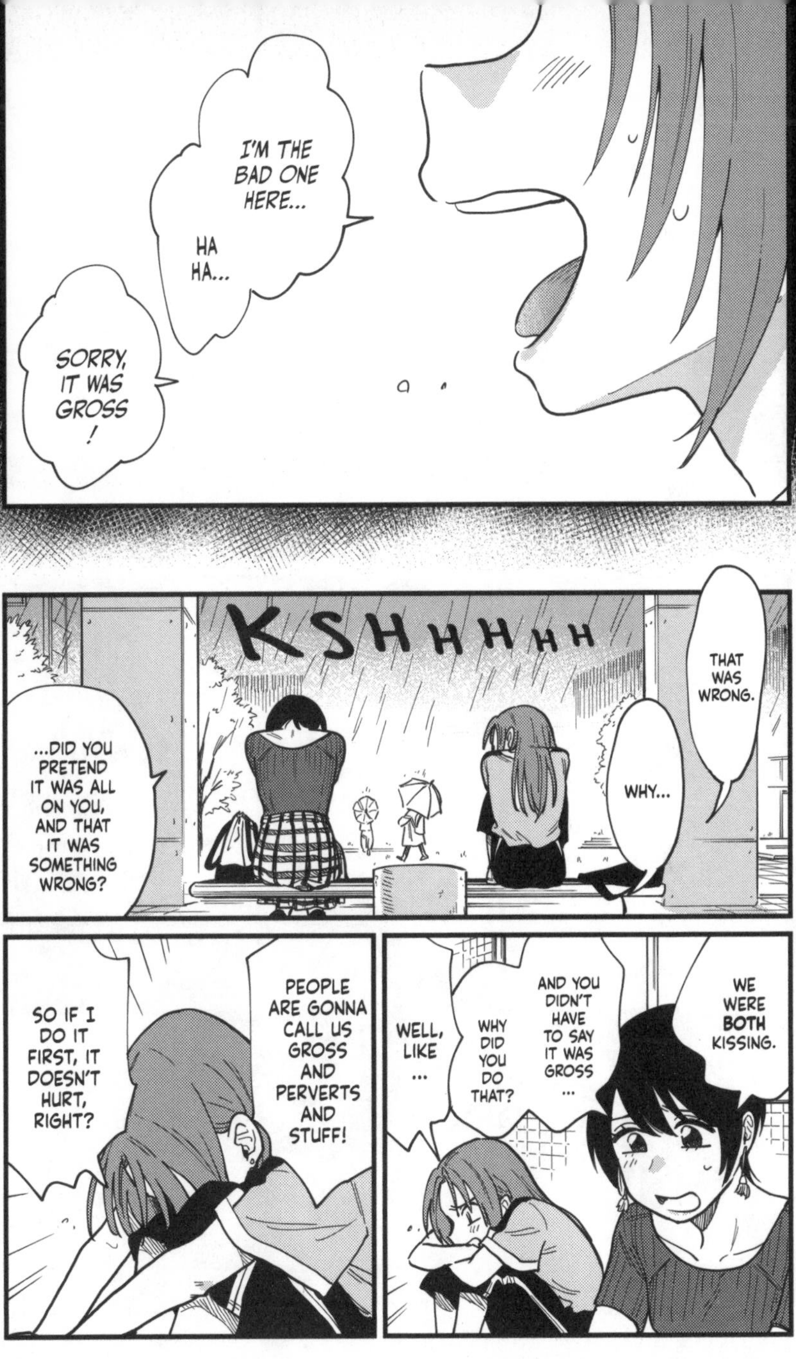
I'M THE BAD ONE HERE...
HA HA...
SORRY, IT WAS GROSS!
KSHHHHHH
THAT WAS WRONG.
WHY...
...DID YOU PRETEND IT WAS ALL ON YOU, AND THAT IT WAS SOMETHING WRONG?
WE WERE **BOTH** KISSING.
AND YOU DIDN'T HAVE TO SAY IT WAS GROSS...
WHY DID YOU DO THAT?
WELL, LIKE...
PEOPLE ARE GONNA CALL US GROSS AND PERVERTS AND STUFF!
SO IF I DO IT FIRST, IT DOESN'T HURT, RIGHT?

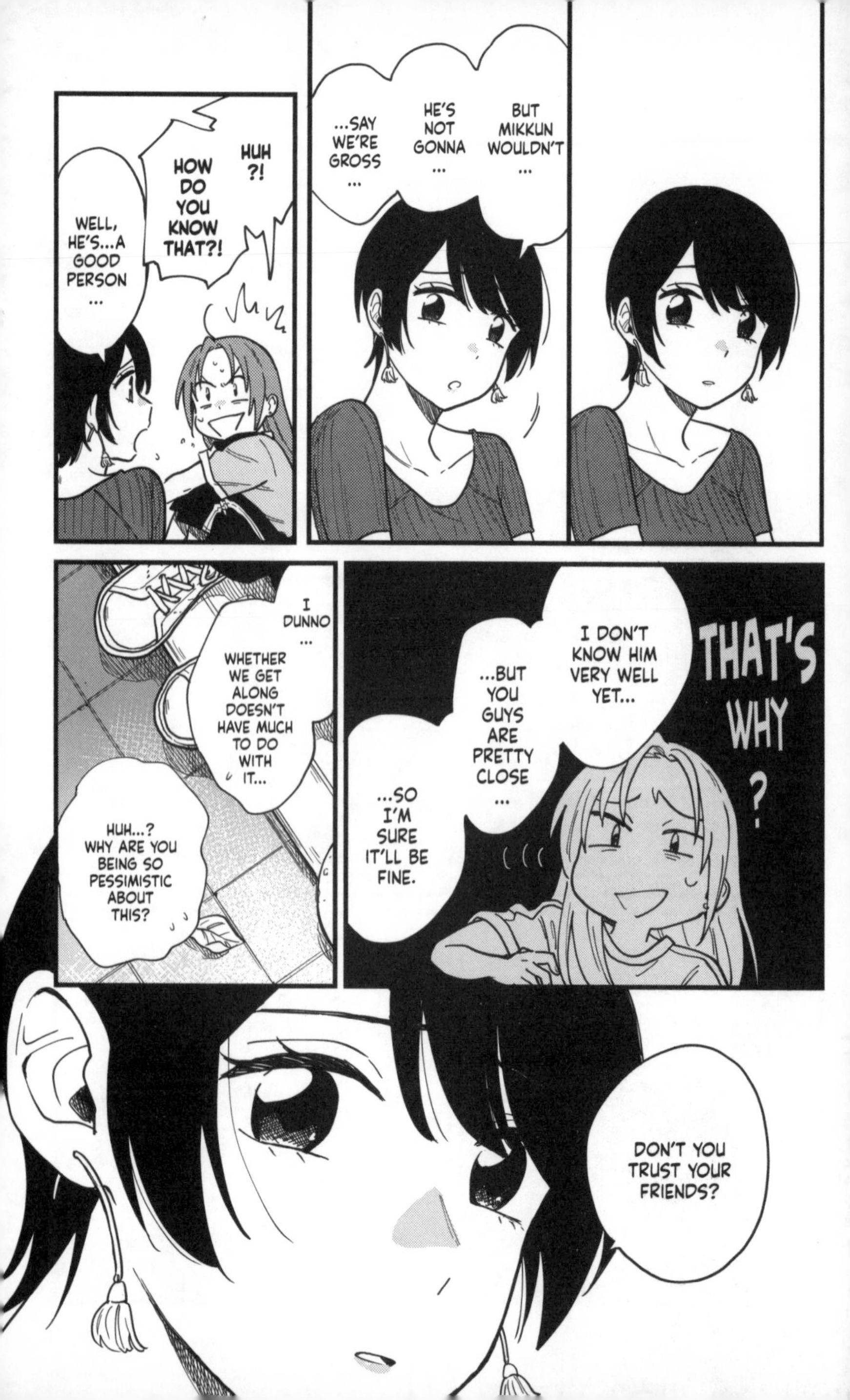
BUT MIKKUN WOULDN'T ... HE'S NOT GONNA ... ...SAY WE'RE GROSS ...
HUH ?!
HOW DO YOU KNOW THAT?!
WELL, HE'S...A GOOD PERSON ...
THAT'S WHY ?
I DON'T KNOW HIM VERY WELL YET...
...BUT YOU GUYS ARE PRETTY CLOSE ...
...SO I'M SURE IT'LL BE FINE.
I DUNNO ... WHETHER WE GET ALONG DOESN'T HAVE MUCH TO DO WITH IT...
HUH...? WHY ARE YOU BEING SO PESSIMISTIC ABOUT THIS?
DON'T YOU TRUST YOUR FRIENDS?

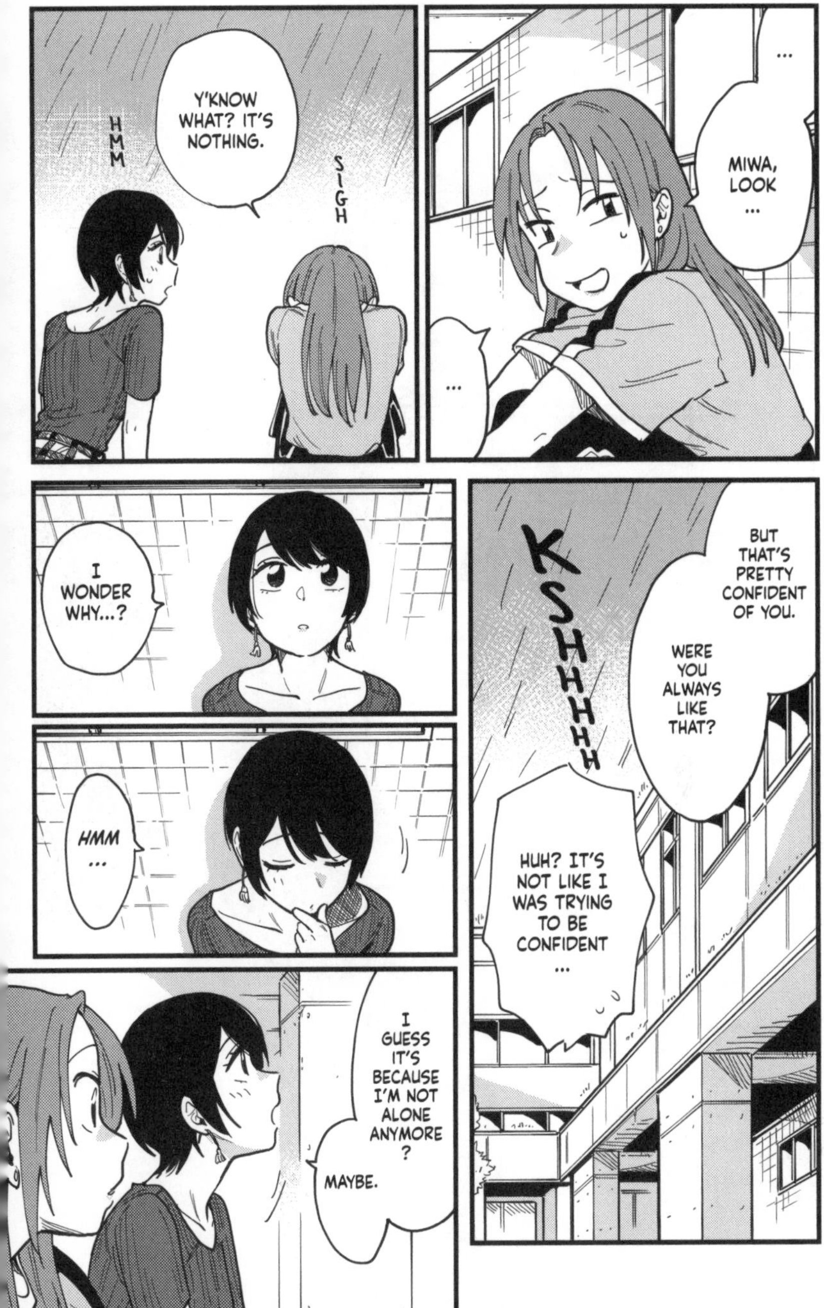
...
MIWA, LOOK ...
...
Y'KNOW WHAT? IT'S NOTHING.
SIGH
HMM
BUT THAT'S PRETTY CONFIDENT OF YOU.
WERE YOU ALWAYS LIKE THAT?
KSHHHHH
HUH? IT'S NOT LIKE I WAS TRYING TO BE CONFIDENT ...
I WONDER WHY...?
HMM ...
I GUESS IT'S BECAUSE I'M NOT ALONE ANYMORE ?
MAYBE.

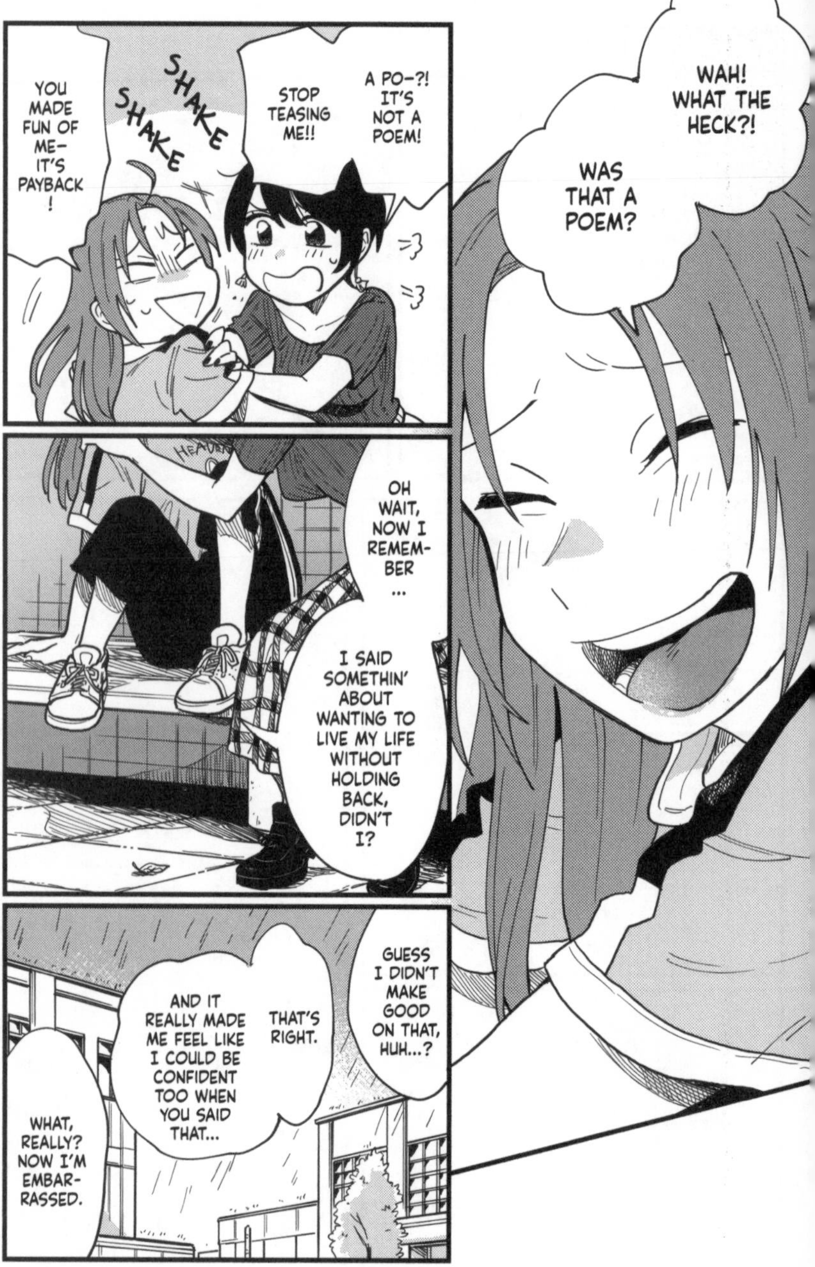
WAH! WHAT THE HECK?!
WAS THAT A POEM?
A PO—?! IT'S NOT A POEM!
STOP TEASING ME!!
SHAKE SHAKE
YOU MADE FUN OF ME—IT'S PAYBACK!
OH WAIT, NOW I REMEMBER...
I SAID SOMETHIN' ABOUT WANTING TO LIVE MY LIFE WITHOUT HOLDING BACK, DIDN'T I?
GUESS I DIDN'T MAKE GOOD ON THAT, HUH...?
THAT'S RIGHT.
AND IT REALLY MADE ME FEEL LIKE I COULD BE CONFIDENT TOO WHEN YOU SAID THAT...
WHAT, REALLY? NOW I'M EMBARRASSED.

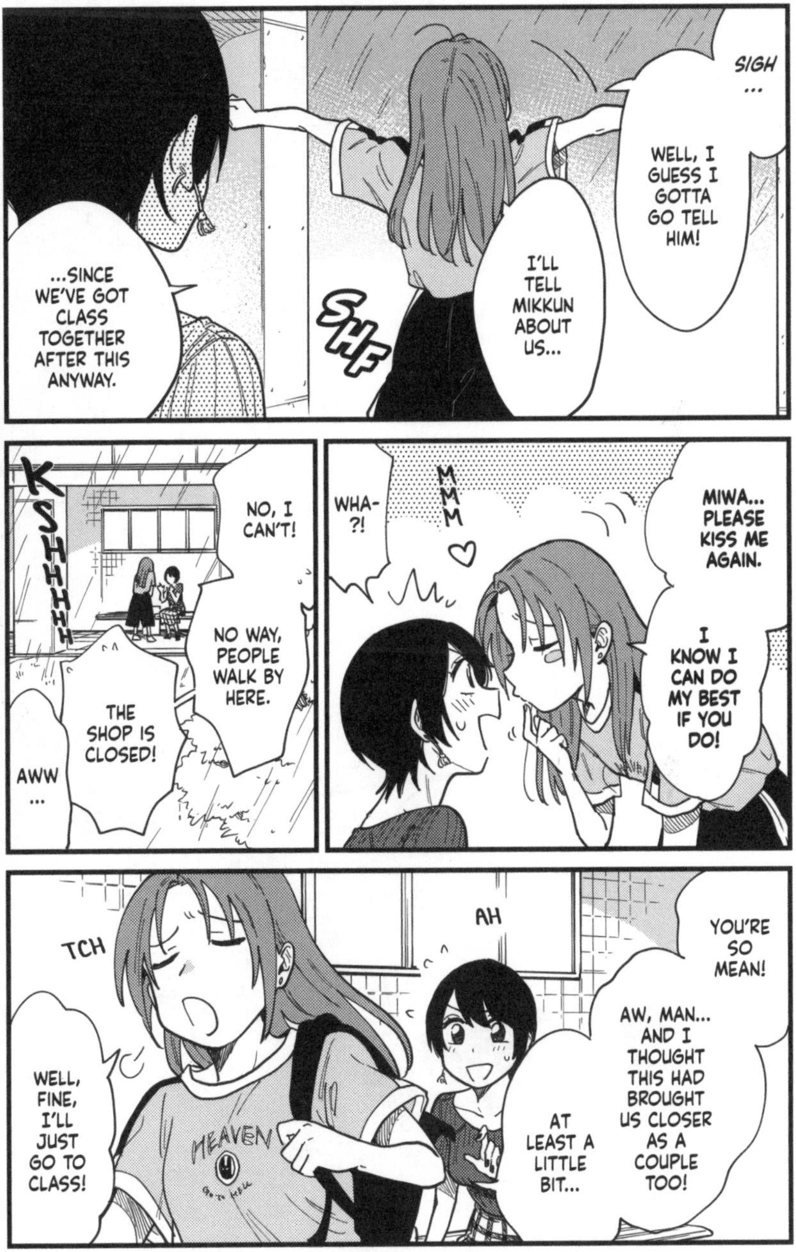
SIGH...
WELL, I GUESS I GOTTA GO TELL HIM!
I'LL TELL MIKKUN ABOUT US...
SHF
...SINCE WE'VE GOT CLASS TOGETHER AFTER THIS ANYWAY.
MIWA... PLEASE KISS ME AGAIN.
I KNOW I CAN DO MY BEST IF YOU DO!
MMM
WHA-?!
KSHHHHH
NO, I CAN'T!
NO WAY, PEOPLE WALK BY HERE.
THE SHOP IS CLOSED!
AWW...
YOU'RE SO MEAN!
AW, MAN... AND I THOUGHT THIS HAD BROUGHT US CLOSER AS A COUPLE TOO!
AH
AT LEAST A LITTLE BIT...
TCH
HEAVEN
WELL, FINE, I'LL JUST GO TO CLASS!

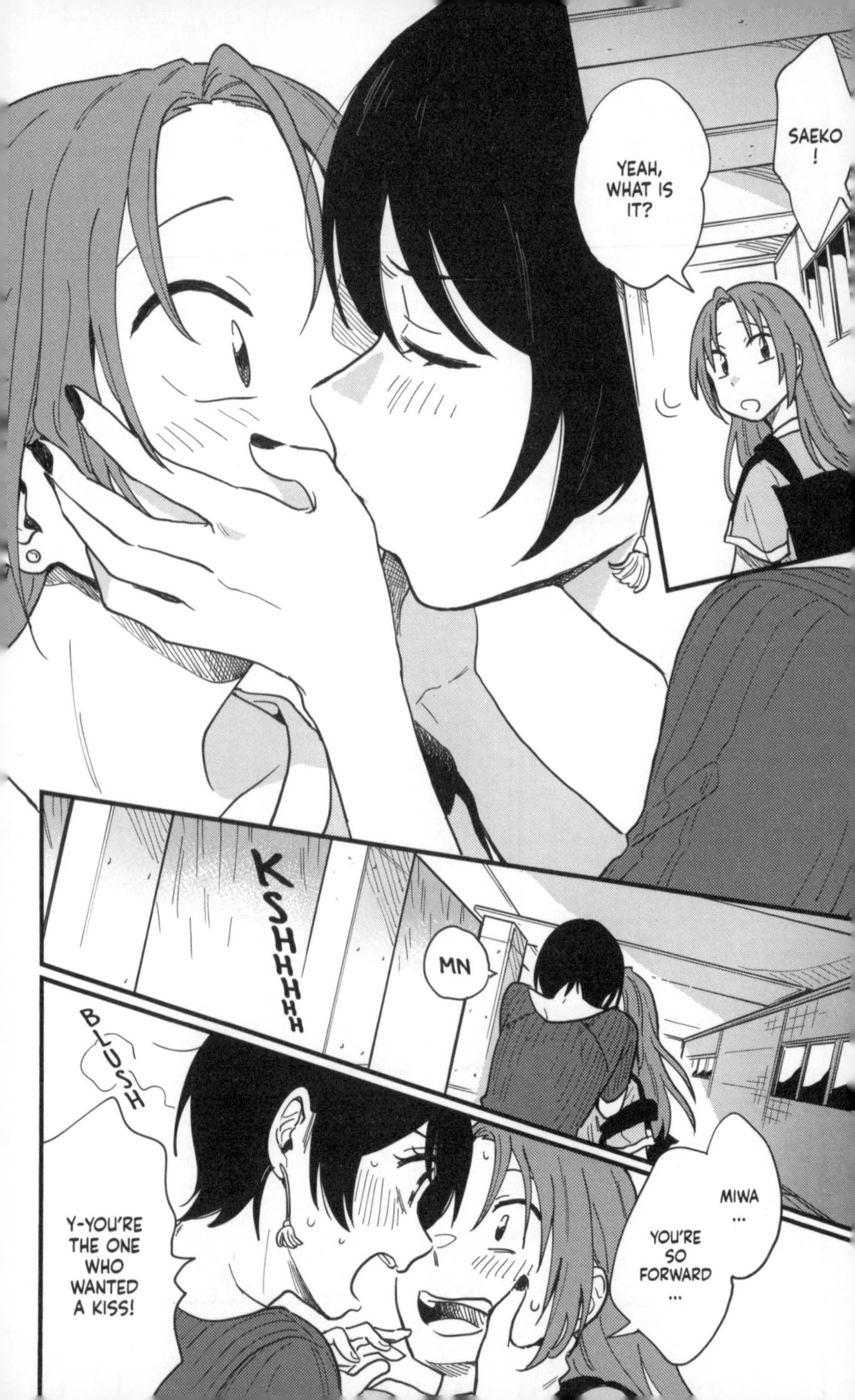
SAEKO!
YEAH, WHAT IS IT?
KSHHHHHH
MN
MIWA...
YOU'RE SO FORWARD...
BLUSH
Y-YOU'RE THE ONE WHO WANTED A KISS!

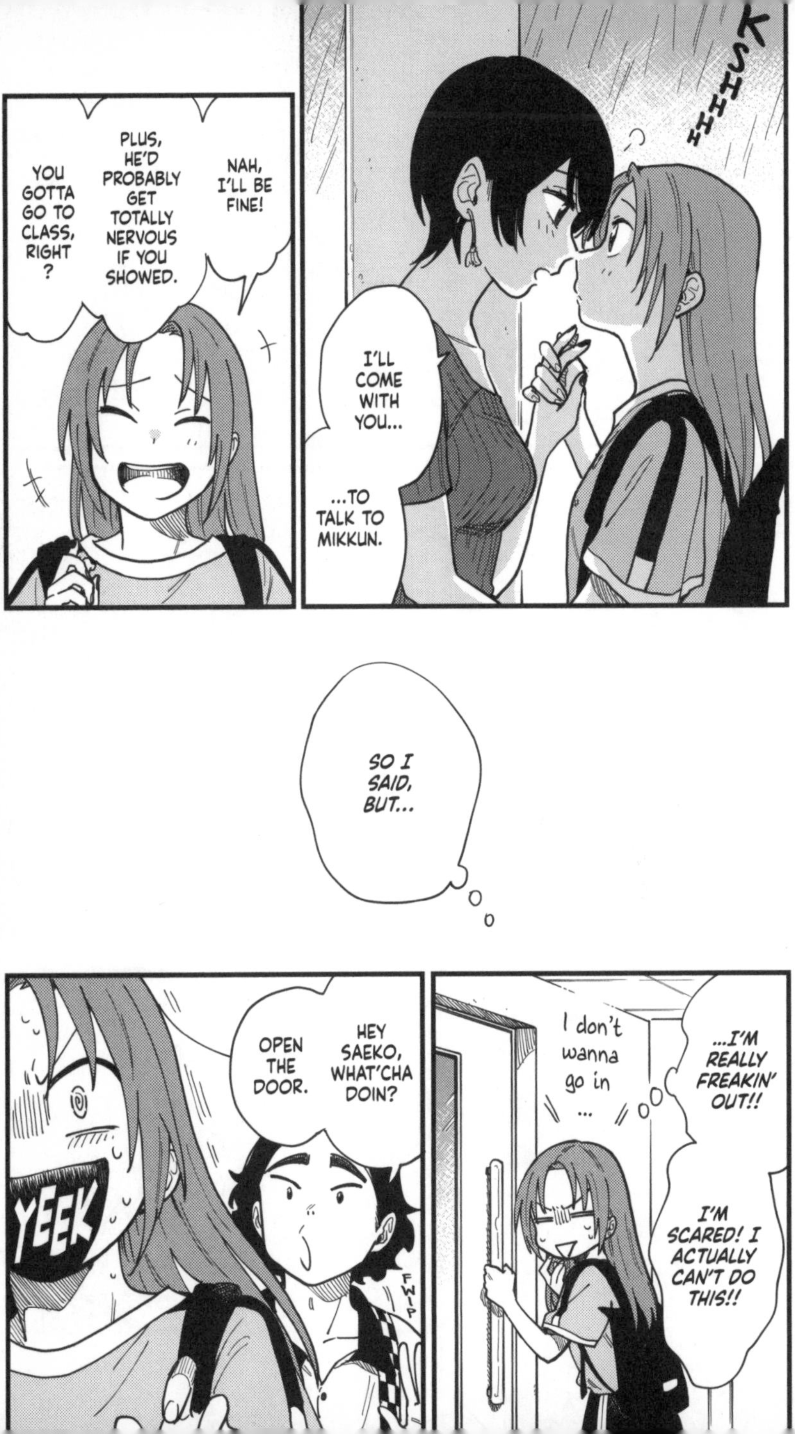
KSHHHHH
I'LL COME WITH YOU...
...TO TALK TO MIKKUN.
NAH, I'LL BE FINE!
PLUS, HE'D PROBABLY GET TOTALLY NERVOUS IF YOU SHOWED.
YOU GOTTA GO TO CLASS, RIGHT?
SO I SAID, BUT...
...I'M REALLY FREAKIN' OUT!!
I don't wanna go in ...
I'M SCARED! I ACTUALLY CAN'T DO THIS!!
HEY SAEKO, WHAT'CHA DOIN?
OPEN THE DOOR.
FWIP
YEEK

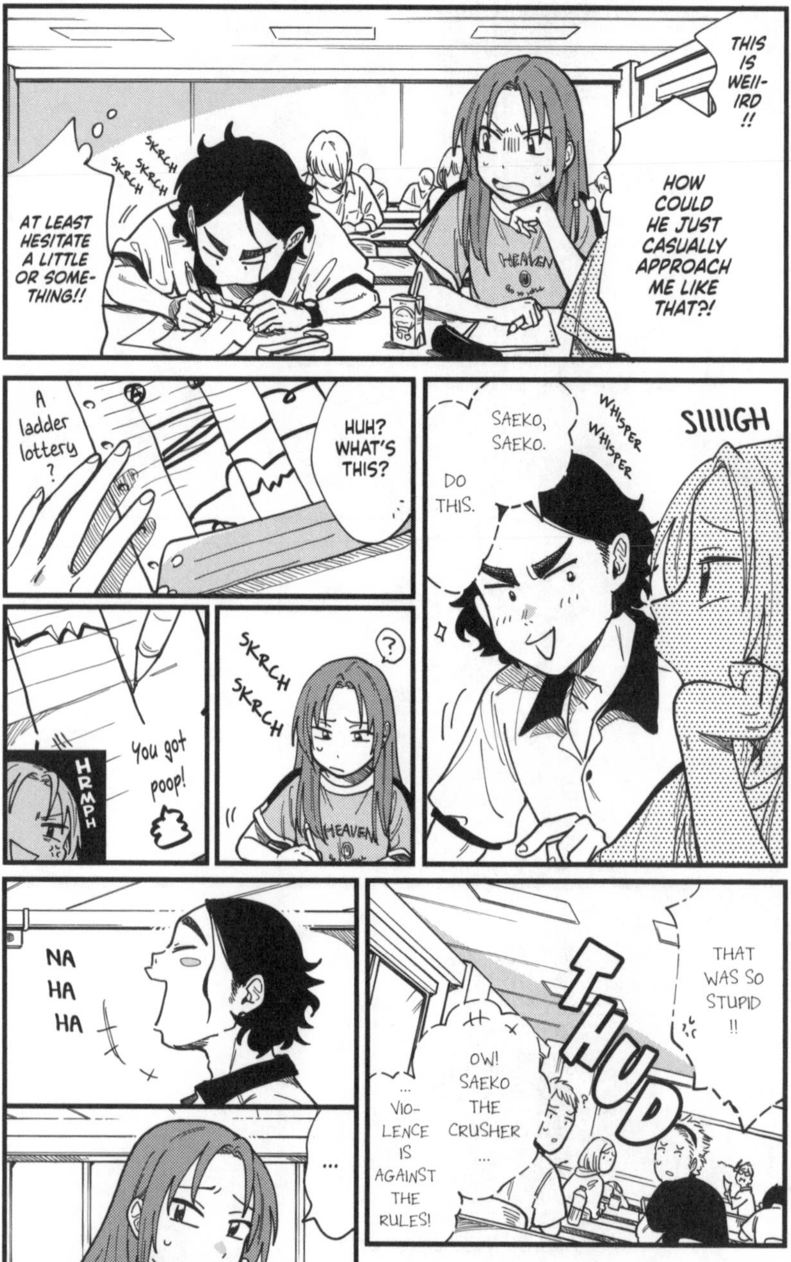
THIS IS WEIIRD!!
HOW COULD HE JUST CASUALLY APPROACH ME LIKE THAT?!
SKRCH SKRCH SKRCH
AT LEAST HESITATE A LITTLE OR SOME-THING!!
SIIIIGH
WHISPER WHISPER
SAEKO, SAEKO.
DO THIS.
HUH? WHAT'S THIS?
A ladder lottery?
?
SKRCH SKRCH
You got poop!
HRMPH
THAT WAS SO STUPID!!
THUD
OW! SAEKO THE CRUSHER...
...VIO-LENCE IS AGAINST THE RULES!
NA HA HA
...

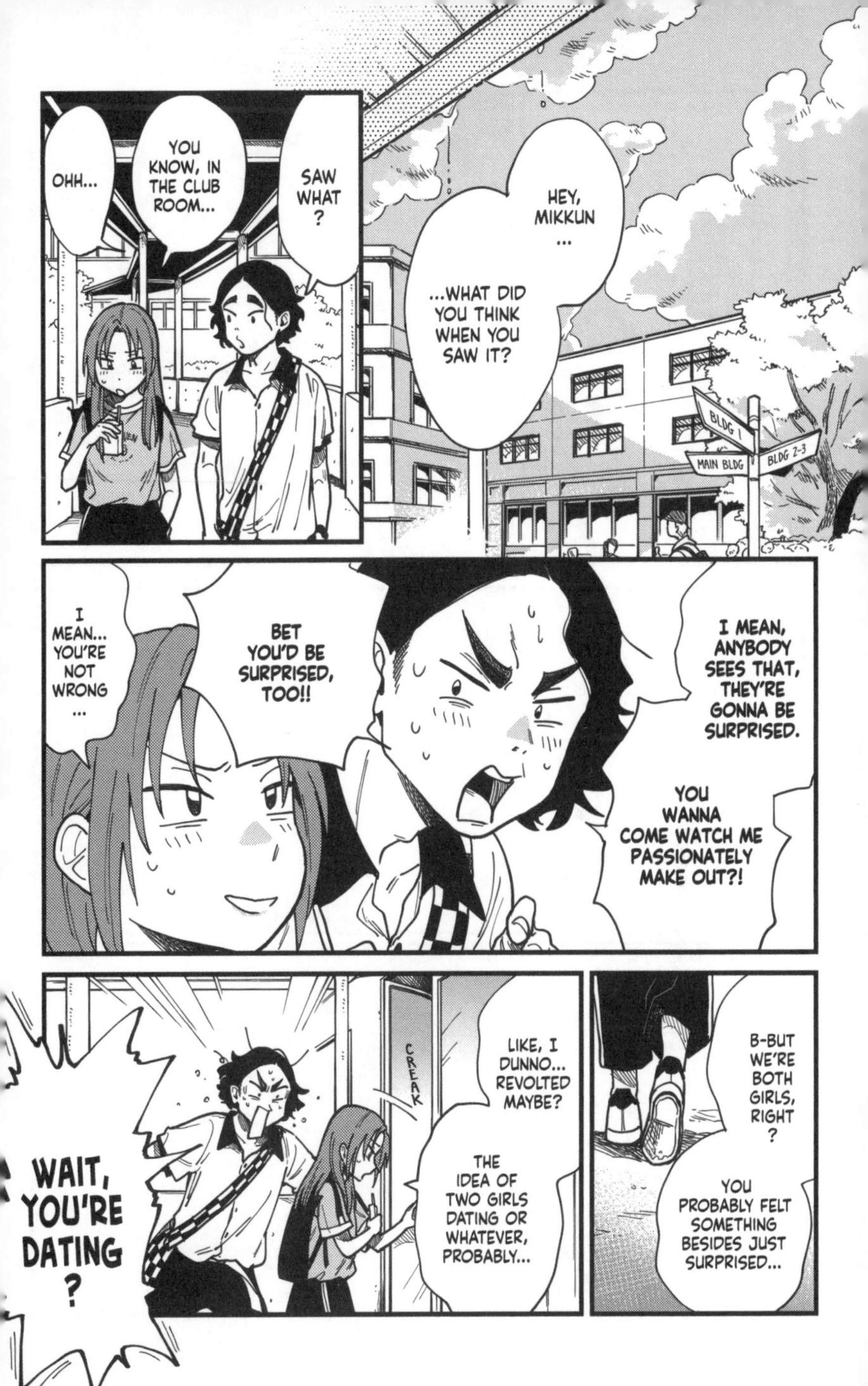
HEY, MIKKUN ...
...WHAT DID YOU THINK WHEN YOU SAW IT?
BLDG 1
BLDG 2-3
MAIN BLDG
SAW WHAT ?
YOU KNOW, IN THE CLUB ROOM...
OHH...
I MEAN, ANYBODY SEES THAT, THEY'RE GONNA BE SURPRISED.
YOU WANNA COME WATCH ME PASSIONATELY MAKE OUT?!
BET YOU'D BE SURPRISED, TOO!!
I MEAN... YOU'RE NOT WRONG ...
B-BUT WE'RE BOTH GIRLS, RIGHT ?
YOU PROBABLY FELT SOMETHING BESIDES JUST SURPRISED...
LIKE, I DUNNO... REVOLTED MAYBE?
THE IDEA OF TWO GIRLS DATING OR WHATEVER, PROBABLY...
CREAK
WAIT, YOU'RE DATING ?

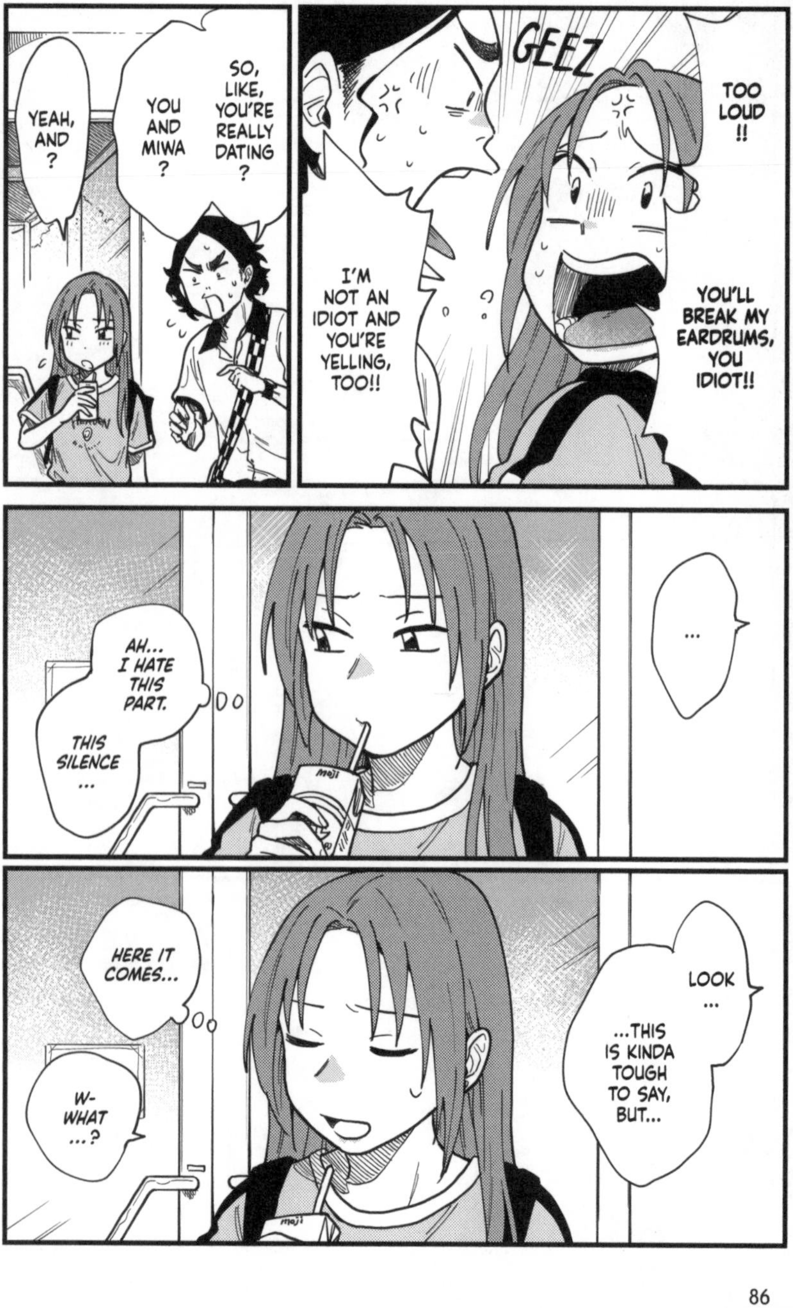
GEEZ
TOO LOUD!!
YOU'LL BREAK MY EARDRUMS, YOU IDIOT!!
I'M NOT AN IDIOT AND YOU'RE YELLING, TOO!!
SO, LIKE, YOU'RE REALLY DATING?
YOU AND MIWA?
YEAH, AND?
...
AH... I HATE THIS PART.
THIS SILENCE...
LOOK...
...THIS IS KINDA TOUGH TO SAY, BUT...
HERE IT COMES...
W-WHAT...?

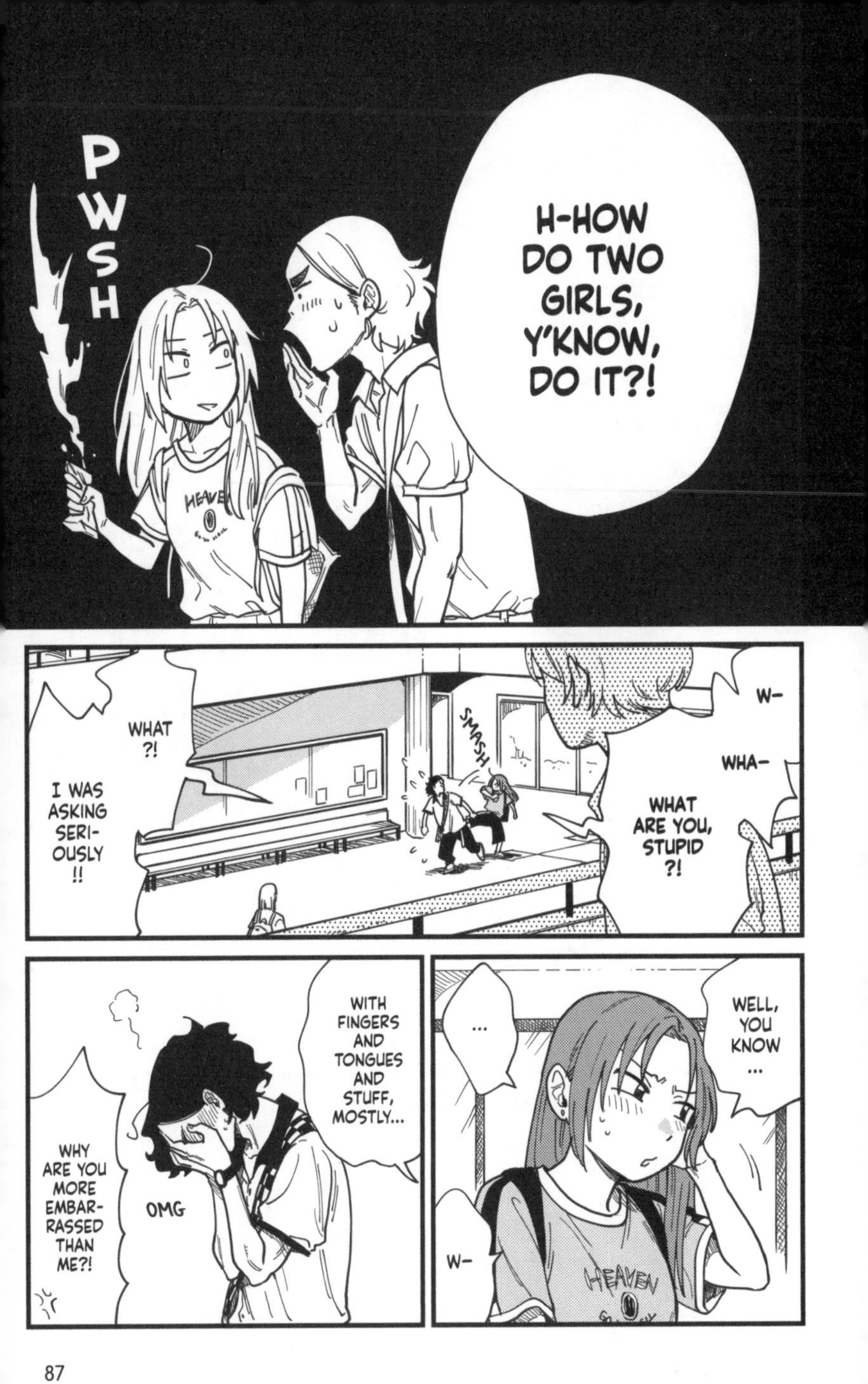
H-HOW DO TWO GIRLS, Y'KNOW, DO IT?!
PWSH
W-
WHA-
WHAT ARE YOU, STUPID ?!
SMASH
WHAT ?!
I WAS ASKING SERI-OUSLY !!
WELL, YOU KNOW ...
...
W-
WITH FINGERS AND TONGUES AND STUFF, MOSTLY...
OMG
WHY ARE YOU MORE EMBAR-RASSED THAN ME?!

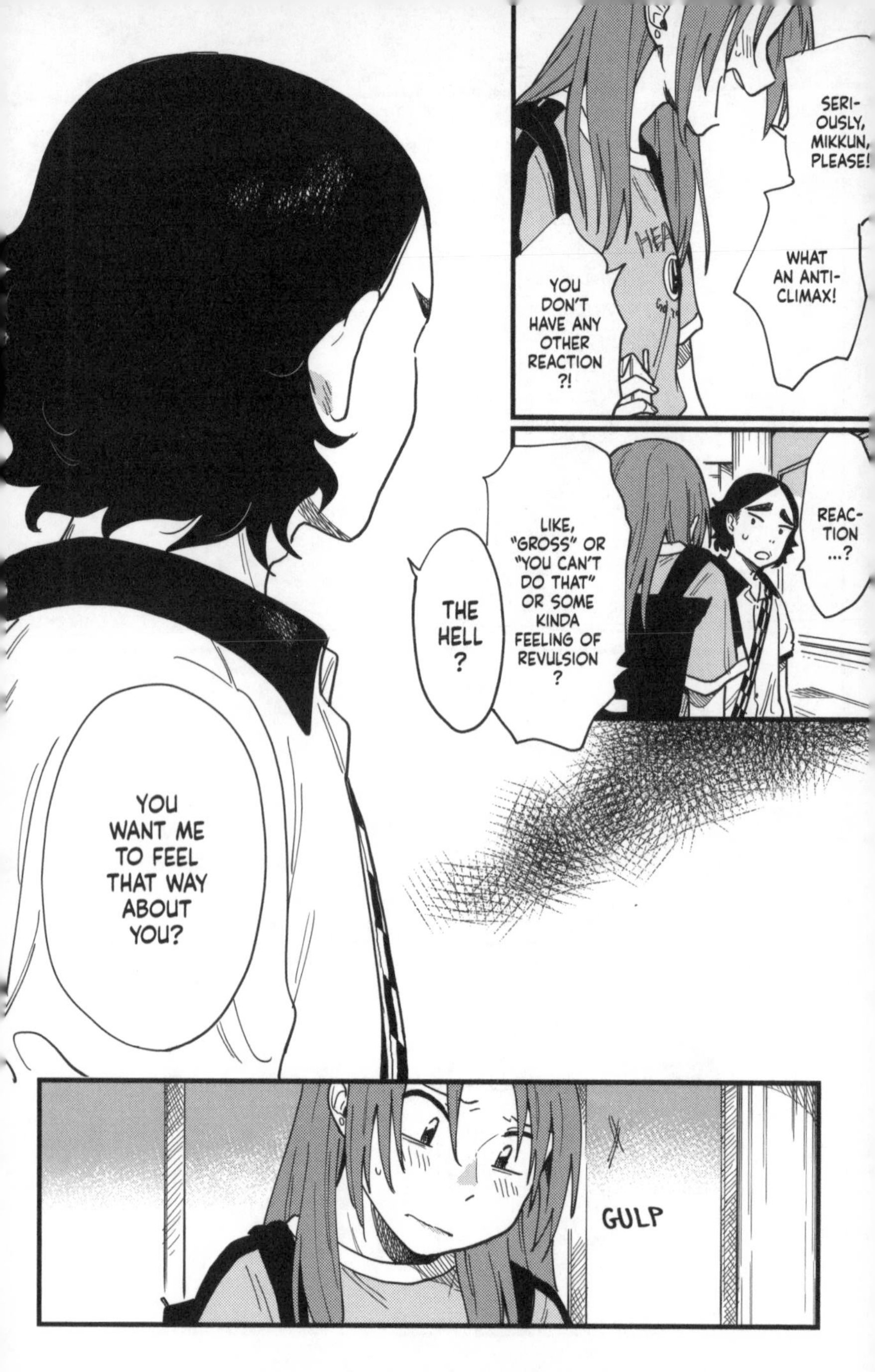
SERI-OUSLY, MIKKUN, PLEASE!
WHAT AN ANTI-CLIMAX!
YOU DON'T HAVE ANY OTHER REACTION ?!
REAC-TION ...?
LIKE, "GROSS" OR "YOU CAN'T DO THAT" OR SOME KINDA FEELING OF REVULSION ?
THE HELL ?
YOU WANT ME TO FEEL THAT WAY ABOUT YOU?
GULP

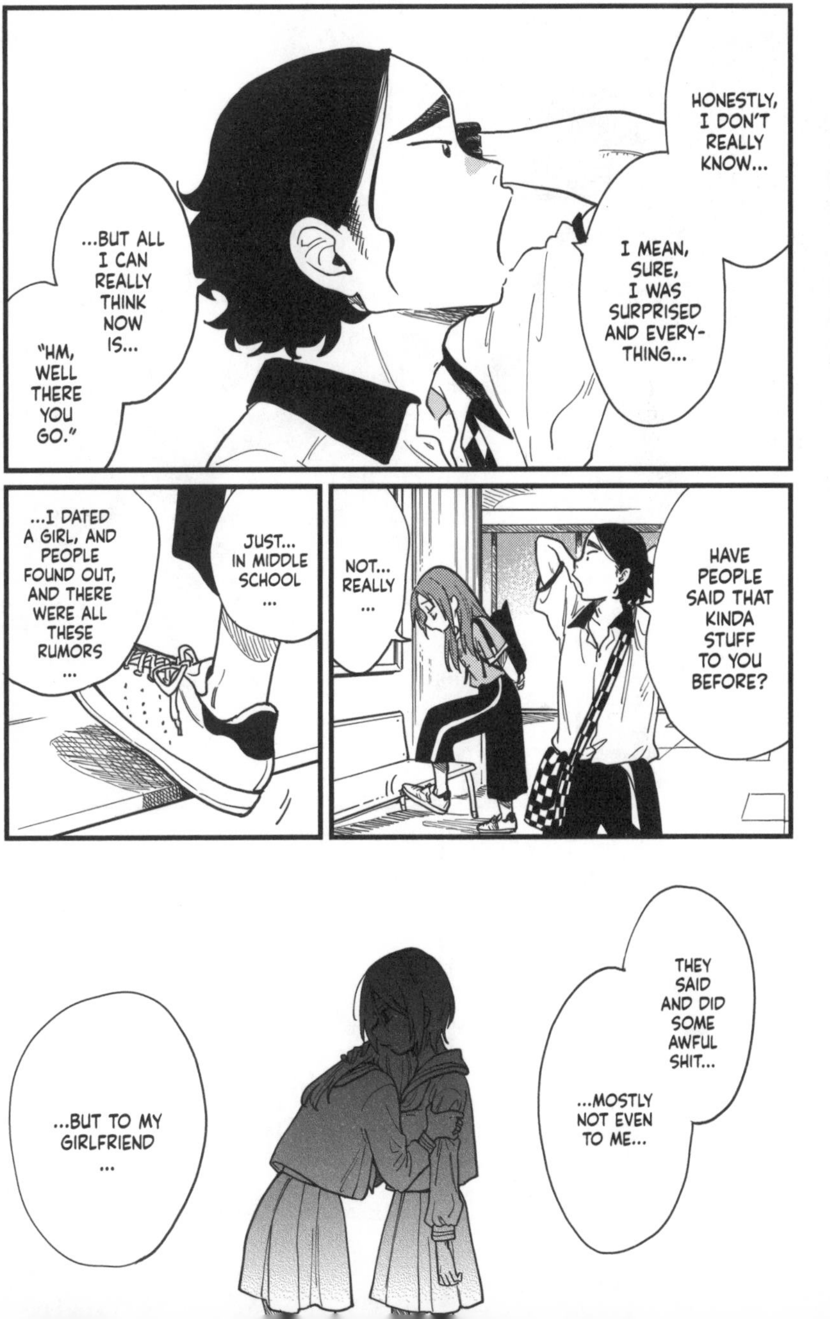
HONESTLY, I DON'T REALLY KNOW...
I MEAN, SURE, I WAS SURPRISED AND EVERY-THING...
...BUT ALL I CAN REALLY THINK NOW IS...
"HM, WELL THERE YOU GO."
HAVE PEOPLE SAID THAT KINDA STUFF TO YOU BEFORE?
NOT... REALLY ...
JUST... IN MIDDLE SCHOOL ...
...I DATED A GIRL, AND PEOPLE FOUND OUT, AND THERE WERE ALL THESE RUMORS ...
THEY SAID AND DID SOME AWFUL SHIT...
...MOSTLY NOT EVEN TO ME...
...BUT TO MY GIRLFRIEND ...

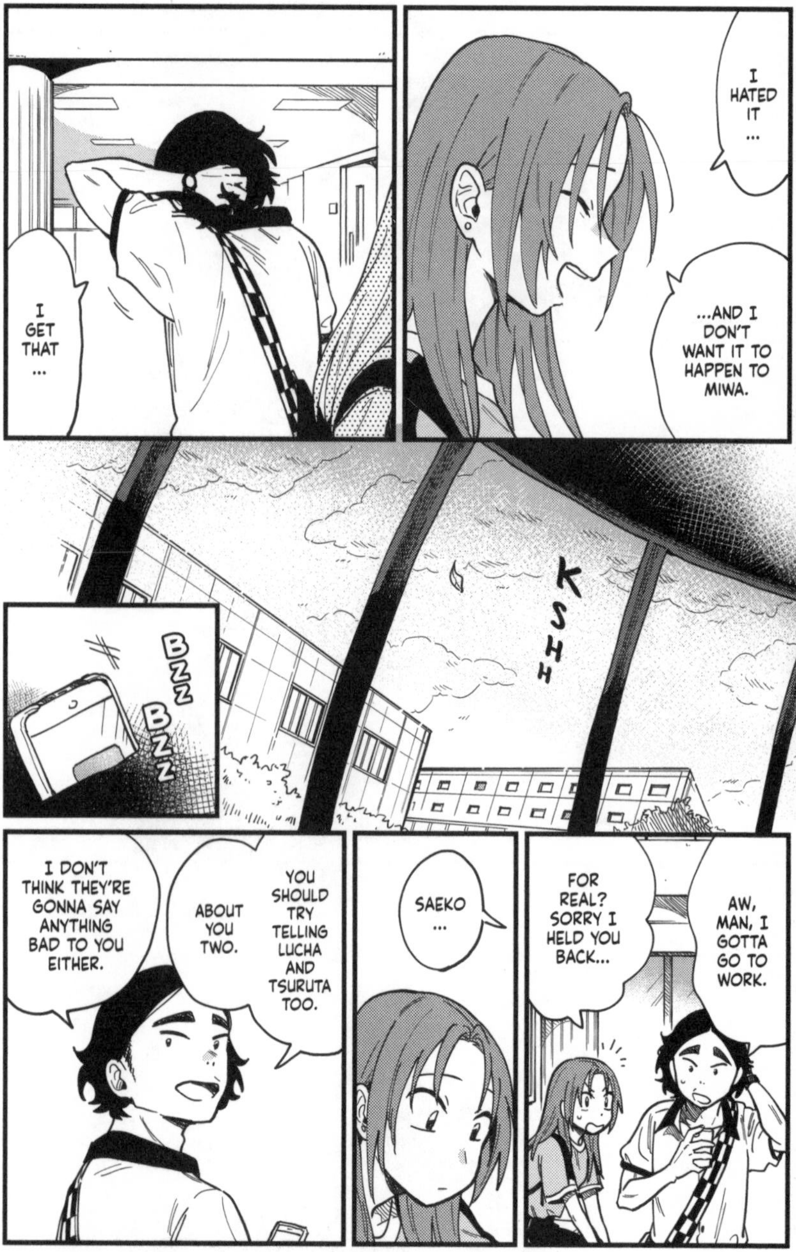
I HATED IT...
...AND I DON'T WANT IT TO HAPPEN TO MIWA.
I GET THAT...
KSHH
BZZ BZZ
AW, MAN, I GOTTA GO TO WORK.
FOR REAL? SORRY I HELD YOU BACK...
SAEKO...
YOU SHOULD TRY TELLING LUCHA AND TSURUTA TOO.
ABOUT YOU TWO.
I DON'T THINK THEY'RE GONNA SAY ANYTHING BAD TO YOU EITHER.

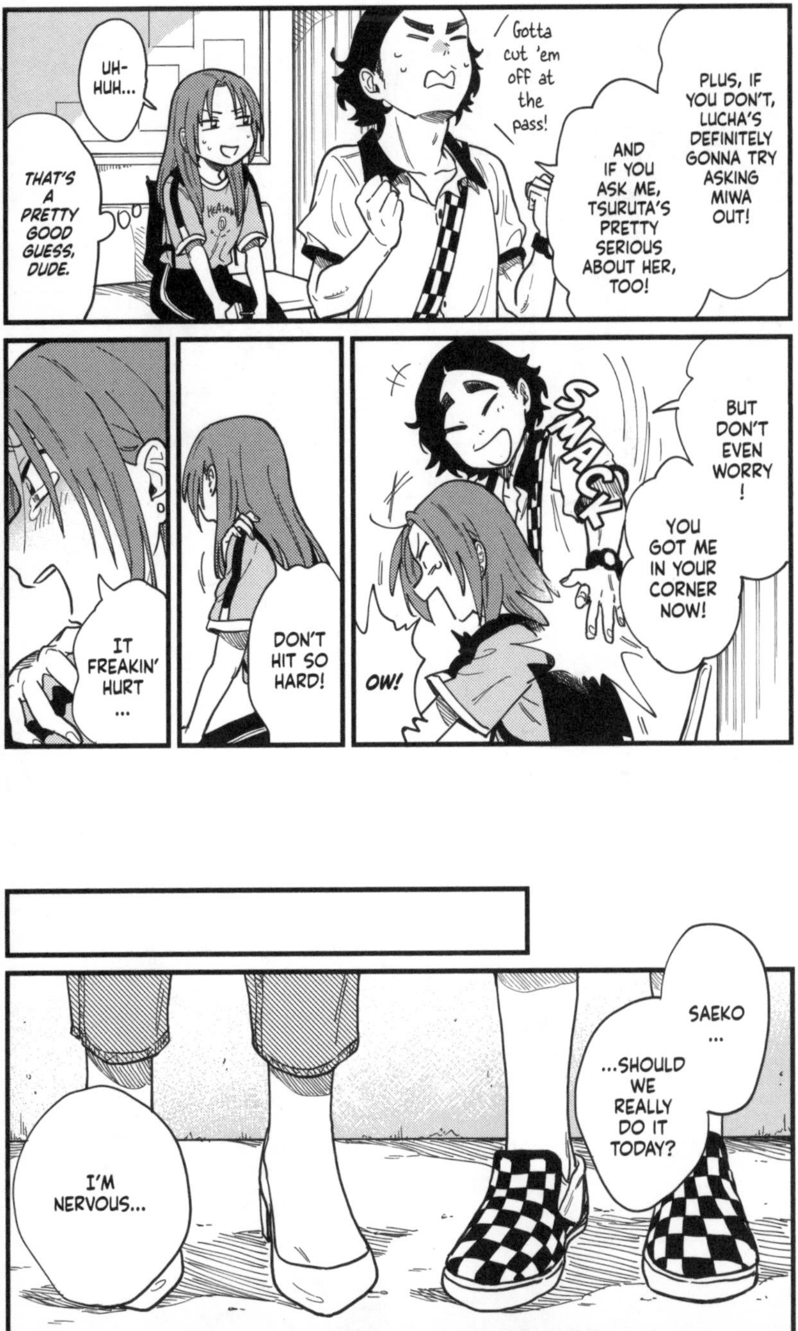
PLUS, IF YOU DON'T, LUCHA'S DEFINITELY GONNA TRY ASKING MIWA OUT!
AND IF YOU ASK ME, TSURUTA'S PRETTY SERIOUS ABOUT HER, TOO!
Gotta cut 'em off at the pass!
UH-HUH...
THAT'S A PRETTY GOOD GUESS, DUDE.
BUT DON'T EVEN WORRY!
SMACK
YOU GOT ME IN YOUR CORNER NOW!
OW!
DON'T HIT SO HARD!
IT FREAKIN' HURT...
SAEKO...
...SHOULD WE REALLY DO IT TODAY?
I'M NERVOUS...

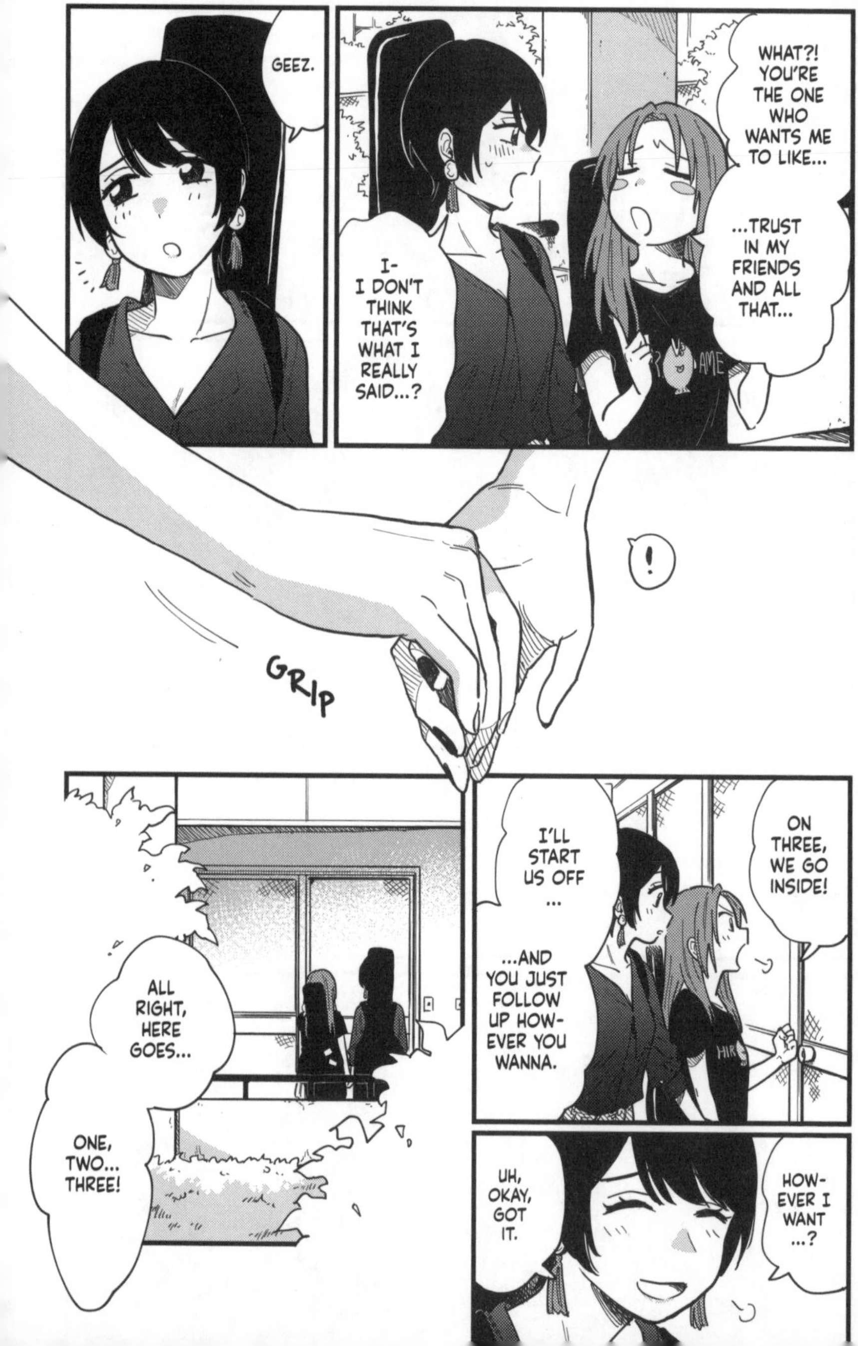
WHAT?! YOU'RE THE ONE WHO WANTS ME TO LIKE...
...TRUST IN MY FRIENDS AND ALL THAT...
I- I DON'T THINK THAT'S WHAT I REALLY SAID...?
GEEZ.
!
GRIP
ON THREE, WE GO INSIDE!
I'LL START US OFF ...
...AND YOU JUST FOLLOW UP HOW-EVER YOU WANNA.
HOW-EVER I WANT ...?
UH, OKAY, GOT IT.
ALL RIGHT, HERE GOES...
ONE, TWO... THREE!

HOW DO WE RELATIONSHIP?

How Do We Relationship?

Chapter 5: I'm a Romantic, You See

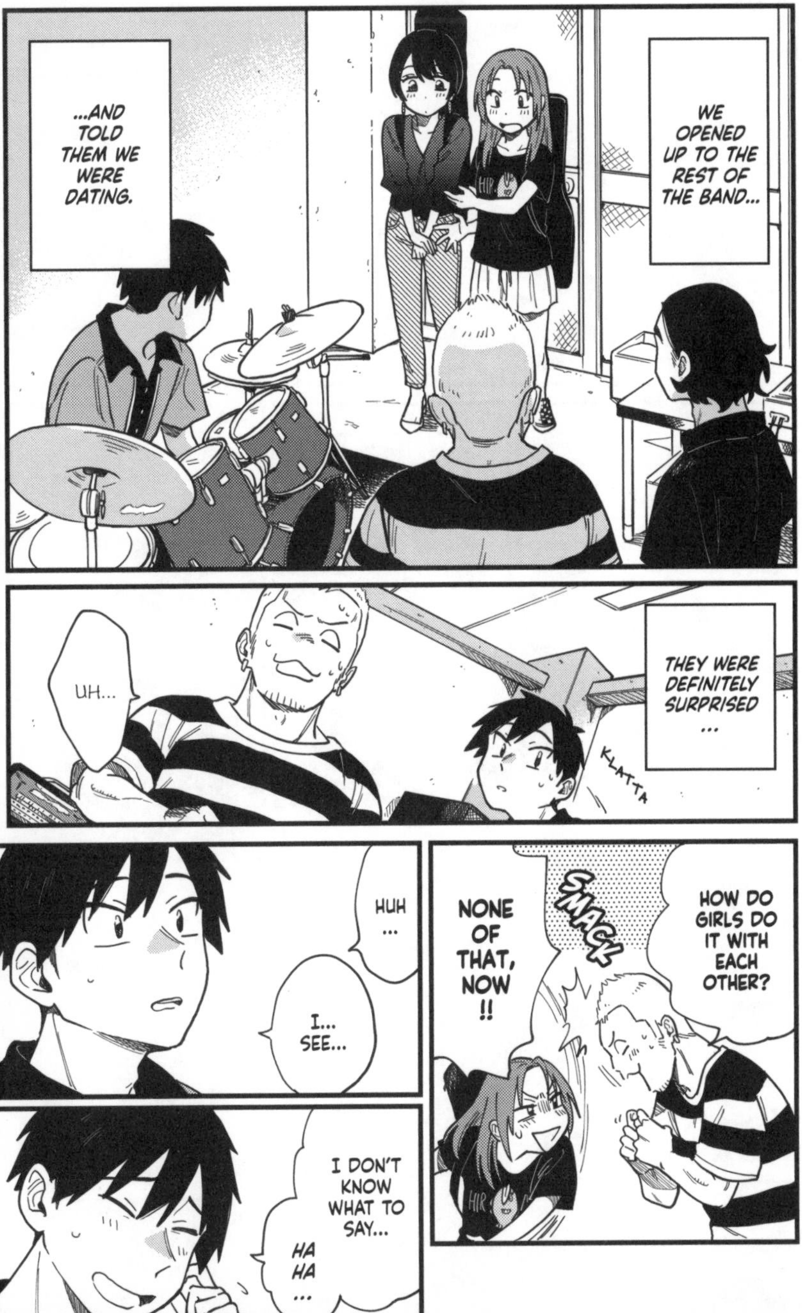
WE OPENED UP TO THE REST OF THE BAND...
...AND TOLD THEM WE WERE DATING.
THEY WERE DEFINITELY SURPRISED ...
KLATTA
UH...
HOW DO GIRLS DO IT WITH EACH OTHER?
SMACK
NONE OF THAT, NOW!!
HUH ...
I... SEE...
I DON'T KNOW WHAT TO SAY...
HA HA ...

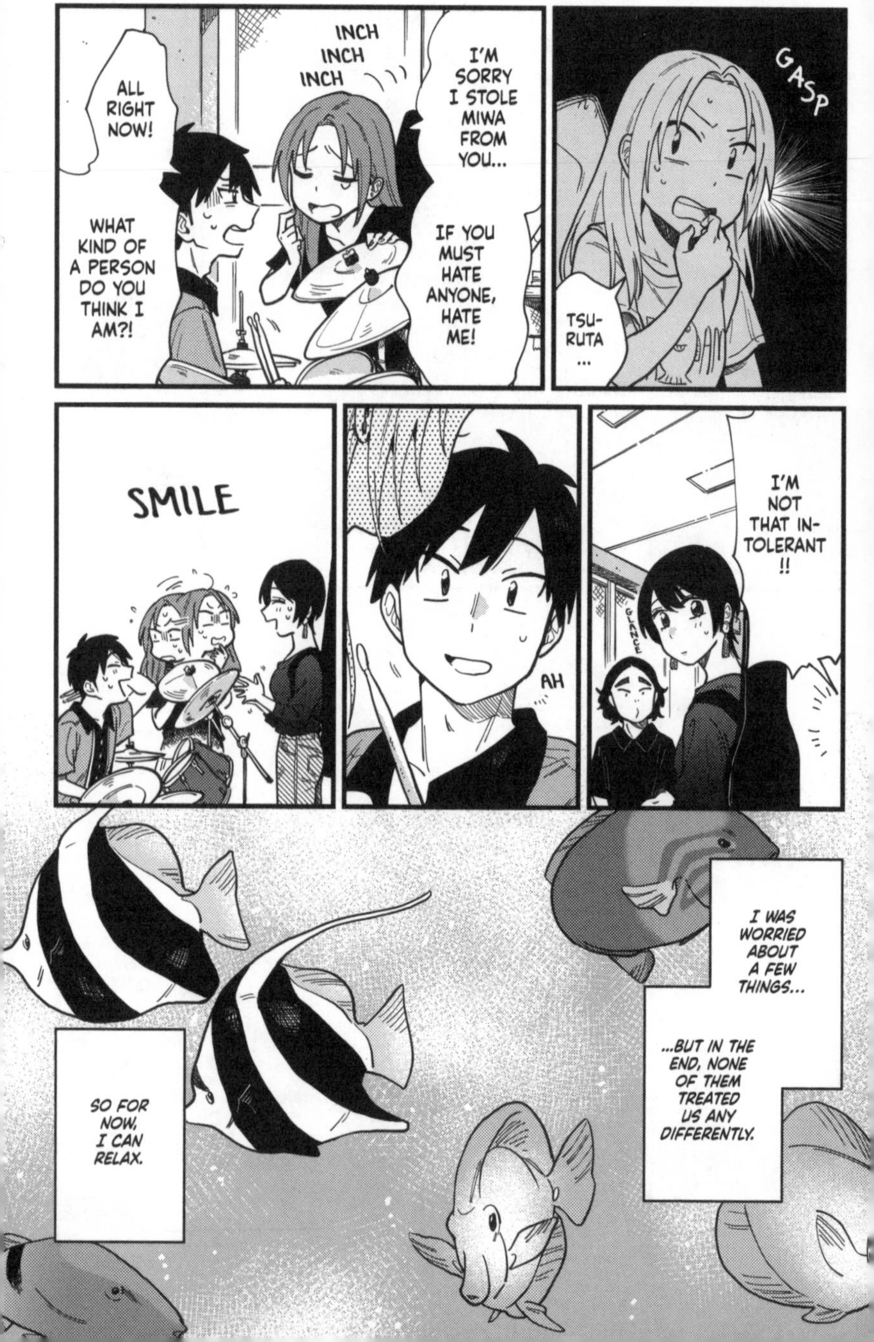
GASP
TSU-RUTA...
I'M SORRY I STOLE MIWA FROM YOU...
INCH INCH INCH
ALL RIGHT NOW!
IF YOU MUST HATE ANYONE, HATE ME!
WHAT KIND OF A PERSON DO YOU THINK I AM?!
I'M NOT THAT IN-TOLERANT!!
GLANCE
AH
SMILE
I WAS WORRIED ABOUT A FEW THINGS...
...BUT IN THE END, NONE OF THEM TREATED US ANY DIFFERENTLY.
SO FOR NOW, I CAN RELAX.

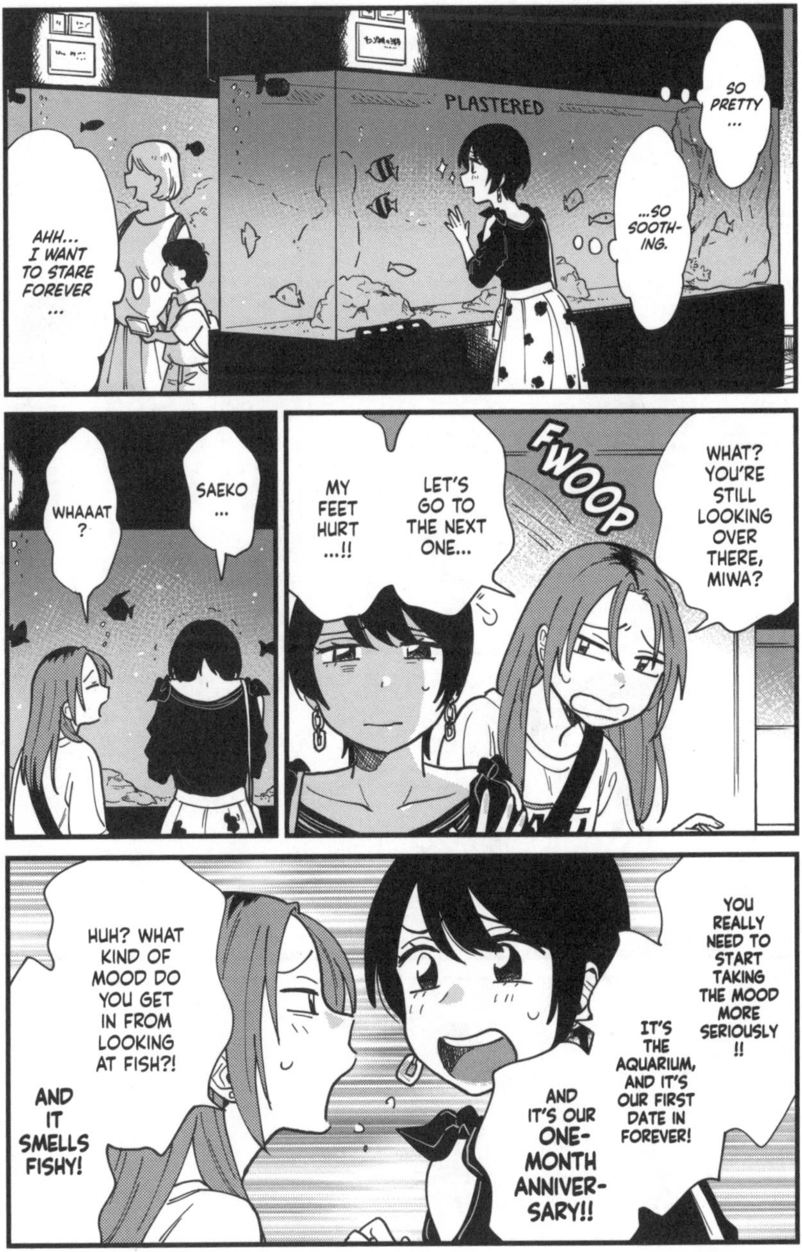
SO PRETTY...
PLASTERED
...SO SOOTHING.
AHH... I WANT TO STARE FOREVER...
WHAT? YOU'RE STILL LOOKING OVER THERE, MIWA?
FWOOP
LET'S GO TO THE NEXT ONE...
MY FEET HURT...!!
SAEKO...
WHAAAT?
YOU REALLY NEED TO START TAKING THE MOOD MORE SERIOUSLY!!
IT'S THE AQUARIUM, AND IT'S OUR FIRST DATE IN FOREVER!
AND IT'S OUR ONE-MONTH ANNIVERSARY!!
HUH? WHAT KIND OF MOOD DO YOU GET IN FROM LOOKING AT FISH?!
AND IT SMELLS FISHY!

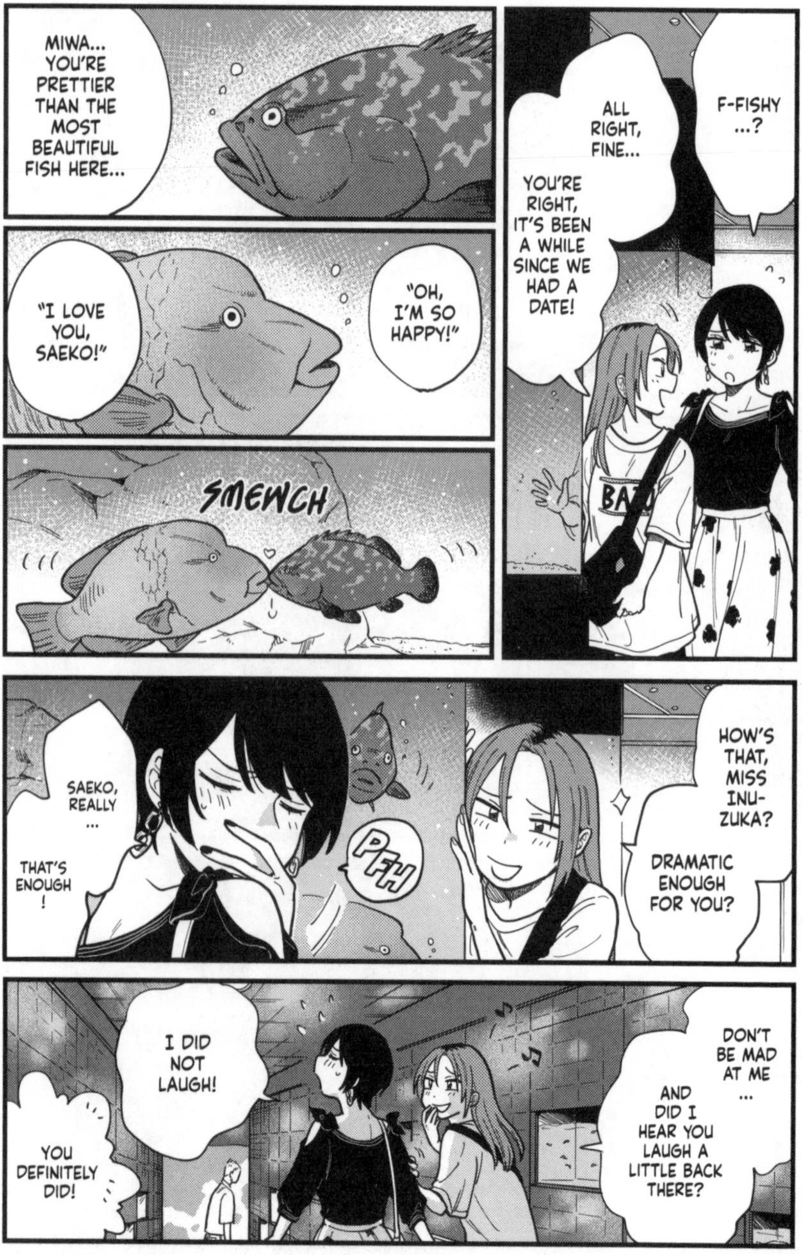
F-FISHY ...?
ALL RIGHT, FINE...
YOU'RE RIGHT, IT'S BEEN A WHILE SINCE WE HAD A DATE!
MIWA... YOU'RE PRETTIER THAN THE MOST BEAUTIFUL FISH HERE...
"OH, I'M SO HAPPY!"
"I LOVE YOU, SAEKO!"
SMEWCH
HOW'S THAT, MISS INU-ZUKA?
DRAMATIC ENOUGH FOR YOU?
PFH
SAEKO, REALLY ...
THAT'S ENOUGH !
DON'T BE MAD AT ME ...
AND DID I HEAR YOU LAUGH A LITTLE BACK THERE?
I DID NOT LAUGH!
YOU DEFINITELY DID!

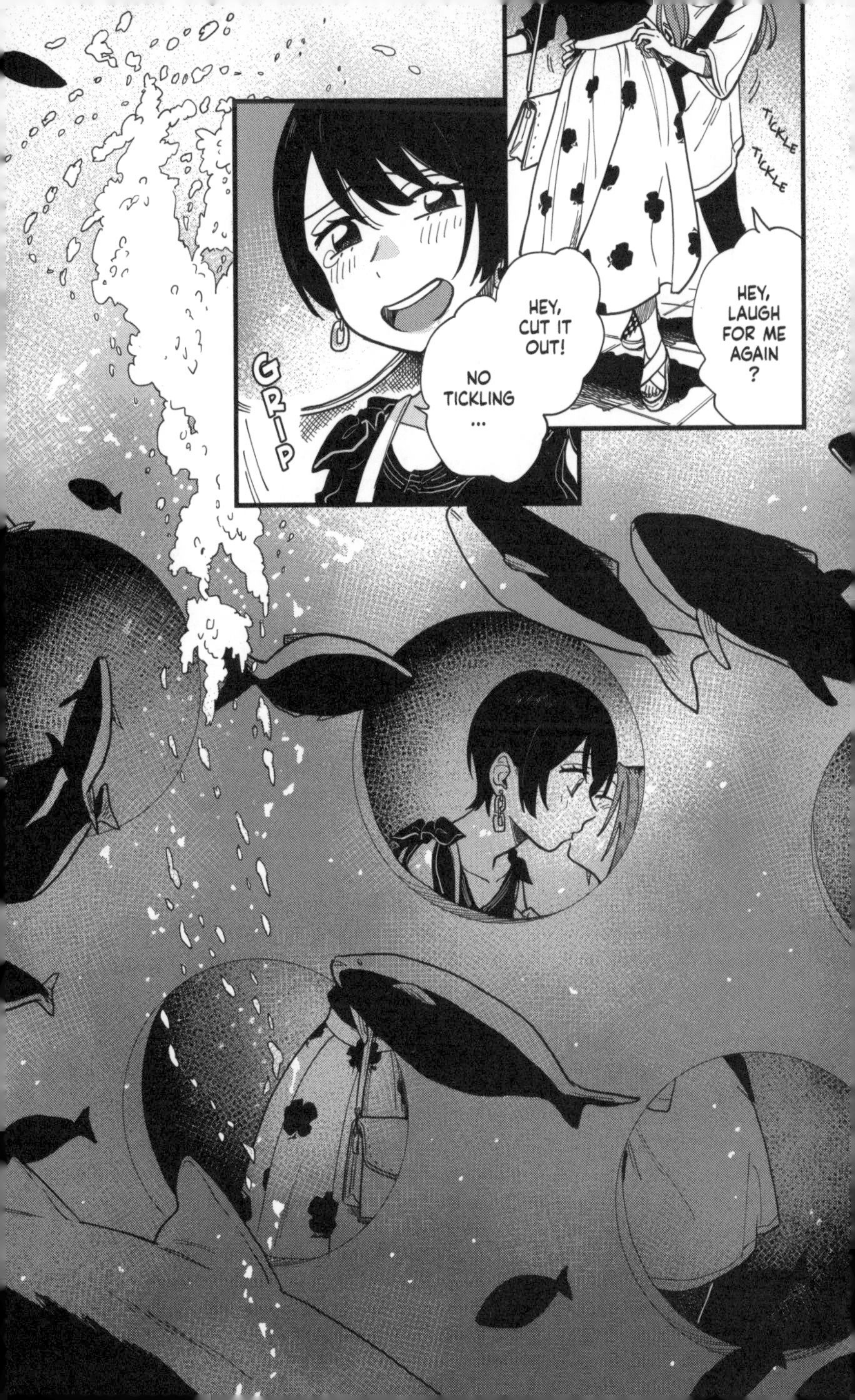
TICKLE TICKLE
HEY, LAUGH FOR ME AGAIN?
HEY, CUT IT OUT!
NO TICKLING ...
GRIP

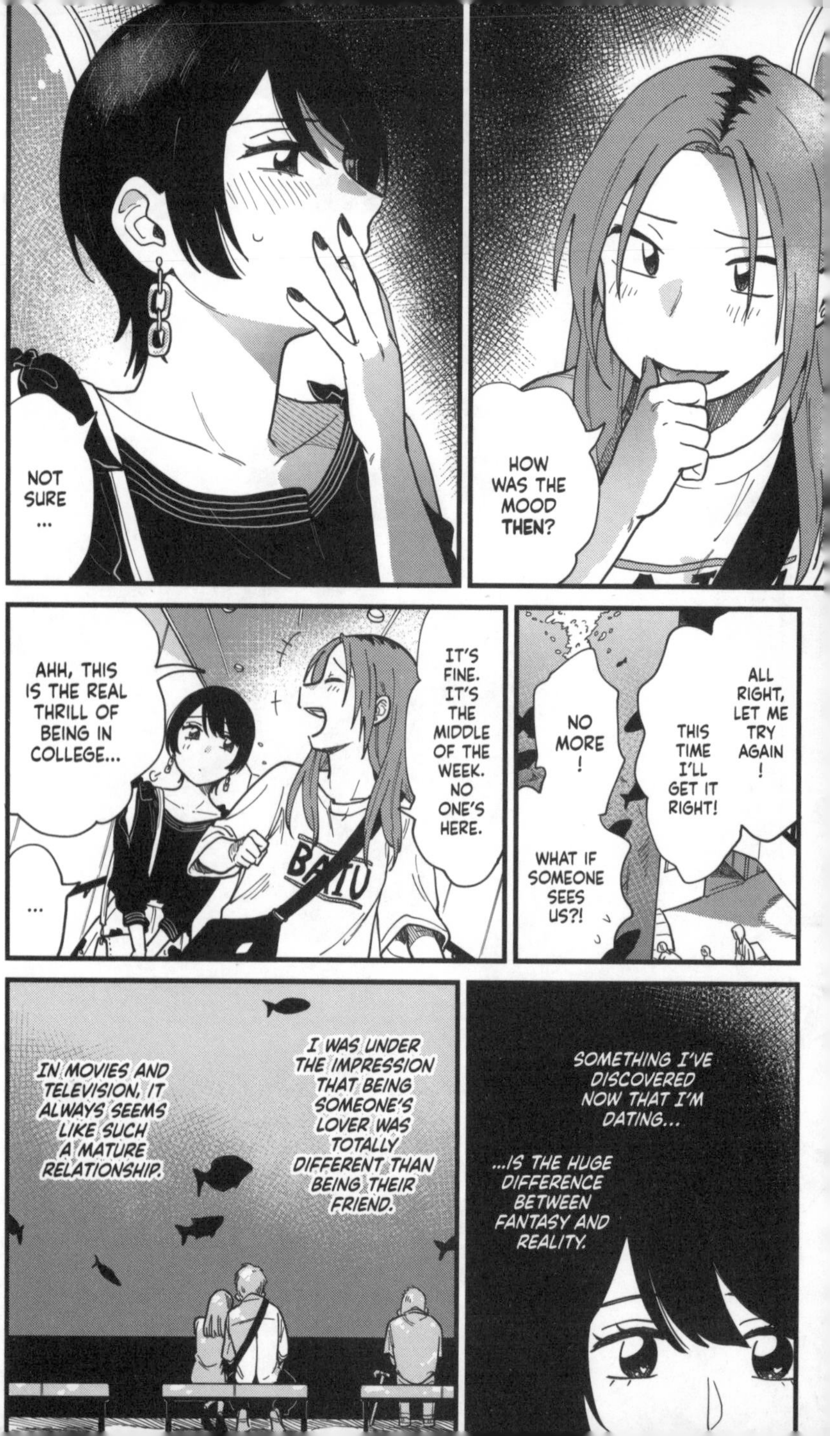
HOW WAS THE MOOD THEN?
NOT SURE ...
ALL RIGHT, LET ME TRY AGAIN!
THIS TIME I'LL GET IT RIGHT!
NO MORE!
WHAT IF SOMEONE SEES US?!
IT'S FINE. IT'S THE MIDDLE OF THE WEEK. NO ONE'S HERE.
AHH, THIS IS THE REAL THRILL OF BEING IN COLLEGE...
...
SOMETHING I'VE DISCOVERED NOW THAT I'M DATING...
...IS THE HUGE DIFFERENCE BETWEEN FANTASY AND REALITY.
I WAS UNDER THE IMPRESSION THAT BEING SOMEONE'S LOVER WAS TOTALLY DIFFERENT THAN BEING THEIR FRIEND.
IN MOVIES AND TELEVISION, IT ALWAYS SEEMS LIKE SUCH A MATURE RELATIONSHIP.

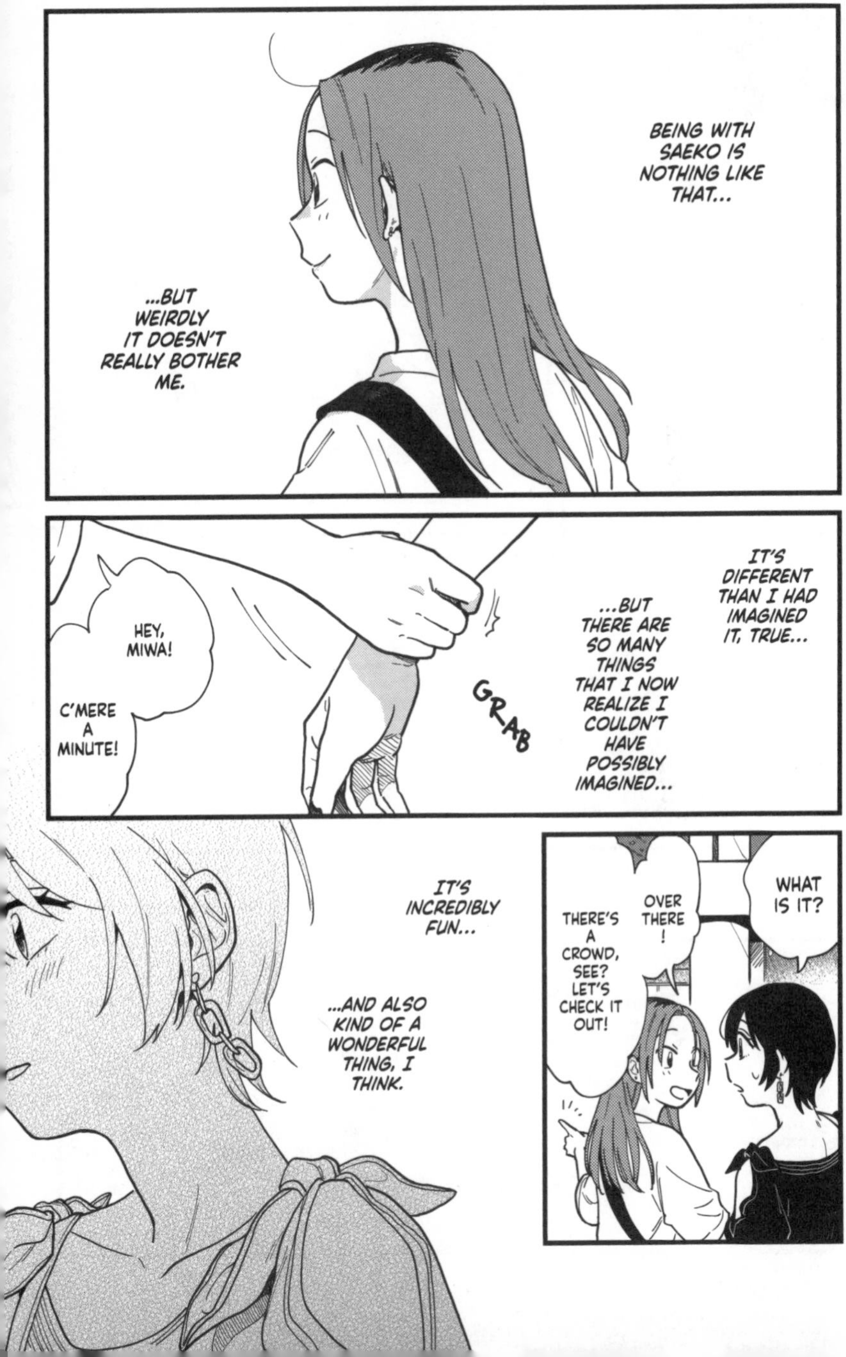
BEING WITH SAEKO IS NOTHING LIKE THAT...
...BUT WEIRDLY IT DOESN'T REALLY BOTHER ME.
IT'S DIFFERENT THAN I HAD IMAGINED IT, TRUE...
...BUT THERE ARE SO MANY THINGS THAT I NOW REALIZE I COULDN'T HAVE POSSIBLY IMAGINED...
GRAB
HEY, MIWA!
C'MERE A MINUTE!
WHAT IS IT?
OVER THERE!
THERE'S A CROWD, SEE? LET'S CHECK IT OUT!
IT'S INCREDIBLY FUN...
...AND ALSO KIND OF A WONDERFUL THING, I THINK.

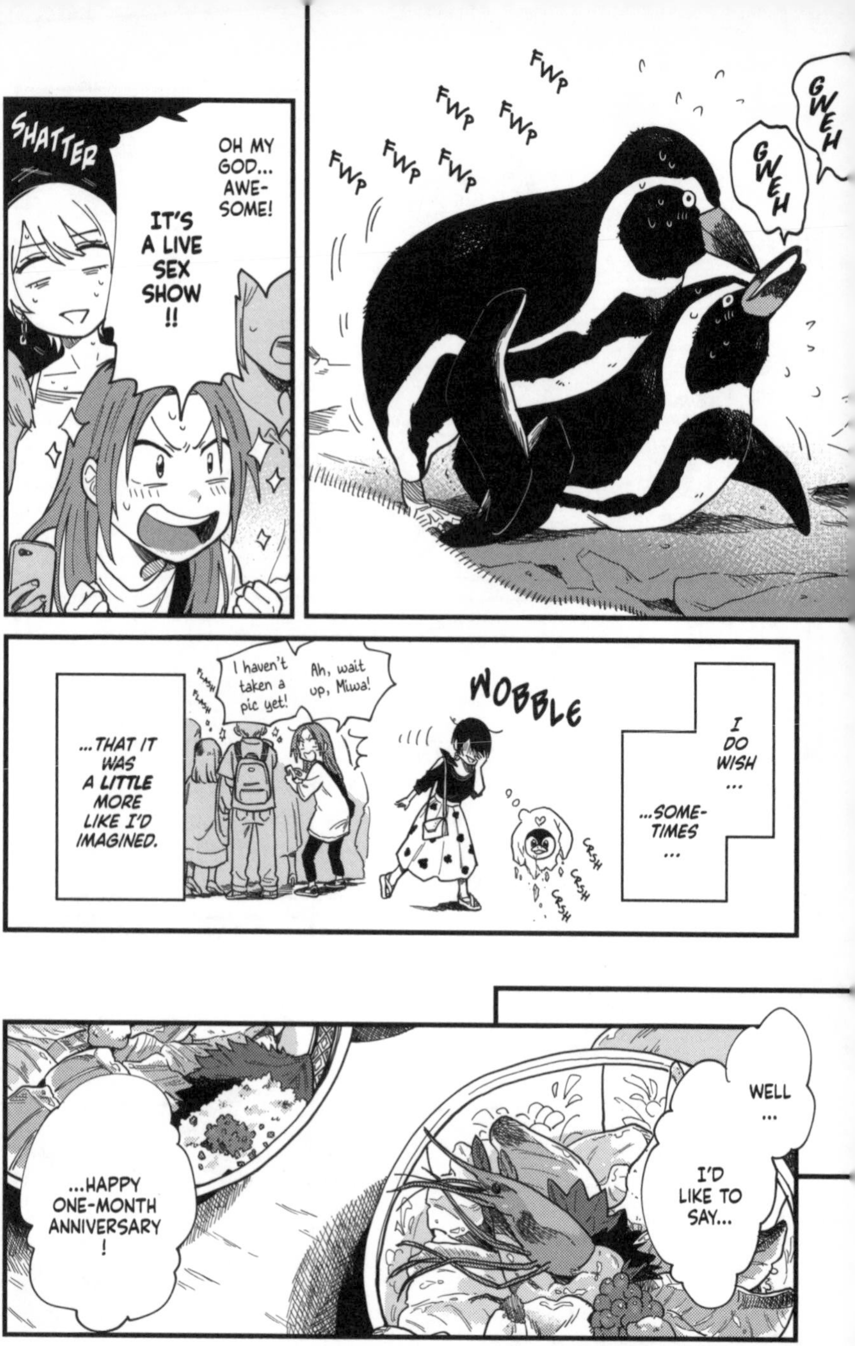
FWP FWP FWP FWP FWP FWP
GWEH
GWEH
OH MY GOD... AWESOME!
SHATTER
IT'S A LIVE SEX SHOW!!
I DO WISH...
...SOMETIMES...
WOBBLE
CRSH CRSH CRSH
Ah, wait up, Miwa!
I haven't taken a pic yet!
FLASH FLASH
...THAT IT WAS A LITTLE MORE LIKE I'D IMAGINED.
WELL...
I'D LIKE TO SAY...
...HAPPY ONE-MONTH ANNIVERSARY!

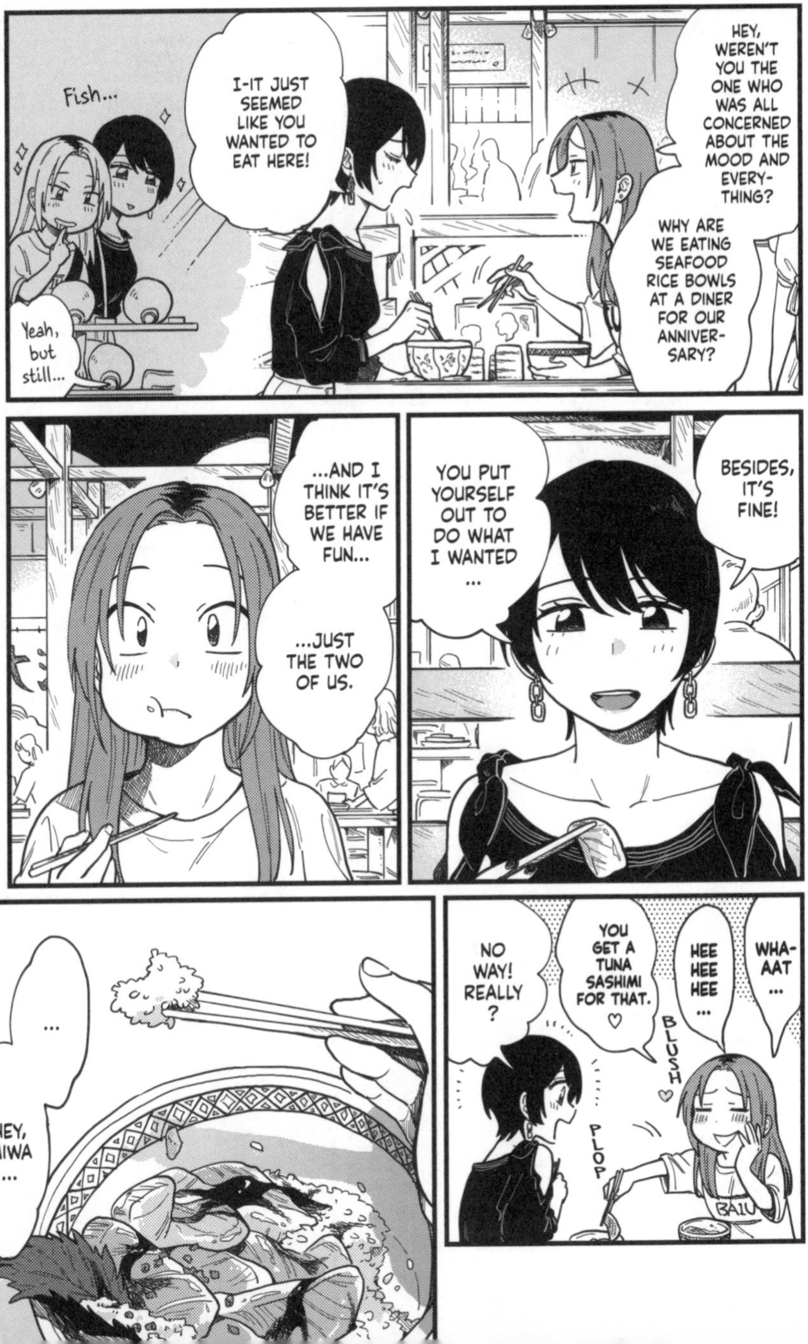
HEY, WEREN'T YOU THE ONE WHO WAS ALL CONCERNED ABOUT THE MOOD AND EVERY-THING?
WHY ARE WE EATING SEAFOOD RICE BOWLS AT A DINER FOR OUR ANNIVER-SARY?
I-IT JUST SEEMED LIKE YOU WANTED TO EAT HERE!
Fish...
Yeah, but still...
BESIDES, IT'S FINE!
YOU PUT YOURSELF OUT TO DO WHAT I WANTED ...
...AND I THINK IT'S BETTER IF WE HAVE FUN...
...JUST THE TWO OF US.
WHA-AAT ...
HEE HEE HEE ...
BLUSH
YOU GET A TUNA SASHIMI FOR THAT. ♡
NO WAY! REALLY ?
PLOP
BAIU
...
HEY, MIWA ...

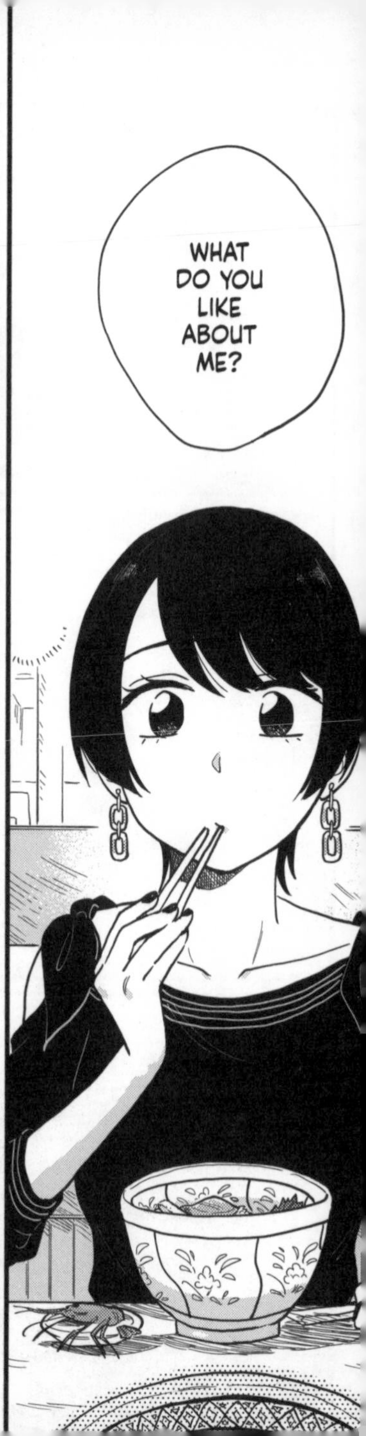
WHAT DO YOU LIKE ABOUT ME?

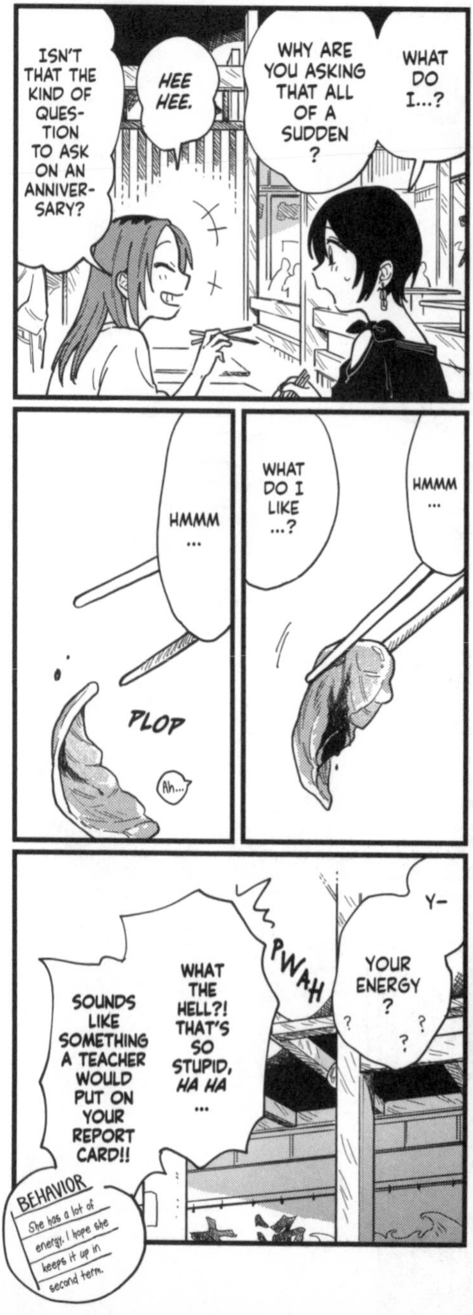
WHAT DO I...?
WHY ARE YOU ASKING THAT ALL OF A SUDDEN?
HEE HEE.
ISN'T THAT THE KIND OF QUESTION TO ASK ON AN ANNIVERSARY?
HMMM...
WHAT DO I LIKE...?
HMMM...
PLOP
Ah...
Y-
YOUR ENERGY?
PWAH
WHAT THE HELL?! THAT'S SO STUPID, HA HA...
SOUNDS LIKE SOMETHING A TEACHER WOULD PUT ON YOUR REPORT CARD!!
BEHAVIOR
She has a lot of energy. I hope she keeps it up in second term.

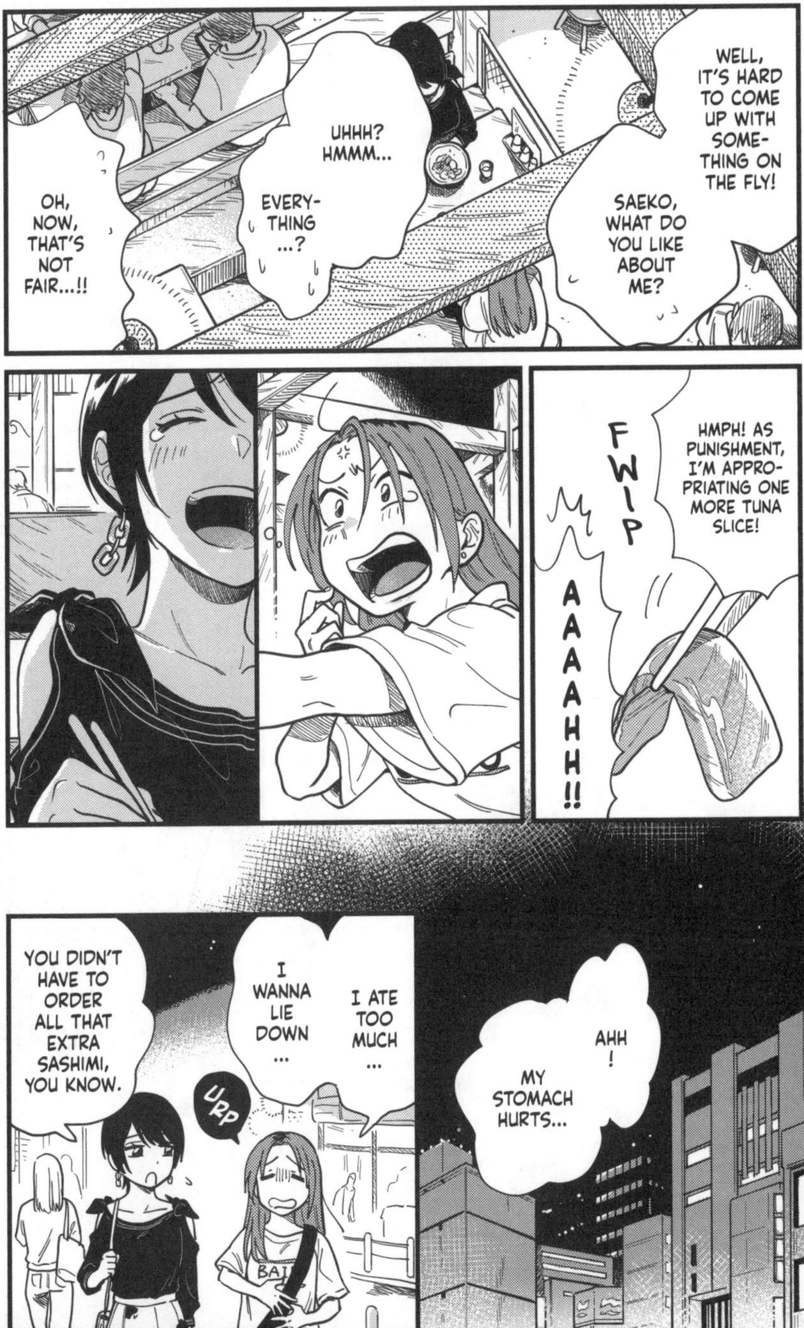
WELL, IT'S HARD TO COME UP WITH SOME-THING ON THE FLY!
SAEKO, WHAT DO YOU LIKE ABOUT ME?
UHHH? HMMM...
EVERY-THING ...?
OH, NOW, THAT'S NOT FAIR...!!
HMPH! AS PUNISHMENT, I'M APPRO-PRIATING ONE MORE TUNA SLICE!
FWIP
AAAAAHH!!
AHH!
MY STOMACH HURTS...
I ATE TOO MUCH ...
I WANNA LIE DOWN ...
URP
YOU DIDN'T HAVE TO ORDER ALL THAT EXTRA SASHIMI, YOU KNOW.

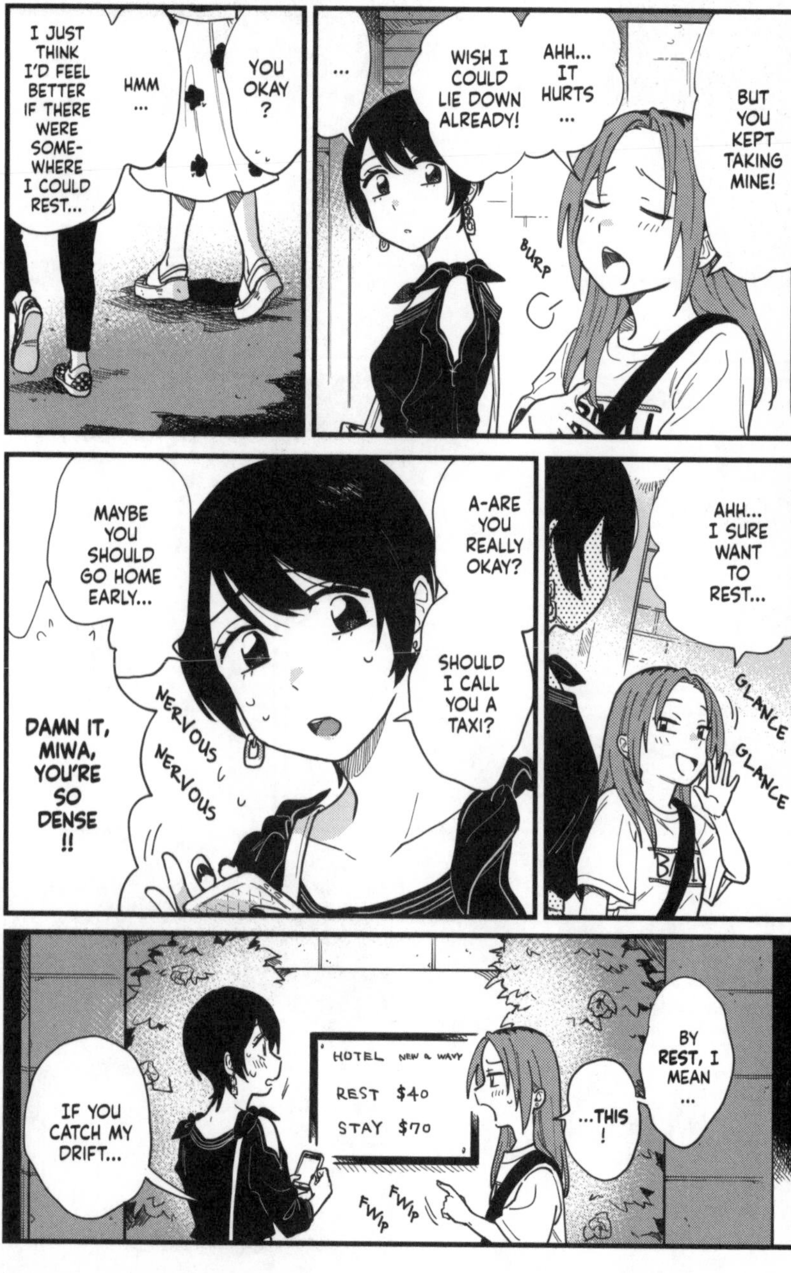
AHH... IT HURTS...
WISH I COULD LIE DOWN ALREADY!
BUT YOU KEPT TAKING MINE!
BURP
...
YOU OKAY?
HMM...
I JUST THINK I'D FEEL BETTER IF THERE WERE SOME-WHERE I COULD REST...
AHH... I SURE WANT TO REST...
GLANCE
GLANCE
A-ARE YOU REALLY OKAY?
SHOULD I CALL YOU A TAXI?
MAYBE YOU SHOULD GO HOME EARLY...
NERVOUS
NERVOUS
DAMN IT, MIWA, YOU'RE SO DENSE!!
BY REST, I MEAN...
...THIS!
HOTEL NEW & WAVY
REST $40
STAY $70
FWIP
FWIP
IF YOU CATCH MY DRIFT...

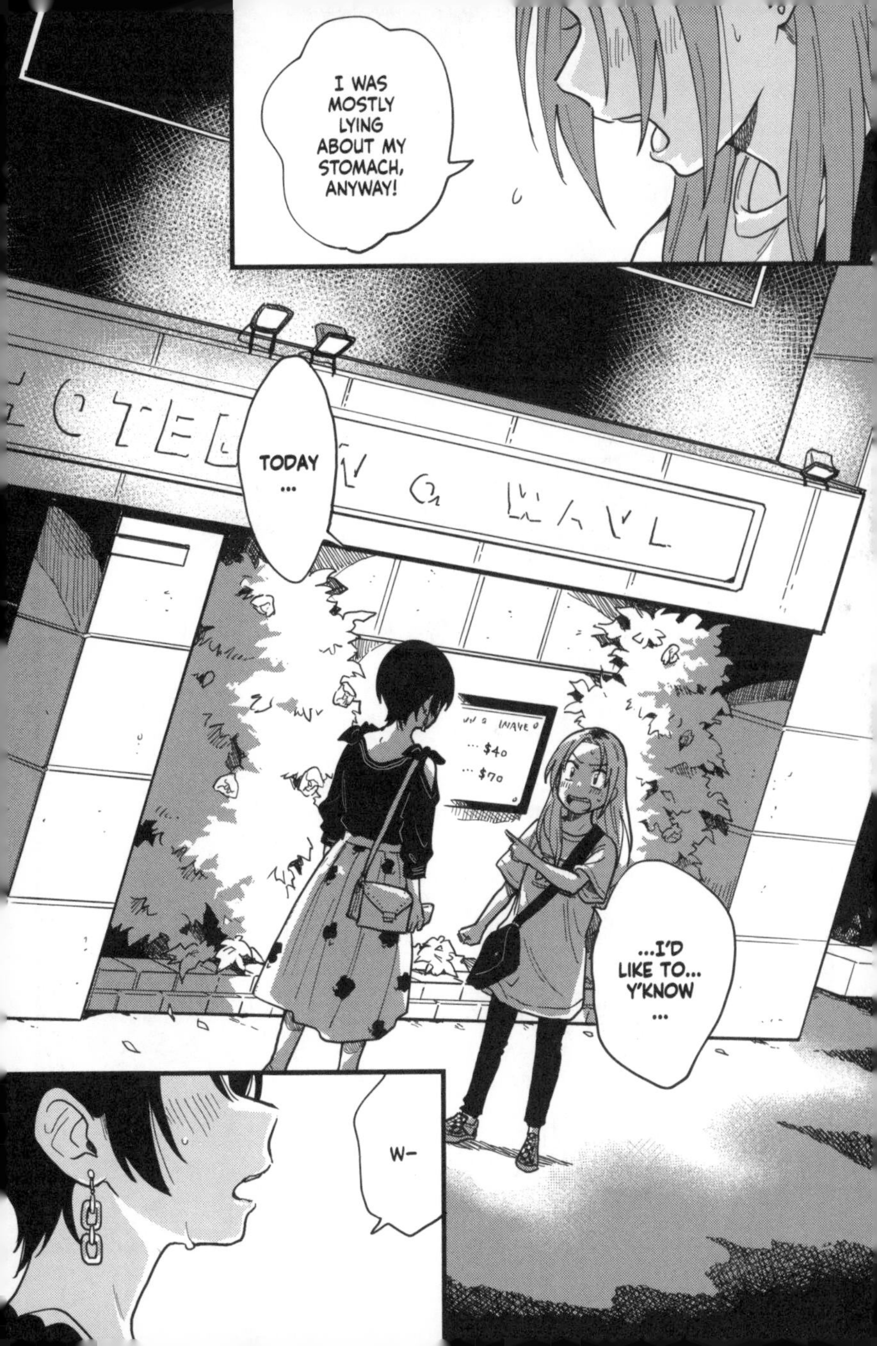
I WAS MOSTLY LYING ABOUT MY STOMACH, ANYWAY!
TODAY ...
... $40
... $70
...I'D LIKE TO... Y'KNOW ...
W-

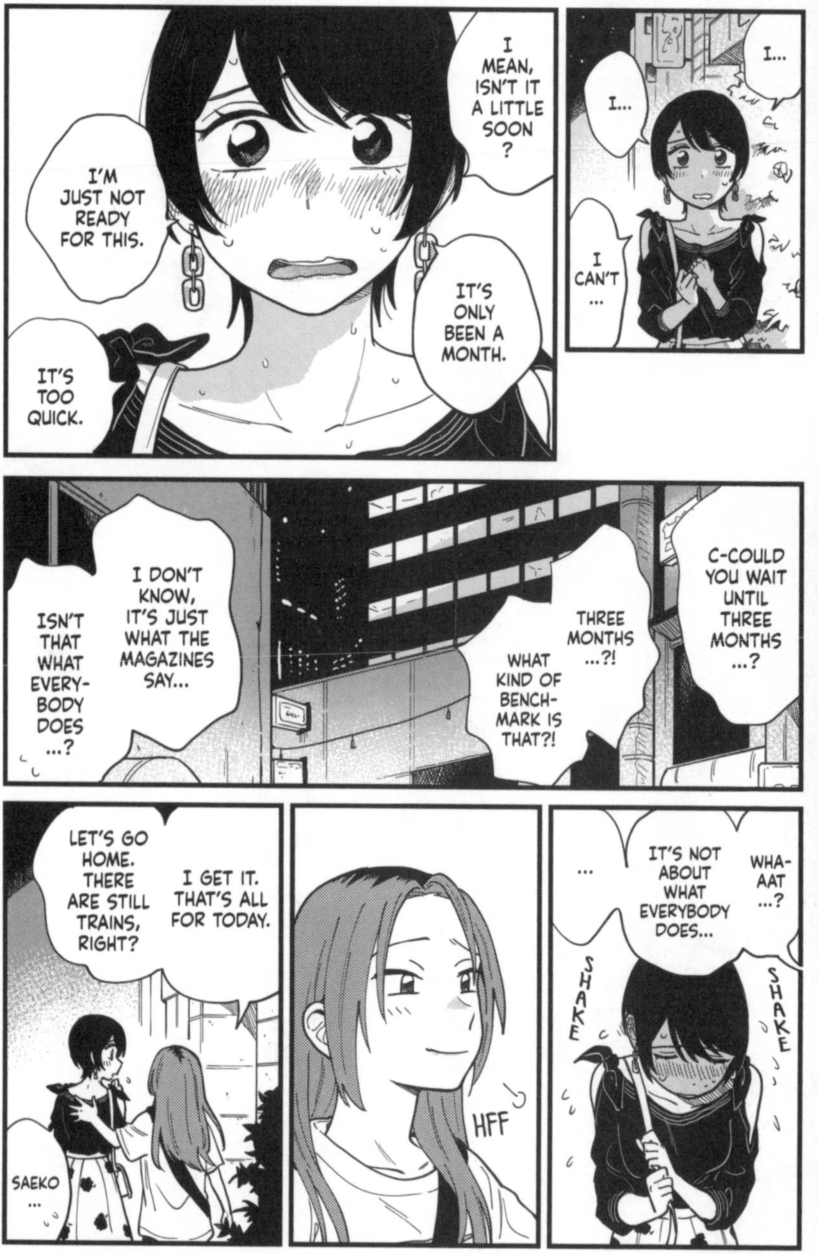
I...
I...
I CAN'T ...
I MEAN, ISN'T IT A LITTLE SOON?
I'M JUST NOT READY FOR THIS.
IT'S ONLY BEEN A MONTH.
IT'S TOO QUICK.
C-COULD YOU WAIT UNTIL THREE MONTHS ...?
THREE MONTHS ...?!
WHAT KIND OF BENCHMARK IS THAT?!
I DON'T KNOW, IT'S JUST WHAT THE MAGAZINES SAY...
ISN'T THAT WHAT EVERYBODY DOES ...?
WHA-AAT ...?
IT'S NOT ABOUT WHAT EVERYBODY DOES...
...
SHAKE
SHAKE
HFF
I GET IT. THAT'S ALL FOR TODAY.
LET'S GO HOME. THERE ARE STILL TRAINS, RIGHT?
SAEKO ...

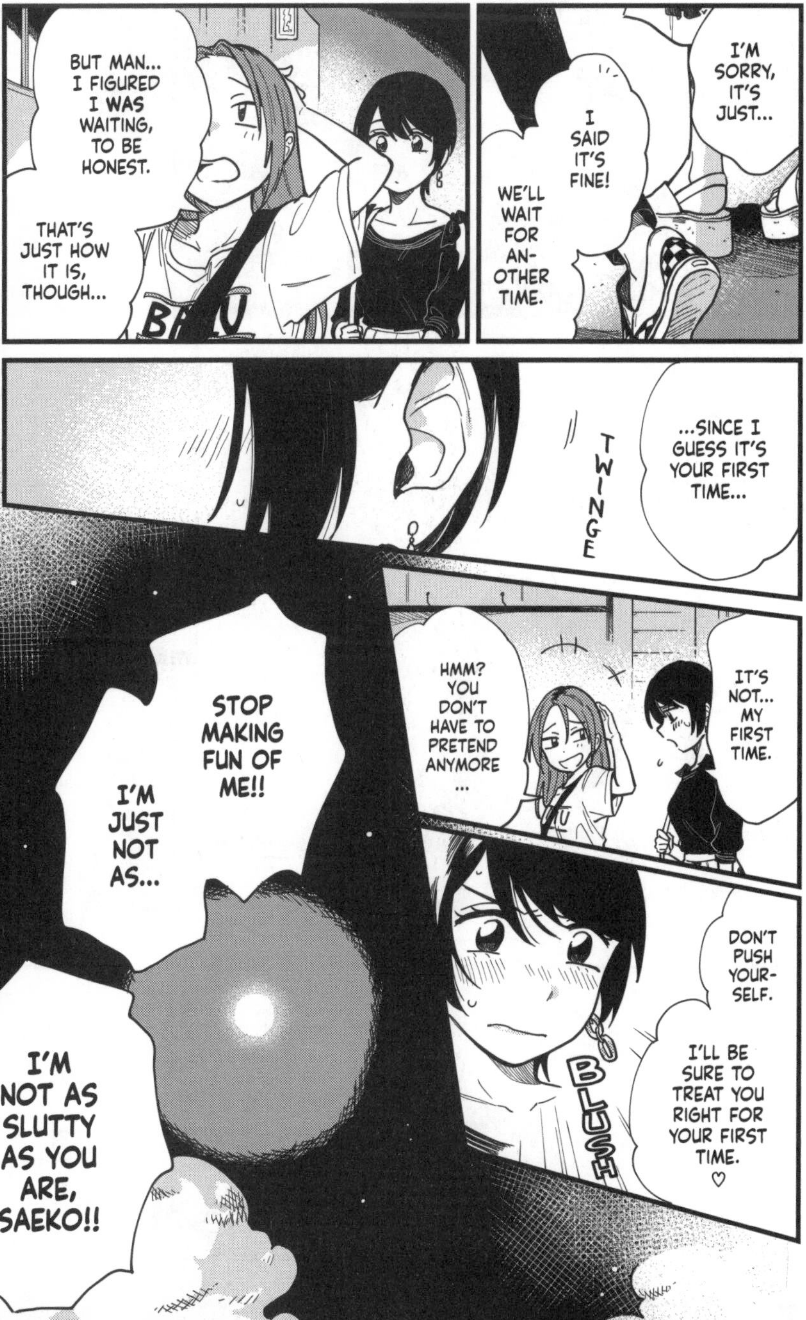
I'M SORRY, IT'S JUST...
I SAID IT'S FINE!
WE'LL WAIT FOR AN-OTHER TIME.
BUT MAN... I FIGURED I WAS WAITING, TO BE HONEST.
THAT'S JUST HOW IT IS, THOUGH...
...SINCE I GUESS IT'S YOUR FIRST TIME...
TWINGE
IT'S NOT... MY FIRST TIME.
HMM? YOU DON'T HAVE TO PRETEND ANYMORE...
DON'T PUSH YOUR-SELF.
I'LL BE SURE TO TREAT YOU RIGHT FOR YOUR FIRST TIME. ♡
BLUSH
STOP MAKING FUN OF ME!!
I'M JUST NOT AS...
I'M NOT AS SLUTTY AS YOU ARE, SAEKO!!

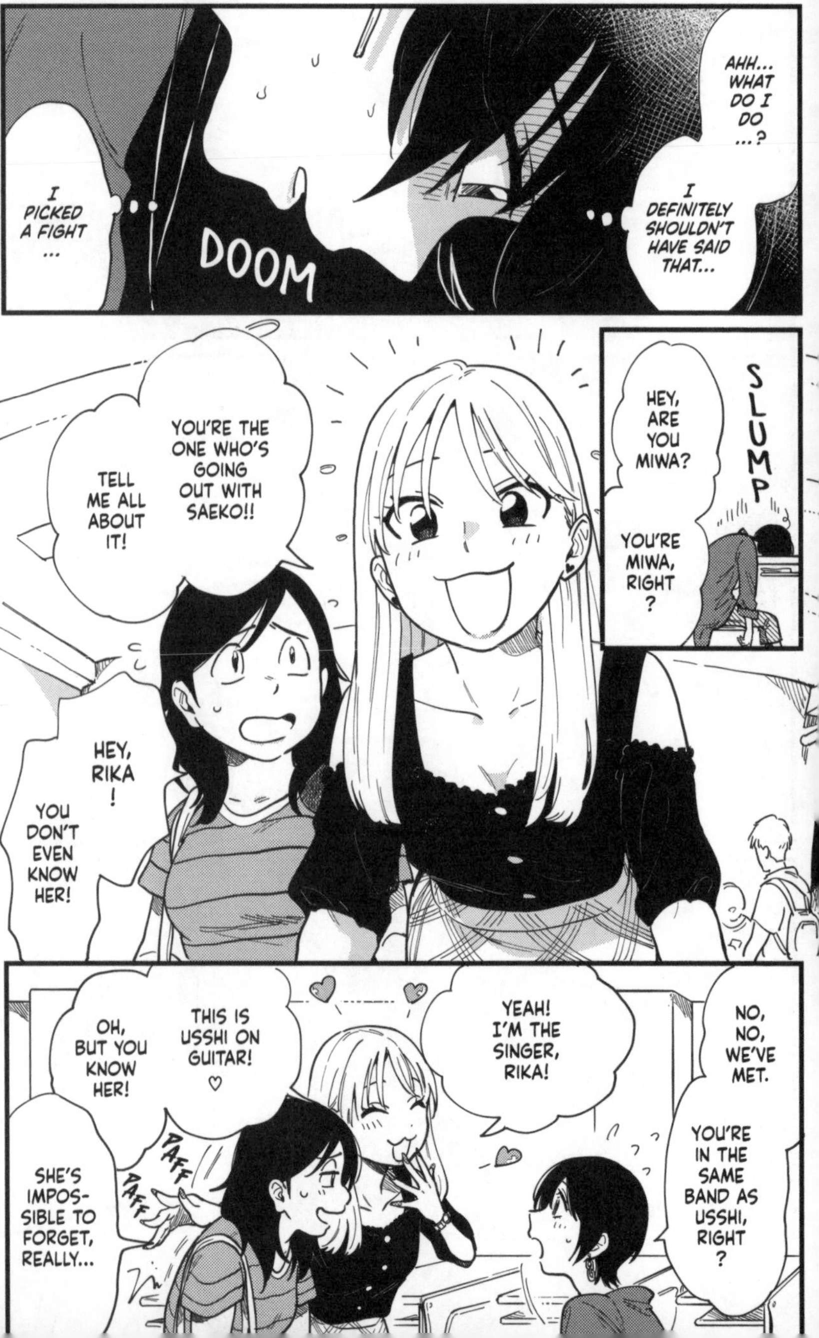
AHH... WHAT DO I DO ...?
I DEFINITELY SHOULDN'T HAVE SAID THAT...
DOOM
I PICKED A FIGHT ...
SLUMP
HEY, ARE YOU MIWA?
YOU'RE MIWA, RIGHT?
YOU'RE THE ONE WHO'S GOING OUT WITH SAEKO!!
TELL ME ALL ABOUT IT!
HEY, RIKA!
YOU DON'T EVEN KNOW HER!
NO, NO, WE'VE MET.
YOU'RE IN THE SAME BAND AS USSHI, RIGHT?
YEAH! I'M THE SINGER, RIKA!
THIS IS USSHI ON GUITAR! ♡
OH, BUT YOU KNOW HER!
PAFF
PAFF
SHE'S IMPOS-SIBLE TO FORGET, REALLY...

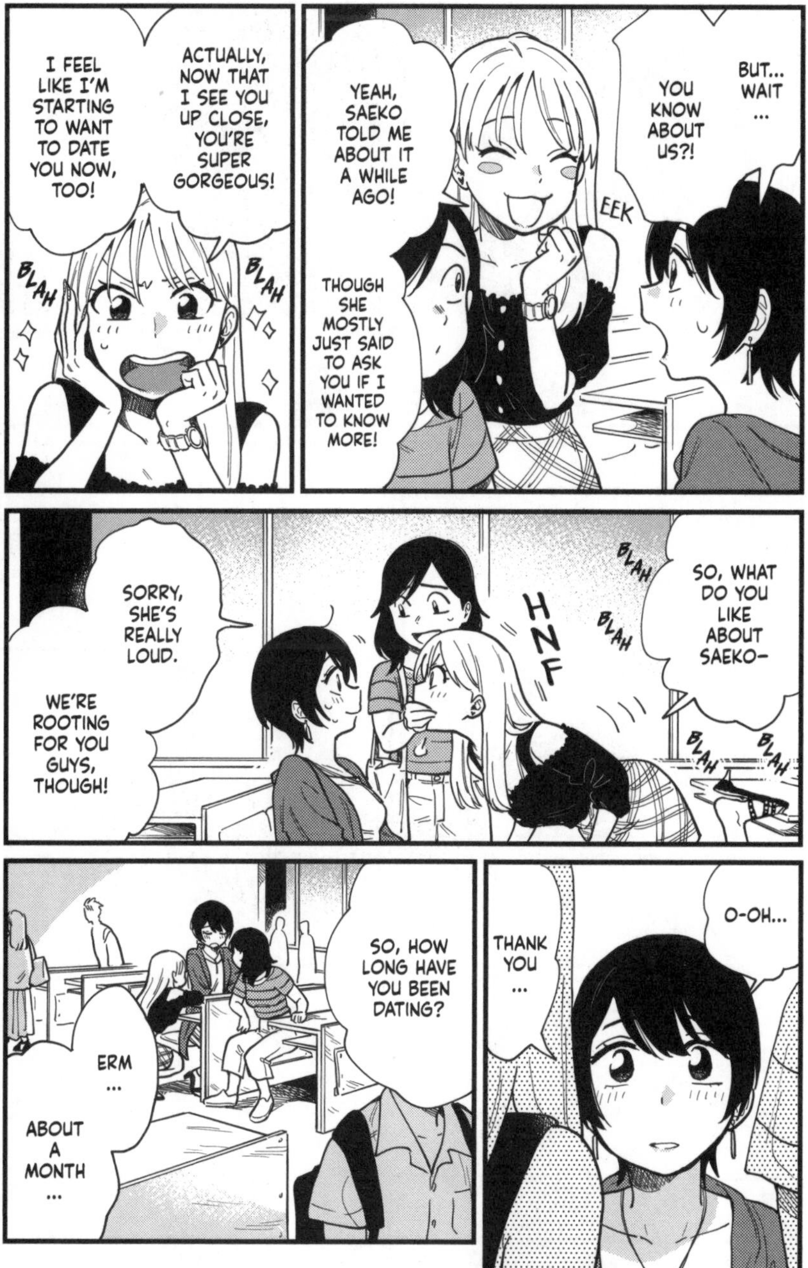
BUT... WAIT ...
YOU KNOW ABOUT US?!
EEK
YEAH, SAEKO TOLD ME ABOUT IT A WHILE AGO!
THOUGH SHE MOSTLY JUST SAID TO ASK YOU IF I WANTED TO KNOW MORE!
ACTUALLY, NOW THAT I SEE YOU UP CLOSE, YOU'RE SUPER GORGEOUS!
I FEEL LIKE I'M STARTING TO WANT TO DATE YOU NOW, TOO!
BLAH
BLAH
SO, WHAT DO YOU LIKE ABOUT SAEKO-
BLAH
BLAH
BLAH
BLAH
HNF
SORRY, SHE'S REALLY LOUD.
WE'RE ROOTING FOR YOU GUYS, THOUGH!
O-OH...
THANK YOU ...
SO, HOW LONG HAVE YOU BEEN DATING?
ERM ...
ABOUT A MONTH ...

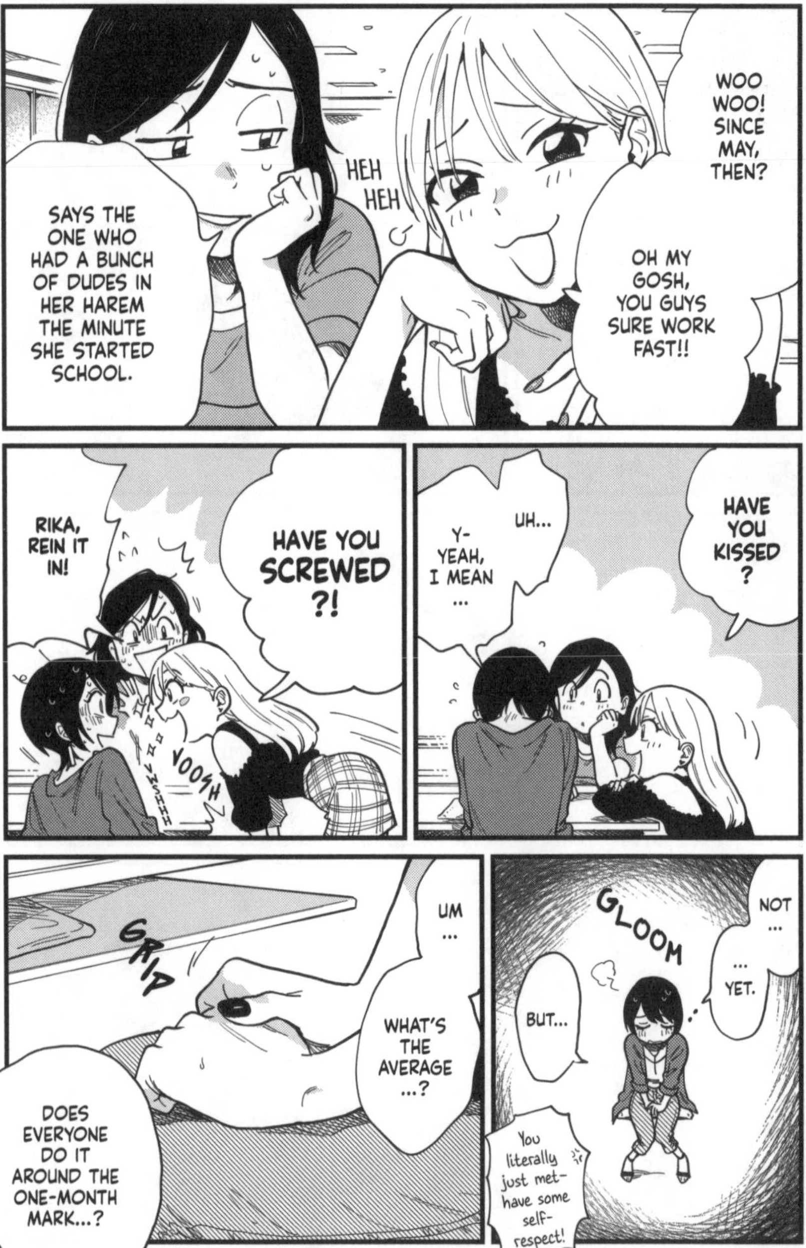
WOO WOO! SINCE MAY, THEN?
OH MY GOSH, YOU GUYS SURE WORK FAST!!
HEH HEH
SAYS THE ONE WHO HAD A BUNCH OF DUDES IN HER HAREM THE MINUTE SHE STARTED SCHOOL.
HAVE YOU KISSED?
UH...
Y- YEAH, I MEAN ...
HAVE YOU SCREWED?!
RIKA, REIN IT IN!
VOOSH
VWSHHH
NOT ...
... YET.
GLOOM
BUT...
You literally just met- have some self-respect!
UM ...
WHAT'S THE AVERAGE ...?
GRIP
DOES EVERYONE DO IT AROUND THE ONE-MONTH MARK...?

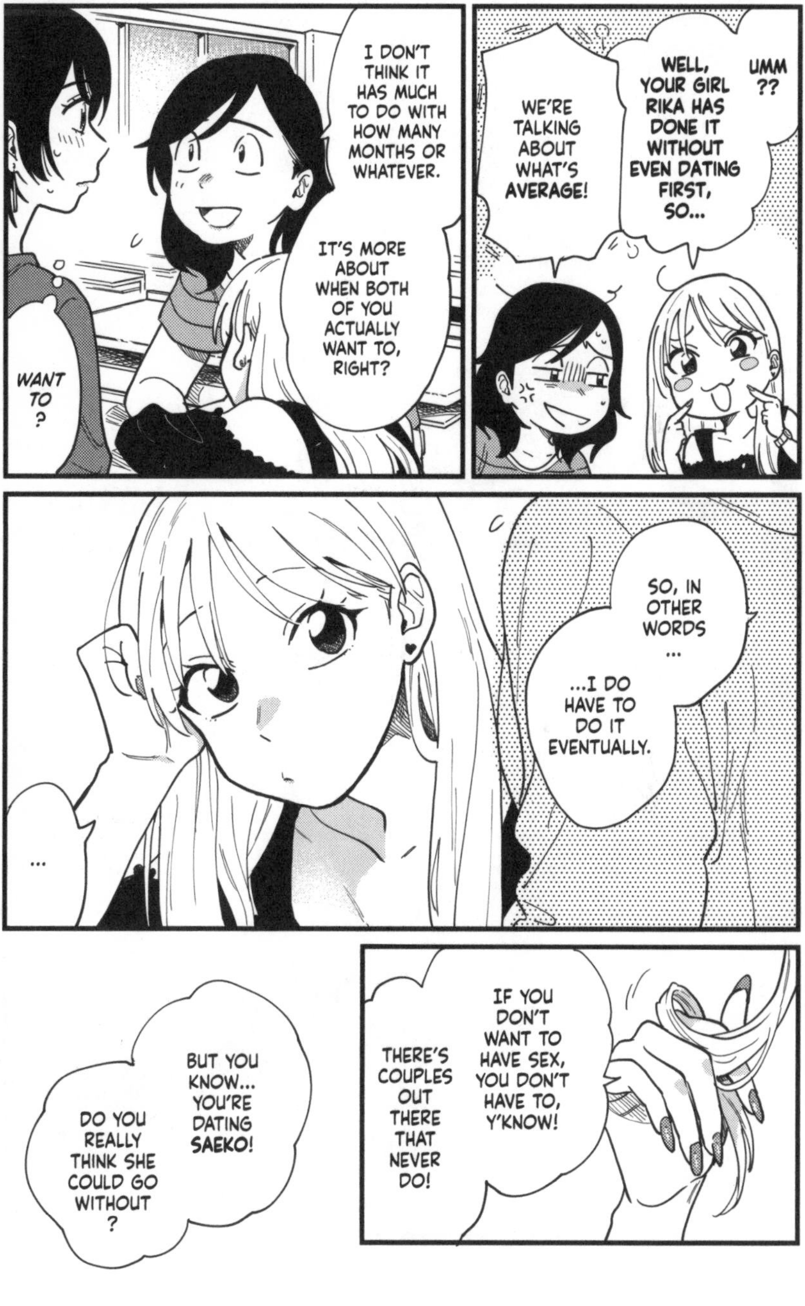
UMM ??
WELL, YOUR GIRL RIKA HAS DONE IT WITHOUT EVEN DATING FIRST, SO...
WE'RE TALKING ABOUT WHAT'S AVERAGE!
I DON'T THINK IT HAS MUCH TO DO WITH HOW MANY MONTHS OR WHATEVER.
IT'S MORE ABOUT WHEN BOTH OF YOU ACTUALLY WANT TO, RIGHT?
WANT TO ?
SO, IN OTHER WORDS ...
...I DO HAVE TO DO IT EVENTUALLY.
...
IF YOU DON'T WANT TO HAVE SEX, YOU DON'T HAVE TO, Y'KNOW!
THERE'S COUPLES OUT THERE THAT NEVER DO!
BUT YOU KNOW... YOU'RE DATING SAEKO!
DO YOU REALLY THINK SHE COULD GO WITHOUT ?

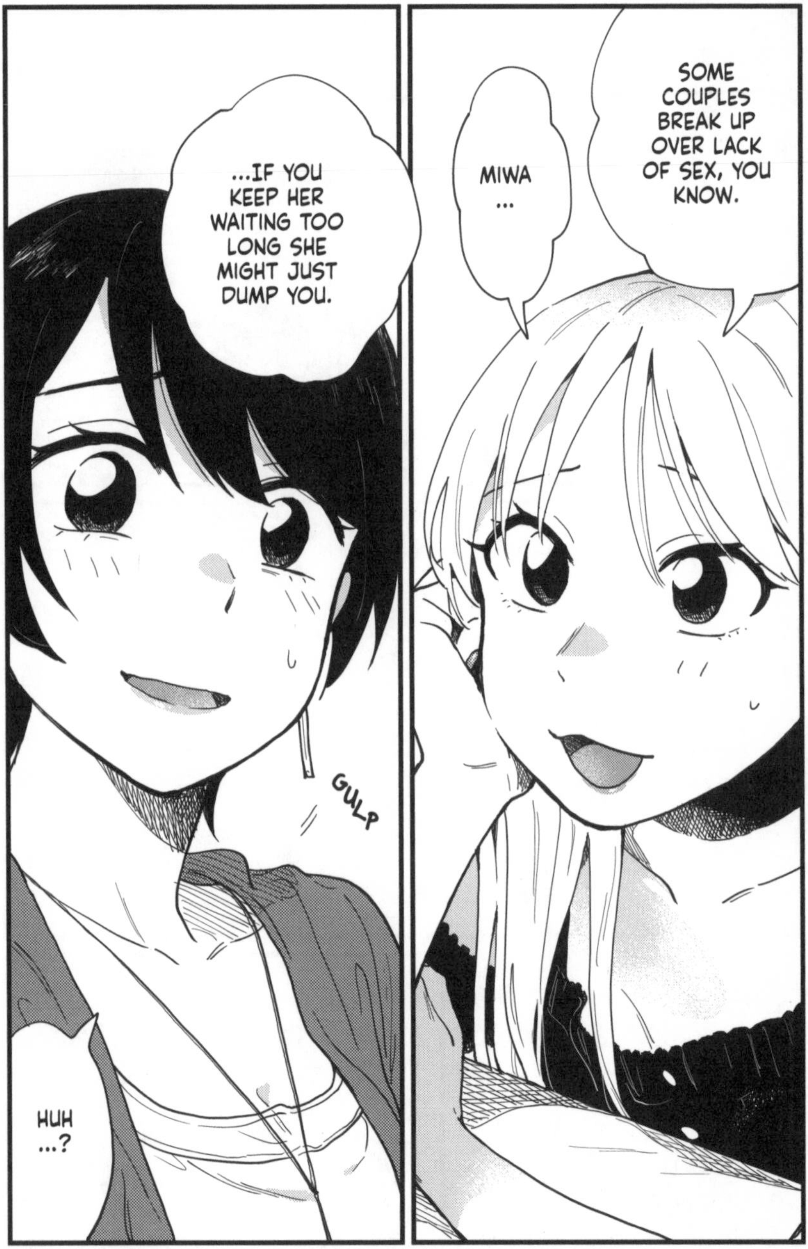
SOME COUPLES BREAK UP OVER LACK OF SEX, YOU KNOW.
MIWA ...
...IF YOU KEEP HER WAITING TOO LONG SHE MIGHT JUST DUMP YOU.
GULP
HUH ...?

How Do We Relationship?

HOW DO WE
RELATIONSHIP?

Chapter 6: This Really Is Love

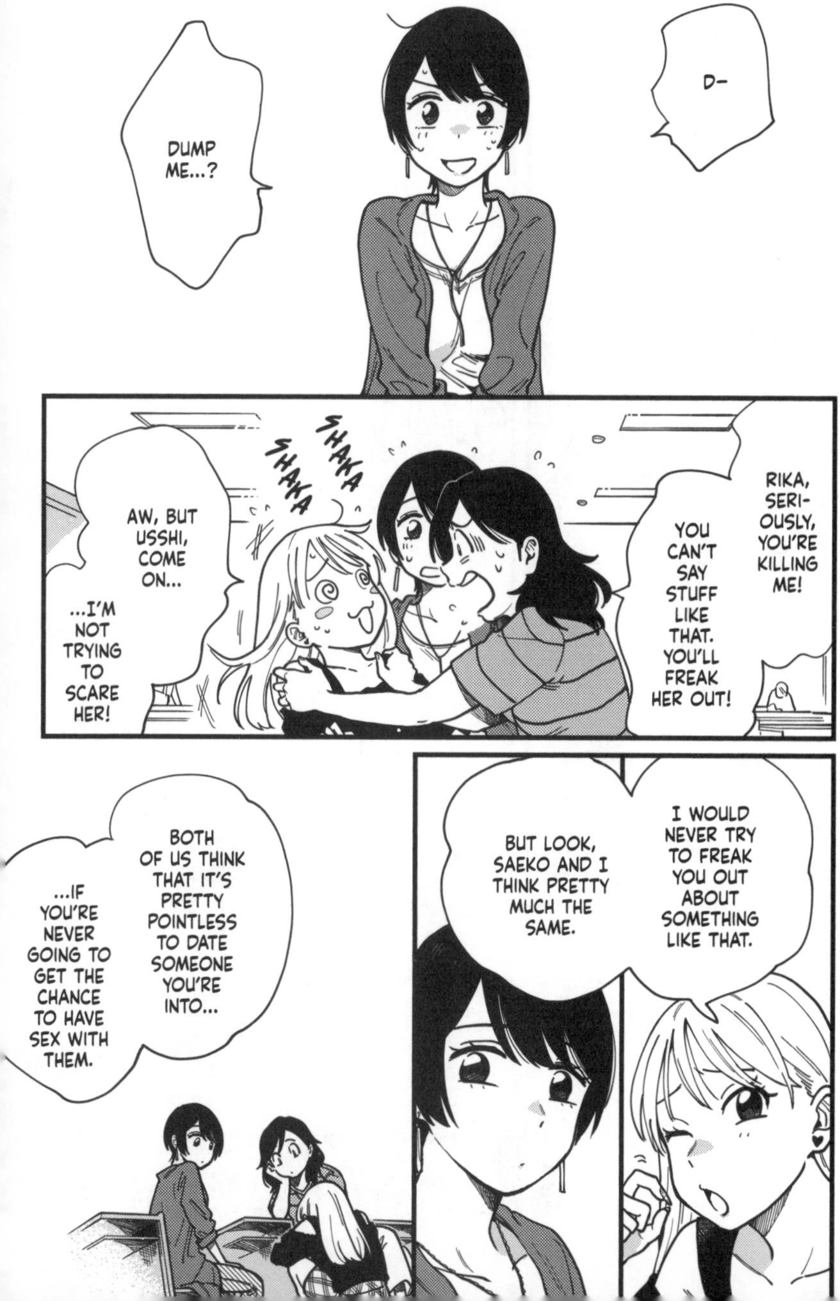
D–
DUMP ME...?
RIKA, SERIOUSLY, YOU'RE KILLING ME!
YOU CAN'T SAY STUFF LIKE THAT. YOU'LL FREAK HER OUT!
SHAKA SHAKA
AW, BUT USSHI, COME ON...
...I'M NOT TRYING TO SCARE HER!
I WOULD NEVER TRY TO FREAK YOU OUT ABOUT SOMETHING LIKE THAT.
BUT LOOK, SAEKO AND I THINK PRETTY MUCH THE SAME.
BOTH OF US THINK THAT IT'S PRETTY POINTLESS TO DATE SOMEONE YOU'RE INTO...
...IF YOU'RE NEVER GOING TO GET THE CHANCE TO HAVE SEX WITH THEM.

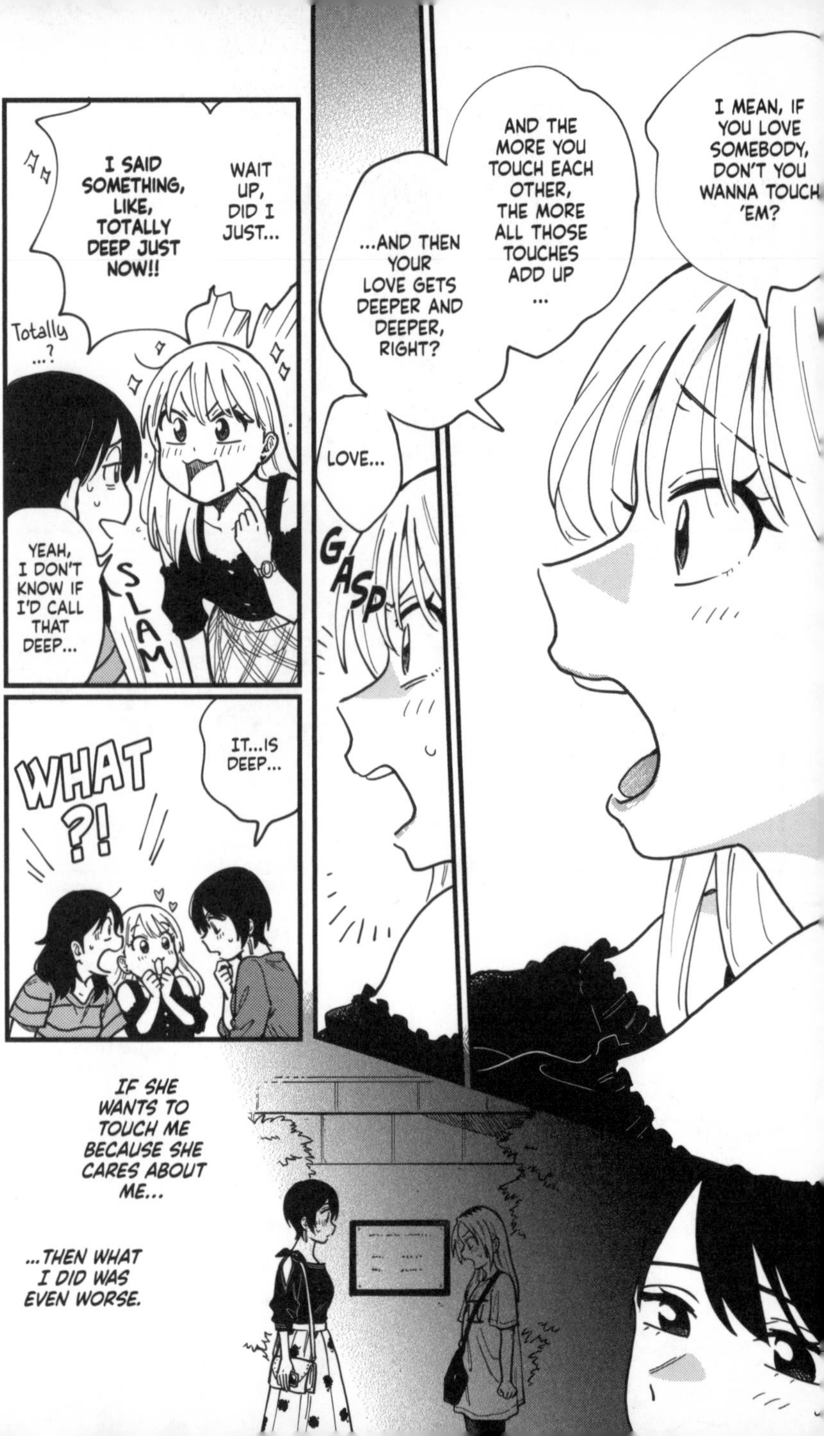
I MEAN, IF YOU LOVE SOMEBODY, DON'T YOU WANNA TOUCH 'EM?
AND THE MORE YOU TOUCH EACH OTHER, THE MORE ALL THOSE TOUCHES ADD UP...
...AND THEN YOUR LOVE GETS DEEPER AND DEEPER, RIGHT?
LOVE...
GASP
WAIT UP, DID I JUST...
I SAID SOMETHING, LIKE, TOTALLY DEEP JUST NOW!!
Totally...?
SLAM
YEAH, I DON'T KNOW IF I'D CALL THAT DEEP...
IT...IS DEEP...
WHAT?!
IF SHE WANTS TO TOUCH ME BECAUSE SHE CARES ABOUT ME...
...THEN WHAT I DID WAS EVEN WORSE.

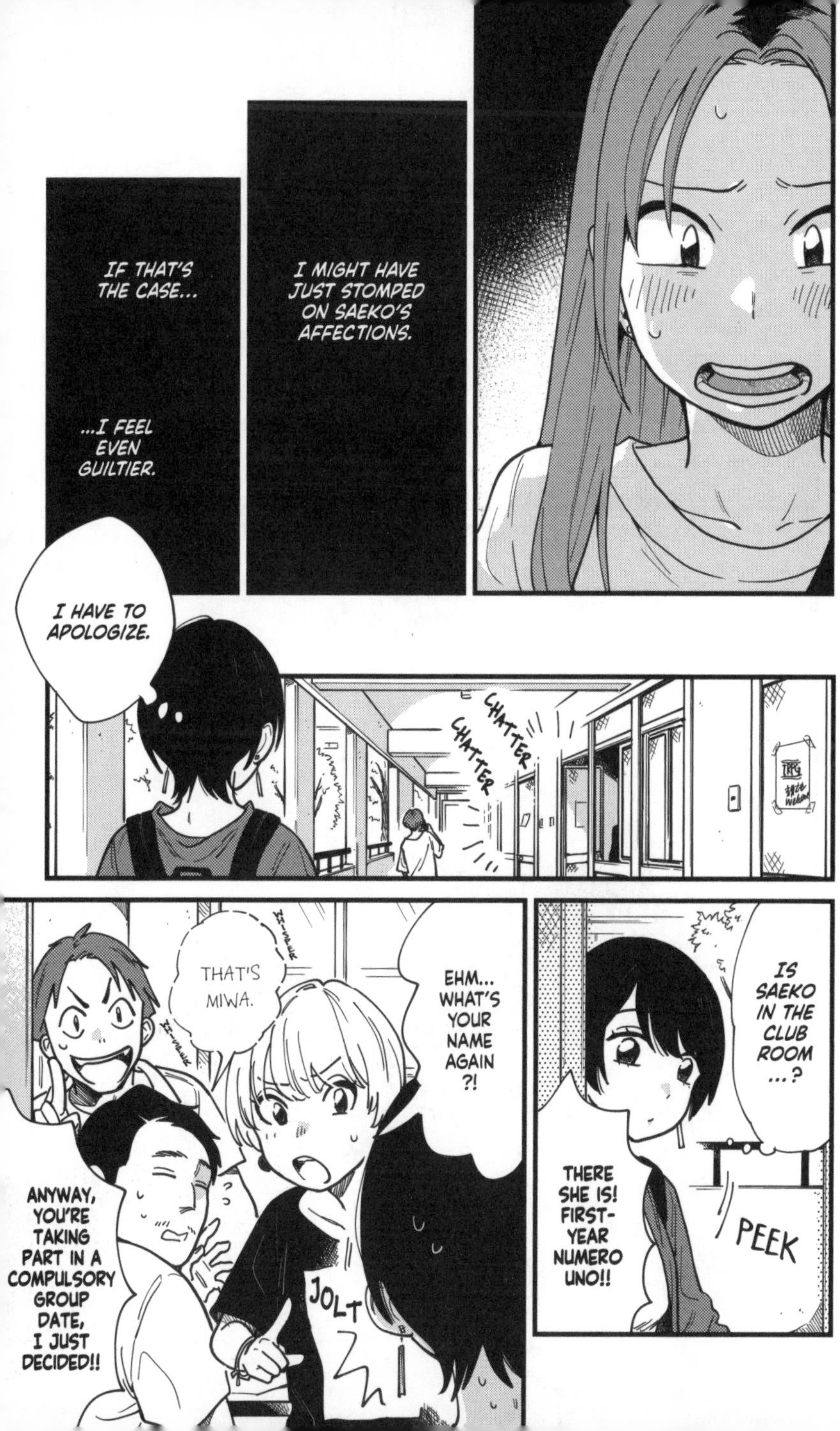
I MIGHT HAVE JUST STOMPED ON SAEKO'S AFFECTIONS.
IF THAT'S THE CASE...
...I FEEL EVEN GUILTIER.
I HAVE TO APOLOGIZE.
CHATTER
CHATTER
IS SAEKO IN THE CLUB ROOM...?
PEEK
THERE SHE IS! FIRST-YEAR NUMERO UNO!!
EHM... WHAT'S YOUR NAME AGAIN?!
THAT'S MIWA.
WHISPER
ANYWAY, YOU'RE TAKING PART IN A COMPULSORY GROUP DATE, I JUST DECIDED!!
JOLT

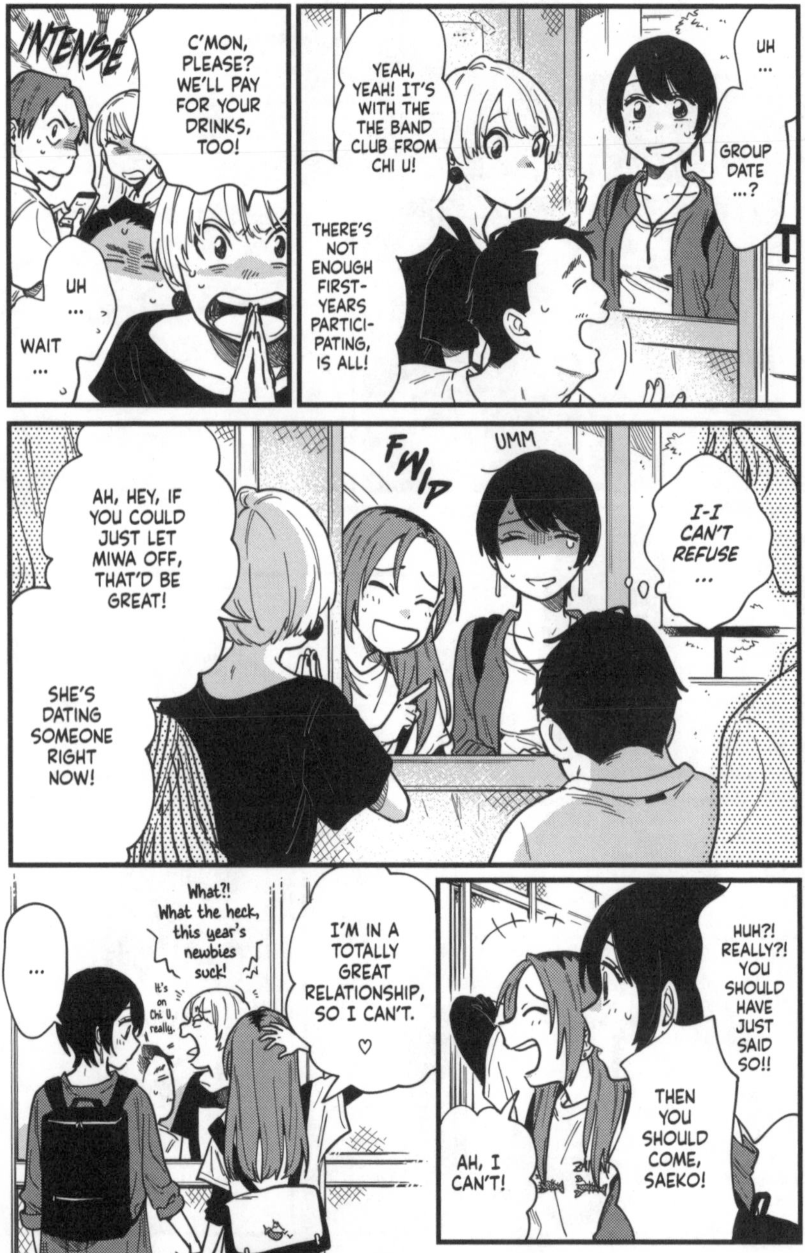
UH ...
GROUP DATE ...?
YEAH, YEAH! IT'S WITH THE THE BAND CLUB FROM CHI U!
THERE'S NOT ENOUGH FIRST-YEARS PARTICIPATING, IS ALL!
INTENSE
C'MON, PLEASE? WE'LL PAY FOR YOUR DRINKS, TOO!
UH ... WAIT ...
UMM
I-I CAN'T REFUSE ...
FWIP
AH, HEY, IF YOU COULD JUST LET MIWA OFF, THAT'D BE GREAT!
SHE'S DATING SOMEONE RIGHT NOW!
HUH?! REALLY?! YOU SHOULD HAVE JUST SAID SO!!
THEN YOU SHOULD COME, SAEKO!
AH, I CAN'T!
I'M IN A TOTALLY GREAT RELATIONSHIP, SO I CAN'T. ♡
What?! What the heck, this year's newbies suck!
It's on Chi U, really.
...

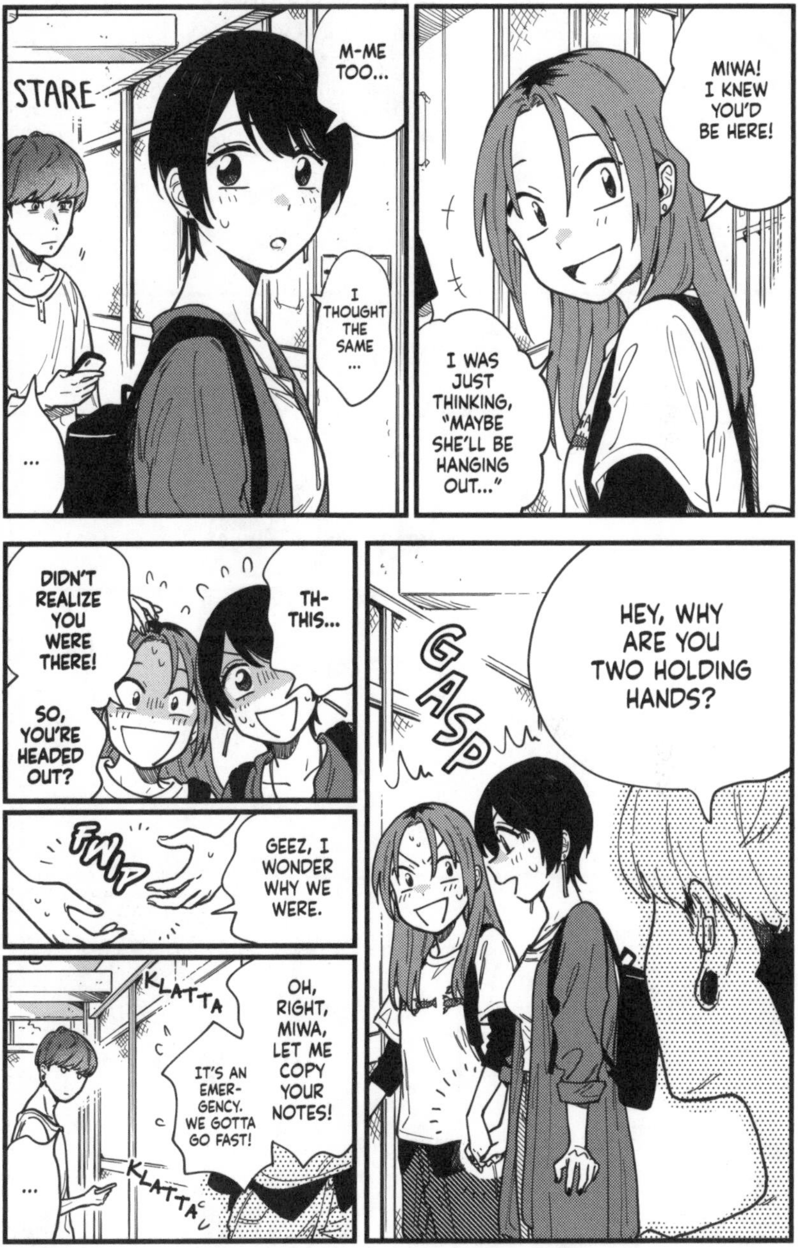
MIWA! I KNEW YOU'D BE HERE!
I WAS JUST THINKING, "MAYBE SHE'LL BE HANGING OUT..."
M-ME TOO...
STARE
I THOUGHT THE SAME ...
...
HEY, WHY ARE YOU TWO HOLDING HANDS?
GASP
TH-THIS...
DIDN'T REALIZE YOU WERE THERE!
SO, YOU'RE HEADED OUT?
GEEZ, I WONDER WHY WE WERE.
FWIP
OH, RIGHT, MIWA, LET ME COPY YOUR NOTES!
KLATTA
IT'S AN EMERGENCY. WE GOTTA GO FAST!
KLATTA
...

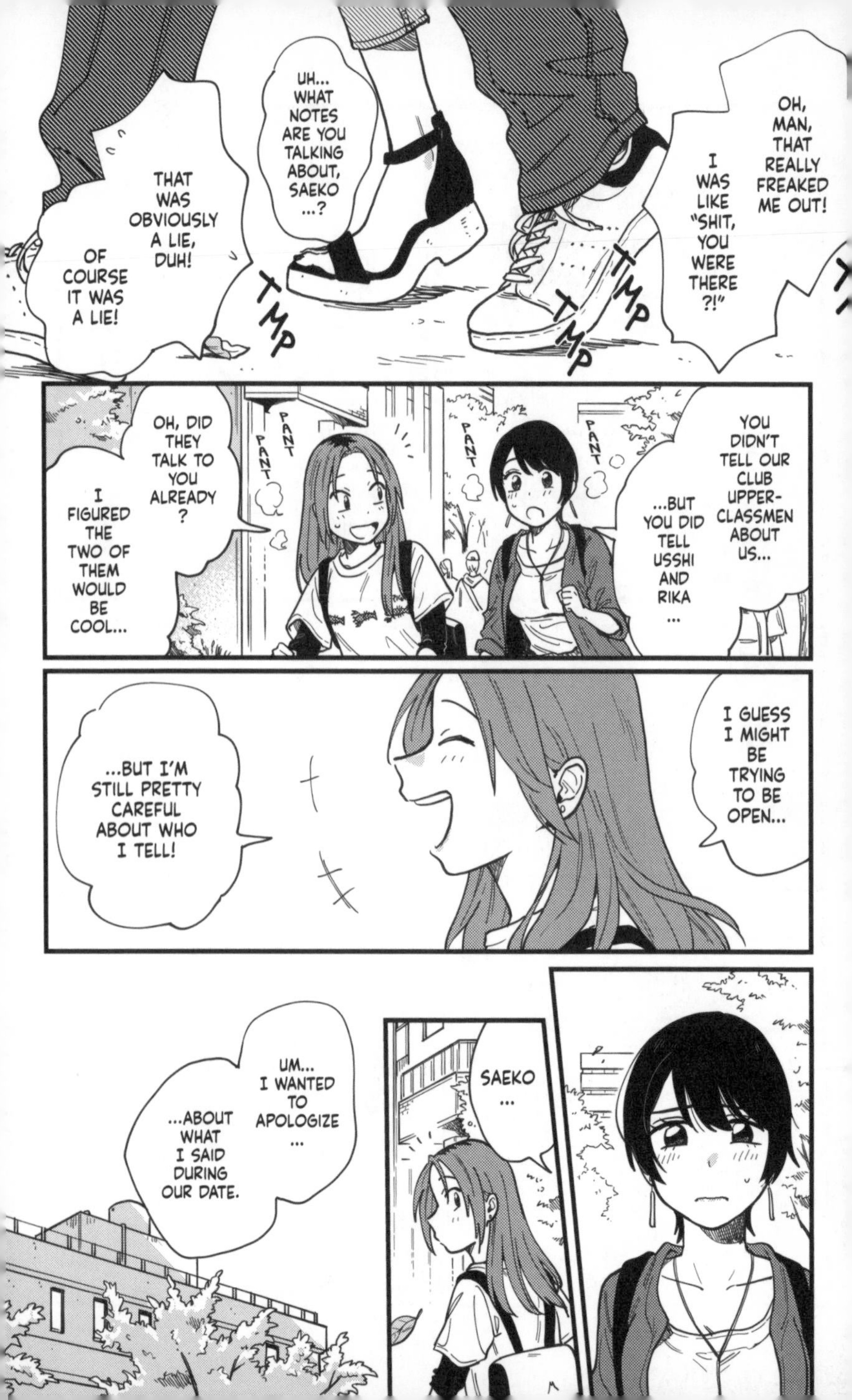
OH, MAN, THAT REALLY FREAKED ME OUT!
I WAS LIKE "SHIT, YOU WERE THERE?!"
TMP TMP
UH... WHAT NOTES ARE YOU TALKING ABOUT, SAEKO...?
THAT WAS OBVIOUSLY A LIE, DUH!
OF COURSE IT WAS A LIE!
TMP
YOU DIDN'T TELL OUR CLUB UPPER-CLASSMEN ABOUT US...
...BUT YOU DID TELL USSHI AND RIKA...
PANT PANT
PANT PANT
OH, DID THEY TALK TO YOU ALREADY?
I FIGURED THE TWO OF THEM WOULD BE COOL...
I GUESS I MIGHT BE TRYING TO BE OPEN...
...BUT I'M STILL PRETTY CAREFUL ABOUT WHO I TELL!
SAEKO...
UM... I WANTED TO APOLOGIZE...
...ABOUT WHAT I SAID DURING OUR DATE.

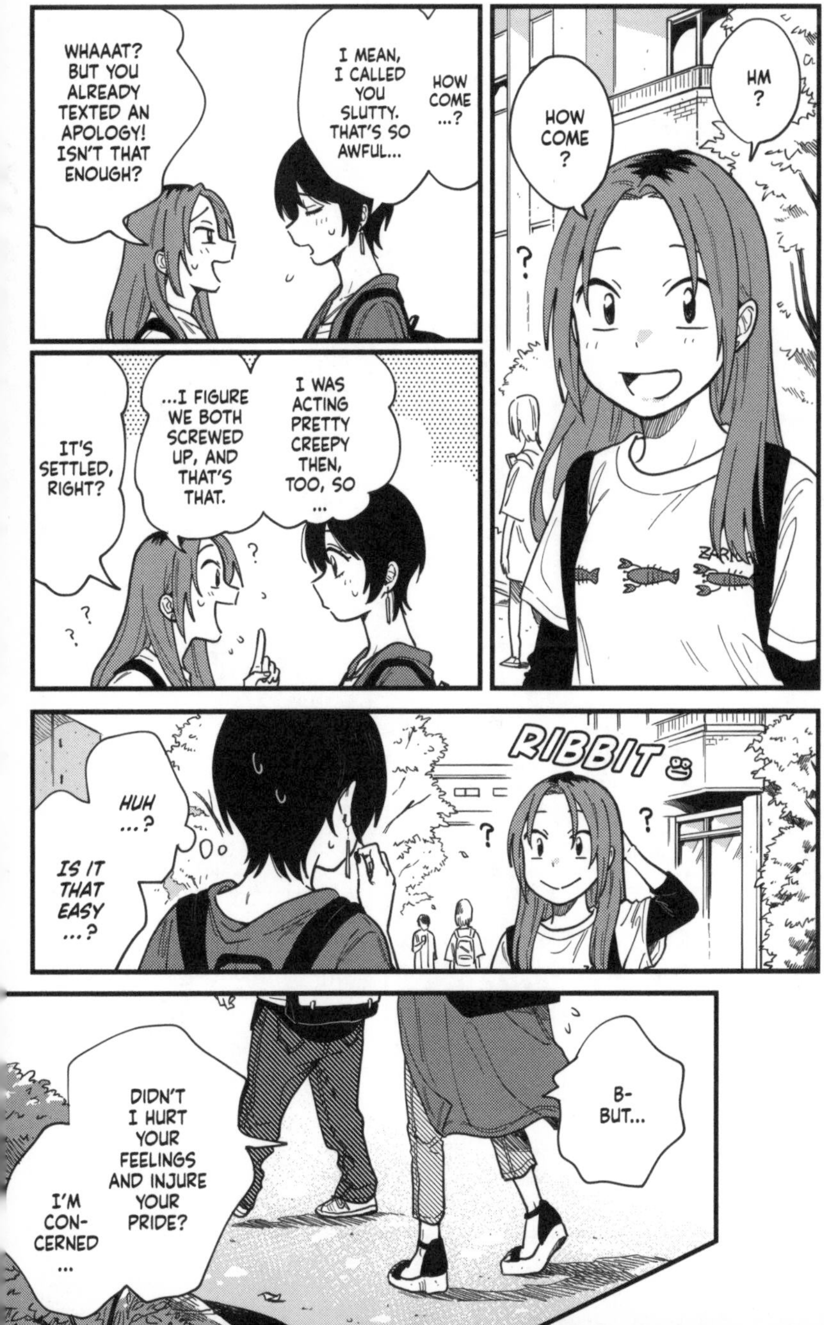
HM ?
HOW COME ?
HOW COME ...?
I MEAN, I CALLED YOU SLUTTY. THAT'S SO AWFUL...
WHAAAT? BUT YOU ALREADY TEXTED AN APOLOGY! ISN'T THAT ENOUGH?
I WAS ACTING PRETTY CREEPY THEN, TOO, SO ...
...I FIGURE WE BOTH SCREWED UP, AND THAT'S THAT.
IT'S SETTLED, RIGHT?
RIBBIT
HUH ...?
IS IT THAT EASY ...?
B- BUT...
DIDN'T I HURT YOUR FEELINGS AND INJURE YOUR PRIDE?
I'M CON- CERNED ...

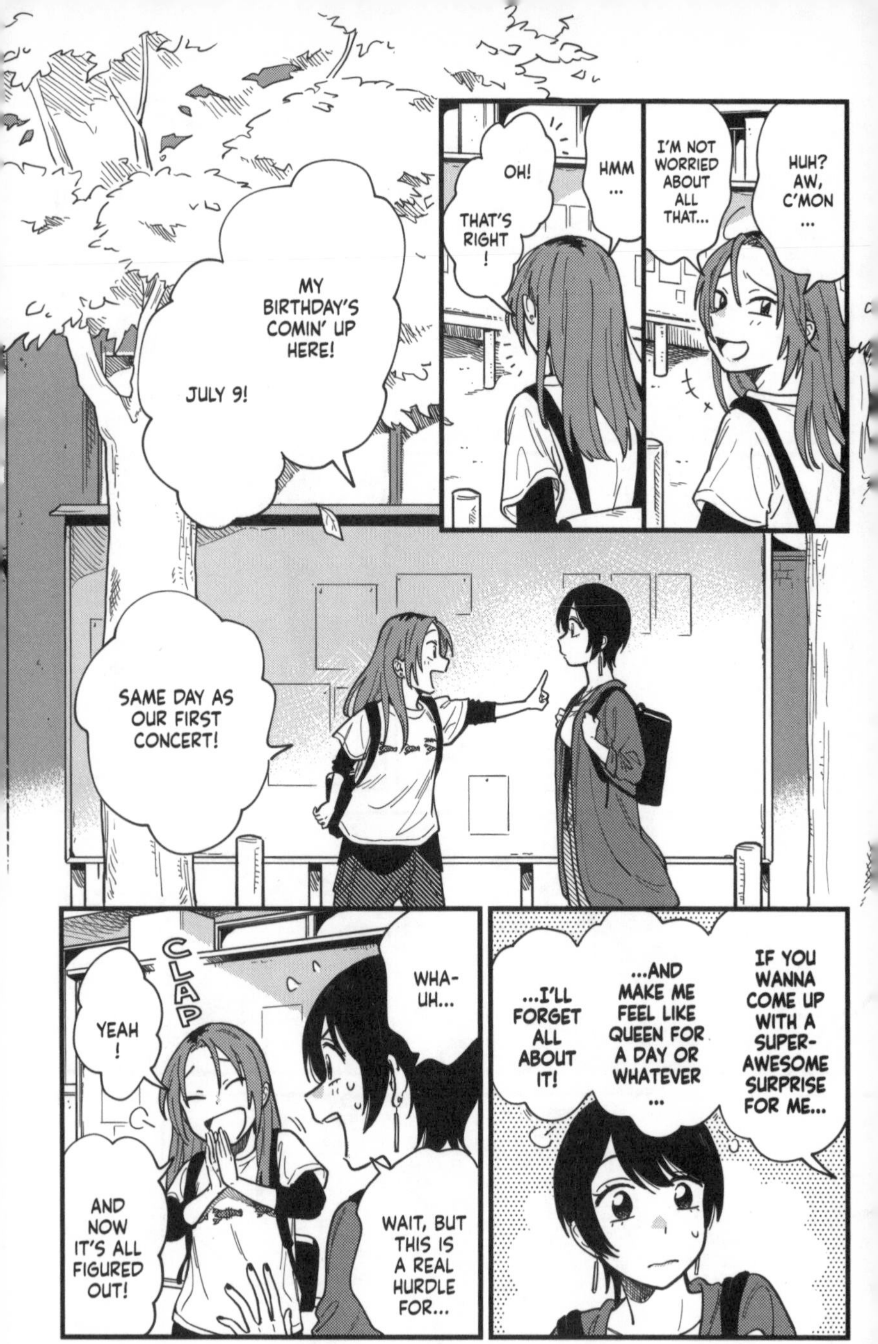
HUH? AW, C'MON...
I'M NOT WORRIED ABOUT ALL THAT...
HMM...
OH!
THAT'S RIGHT!
MY BIRTHDAY'S COMIN' UP HERE!
JULY 9!
SAME DAY AS OUR FIRST CONCERT!
IF YOU WANNA COME UP WITH A SUPER-AWESOME SURPRISE FOR ME...
...AND MAKE ME FEEL LIKE QUEEN FOR A DAY OR WHATEVER...
...I'LL FORGET ALL ABOUT IT!
WHA-UH...
CLAP
YEAH!
WAIT, BUT THIS IS A REAL HURDLE FOR...
AND NOW IT'S ALL FIGURED OUT!

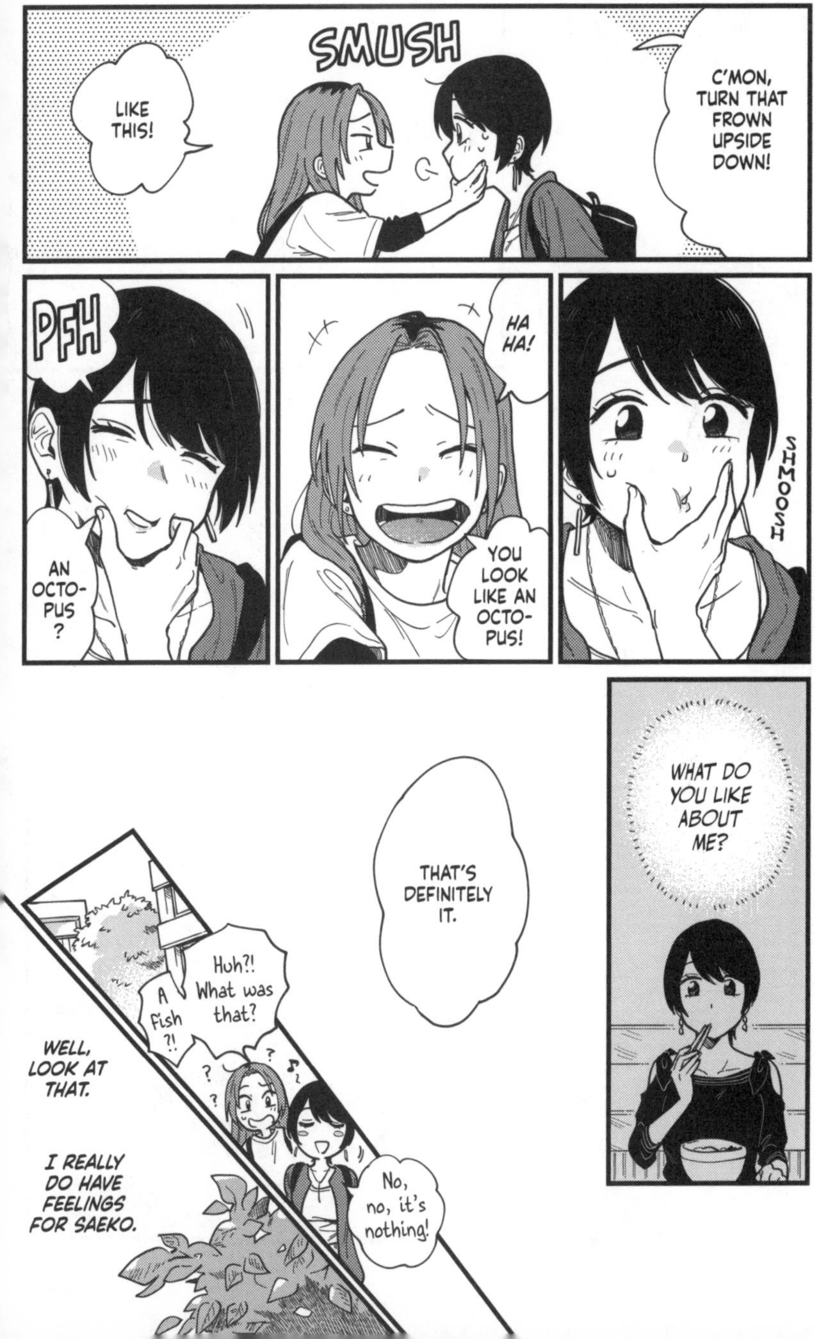
C'MON, TURN THAT FROWN UPSIDE DOWN!
SMUSH
LIKE THIS!
SHMOOSH
HA HA!
YOU LOOK LIKE AN OCTO-PUS!
PFH
AN OCTO-PUS?
WHAT DO YOU LIKE ABOUT ME?
THAT'S DEFINITELY IT.
Huh?! What was that?
A Fish?!
No, no, it's nothing!
WELL, LOOK AT THAT.
I REALLY DO HAVE FEELINGS FOR SAEKO.

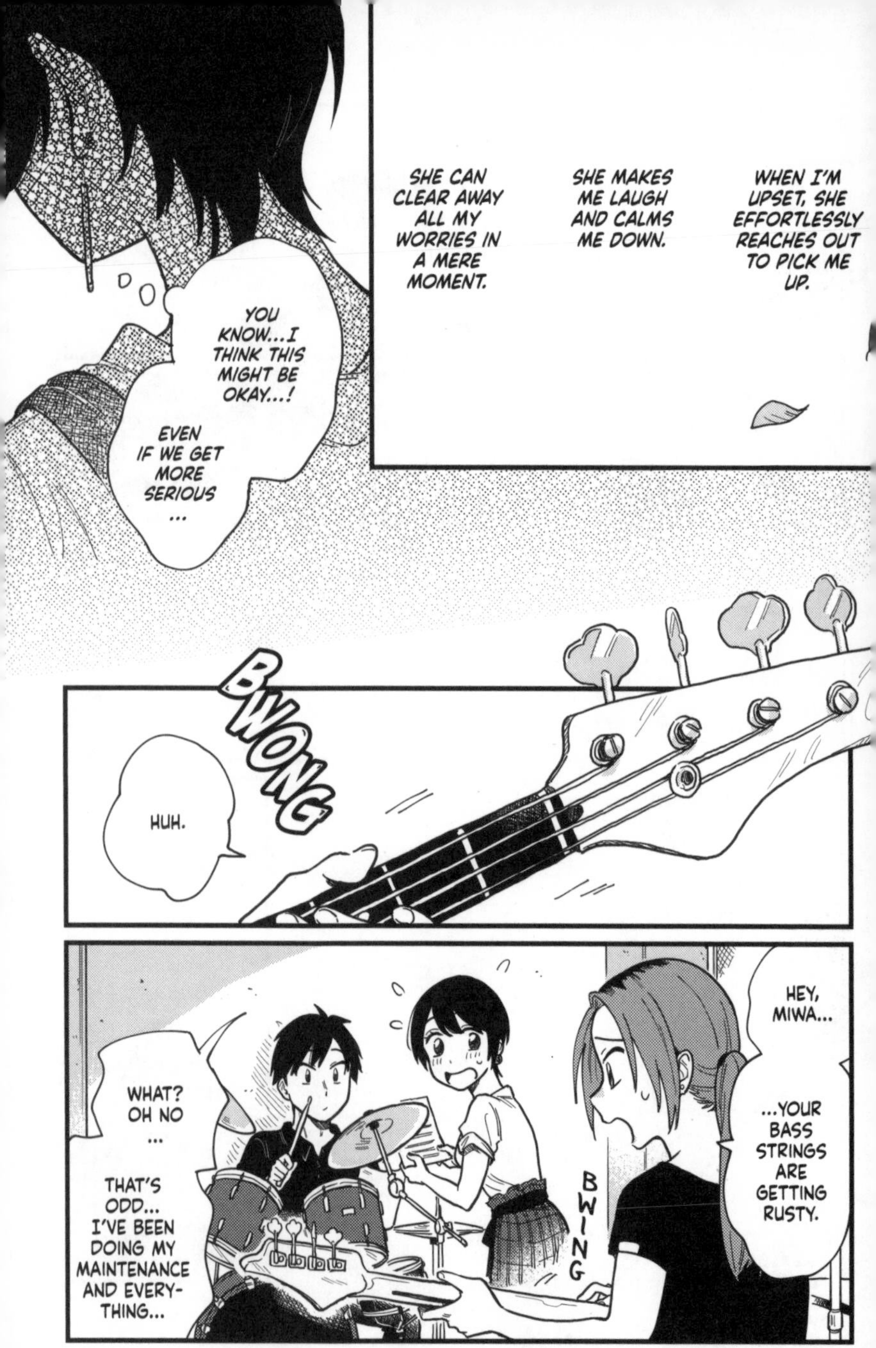
WHEN I'M UPSET, SHE EFFORTLESSLY REACHES OUT TO PICK ME UP.
SHE MAKES ME LAUGH AND CALMS ME DOWN.
SHE CAN CLEAR AWAY ALL MY WORRIES IN A MERE MOMENT.
YOU KNOW...I THINK THIS MIGHT BE OKAY...!
EVEN IF WE GET MORE SERIOUS...
BWONG
HUH.
HEY, MIWA...
...YOUR BASS STRINGS ARE GETTING RUSTY.
BWING
WHAT? OH NO...
THAT'S ODD... I'VE BEEN DOING MY MAINTENANCE AND EVERYTHING...

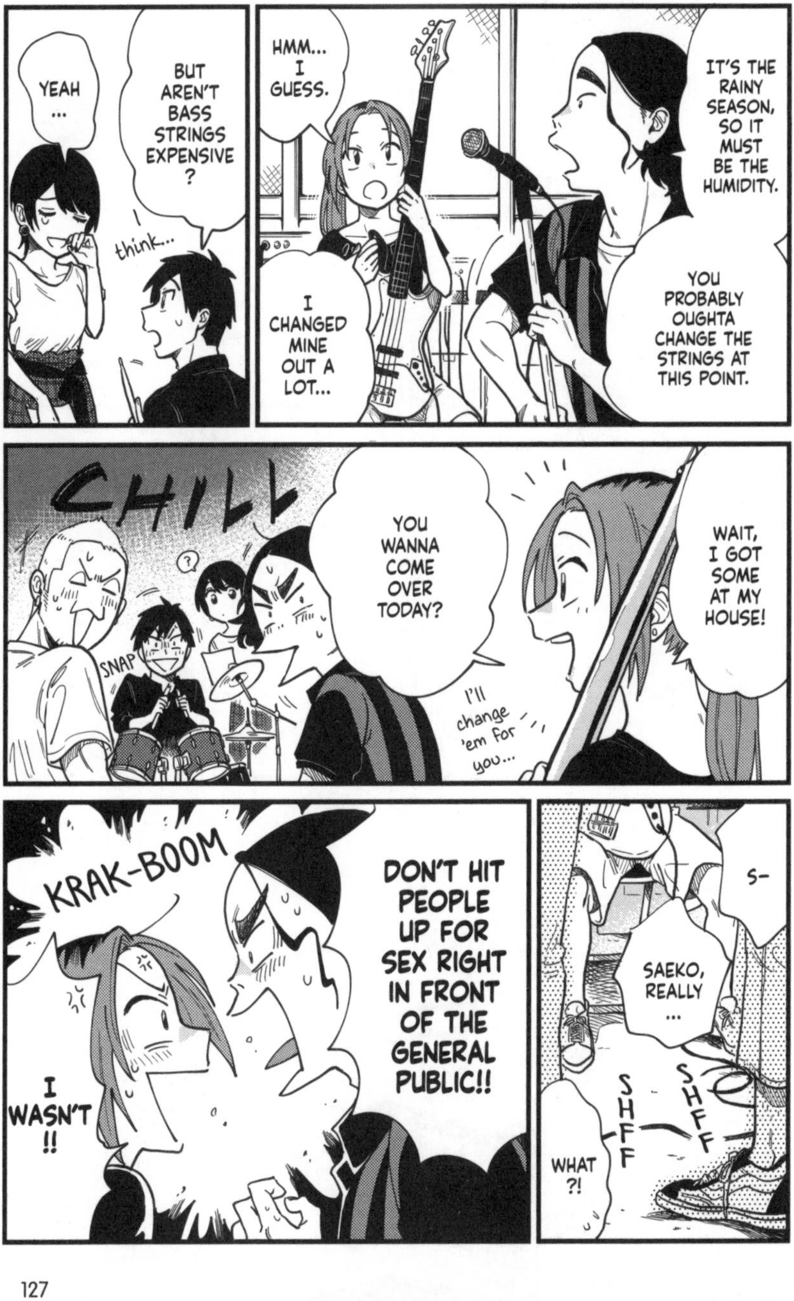

IT'S THE RAINY SEASON, SO IT MUST BE THE HUMIDITY.
YOU PROBABLY OUGHTA CHANGE THE STRINGS AT THIS POINT.
HMM... I GUESS.
I CHANGED MINE OUT A LOT...
BUT AREN'T BASS STRINGS EXPENSIVE?
I think...
YEAH...
WAIT, I GOT SOME AT MY HOUSE!
YOU WANNA COME OVER TODAY?
I'll change 'em for you...
CHILL
?
SNAP
S-
SAEKO, REALLY...
SHFF
SHFF
WHAT?!
KRAK-BOOM
DON'T HIT PEOPLE UP FOR SEX RIGHT IN FRONT OF THE GENERAL PUBLIC!!
I WASN'T!!

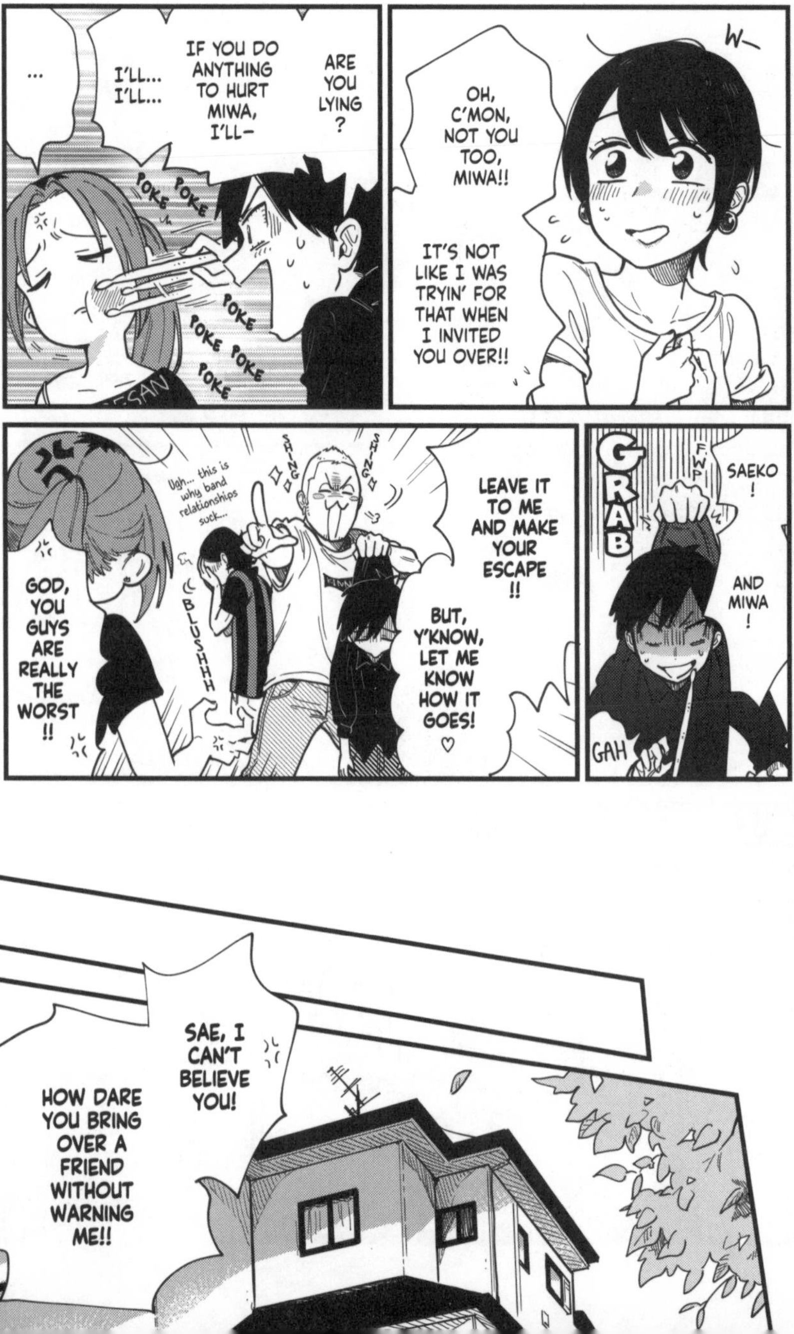
W—
OH, C'MON, NOT YOU TOO, MIWA!!
IT'S NOT LIKE I WAS TRYIN' FOR THAT WHEN I INVITED YOU OVER!!
ARE YOU LYING?
IF YOU DO ANYTHING TO HURT MIWA, I'LL—
I'LL... I'LL...
...
POKE POKE
POKE POKE POKE POKE
GRAB
FWP
SAEKO!
AND MIWA!
GAH
LEAVE IT TO ME AND MAKE YOUR ESCAPE!!
BUT, Y'KNOW, LET ME KNOW HOW IT GOES! ♡
SHING SHING
Ugh... this is why band relationships suck...
BLUSHHH
GOD, YOU GUYS ARE REALLY THE WORST!!
SAE, I CAN'T BELIEVE YOU!
HOW DARE YOU BRING OVER A FRIEND WITHOUT WARNING ME!!

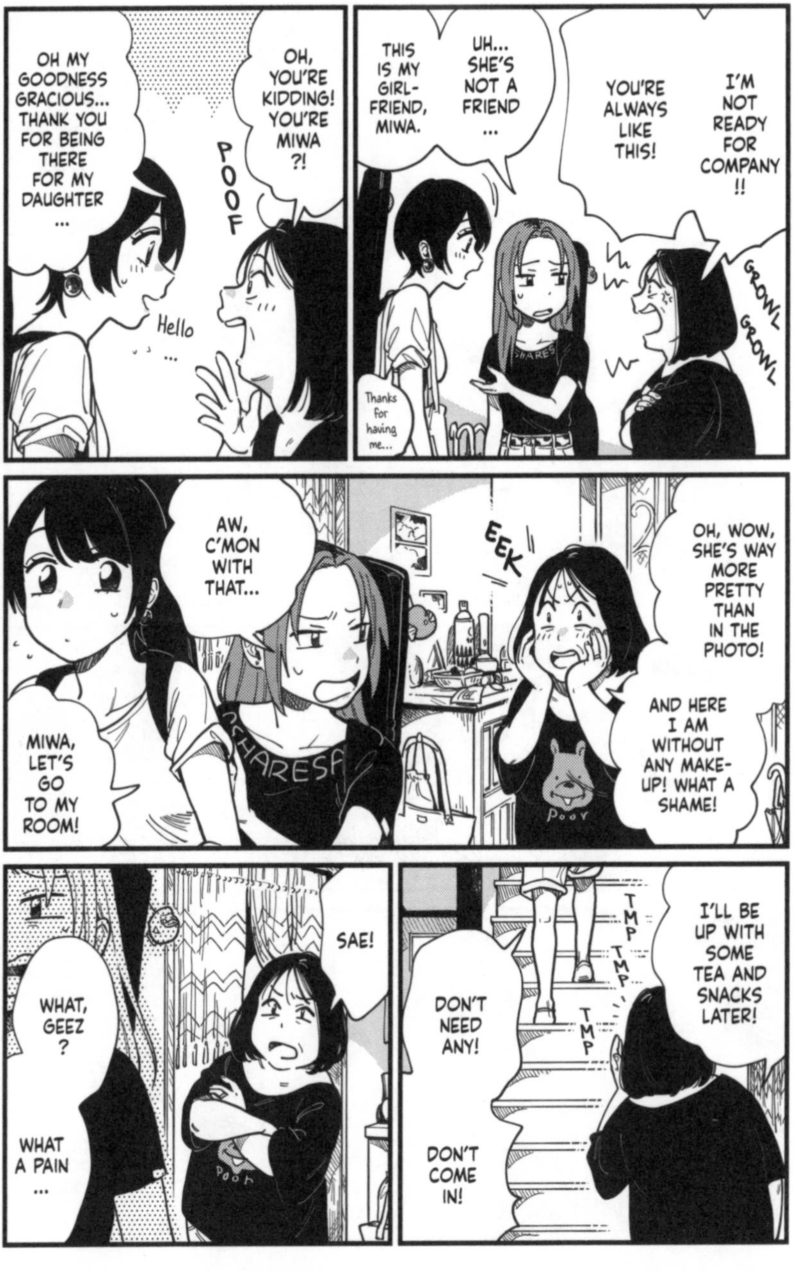
I'M NOT READY FOR COMPANY !!
YOU'RE ALWAYS LIKE THIS!
UH... SHE'S NOT A FRIEND ...
THIS IS MY GIRL-FRIEND, MIWA.
GROWL GROWL
Thanks for having me...
OH, YOU'RE KIDDING! YOU'RE MIWA ?!
POOF
OH MY GOODNESS GRACIOUS... THANK YOU FOR BEING THERE FOR MY DAUGHTER ...
Hello ...
OH, WOW, SHE'S WAY MORE PRETTY THAN IN THE PHOTO!
EEK
AND HERE I AM WITHOUT ANY MAKE-UP! WHAT A SHAME!
AW, C'MON WITH THAT...
MIWA, LET'S GO TO MY ROOM!
I'LL BE UP WITH SOME TEA AND SNACKS LATER!
TMP TMP TMP
DON'T NEED ANY!
DON'T COME IN!
SAE!
WHAT, GEEZ ?
WHAT A PAIN ...

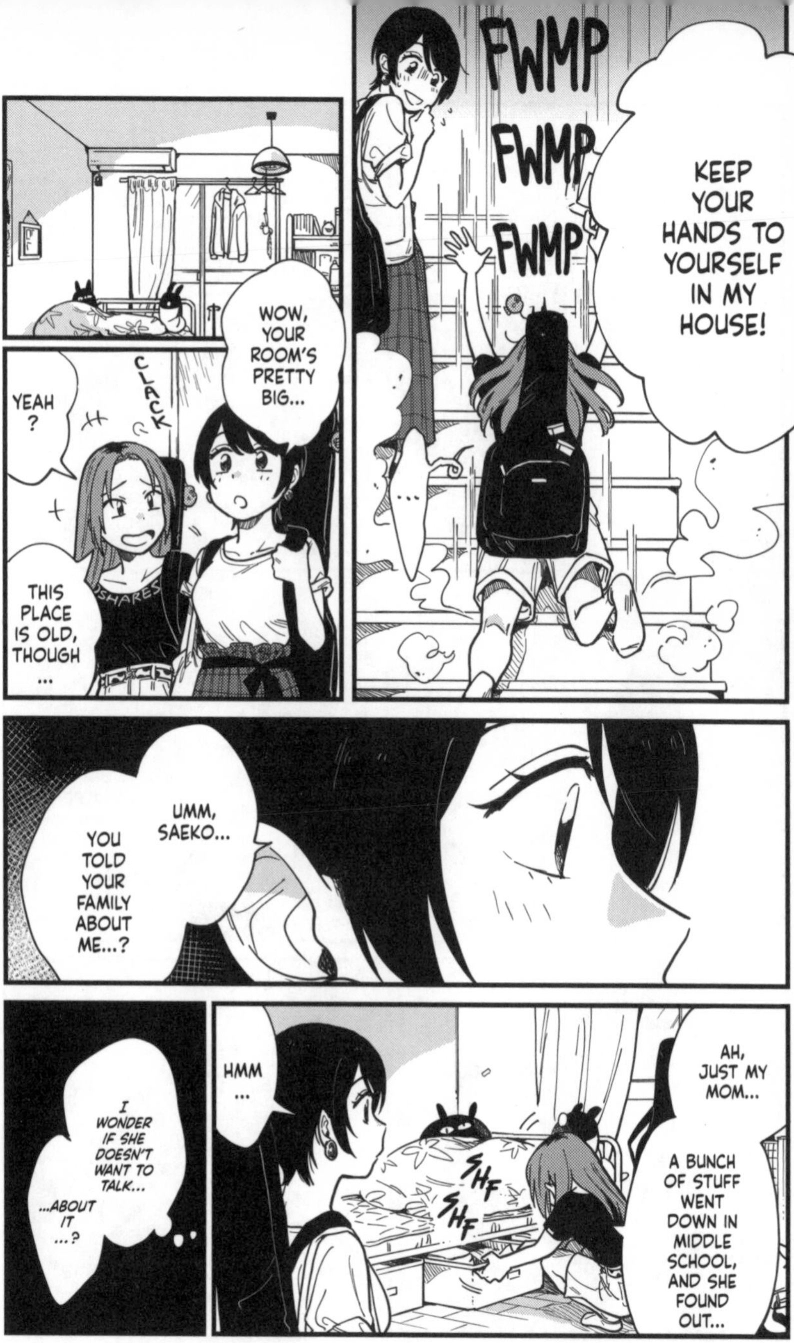
FWMP
FWMP
FWMP
KEEP YOUR HANDS TO YOURSELF IN MY HOUSE!
...
WOW, YOUR ROOM'S PRETTY BIG...
CLACK
YEAH?
THIS PLACE IS OLD, THOUGH...
UMM, SAEKO...
YOU TOLD YOUR FAMILY ABOUT ME...?
AH, JUST MY MOM...
A BUNCH OF STUFF WENT DOWN IN MIDDLE SCHOOL, AND SHE FOUND OUT...
SHF
SHF
HMM...
I WONDER IF SHE DOESN'T WANT TO TALK...
...ABOUT IT...?

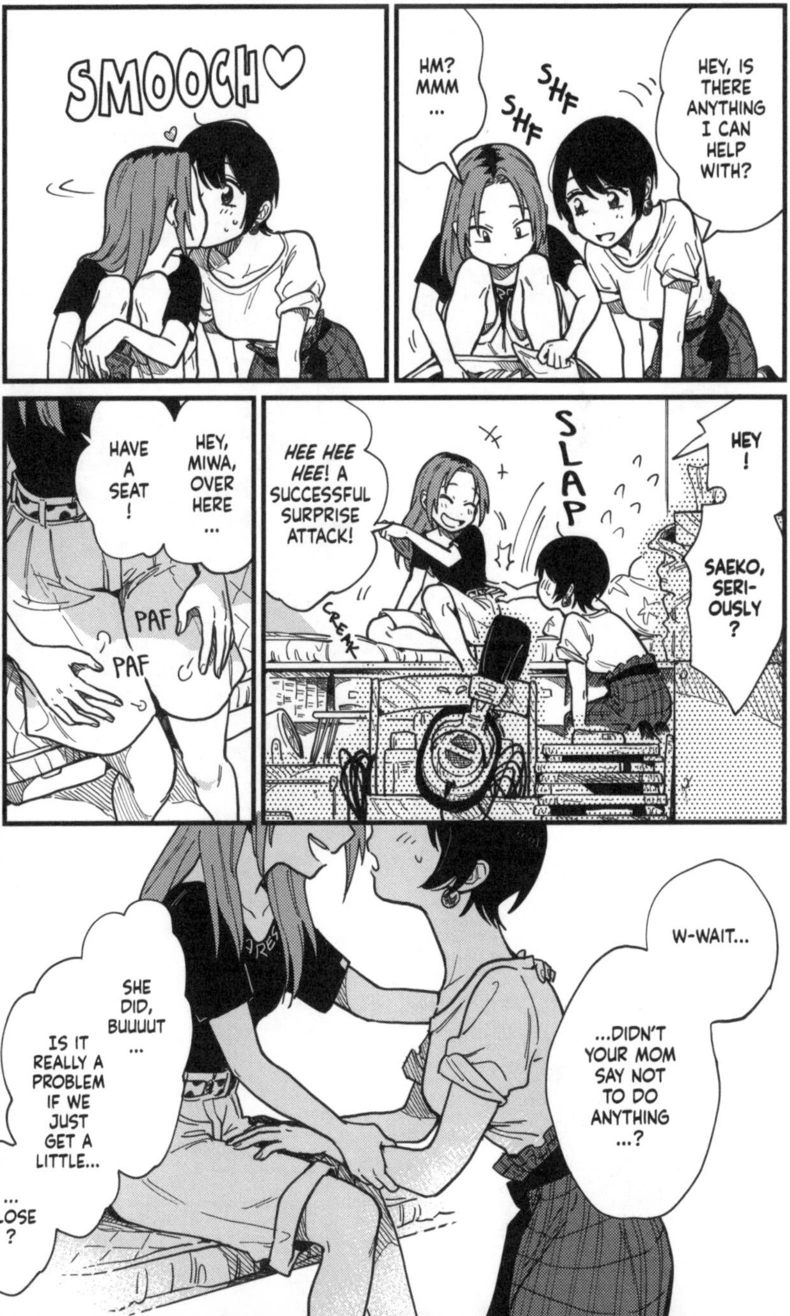
HEY, IS THERE ANYTHING I CAN HELP WITH?
SHF
SHF
HM? MMM ...
SMOOCH♡
HEY!
SAEKO, SERIOUSLY?
SLAP
HEE HEE HEE! A SUCCESSFUL SURPRISE ATTACK!
CREAK
HEY, MIWA, OVER HERE ...
HAVE A SEAT!
PAF
PAF
W-WAIT...
...DIDN'T YOUR MOM SAY NOT TO DO ANYTHING ...?
SHE DID, BUUUUT ...
IS IT REALLY A PROBLEM IF WE JUST GET A LITTLE...
... CLOSE?

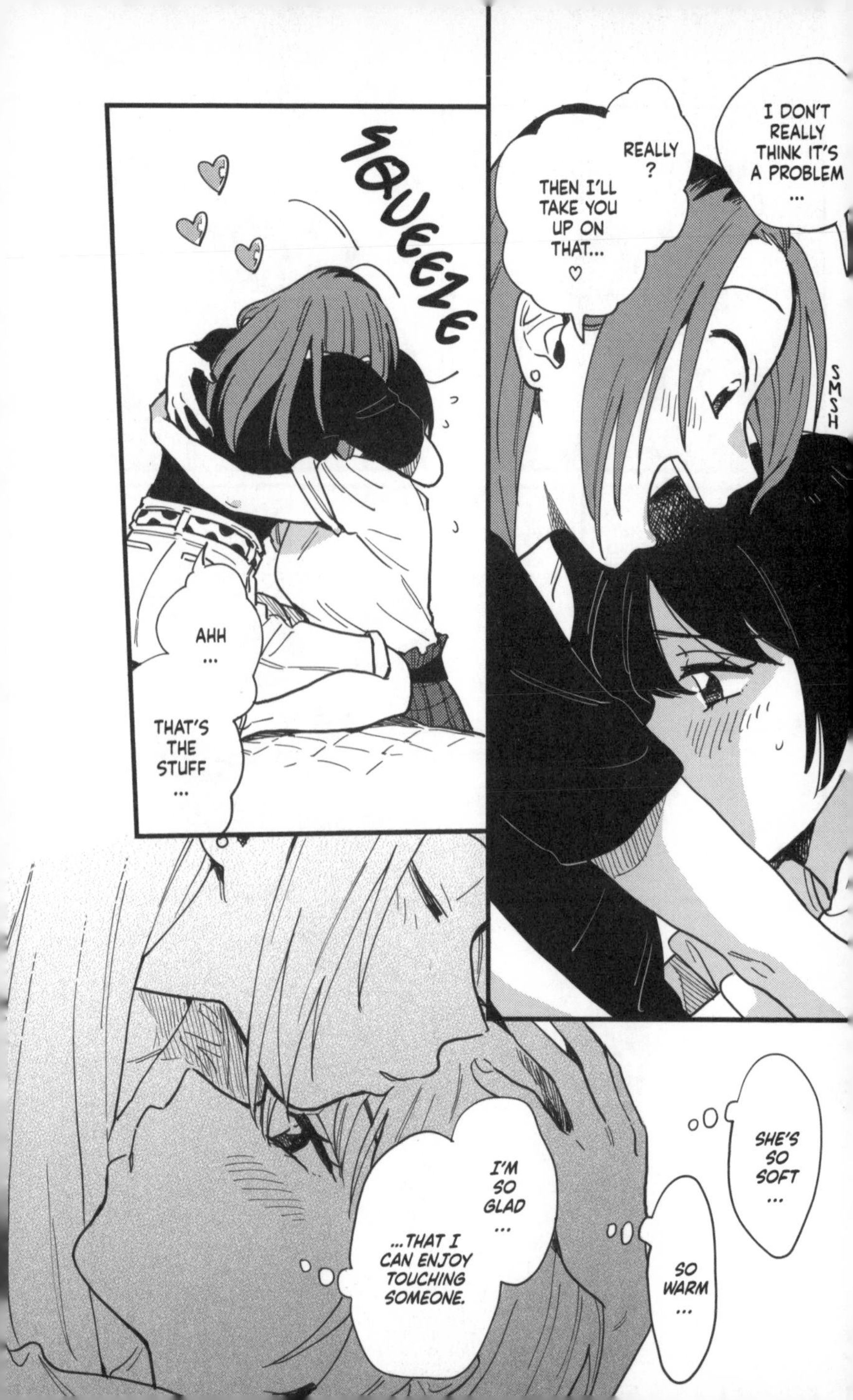
I DON'T REALLY THINK IT'S A PROBLEM ...
SMSH
REALLY ?
THEN I'LL TAKE YOU UP ON THAT... ♡
SQUEEZE
AHH ...
THAT'S THE STUFF ...
SHE'S SO SOFT ...
SO WARM ...
I'M SO GLAD ...
...THAT I CAN ENJOY TOUCHING SOMEONE.

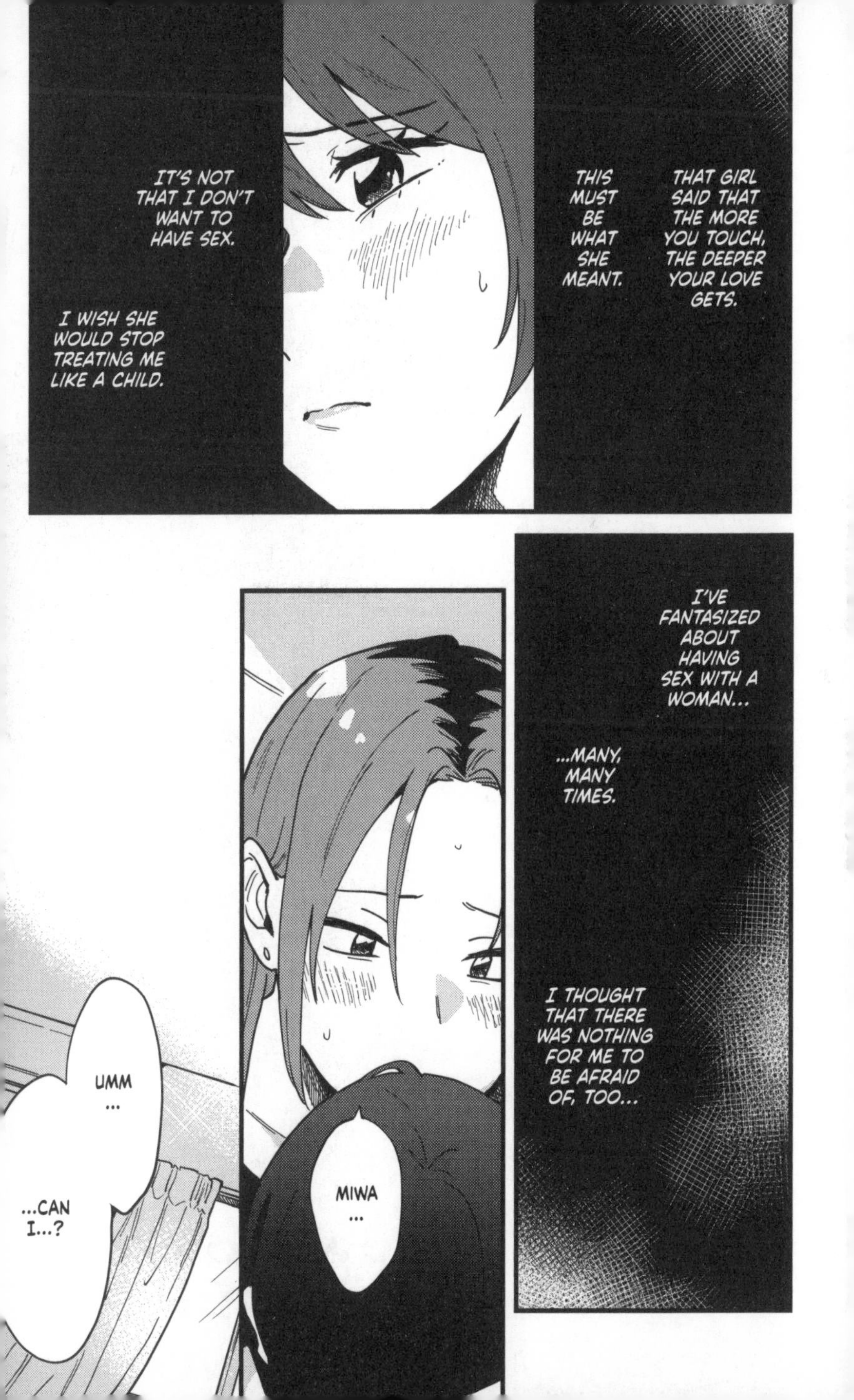
THAT GIRL SAID THAT THE MORE YOU TOUCH, THE DEEPER YOUR LOVE GETS.
THIS MUST BE WHAT SHE MEANT.
IT'S NOT THAT I DON'T WANT TO HAVE SEX.
I WISH SHE WOULD STOP TREATING ME LIKE A CHILD.
I'VE FANTASIZED ABOUT HAVING SEX WITH A WOMAN...
...MANY, MANY TIMES.
I THOUGHT THAT THERE WAS NOTHING FOR ME TO BE AFRAID OF, TOO...
MIWA...
UMM...
...CAN I...?

How Do We Relationship?

Chapter 7: We're Not in Sync!

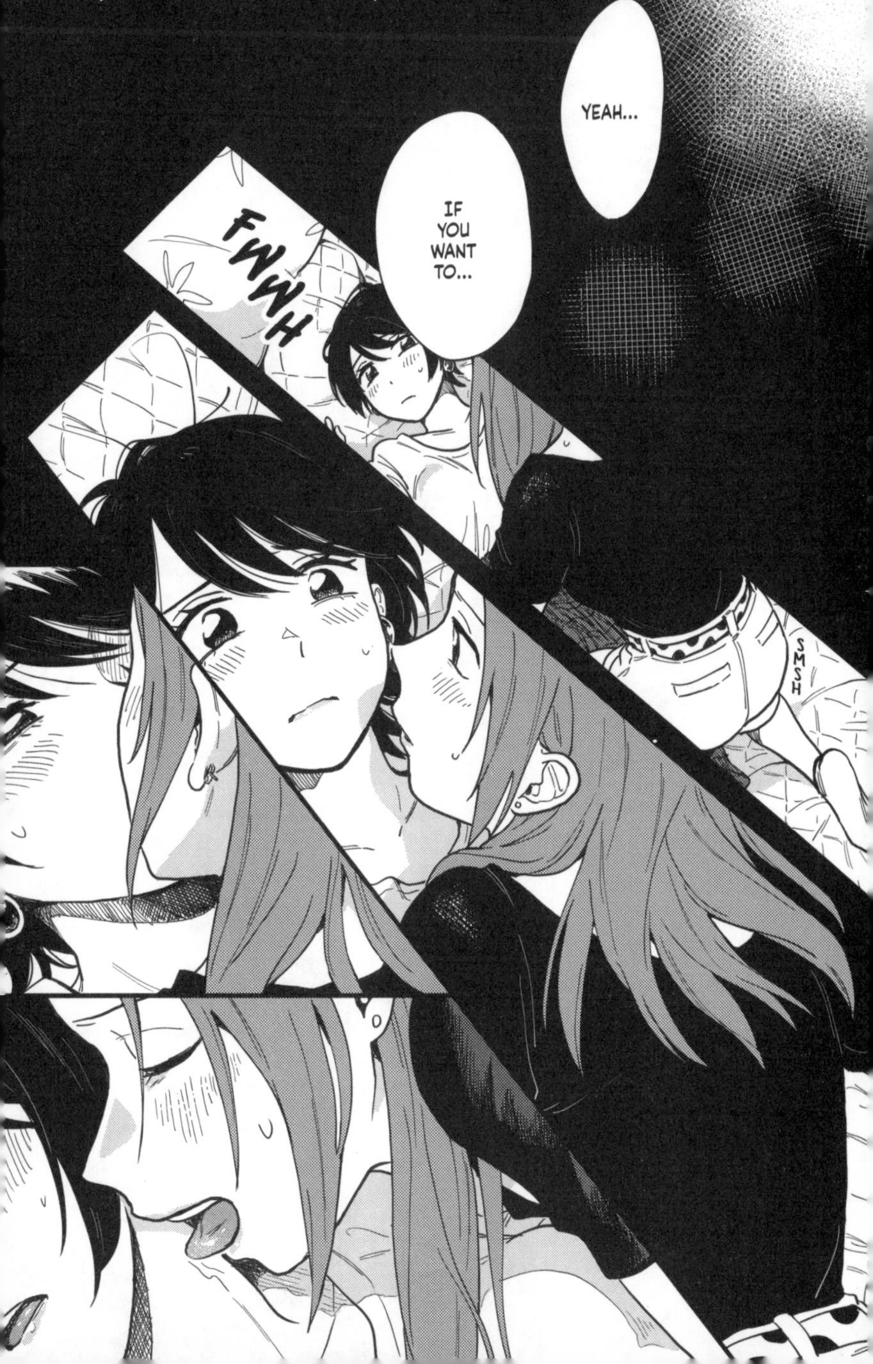
YEAH...
IF YOU WANT TO...
FWWH
SMSH

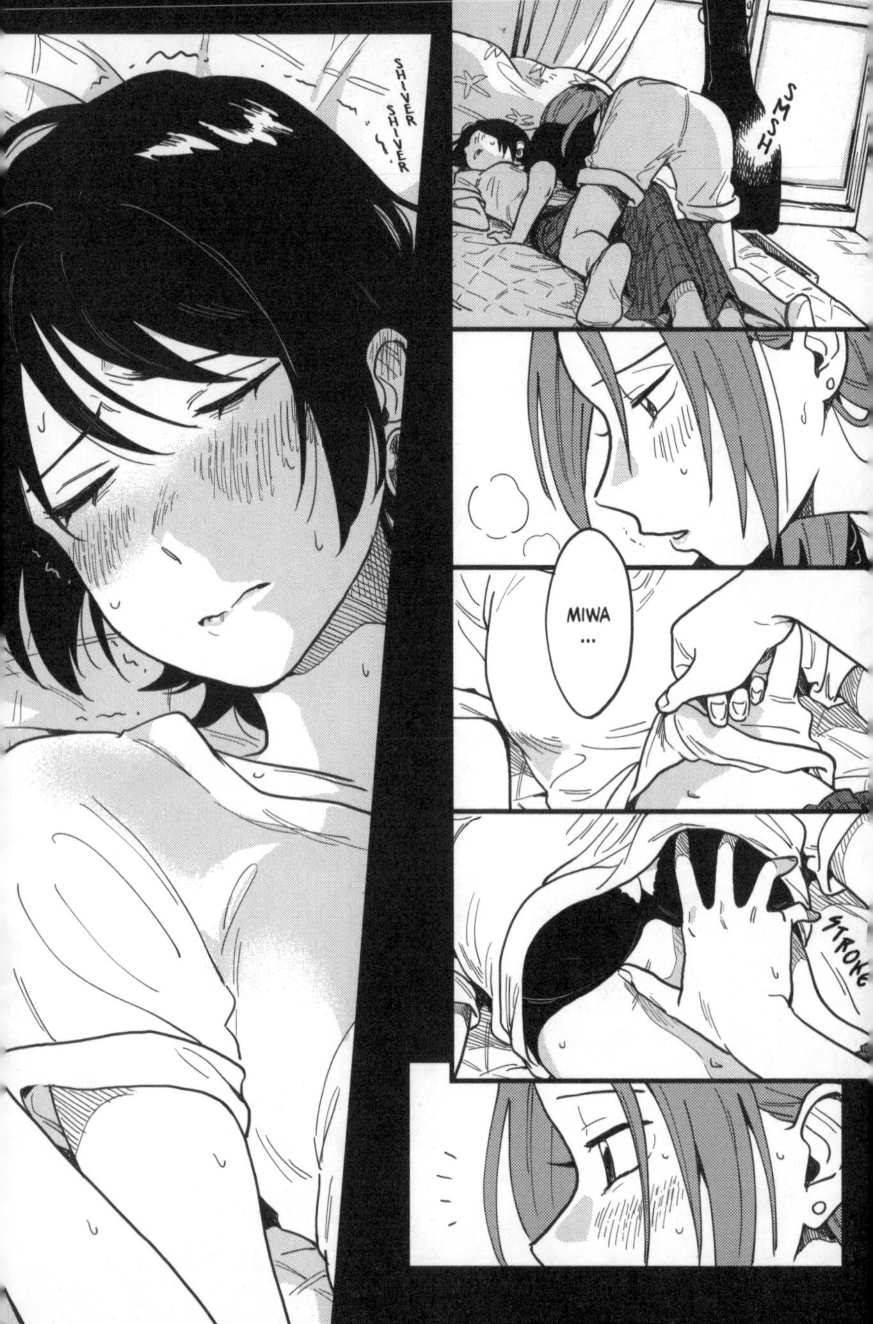
SHUSH
MIWA...
STROKE
SHIVER SHIVER

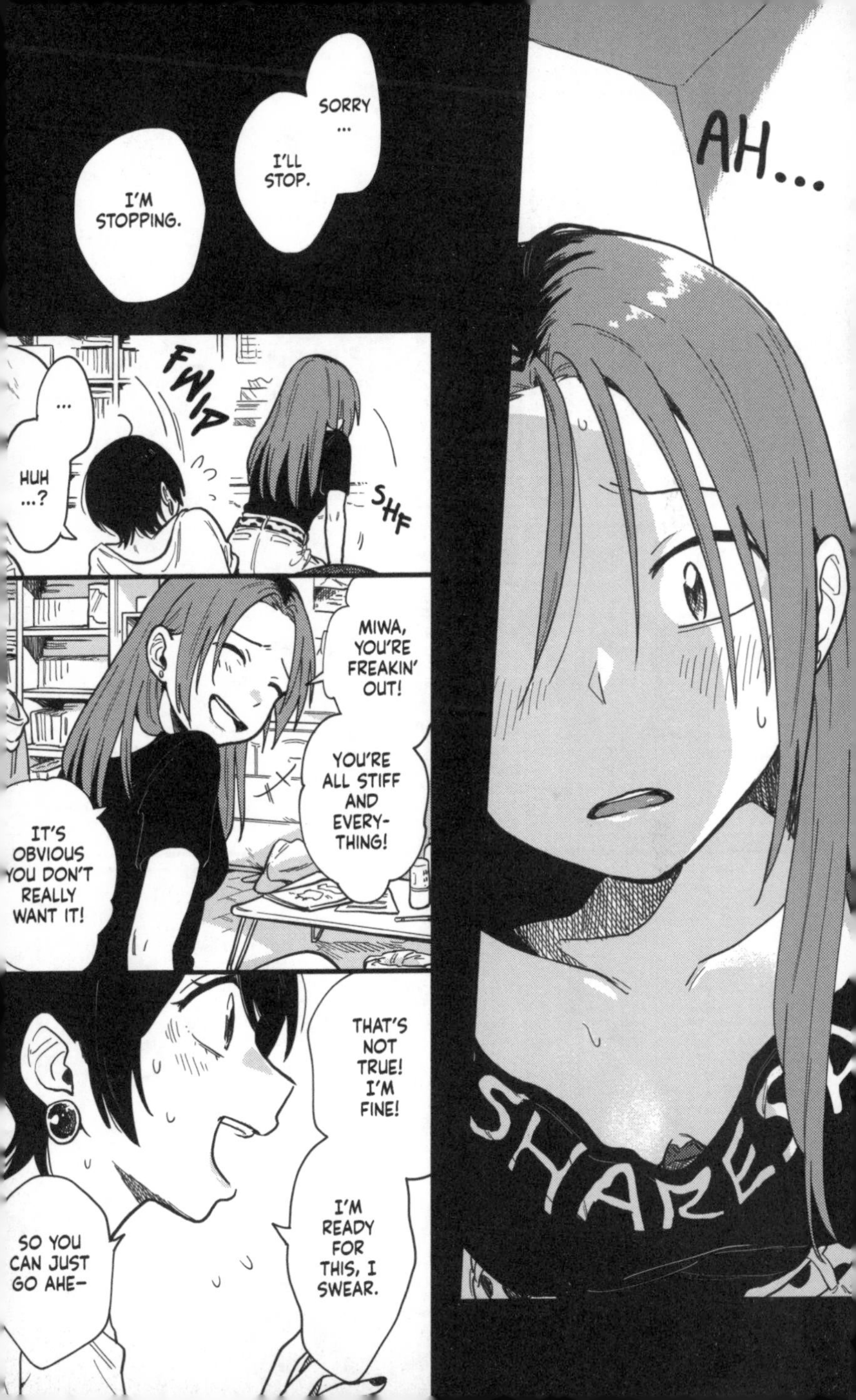

AH...
SORRY ...
I'LL STOP.
I'M STOPPING.
FWIP
SHF
... HUH ...?
MIWA, YOU'RE FREAKIN' OUT!
YOU'RE ALL STIFF AND EVERYTHING!
IT'S OBVIOUS YOU DON'T REALLY WANT IT!
THAT'S NOT TRUE! I'M FINE!
I'M READY FOR THIS, I SWEAR.
SO YOU CAN JUST GO AHE-

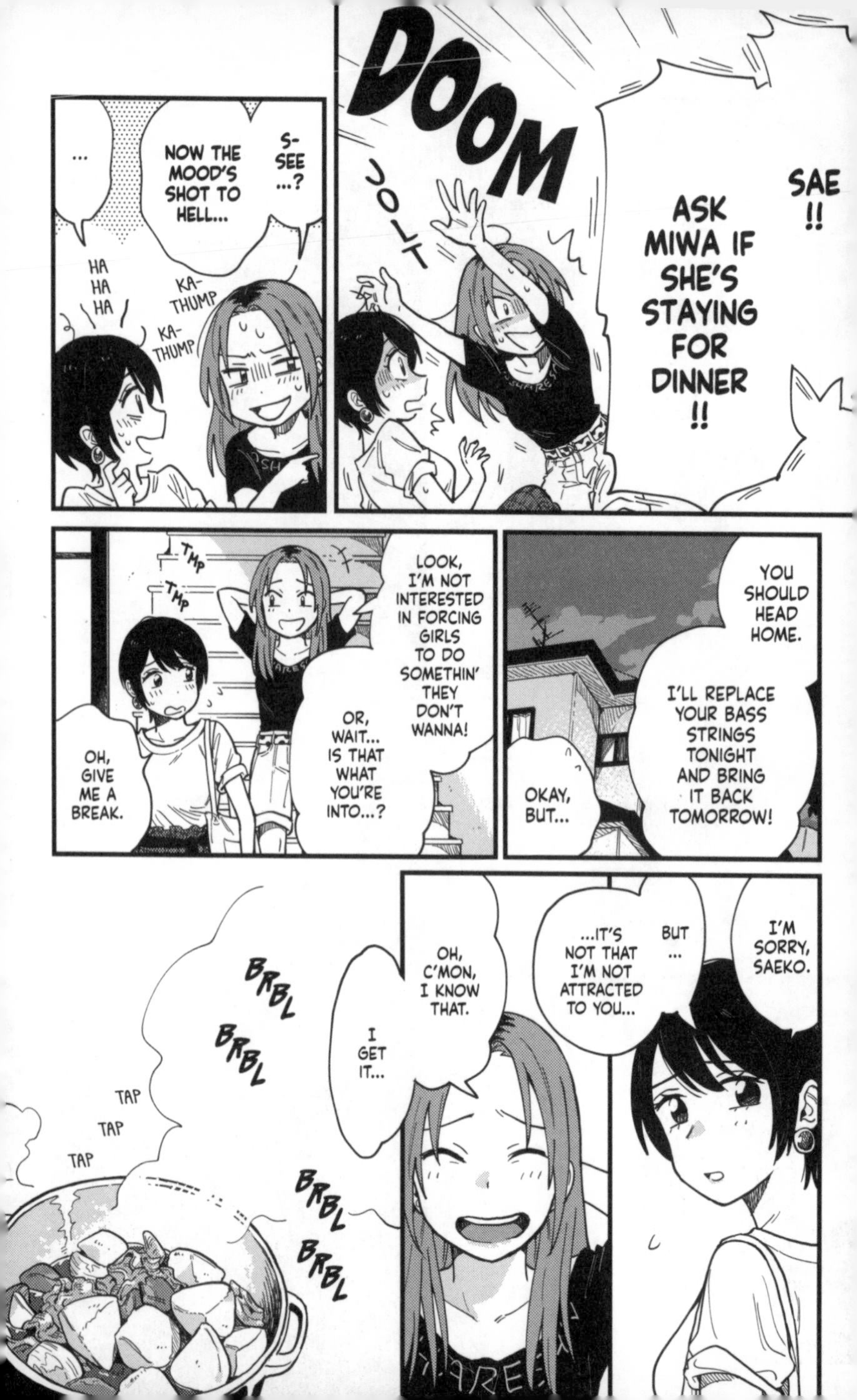
SAE !!
ASK MIWA IF SHE'S STAYING FOR DINNER !!
DOOM
JOLT
S-SEE ...?
NOW THE MOOD'S SHOT TO HELL...
...
KA-THUMP
KA-THUMP
HA HA HA
YOU SHOULD HEAD HOME.
I'LL REPLACE YOUR BASS STRINGS TONIGHT AND BRING IT BACK TOMORROW!
OKAY, BUT...
LOOK, I'M NOT INTERESTED IN FORCING GIRLS TO DO SOMETHIN' THEY DON'T WANNA!
TMP
TMP
OR, WAIT... IS THAT WHAT YOU'RE INTO...?
OH, GIVE ME A BREAK.
I'M SORRY, SAEKO.
BUT ...
...IT'S NOT THAT I'M NOT ATTRACTED TO YOU...
OH, C'MON, I KNOW THAT.
I GET IT...
BRBL
BRBL
TAP
TAP
TAP
BRBL
BRBL

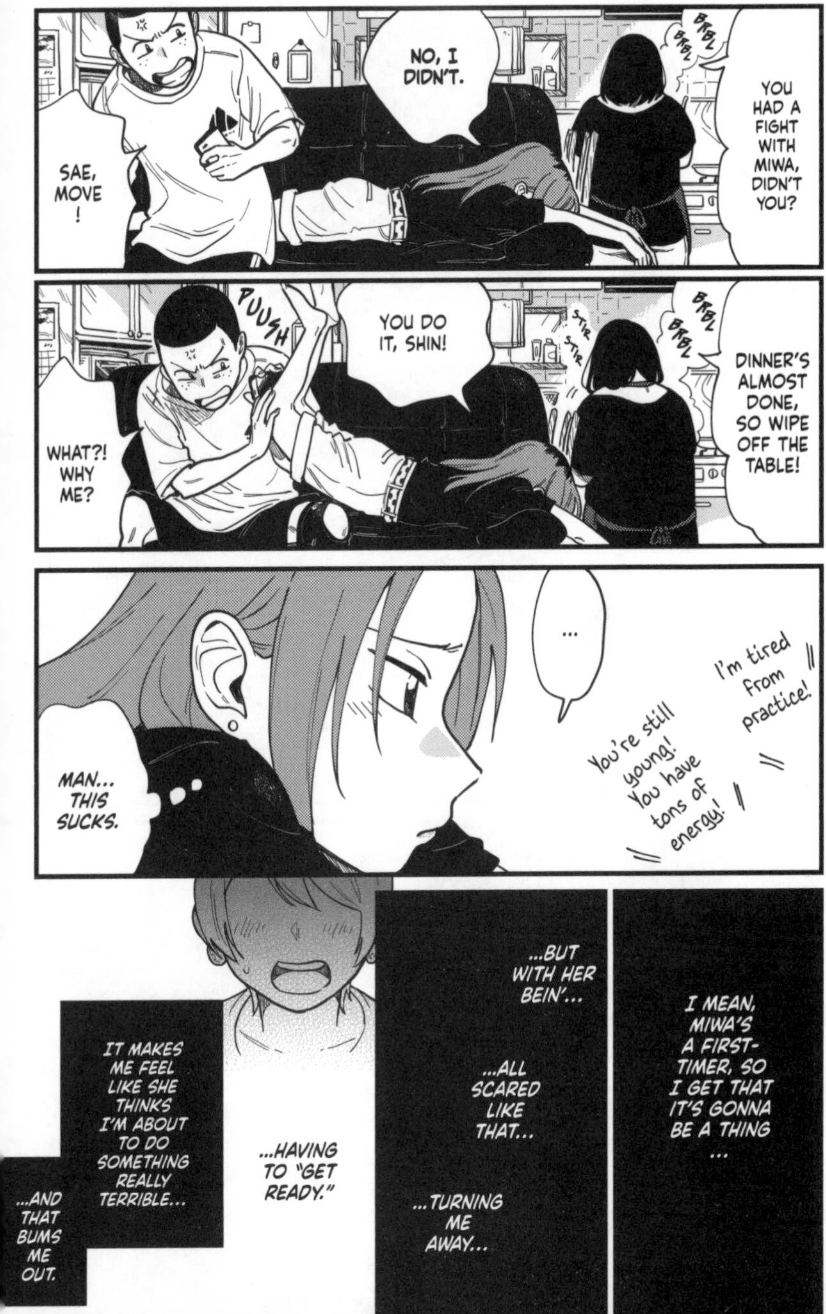
BRBL BRBL
YOU HAD A FIGHT WITH MIWA, DIDN'T YOU?
NO, I DIDN'T.
SAE, MOVE!
BRBL BRBL
DINNER'S ALMOST DONE, SO WIPE OFF THE TABLE!
STIR STIR
YOU DO IT, SHIN!
PUUSH
WHAT?! WHY ME?
I'm tired from practice!
You're still young! You have tons of energy!
...
MAN... THIS SUCKS.
I MEAN, MIWA'S A FIRST-TIMER, SO I GET THAT IT'S GONNA BE A THING...
...BUT WITH HER BEIN'...
...ALL SCARED LIKE THAT...
...TURNING ME AWAY...
...HAVING TO "GET READY."
IT MAKES ME FEEL LIKE SHE THINKS I'M ABOUT TO DO SOMETHING REALLY TERRIBLE...
...AND THAT BUMS ME OUT.

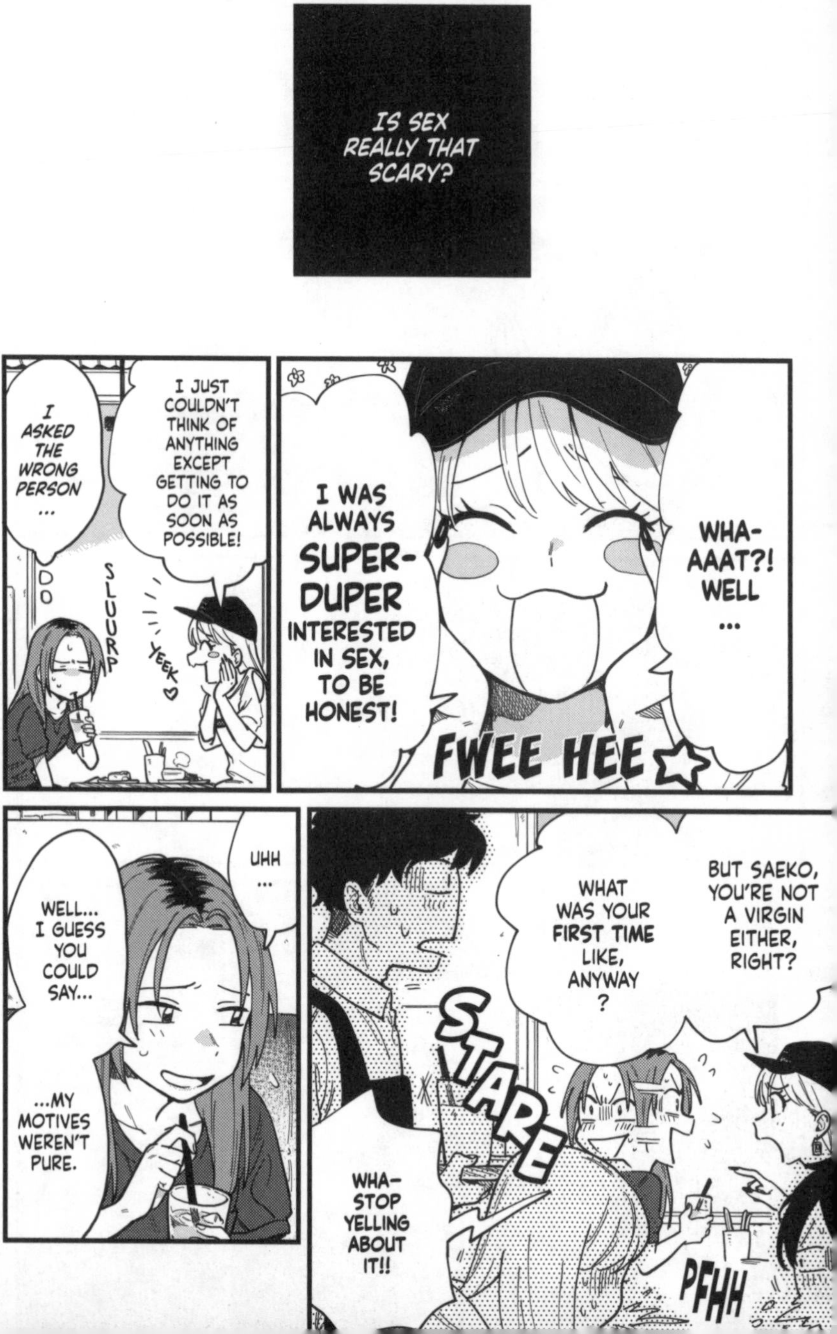
IS SEX REALLY THAT SCARY?
WHA-AAAT?! WELL...
I WAS ALWAYS SUPER-DUPER INTERESTED IN SEX, TO BE HONEST!
FWEE HEE
I JUST COULDN'T THINK OF ANYTHING EXCEPT GETTING TO DO IT AS SOON AS POSSIBLE!
I ASKED THE WRONG PERSON...
SLUURP
YEEK
BUT SAEKO, YOU'RE NOT A VIRGIN EITHER, RIGHT?
WHAT WAS YOUR FIRST TIME LIKE, ANYWAY?
STARE
WHA- STOP YELLING ABOUT IT!!
PFHH
UHH...
WELL... I GUESS YOU COULD SAY...
...MY MOTIVES WEREN'T PURE.

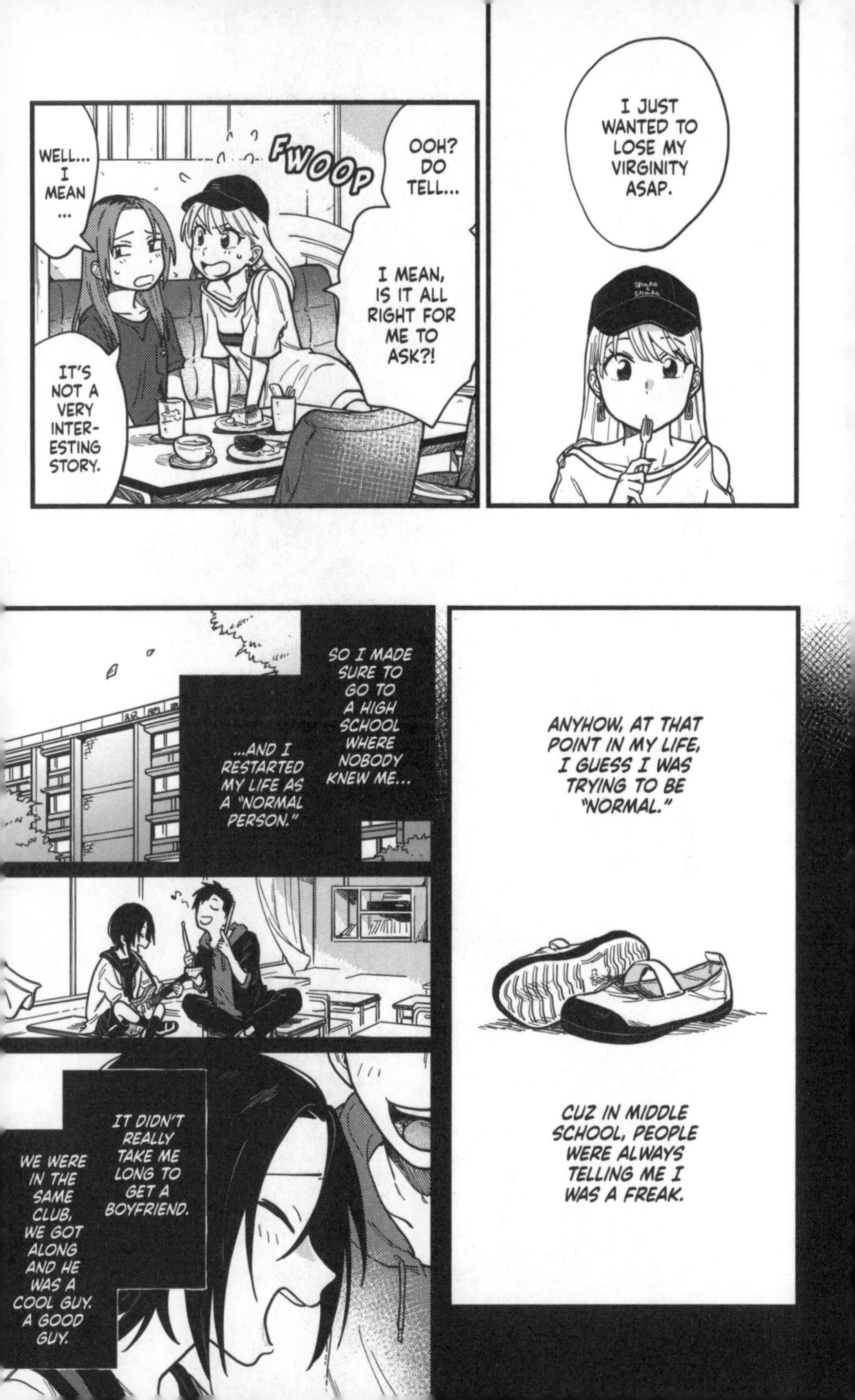
I JUST WANTED TO LOSE MY VIRGINITY ASAP.
OOH? DO TELL...
I MEAN, IS IT ALL RIGHT FOR ME TO ASK?!
FWOOP
WELL... I MEAN...
IT'S NOT A VERY INTERESTING STORY.
ANYHOW, AT THAT POINT IN MY LIFE, I GUESS I WAS TRYING TO BE "NORMAL."
CUZ IN MIDDLE SCHOOL, PEOPLE WERE ALWAYS TELLING ME I WAS A FREAK.
SO I MADE SURE TO GO TO A HIGH SCHOOL WHERE NOBODY KNEW ME...
...AND I RESTARTED MY LIFE AS A "NORMAL PERSON."
IT DIDN'T REALLY TAKE ME LONG TO GET A BOYFRIEND.
WE WERE IN THE SAME CLUB, WE GOT ALONG AND HE WAS A COOL GUY. A GOOD GUY.

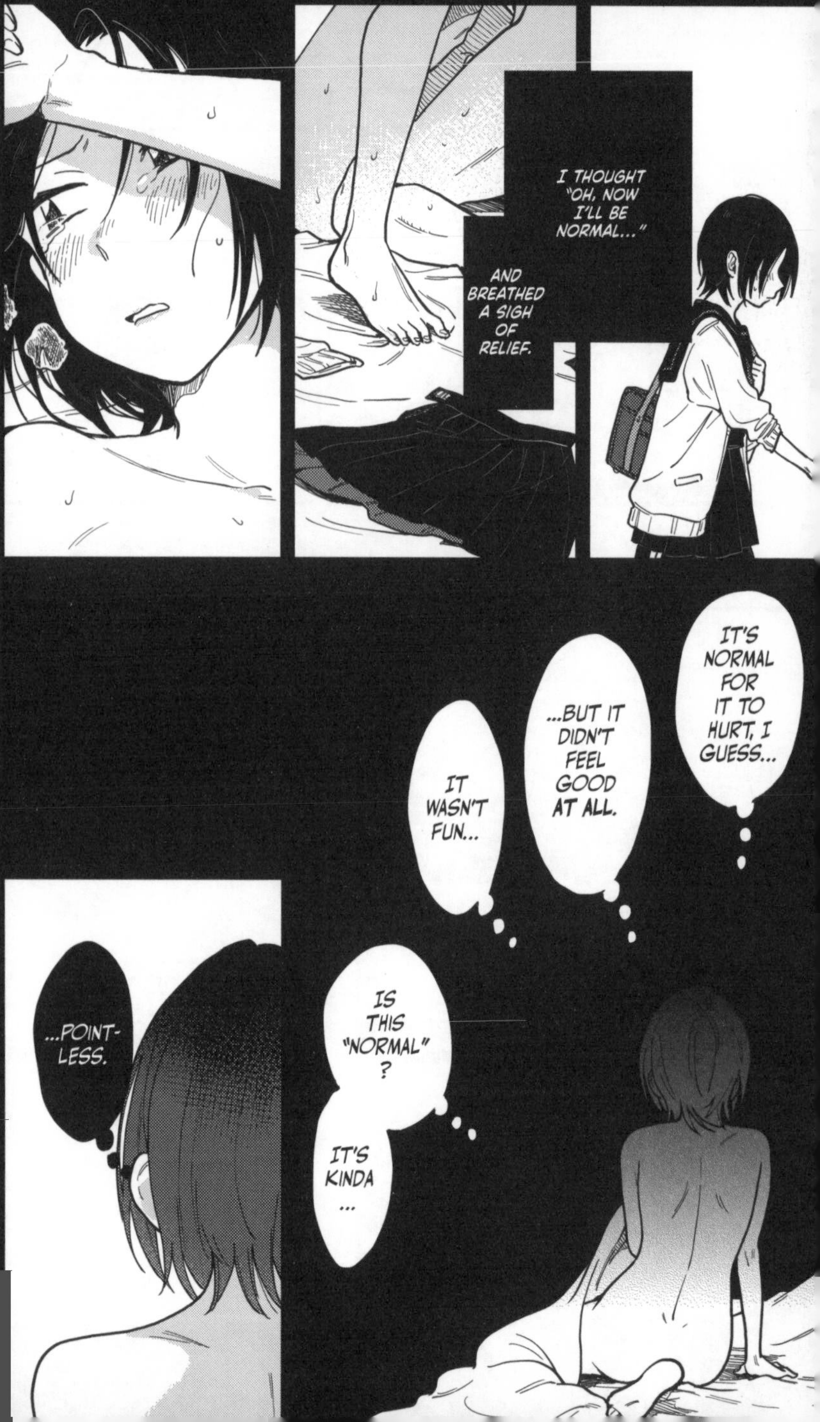
I THOUGHT "OH, NOW I'LL BE NORMAL..."
AND BREATHED A SIGH OF RELIEF.
IT'S NORMAL FOR IT TO HURT, I GUESS...
...BUT IT DIDN'T FEEL GOOD AT ALL.
IT WASN'T FUN...
IS THIS "NORMAL"?
IT'S KINDA...
...POINT-LESS.

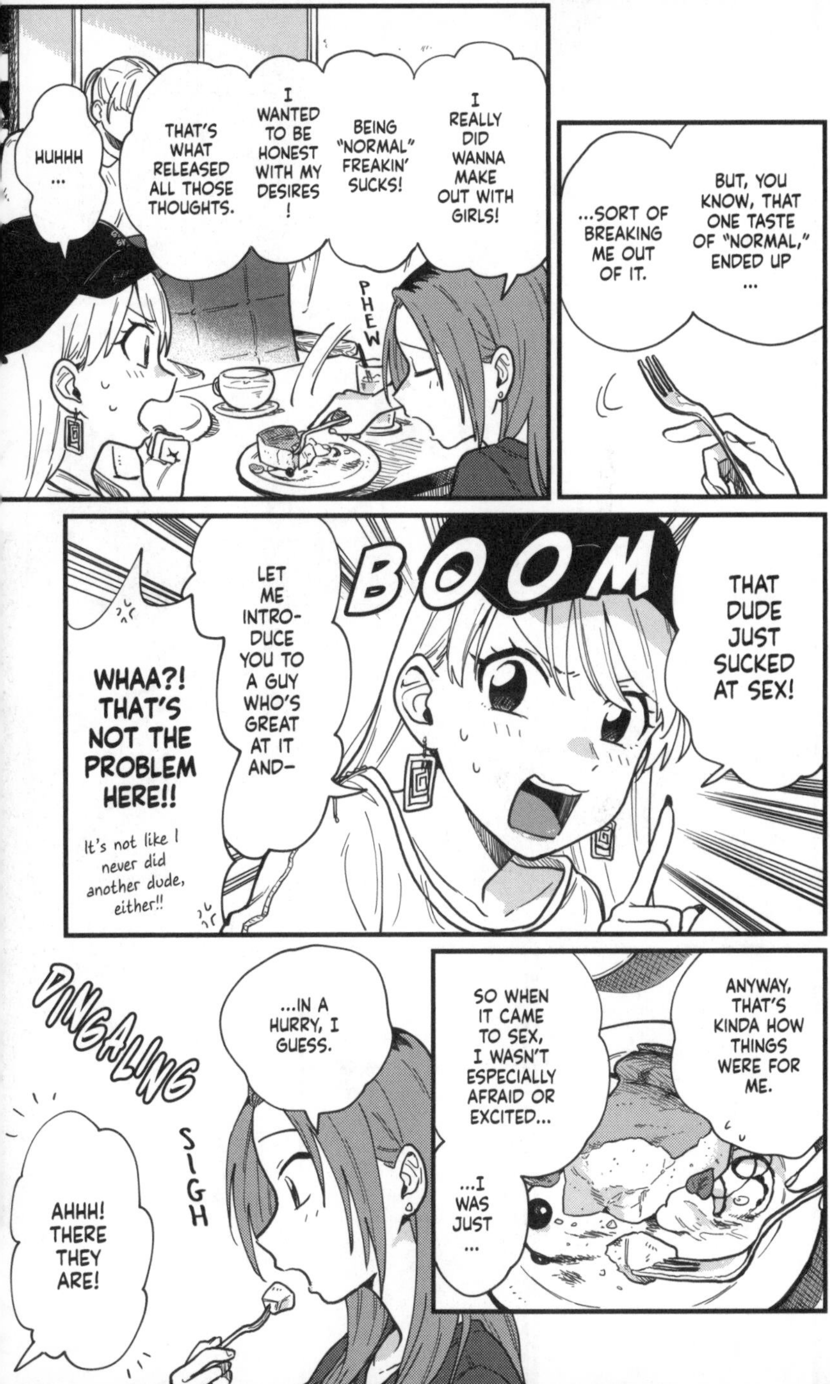
BUT, YOU KNOW, THAT ONE TASTE OF "NORMAL," ENDED UP ...
...SORT OF BREAKING ME OUT OF IT.
I REALLY DID WANNA MAKE OUT WITH GIRLS!
BEING "NORMAL" FREAKIN' SUCKS!
I WANTED TO BE HONEST WITH MY DESIRES!
THAT'S WHAT RELEASED ALL THOSE THOUGHTS.
PHEW
HUHHH ...
THAT DUDE JUST SUCKED AT SEX!
BOOM
LET ME INTRO-DUCE YOU TO A GUY WHO'S GREAT AT IT AND–
WHAA?! THAT'S NOT THE PROBLEM HERE!!
It's not like I never did another dude, either!!
ANYWAY, THAT'S KINDA HOW THINGS WERE FOR ME.
SO WHEN IT CAME TO SEX, I WASN'T ESPECIALLY AFRAID OR EXCITED...
...I WAS JUST ...
...IN A HURRY, I GUESS.
SIGH
DINGALING
AHHH! THERE THEY ARE!

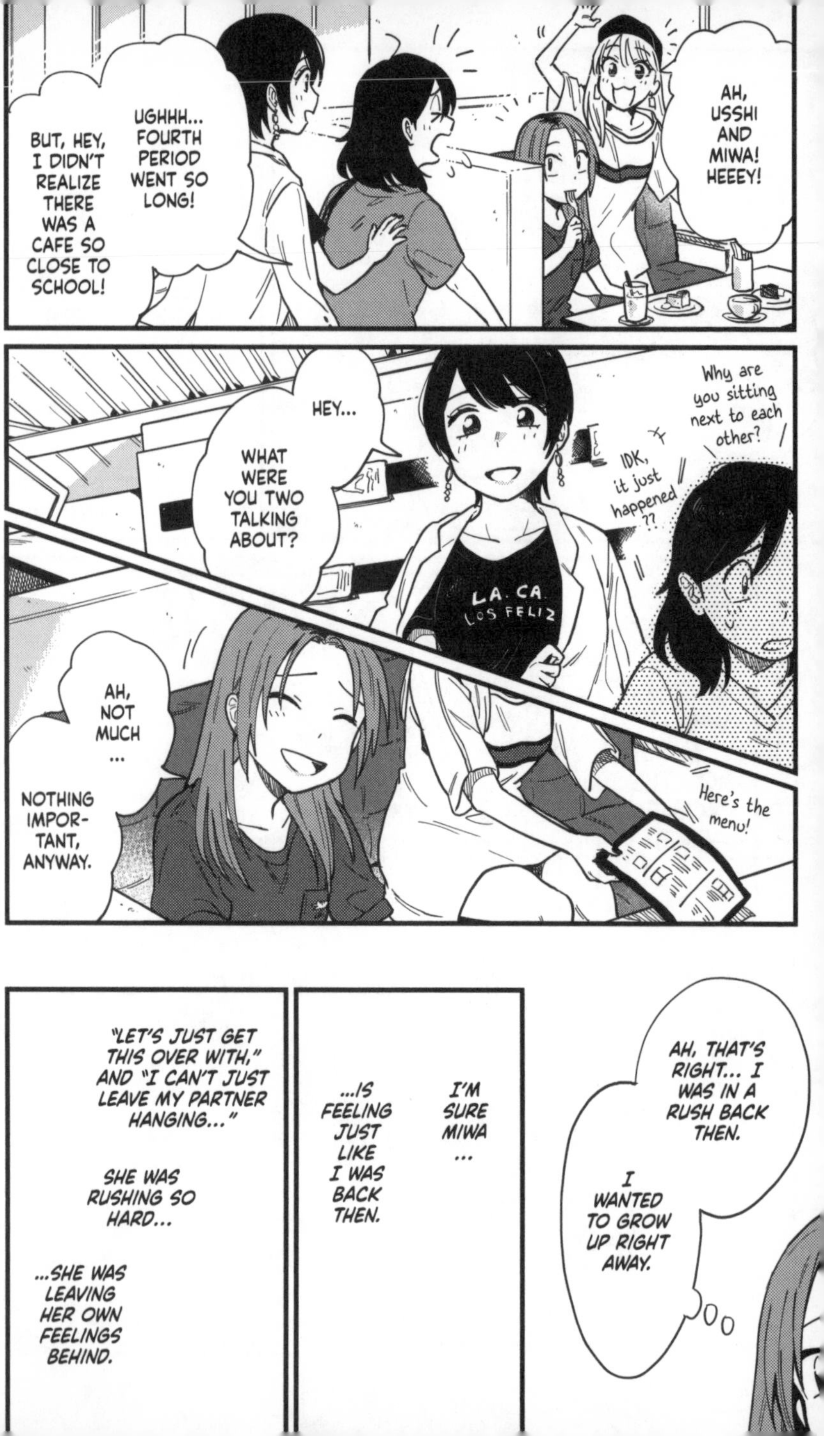
AH, USSHI AND MIWA! HEEEY!
UGHHH... FOURTH PERIOD WENT SO LONG!
BUT, HEY, I DIDN'T REALIZE THERE WAS A CAFE SO CLOSE TO SCHOOL!
Why are you sitting next to each other?
IDK, it just happened ??
HEY...
WHAT WERE YOU TWO TALKING ABOUT?
Here's the menu!
AH, NOT MUCH ...
NOTHING IMPORTANT, ANYWAY.
AH, THAT'S RIGHT... I WAS IN A RUSH BACK THEN.
I WANTED TO GROW UP RIGHT AWAY.
I'M SURE MIWA ...
...IS FEELING JUST LIKE I WAS BACK THEN.
"LET'S JUST GET THIS OVER WITH," AND "I CAN'T JUST LEAVE MY PARTNER HANGING..."
SHE WAS RUSHING SO HARD...
...SHE WAS LEAVING HER OWN FEELINGS BEHIND.

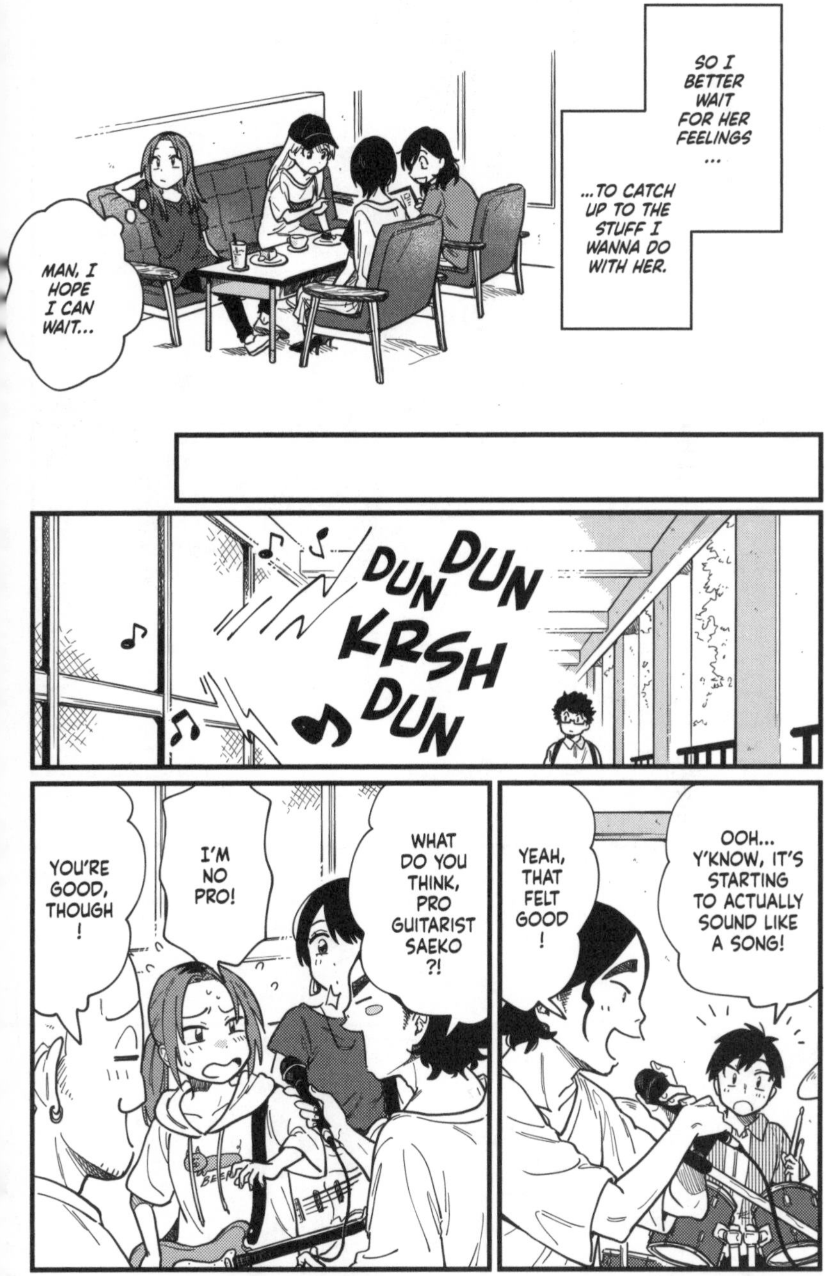
SO I BETTER WAIT FOR HER FEELINGS...
...TO CATCH UP TO THE STUFF I WANNA DO WITH HER.
MAN, I HOPE I CAN WAIT...
DUN DUN
KRSH
DUN
OOH... Y'KNOW, IT'S STARTING TO ACTUALLY SOUND LIKE A SONG!
YEAH, THAT FELT GOOD!
WHAT DO YOU THINK, PRO GUITARIST SAEKO?!
I'M NO PRO!
YOU'RE GOOD, THOUGH!

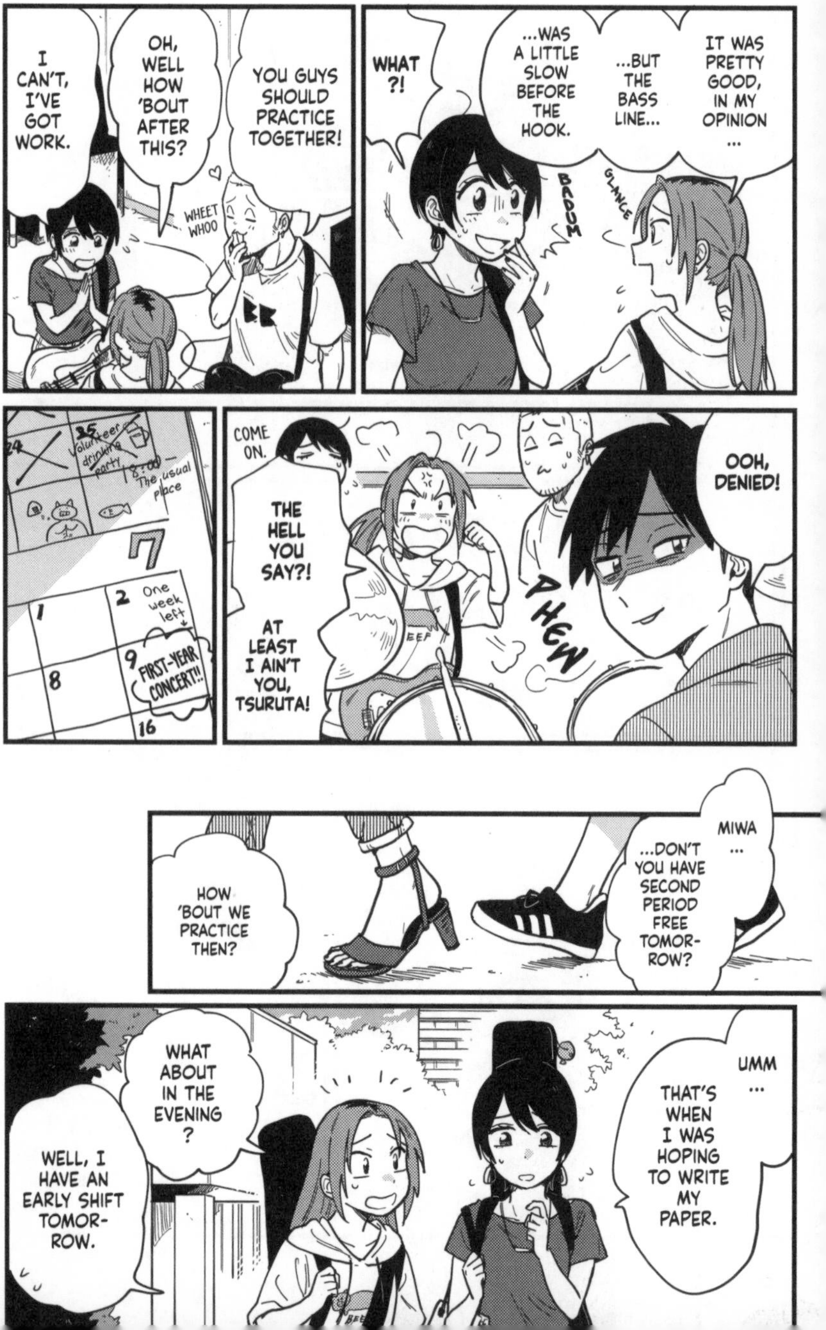
IT WAS PRETTY GOOD, IN MY OPINION ...
...BUT THE BASS LINE...
...WAS A LITTLE SLOW BEFORE THE HOOK.
GLANCE
BADUM
WHAT ?!
YOU GUYS SHOULD PRACTICE TOGETHER!
WHEET WHOO
OH, WELL HOW 'BOUT AFTER THIS?
I CAN'T, I'VE GOT WORK.
OOH, DENIED!
PHEW
THE HELL YOU SAY?!
AT LEAST I AIN'T YOU, TSURUTA!
COME ON.
24
25 Volunteer drinking party 18:00 — The usual place
7
1
2 One week left
8
9 FIRST-YEAR CONCERT!!
16
MIWA ...
...DON'T YOU HAVE SECOND PERIOD FREE TOMOR-ROW?
HOW 'BOUT WE PRACTICE THEN?
UMM ...
THAT'S WHEN I WAS HOPING TO WRITE MY PAPER.
WHAT ABOUT IN THE EVENING ?
WELL, I HAVE AN EARLY SHIFT TOMOR-ROW.

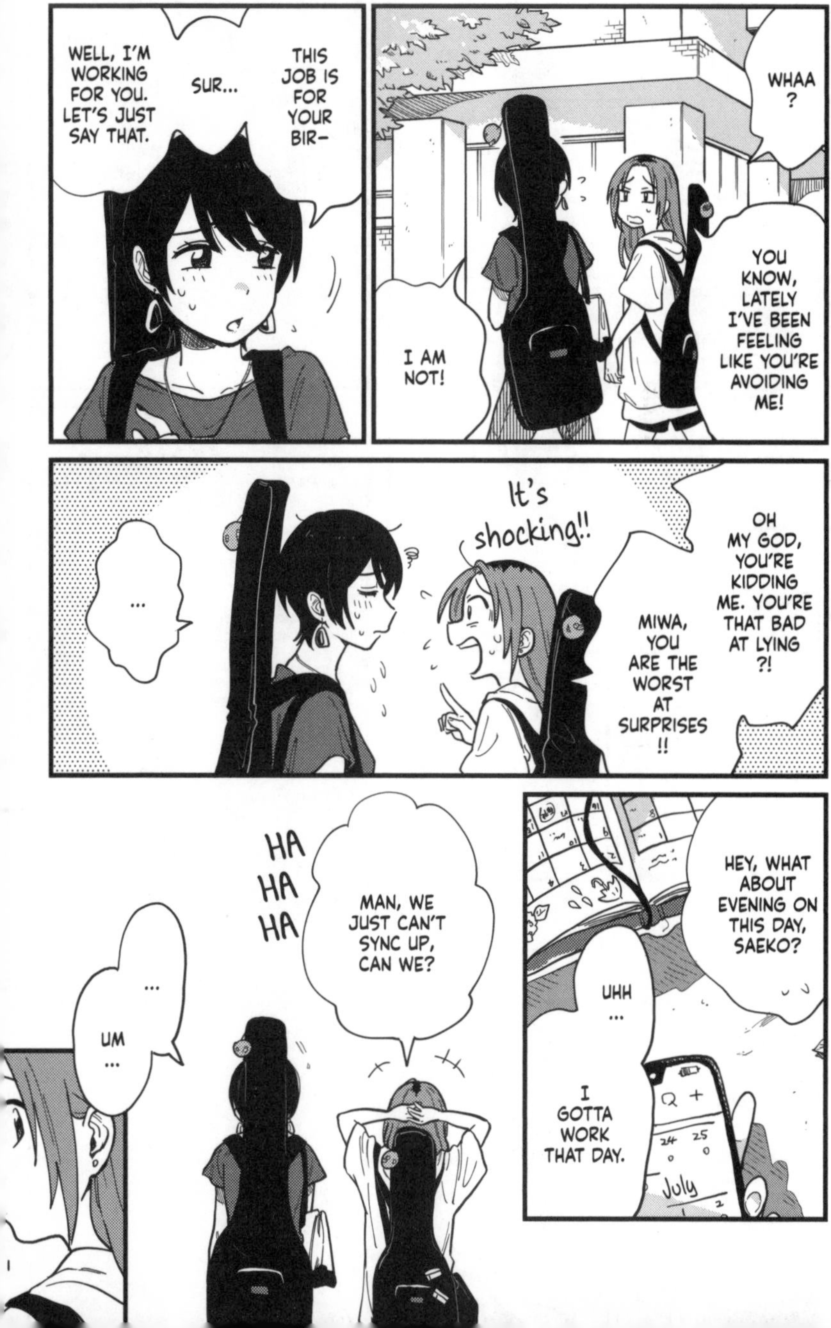
WHAA?
YOU KNOW, LATELY I'VE BEEN FEELING LIKE YOU'RE AVOIDING ME!
I AM NOT!
THIS JOB IS FOR YOUR BIR–
SUR...
WELL, I'M WORKING FOR YOU. LET'S JUST SAY THAT.
OH MY GOD, YOU'RE KIDDING ME. YOU'RE THAT BAD AT LYING ?!
MIWA, YOU ARE THE WORST AT SURPRISES !!
It's shocking!!
...
HEY, WHAT ABOUT EVENING ON THIS DAY, SAEKO?
UHH ...
I GOTTA WORK THAT DAY.
July
MAN, WE JUST CAN'T SYNC UP, CAN WE?
HA HA HA
...
UM ...

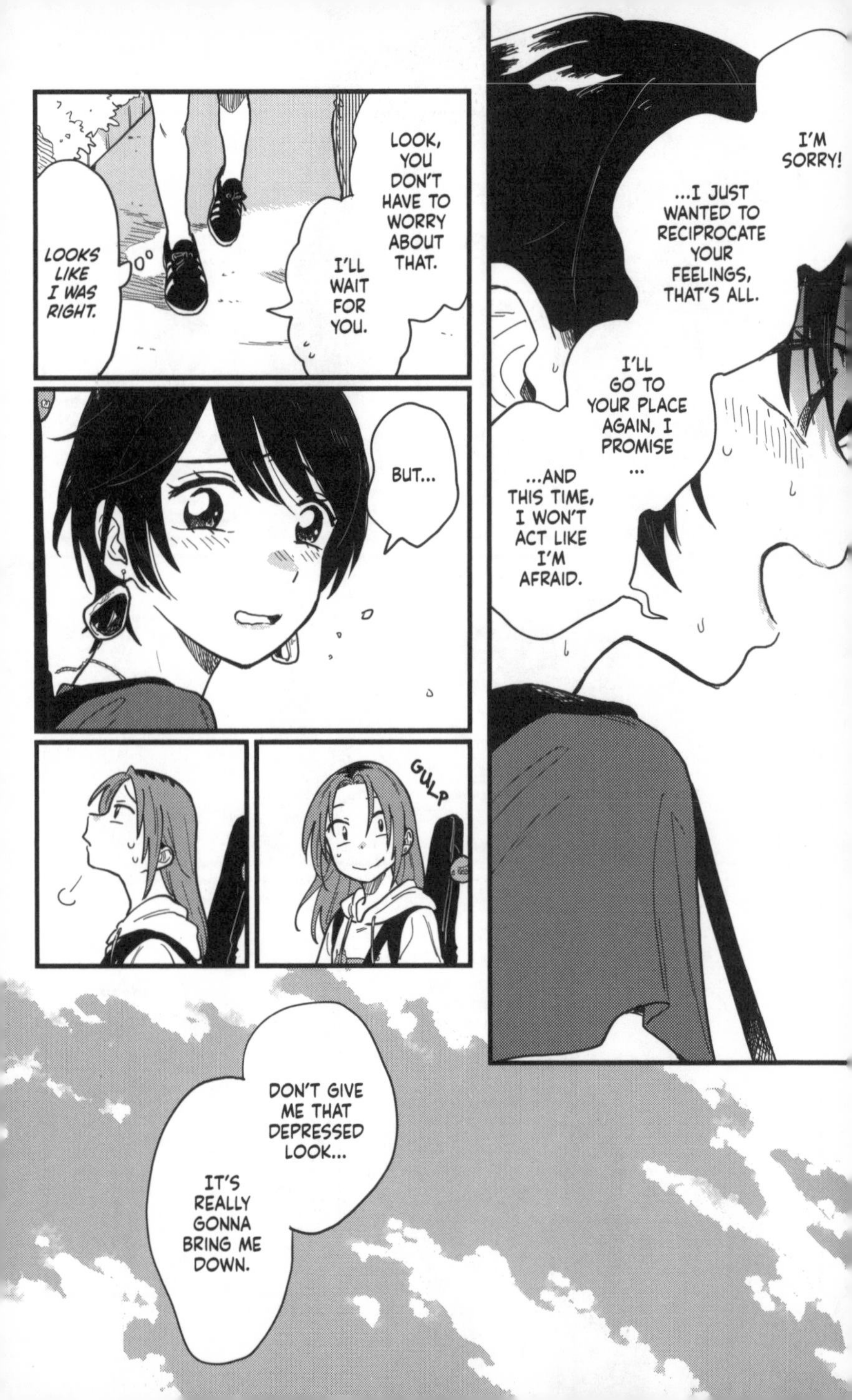
I'M SORRY!
...I JUST WANTED TO RECIPROCATE YOUR FEELINGS, THAT'S ALL.
I'LL GO TO YOUR PLACE AGAIN, I PROMISE...
...AND THIS TIME, I WON'T ACT LIKE I'M AFRAID.
LOOK, YOU DON'T HAVE TO WORRY ABOUT THAT.
I'LL WAIT FOR YOU.
LOOKS LIKE I WAS RIGHT.
BUT...
GULP
DON'T GIVE ME THAT DEPRESSED LOOK...
IT'S REALLY GONNA BRING ME DOWN.

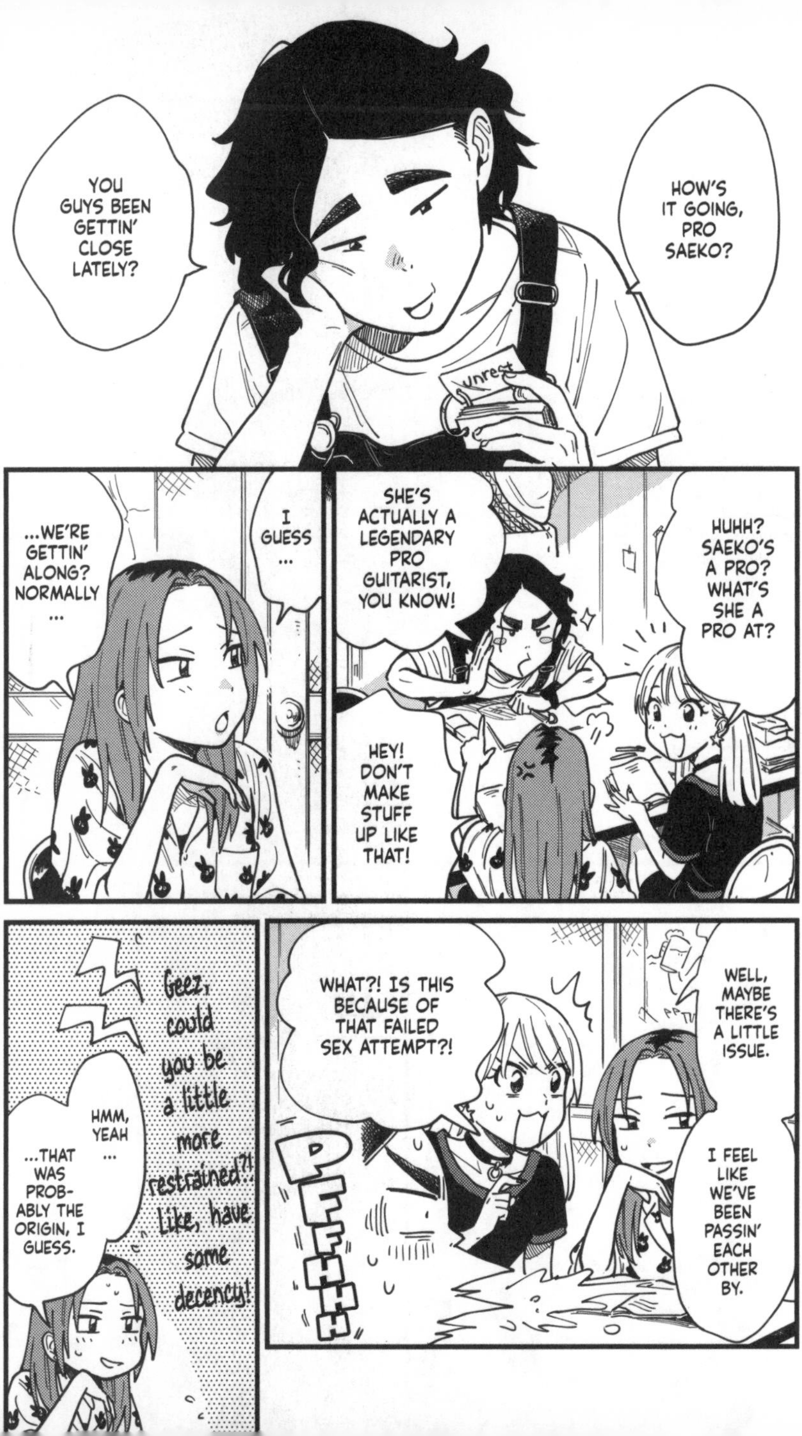
HOW'S IT GOING, PRO SAEKO?
YOU GUYS BEEN GETTIN' CLOSE LATELY?
Unrest
HUHH? SAEKO'S A PRO? WHAT'S SHE A PRO AT?
SHE'S ACTUALLY A LEGENDARY PRO GUITARIST, YOU KNOW!
HEY! DON'T MAKE STUFF UP LIKE THAT!
I GUESS ...
...WE'RE GETTIN' ALONG? NORMALLY ...
WELL, MAYBE THERE'S A LITTLE ISSUE.
I FEEL LIKE WE'VE BEEN PASSIN' EACH OTHER BY.
WHAT?! IS THIS BECAUSE OF THAT FAILED SEX ATTEMPT?!
PFFHHHH
Geez, could you be a little more restrained?!.. Like, have some decency!
HMM, YEAH ...
...THAT WAS PROBABLY THE ORIGIN, I GUESS.

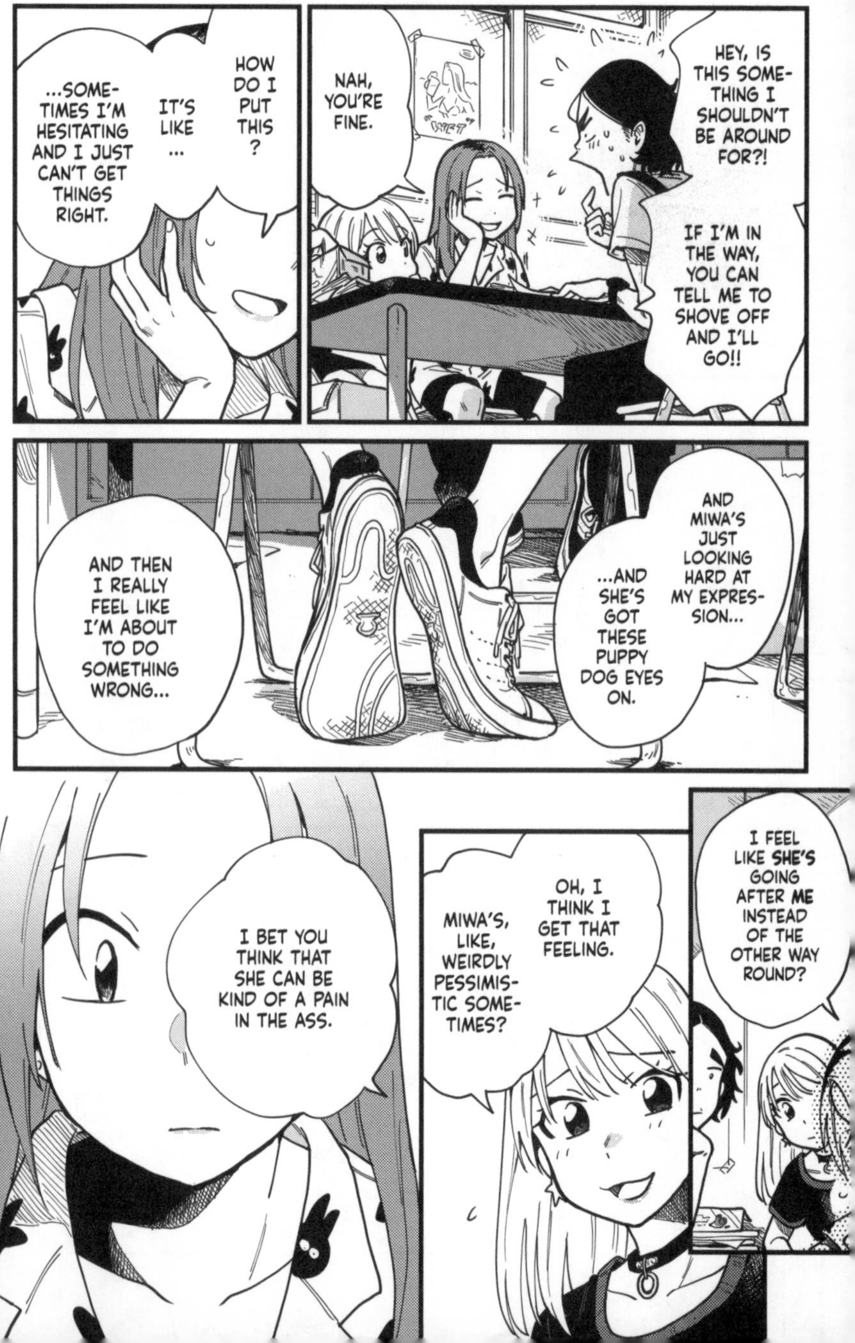
HEY, IS THIS SOMETHING I SHOULDN'T BE AROUND FOR?!
IF I'M IN THE WAY, YOU CAN TELL ME TO SHOVE OFF AND I'LL GO!!
NAH, YOU'RE FINE.
HOW DO I PUT THIS?
IT'S LIKE...
...SOMETIMES I'M HESITATING AND I JUST CAN'T GET THINGS RIGHT.
AND MIWA'S JUST LOOKING HARD AT MY EXPRESSION...
...AND SHE'S GOT THESE PUPPY DOG EYES ON.
AND THEN I REALLY FEEL LIKE I'M ABOUT TO DO SOMETHING WRONG...
I FEEL LIKE **SHE'S** GOING AFTER **ME** INSTEAD OF THE OTHER WAY ROUND?
OH, I THINK I GET THAT FEELING.
MIWA'S, LIKE, WEIRDLY PESSIMISTIC SOMETIMES?
I BET YOU THINK THAT SHE CAN BE KIND OF A PAIN IN THE ASS.

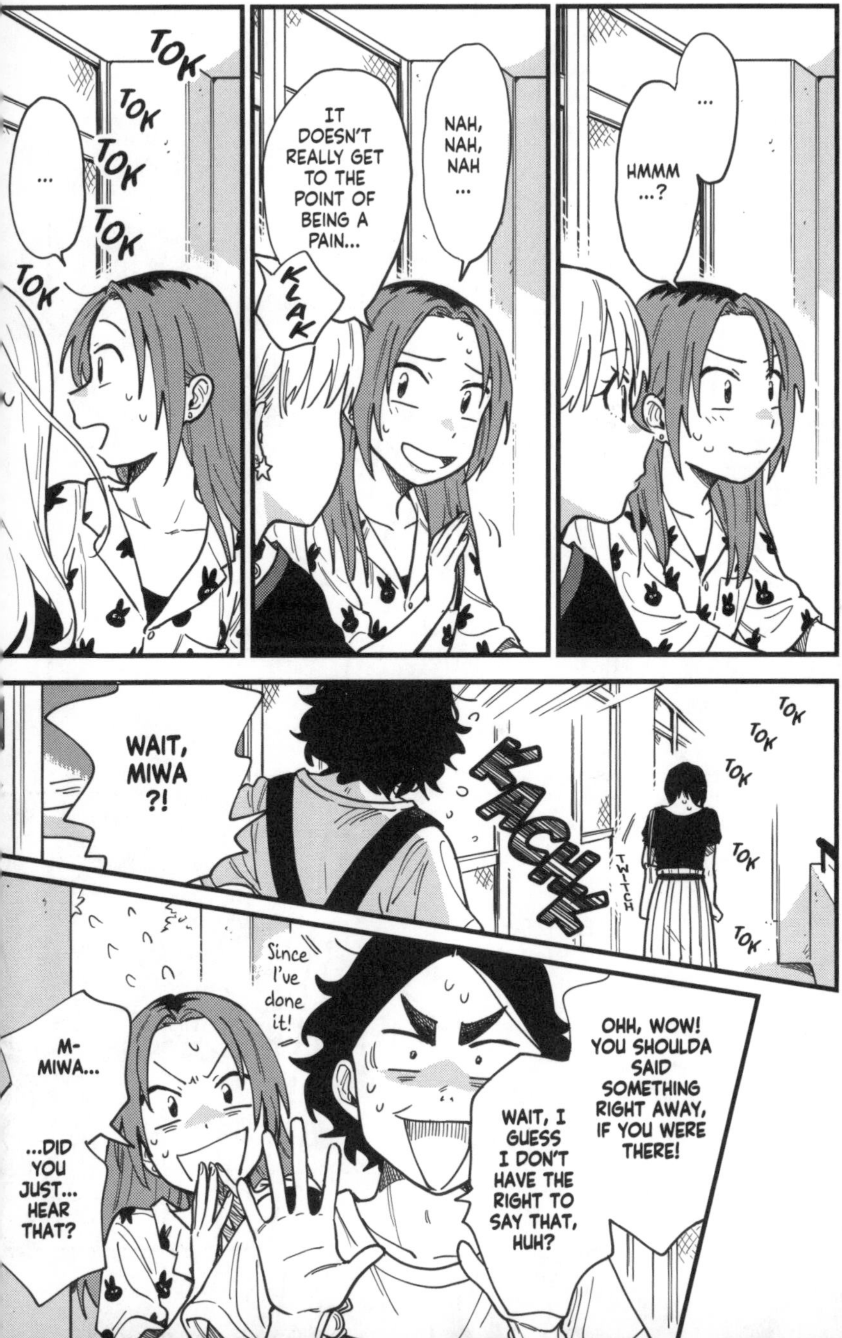
...
HMMM ...?
NAH, NAH, NAH ...
IT DOESN'T REALLY GET TO THE POINT OF BEING A PAIN...
KLAK
TOK
TOK
TOK
TOK
TOK
...
TOK
TOK
TOK
TOK
TOK
KACHK
TWITCH
WAIT, MIWA ?!
OHH, WOW! YOU SHOULDA SAID SOMETHING RIGHT AWAY, IF YOU WERE THERE!
WAIT, I GUESS I DON'T HAVE THE RIGHT TO SAY THAT, HUH?
Since I've done it!
M-MIWA...
...DID YOU JUST... HEAR THAT?

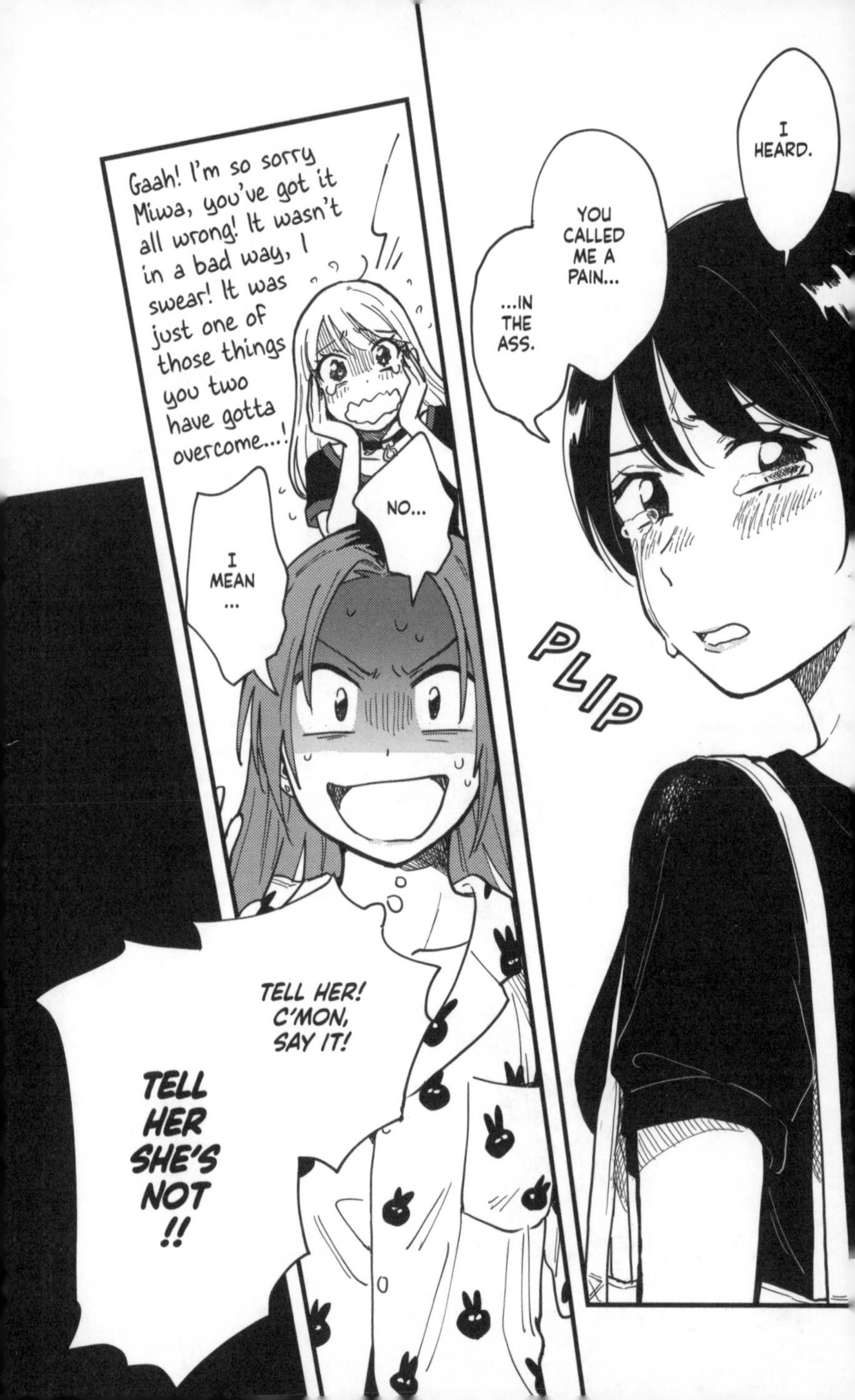
I HEARD.
YOU CALLED ME A PAIN...
...IN THE ASS.
PLIP
Gaah! I'm so sorry Miwa, you've got it all wrong! It wasn't in a bad way, I swear! It was just one of those things you two have gotta overcome...!
NO...
I MEAN ...
TELL HER! C'MON, SAY IT!
TELL HER SHE'S NOT !!

HOW DO WE RELATIONSHIP?

How Do We
Relationship?

Chapter 8: A Pain in the Ass

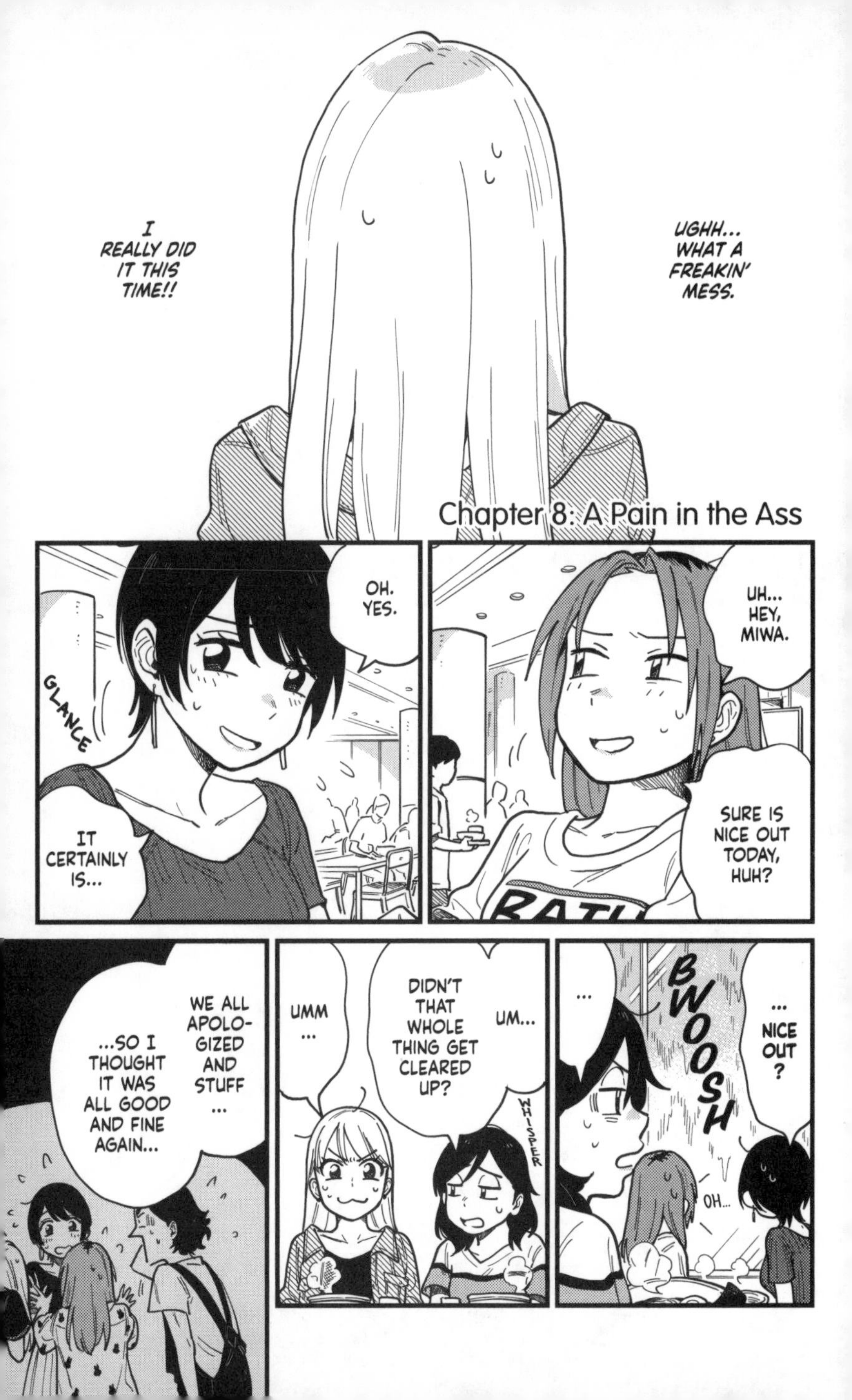
UGHH... WHAT A FREAKIN' MESS.
I REALLY DID IT THIS TIME!!
UH... HEY, MIWA.
SURE IS NICE OUT TODAY, HUH?
OH. YES.
GLANCE
IT CERTAINLY IS...
... NICE OUT?
BWOOSH
...
OH...
UM...
DIDN'T THAT WHOLE THING GET CLEARED UP?
WHISPER
UMM ...
WE ALL APOLO-GIZED AND STUFF ...
...SO I THOUGHT IT WAS ALL GOOD AND FINE AGAIN...

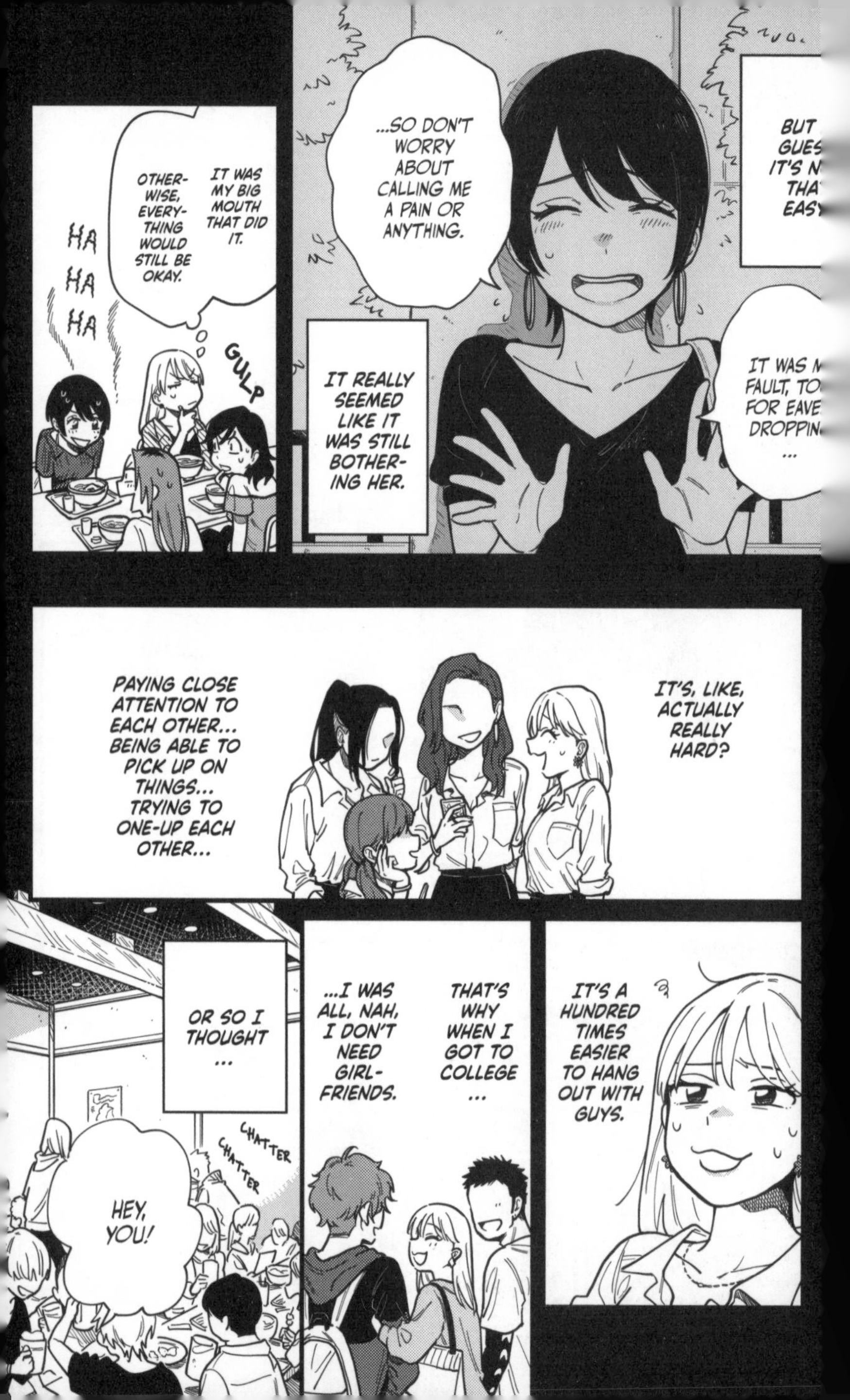
BUT GUES IT'S N THA EAS
IT WAS M FAULT, TO FOR EAVE DROPPIN ...
...SO DON'T WORRY ABOUT CALLING ME A PAIN OR ANYTHING.
IT REALLY SEEMED LIKE IT WAS STILL BOTHERING HER.
IT WAS MY BIG MOUTH THAT DID IT.
OTHERWISE, EVERYTHING WOULD STILL BE OKAY.
HA HA HA
GULP
IT'S, LIKE, ACTUALLY REALLY HARD?
PAYING CLOSE ATTENTION TO EACH OTHER... BEING ABLE TO PICK UP ON THINGS... TRYING TO ONE-UP EACH OTHER...
IT'S A HUNDRED TIMES EASIER TO HANG OUT WITH GUYS.
THAT'S WHY WHEN I GOT TO COLLEGE...
...I WAS ALL, NAH, I DON'T NEED GIRLFRIENDS.
OR SO I THOUGHT...
CHATTER CHATTER
HEY, YOU!

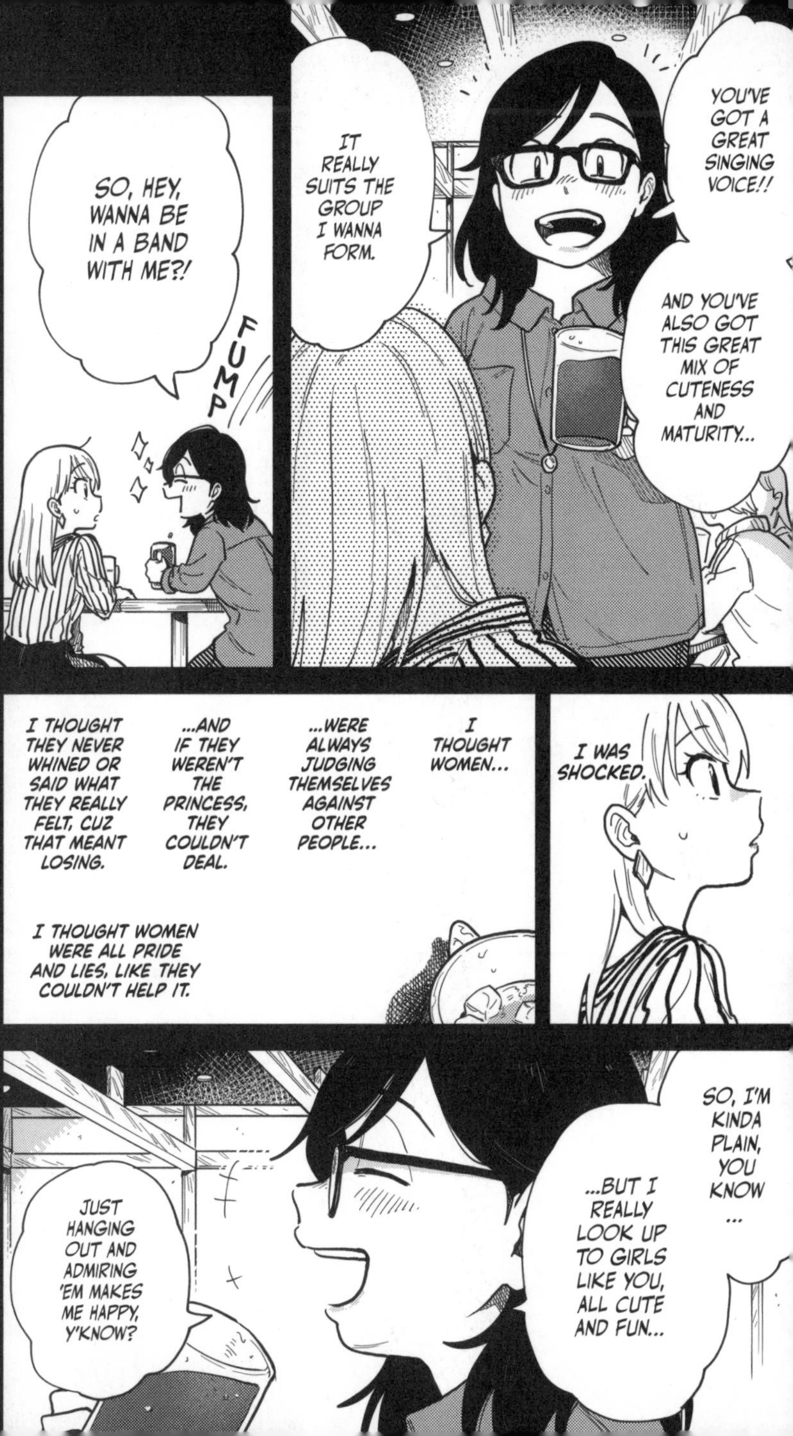
YOU'VE GOT A GREAT SINGING VOICE!!
AND YOU'VE ALSO GOT THIS GREAT MIX OF CUTENESS AND MATURITY...
IT REALLY SUITS THE GROUP I WANNA FORM.
FUMP
SO, HEY, WANNA BE IN A BAND WITH ME?!
I WAS SHOCKED.
I THOUGHT WOMEN...
...WERE ALWAYS JUDGING THEMSELVES AGAINST OTHER PEOPLE...
...AND IF THEY WEREN'T THE PRINCESS, THEY COULDN'T DEAL.
I THOUGHT THEY NEVER WHINED OR SAID WHAT THEY REALLY FELT, CUZ THAT MEANT LOSING.
I THOUGHT WOMEN WERE ALL PRIDE AND LIES, LIKE THEY COULDN'T HELP IT.
SO, I'M KINDA PLAIN, YOU KNOW...
...BUT I REALLY LOOK UP TO GIRLS LIKE YOU, ALL CUTE AND FUN...
JUST HANGING OUT AND ADMIRING 'EM MAKES ME HAPPY, Y'KNOW?

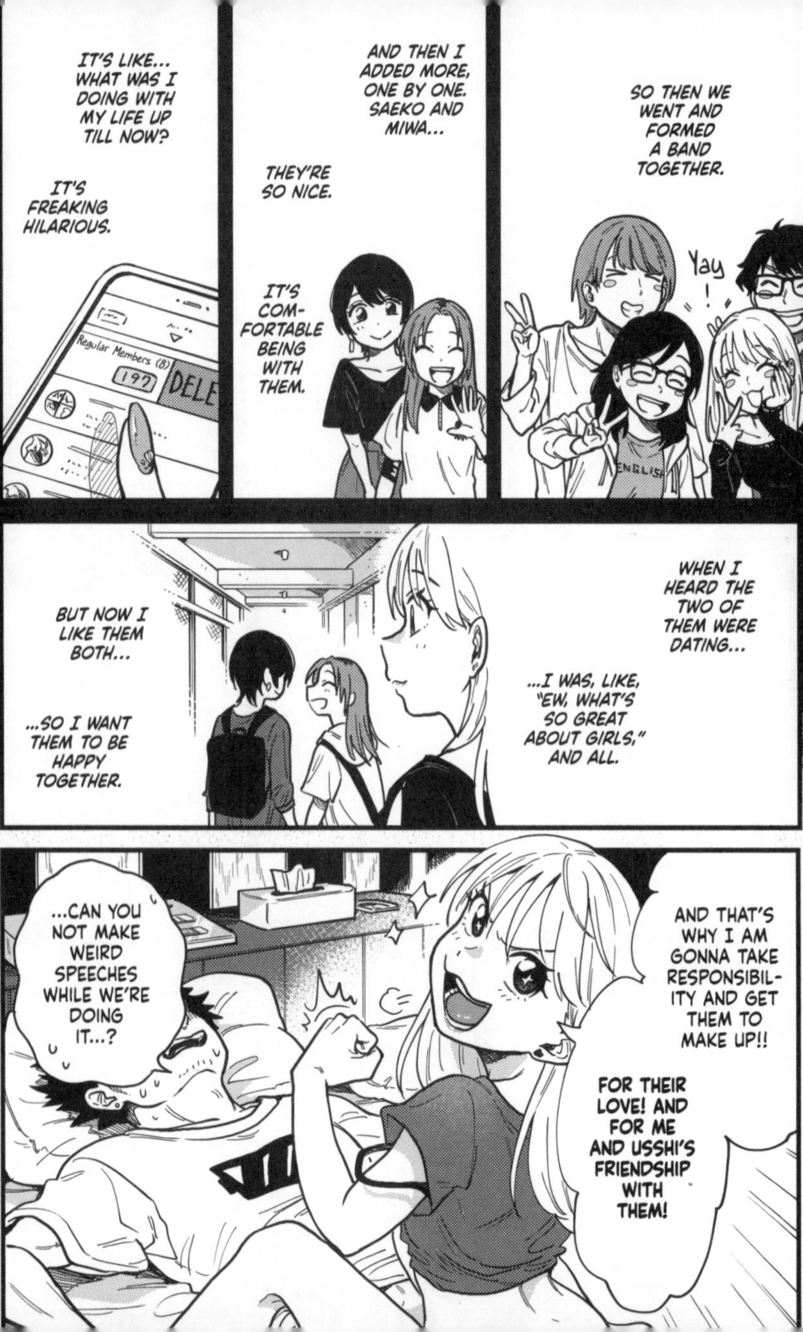
SO THEN WE WENT AND FORMED A BAND TOGETHER.
Yay!
AND THEN I ADDED MORE, ONE BY ONE. SAEKO AND MIWA...
THEY'RE SO NICE.
IT'S COM-FORTABLE BEING WITH THEM.
IT'S LIKE... WHAT WAS I DOING WITH MY LIFE UP TILL NOW?
IT'S FREAKING HILARIOUS.
Regular Members (8)
197
DELE
WHEN I HEARD THE TWO OF THEM WERE DATING...
...I WAS, LIKE, "EW, WHAT'S SO GREAT ABOUT GIRLS," AND ALL.
BUT NOW I LIKE THEM BOTH...
...SO I WANT THEM TO BE HAPPY TOGETHER.
AND THAT'S WHY I AM GONNA TAKE RESPONSIBIL-ITY AND GET THEM TO MAKE UP!!
FOR THEIR LOVE! AND FOR ME AND USSHI'S FRIENDSHIP WITH THEM!
...CAN YOU NOT MAKE WEIRD SPEECHES WHILE WE'RE DOING IT...?

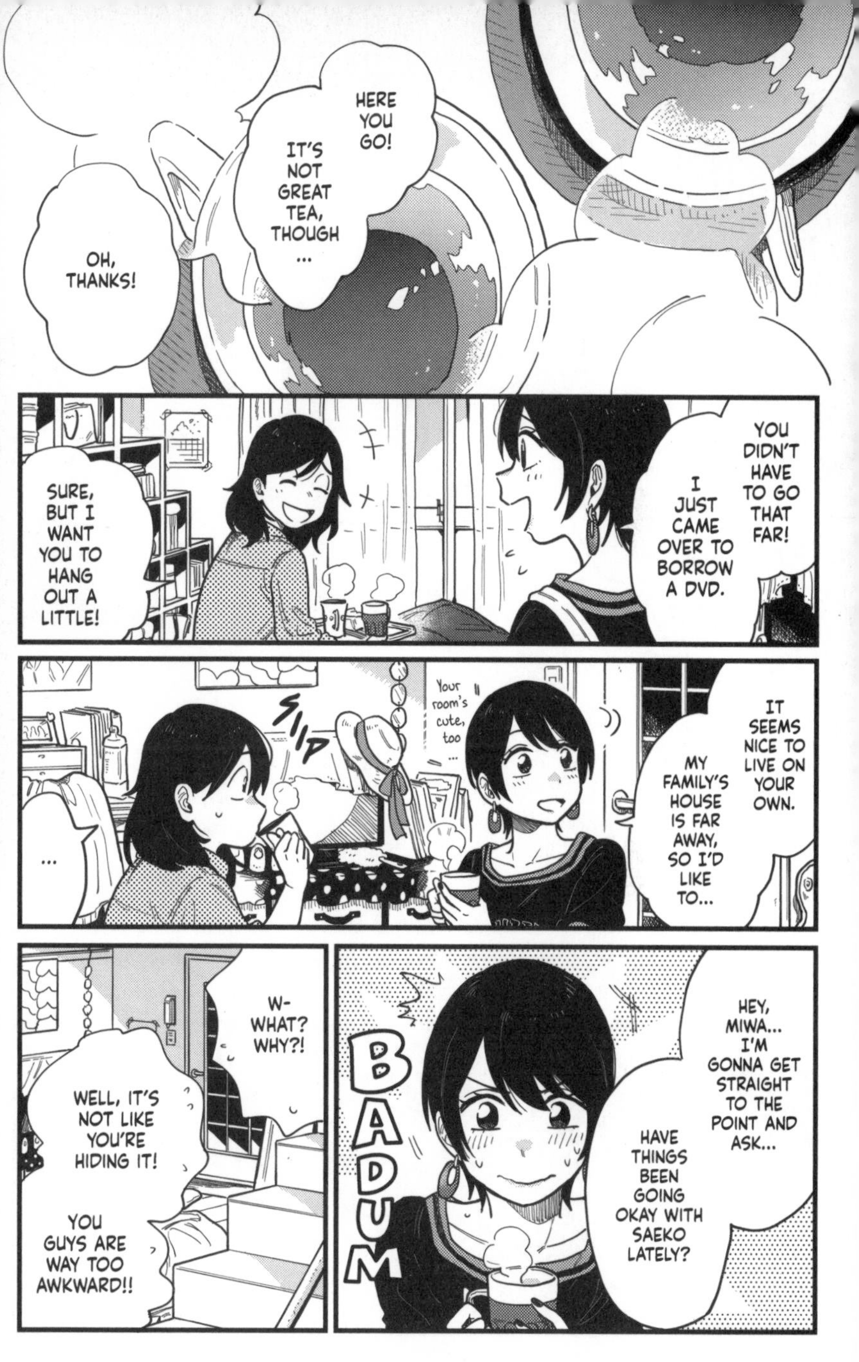
HERE YOU GO!
IT'S NOT GREAT TEA, THOUGH ...
OH, THANKS!
YOU DIDN'T HAVE TO GO THAT FAR!
I JUST CAME OVER TO BORROW A DVD.
SURE, BUT I WANT YOU TO HANG OUT A LITTLE!
IT SEEMS NICE TO LIVE ON YOUR OWN.
MY FAMILY'S HOUSE IS FAR AWAY, SO I'D LIKE TO...
Your room's cute, too ...
SIIP
...
HEY, MIWA... I'M GONNA GET STRAIGHT TO THE POINT AND ASK...
HAVE THINGS BEEN GOING OKAY WITH SAEKO LATELY?
BADUM
W-WHAT? WHY?!
WELL, IT'S NOT LIKE YOU'RE HIDING IT!
YOU GUYS ARE WAY TOO AWKWARD!!

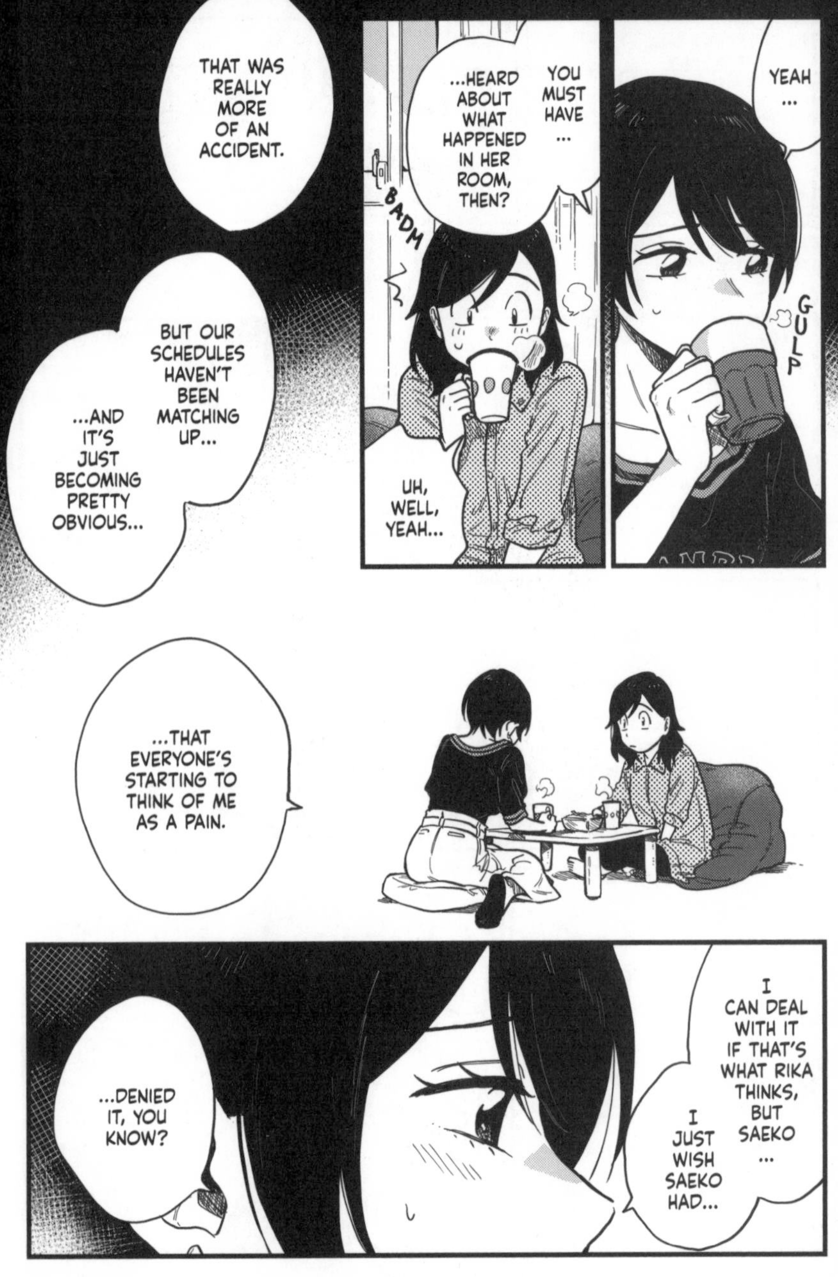
YEAH ...
GULP
YOU MUST HAVE ...
...HEARD ABOUT WHAT HAPPENED IN HER ROOM, THEN?
BADM
UH, WELL, YEAH...
THAT WAS REALLY MORE OF AN ACCIDENT.
BUT OUR SCHEDULES HAVEN'T BEEN MATCHING UP...
...AND IT'S JUST BECOMING PRETTY OBVIOUS...
...THAT EVERYONE'S STARTING TO THINK OF ME AS A PAIN.
I CAN DEAL WITH IT IF THAT'S WHAT RIKA THINKS, BUT SAEKO ...
I JUST WISH SAEKO HAD...
...DENIED IT, YOU KNOW?

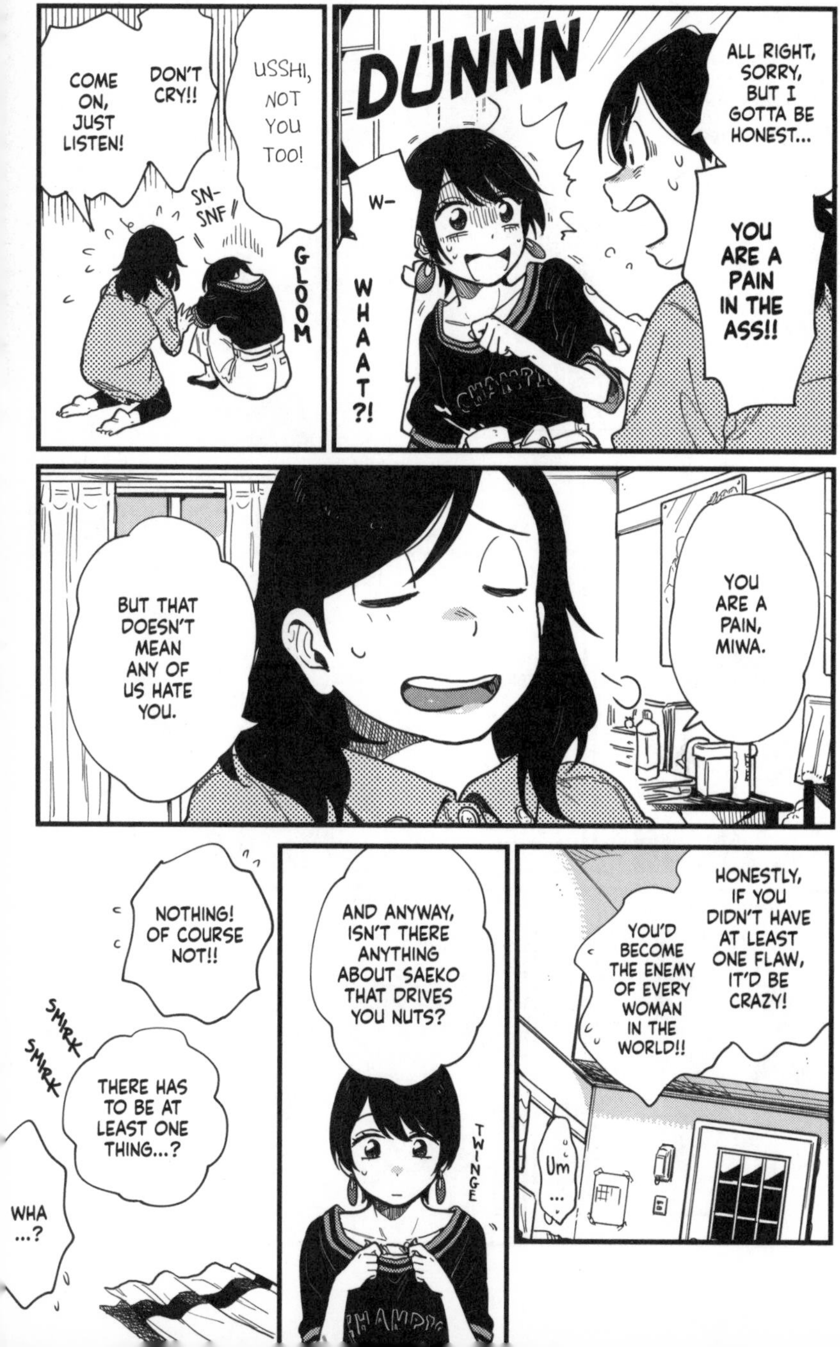

ALL RIGHT, SORRY, BUT I GOTTA BE HONEST...
YOU ARE A PAIN IN THE ASS!!
DUNNN
W-
WHAAAT?!
USSHI, NOT YOU TOO!
DON'T CRY!!
COME ON, JUST LISTEN!
SN-SNF
GLOOM
YOU ARE A PAIN, MIWA.
BUT THAT DOESN'T MEAN ANY OF US HATE YOU.
HONESTLY, IF YOU DIDN'T HAVE AT LEAST ONE FLAW, IT'D BE CRAZY!
YOU'D BECOME THE ENEMY OF EVERY WOMAN IN THE WORLD!!
Um ...
AND ANYWAY, ISN'T THERE ANYTHING ABOUT SAEKO THAT DRIVES YOU NUTS?
TWINGE
NOTHING! OF COURSE NOT!!
SMIRK SMIRK
THERE HAS TO BE AT LEAST ONE THING...?
WHA ...?

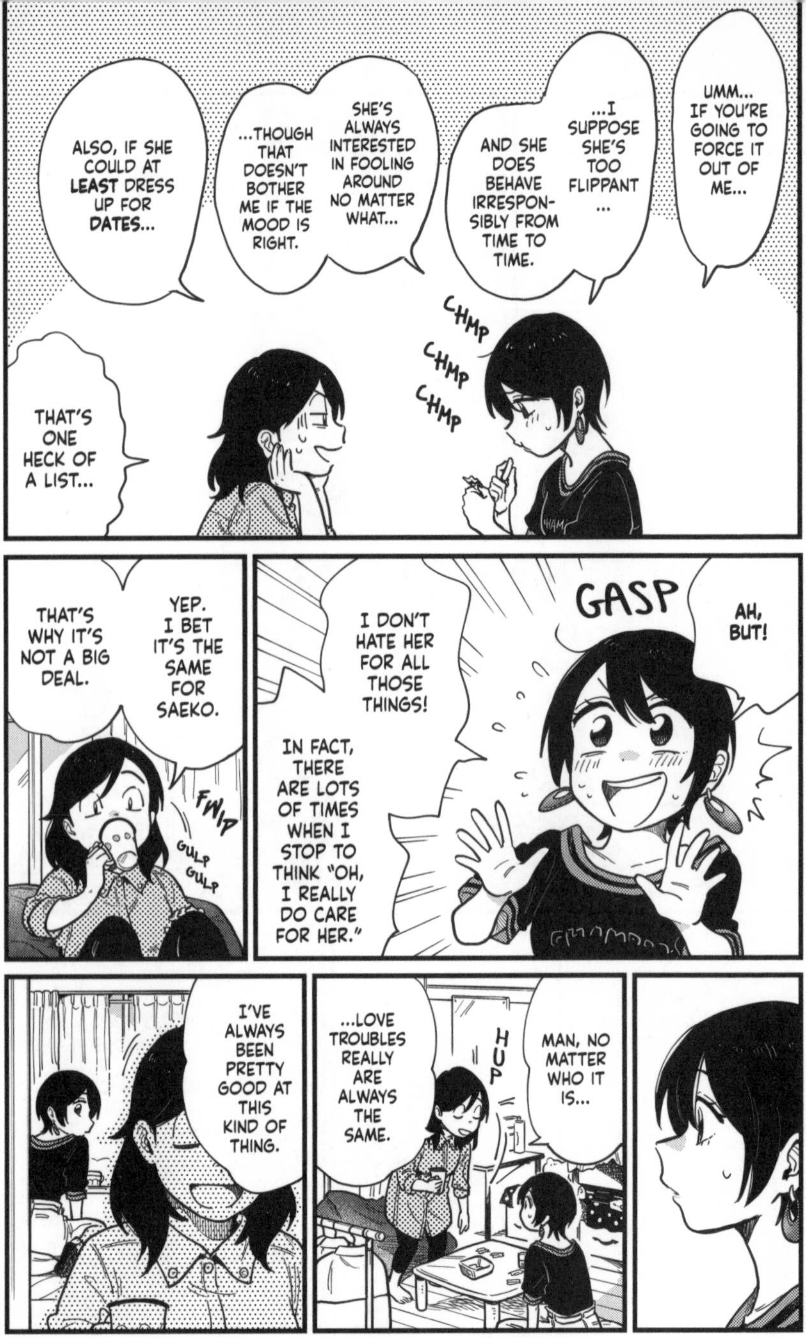
UMM... IF YOU'RE GOING TO FORCE IT OUT OF ME...
...I SUPPOSE SHE'S TOO FLIPPANT ...
AND SHE DOES BEHAVE IRRESPONSIBLY FROM TIME TO TIME.
SHE'S ALWAYS INTERESTED IN FOOLING AROUND NO MATTER WHAT...
...THOUGH THAT DOESN'T BOTHER ME IF THE MOOD IS RIGHT.
ALSO, IF SHE COULD AT **LEAST** DRESS UP FOR **DATES**...
CHMP
CHMP
CHMP
THAT'S ONE HECK OF A LIST...
GASP
AH, BUT!
I DON'T HATE HER FOR ALL THOSE THINGS!
IN FACT, THERE ARE LOTS OF TIMES WHEN I STOP TO THINK "OH, I REALLY DO CARE FOR HER."
YEP. I BET IT'S THE SAME FOR SAEKO.
THAT'S WHY IT'S NOT A BIG DEAL.
FWIP
GULP GULP
MAN, NO MATTER WHO IT IS...
HUP
...LOVE TROUBLES REALLY ARE ALWAYS THE SAME.
I'VE ALWAYS BEEN PRETTY GOOD AT THIS KIND OF THING.

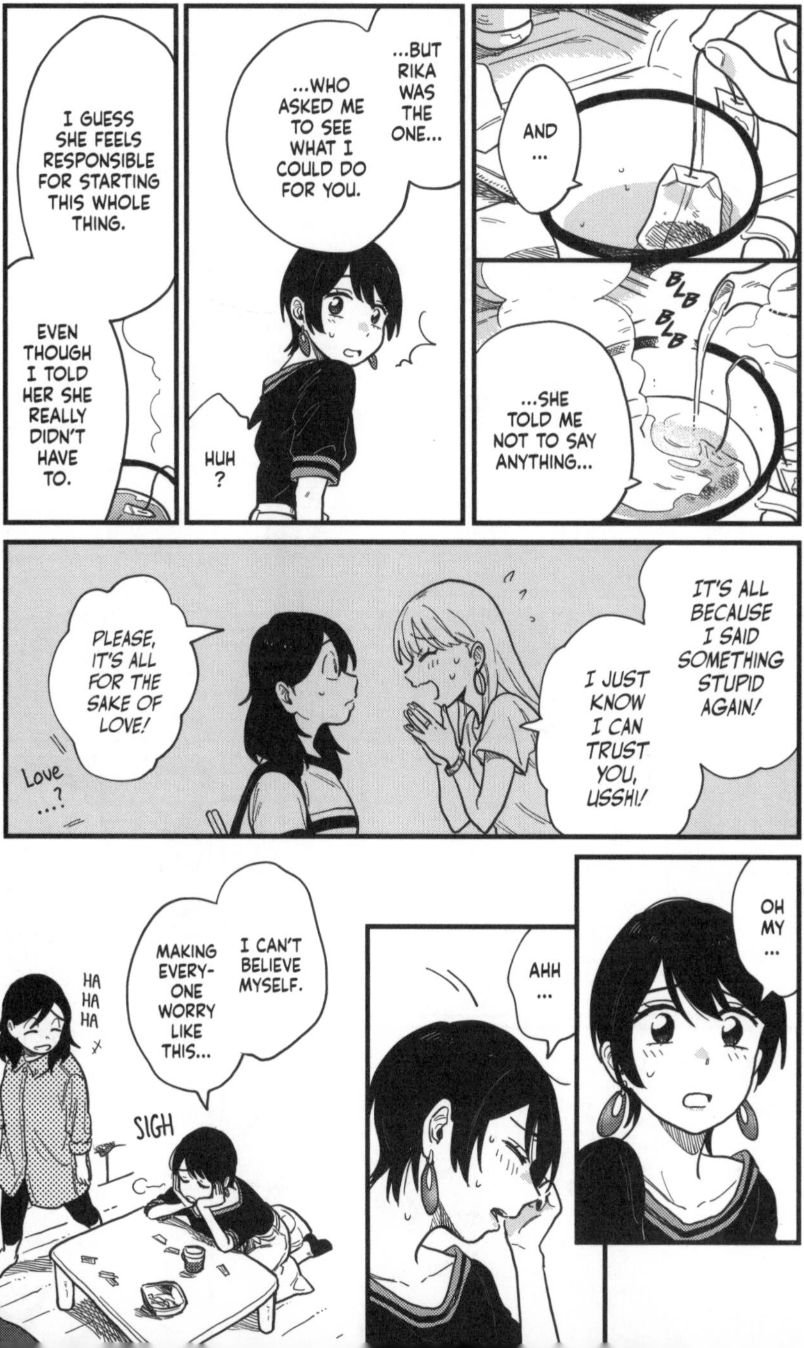
AND ...
BLB BLB
...SHE TOLD ME NOT TO SAY ANYTHING...
...BUT RIKA WAS THE ONE...
...WHO ASKED ME TO SEE WHAT I COULD DO FOR YOU.
HUH?
I GUESS SHE FEELS RESPONSIBLE FOR STARTING THIS WHOLE THING.
EVEN THOUGH I TOLD HER SHE REALLY DIDN'T HAVE TO.
IT'S ALL BECAUSE I SAID SOMETHING STUPID AGAIN!
I JUST KNOW I CAN TRUST YOU, USSHI!
PLEASE, IT'S ALL FOR THE SAKE OF LOVE!
Love ...?
OH MY ...
AHH ...
I CAN'T BELIEVE MYSELF.
MAKING EVERY-ONE WORRY LIKE THIS...
SIGH
HA HA HA

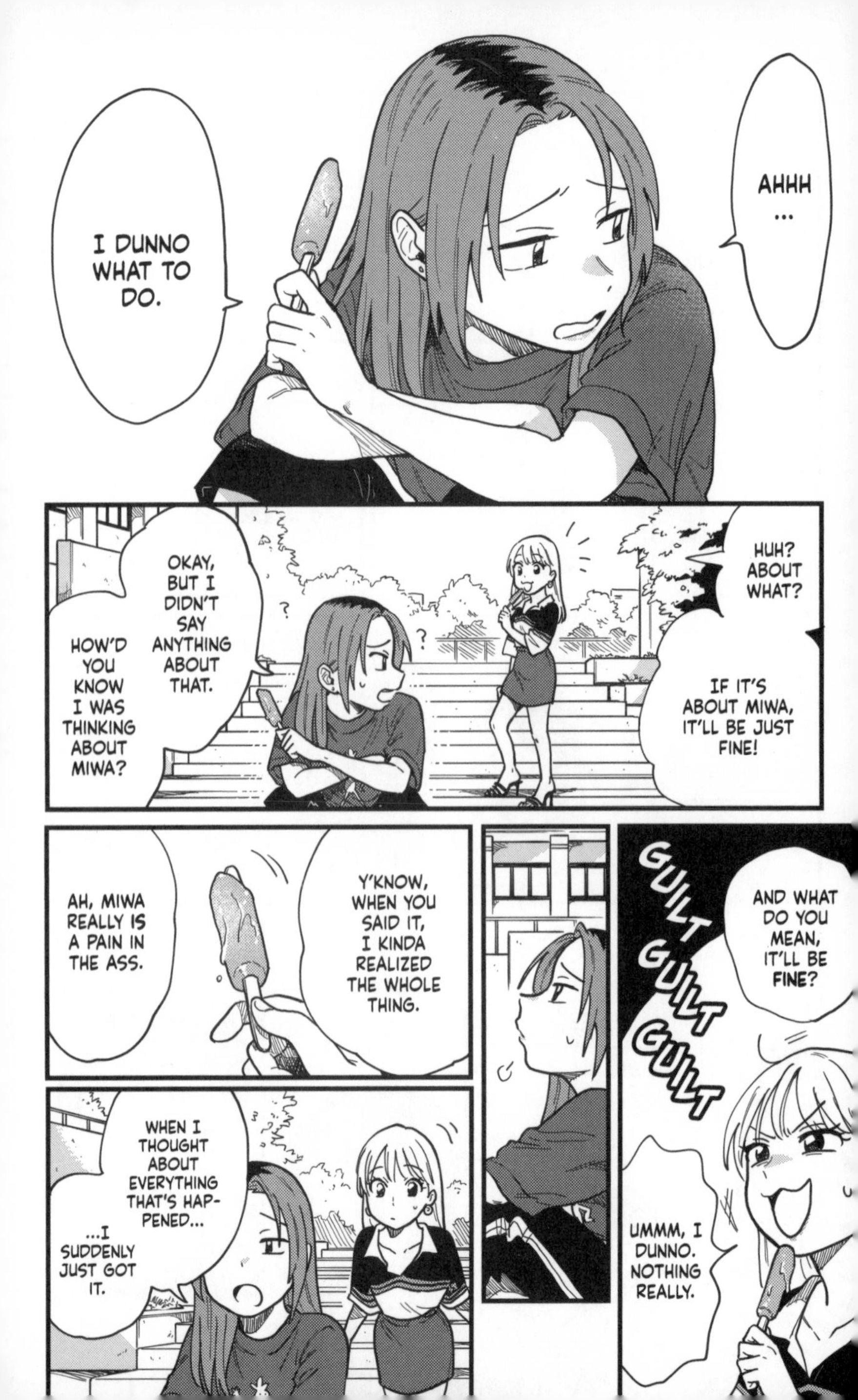
AHHH ...
I DUNNO WHAT TO DO.
HUH? ABOUT WHAT?
IF IT'S ABOUT MIWA, IT'LL BE JUST FINE!
OKAY, BUT I DIDN'T SAY ANYTHING ABOUT THAT.
HOW'D YOU KNOW I WAS THINKING ABOUT MIWA?
AND WHAT DO YOU MEAN, IT'LL BE FINE?
GUILT GUILT GUILT
UMMM, I DUNNO. NOTHING REALLY.
Y'KNOW, WHEN YOU SAID IT, I KINDA REALIZED THE WHOLE THING.
AH, MIWA REALLY IS A PAIN IN THE ASS.
WHEN I THOUGHT ABOUT EVERYTHING THAT'S HAP-PENED...
...I SUDDENLY JUST GOT IT.

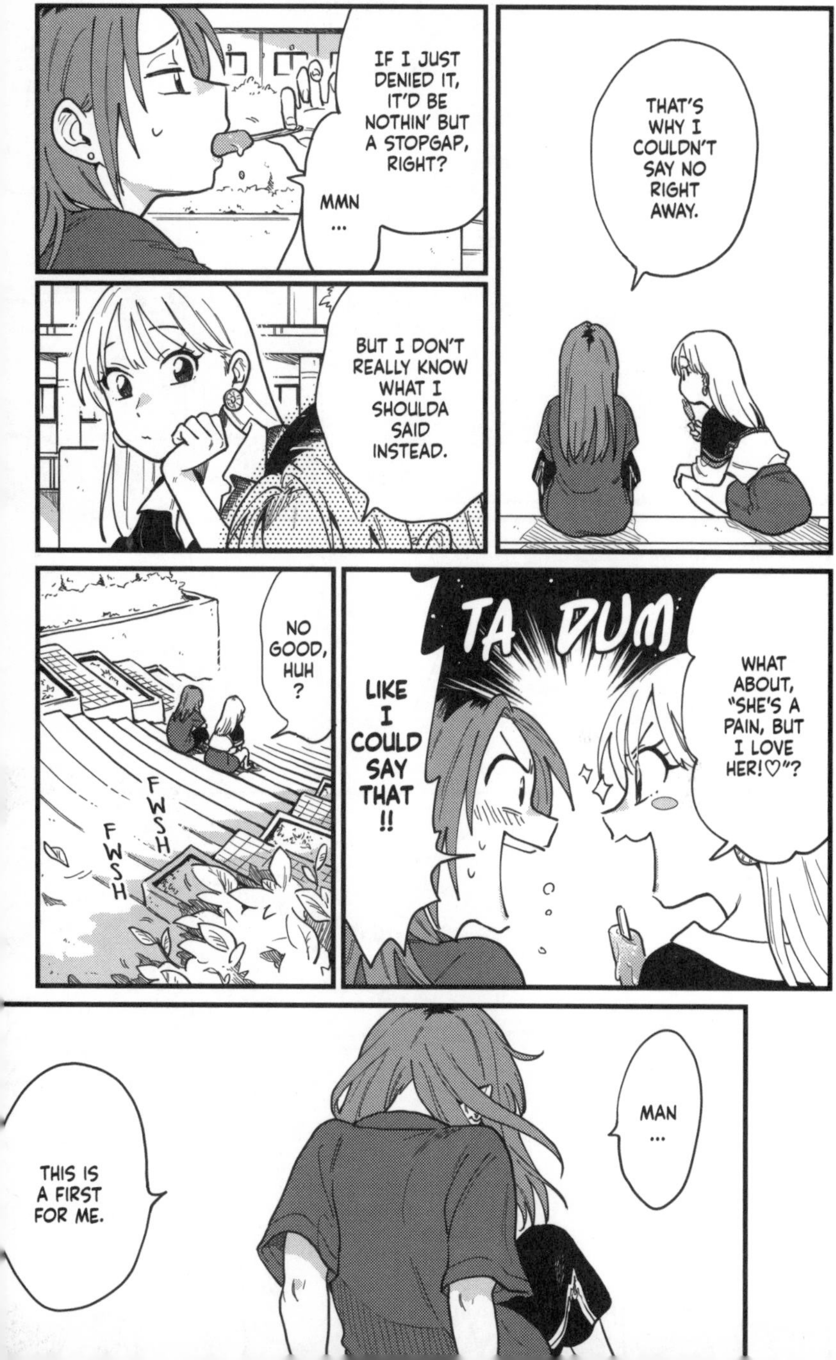
THAT'S WHY I COULDN'T SAY NO RIGHT AWAY.
IF I JUST DENIED IT, IT'D BE NOTHIN' BUT A STOPGAP, RIGHT?
MMN ...
BUT I DON'T REALLY KNOW WHAT I SHOULDA SAID INSTEAD.
TA DUM
WHAT ABOUT, "SHE'S A PAIN, BUT I LOVE HER!♡"?
LIKE I COULD SAY THAT !!
NO GOOD, HUH ?
FWSH
FWSH
MAN ...
THIS IS A FIRST FOR ME.

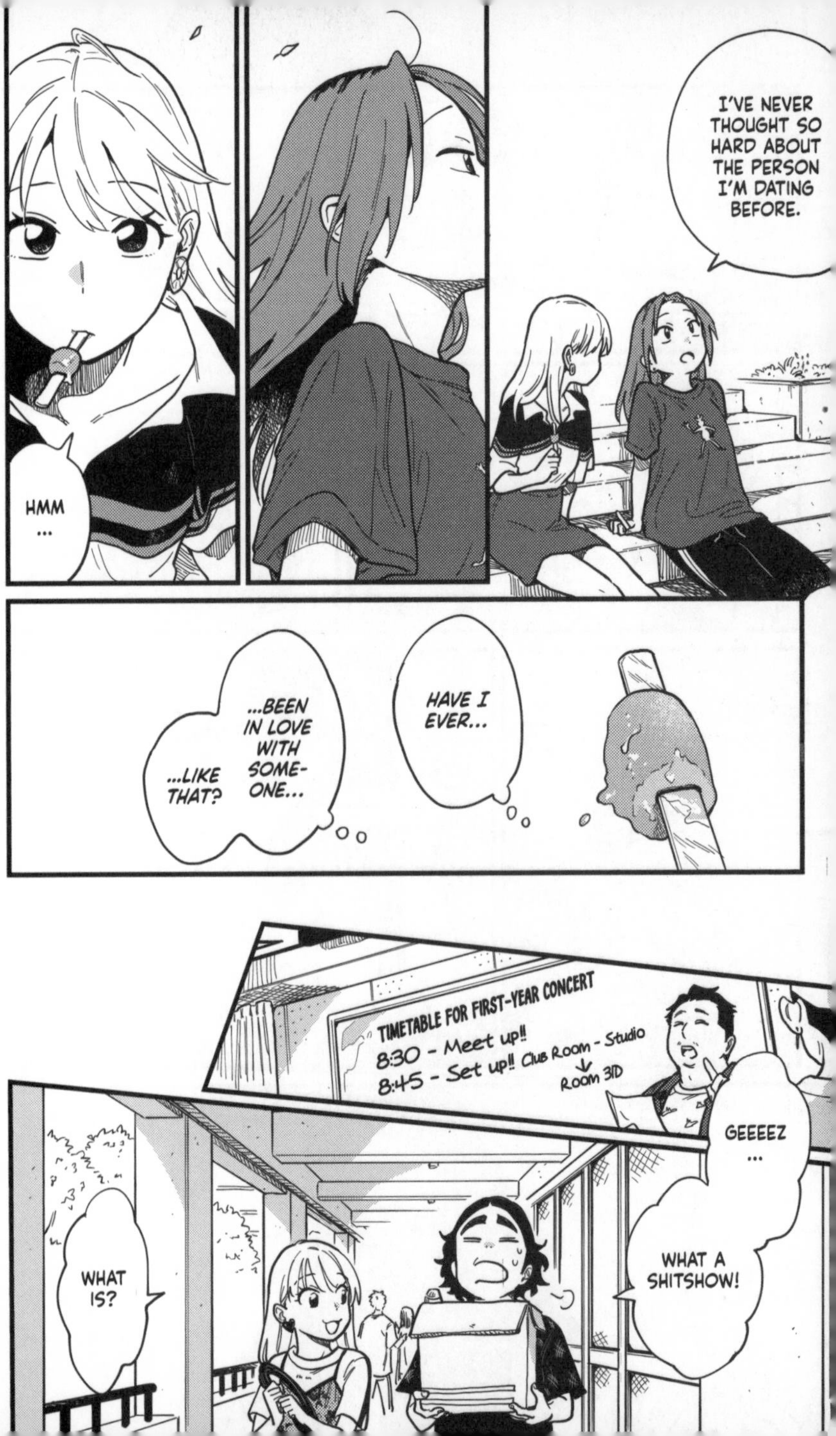
I'VE NEVER THOUGHT SO HARD ABOUT THE PERSON I'M DATING BEFORE.
HMM ...
HAVE I EVER...
...BEEN IN LOVE WITH SOMEONE...
...LIKE THAT?
TIMETABLE FOR FIRST-YEAR CONCERT
8:30 - Meet up!!
8:45 - Set up!! Club Room - Studio → Room 31D
GEEEEZ ...
WHAT A SHITSHOW!
WHAT IS?

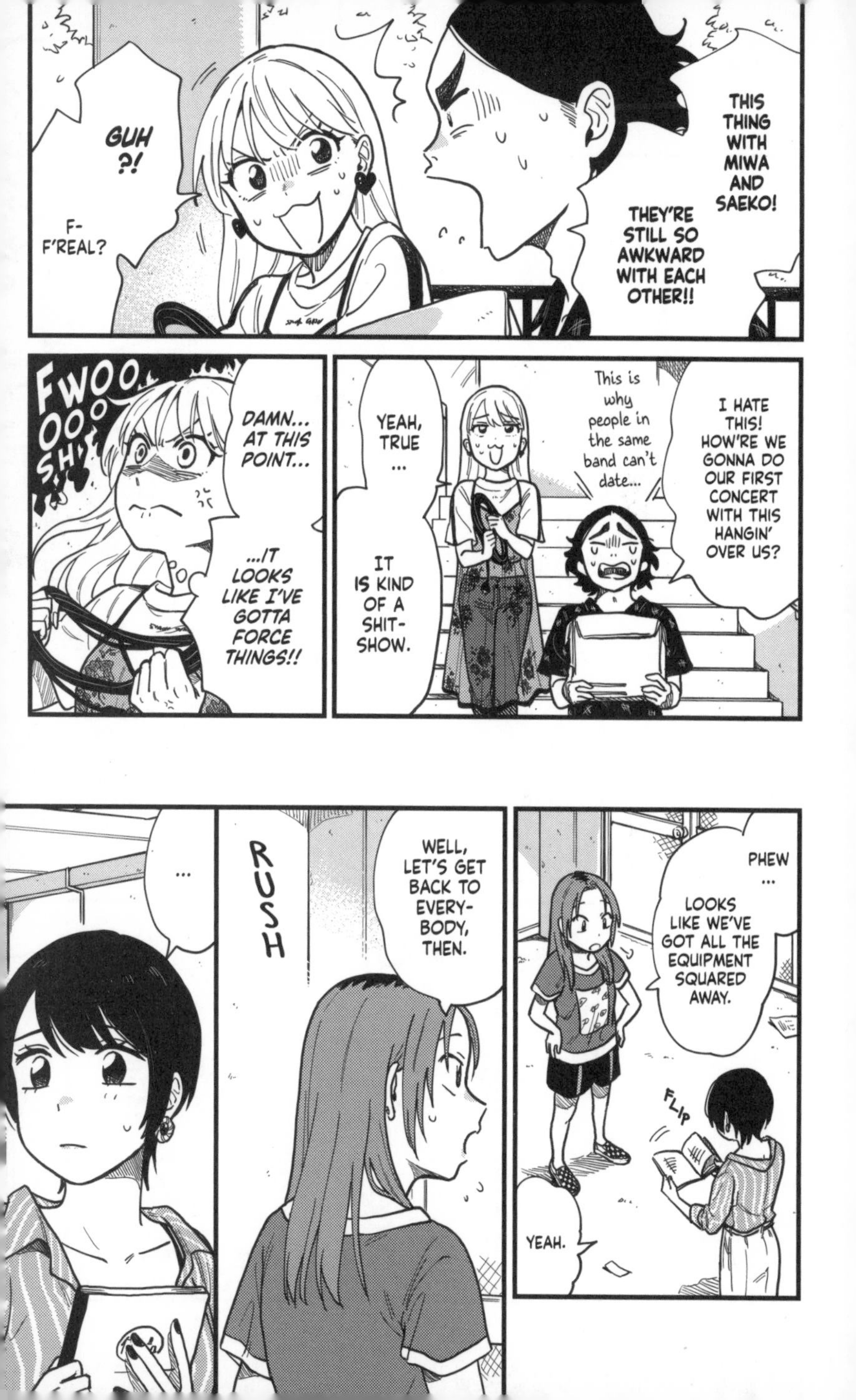
THIS THING WITH MIWA AND SAEKO!
THEY'RE STILL SO AWKWARD WITH EACH OTHER!!
GUH ?!
F- F'REAL?
I HATE THIS! HOW'RE WE GONNA DO OUR FIRST CONCERT WITH THIS HANGIN' OVER US?
This is why people in the same band can't date...
YEAH, TRUE ...
IT IS KIND OF A SHIT-SHOW.
DAMN... AT THIS POINT...
...IT LOOKS LIKE I'VE GOTTA FORCE THINGS!!
FWOOOOOSH
PHEW ...
LOOKS LIKE WE'VE GOT ALL THE EQUIPMENT SQUARED AWAY.
FLIP
YEAH.
WELL, LET'S GET BACK TO EVERYBODY, THEN.
RUSH
...

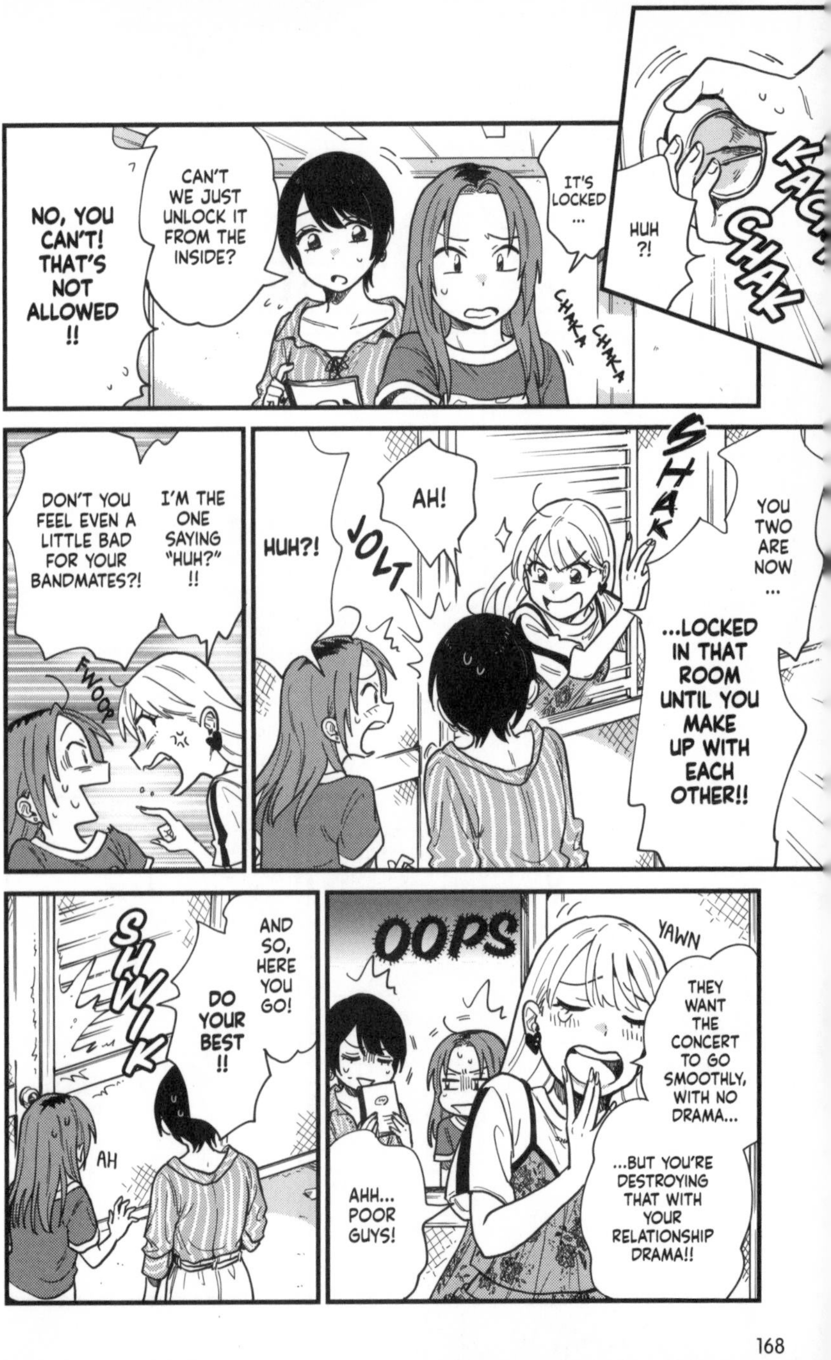
HUH ?!
KACHAK
IT'S LOCKED ...
CHAKA CHAKA
CAN'T WE JUST UNLOCK IT FROM THE INSIDE?
NO, YOU CAN'T! THAT'S NOT ALLOWED !!
SHAK
YOU TWO ARE NOW ...
...LOCKED IN THAT ROOM UNTIL YOU MAKE UP WITH EACH OTHER!!
AH!
JOLT
HUH?!
I'M THE ONE SAYING "HUH?" !!
DON'T YOU FEEL EVEN A LITTLE BAD FOR YOUR BANDMATES?!
FWOOP
OOPS
YAWN
THEY WANT THE CONCERT TO GO SMOOTHLY, WITH NO DRAMA...
...BUT YOU'RE DESTROYING THAT WITH YOUR RELATIONSHIP DRAMA!!
AHH... POOR GUYS!
AND SO, HERE YOU GO!
DO YOUR BEST !!
SHWIK
AH

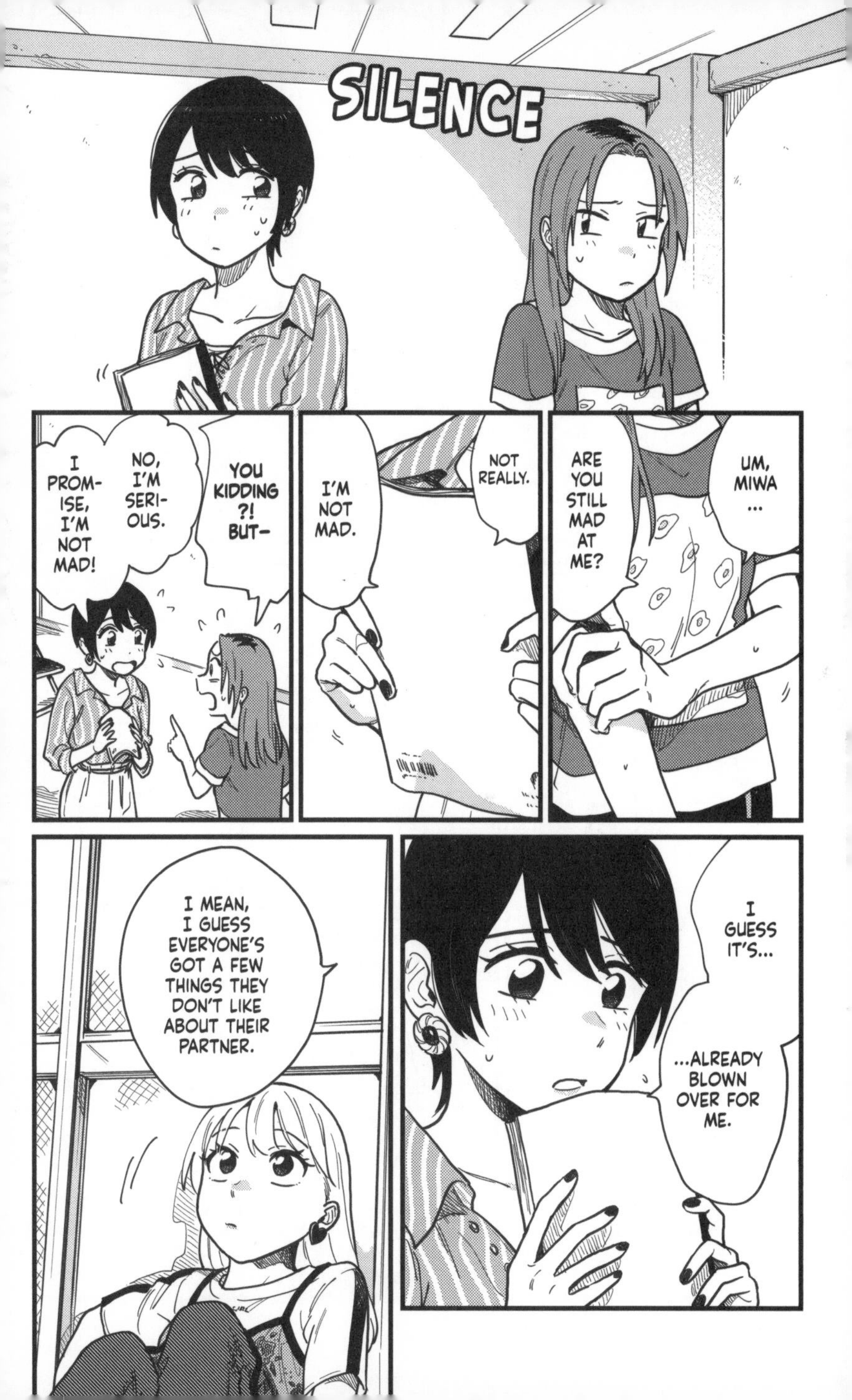
SILENCE
UM, MIWA...
ARE YOU STILL MAD AT ME?
NOT REALLY.
I'M NOT MAD.
YOU KIDDING?! BUT—
NO, I'M SERIOUS.
I PROMISE, I'M NOT MAD!
I GUESS IT'S...
...ALREADY BLOWN OVER FOR ME.
I MEAN, I GUESS EVERYONE'S GOT A FEW THINGS THEY DON'T LIKE ABOUT THEIR PARTNER.

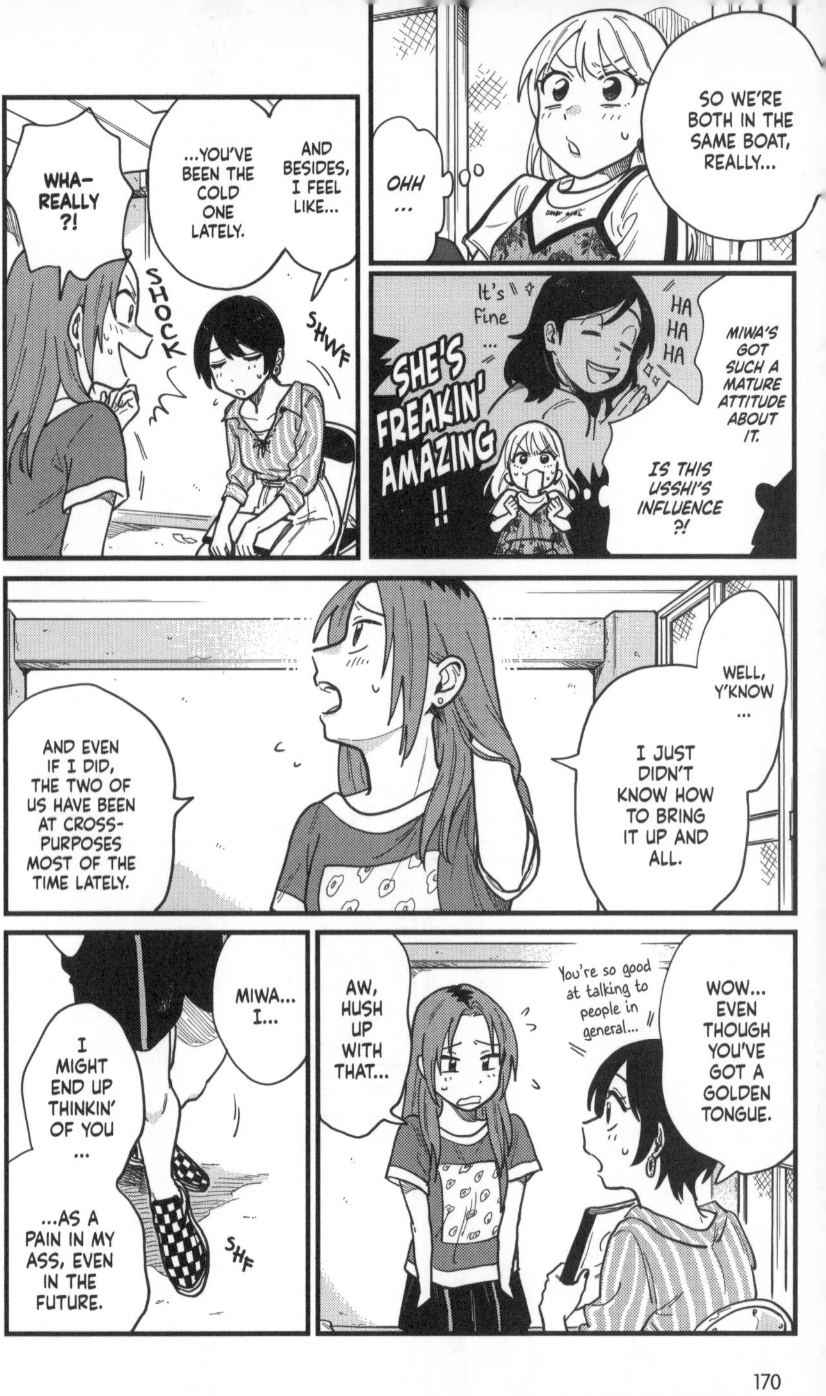
SO WE'RE BOTH IN THE SAME BOAT, REALLY...
OHH ...
HA HA HA
MIWA'S GOT SUCH A MATURE ATTITUDE ABOUT IT.
It's fine ...
SHE'S FREAKIN' AMAZING !!
IS THIS USSHI'S INFLUENCE ?!
AND BESIDES, I FEEL LIKE...
...YOU'VE BEEN THE COLD ONE LATELY.
SHWF
WHA- REALLY ?!
SHOCK
WELL, Y'KNOW ...
I JUST DIDN'T KNOW HOW TO BRING IT UP AND ALL.
AND EVEN IF I DID, THE TWO OF US HAVE BEEN AT CROSS-PURPOSES MOST OF THE TIME LATELY.
WOW... EVEN THOUGH YOU'VE GOT A GOLDEN TONGUE.
You're so good at talking to people in general...
AW, HUSH UP WITH THAT...
MIWA... I...
I MIGHT END UP THINKIN' OF YOU ...
...AS A PAIN IN MY ASS, EVEN IN THE FUTURE.
SHF

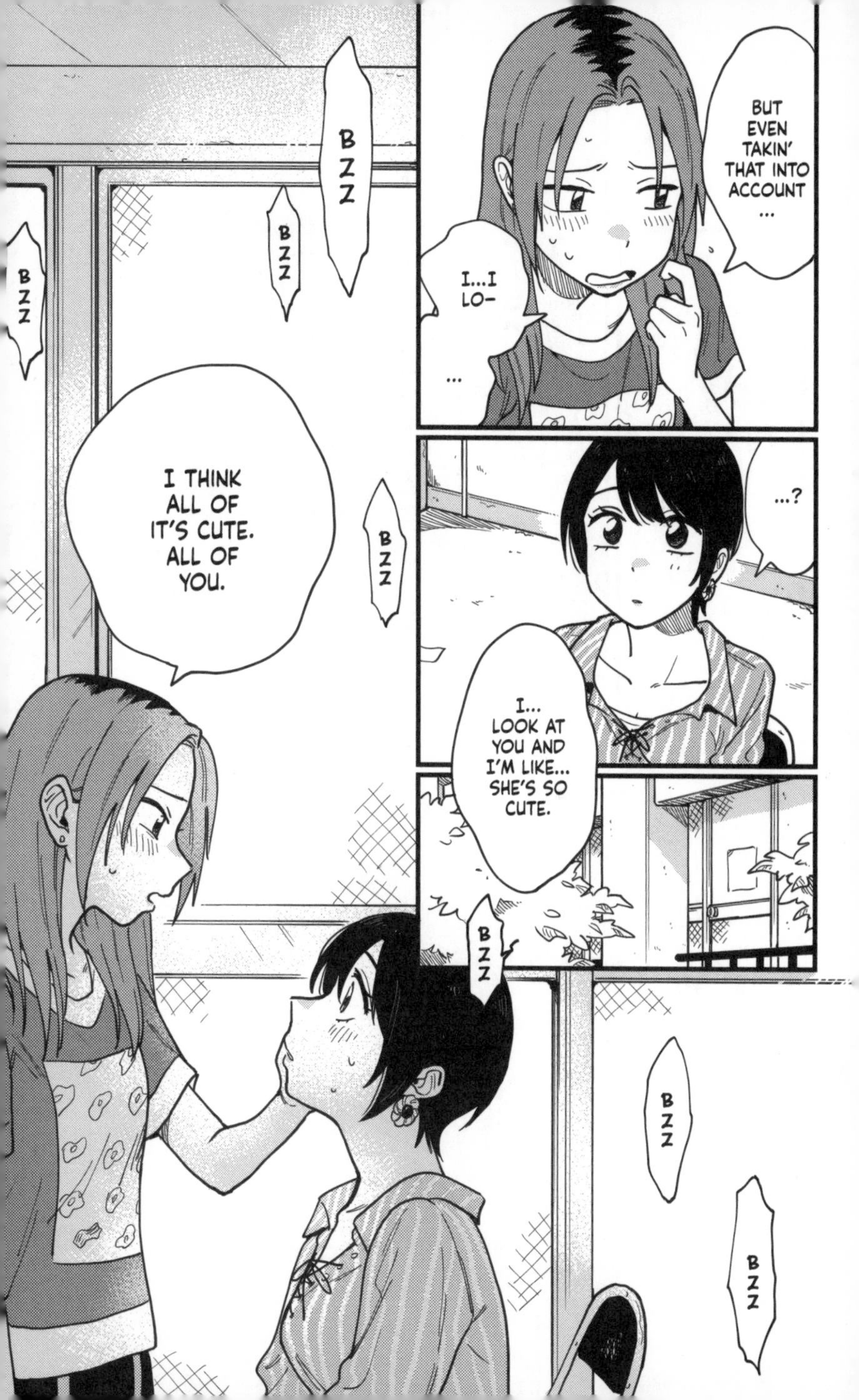
BUT EVEN TAKIN' THAT INTO ACCOUNT...
I...I LO-
...
...?
I... LOOK AT YOU AND I'M LIKE... SHE'S SO CUTE.
BZZ
BZZ
BZZ
BZZ
I THINK ALL OF IT'S CUTE. ALL OF YOU.
BZZ
BZZ
BZZ

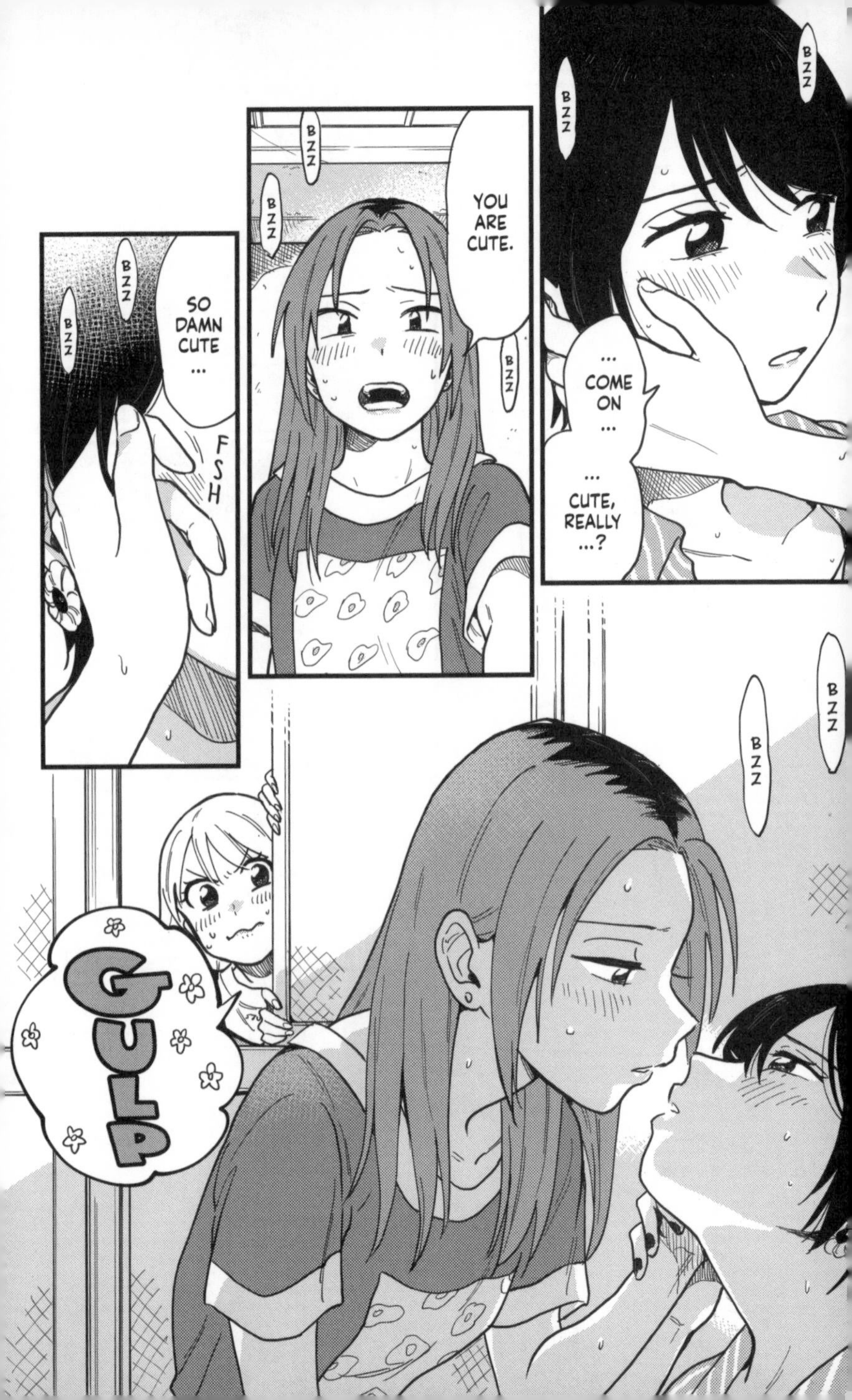
BZZ
BZZ
... COME ON ...
... CUTE, REALLY ...?
BZZ
BZZ
YOU ARE CUTE.
BZZ
BZZ
BZZ
SO DAMN CUTE ...
FSH
BZZ
BZZ
GULP

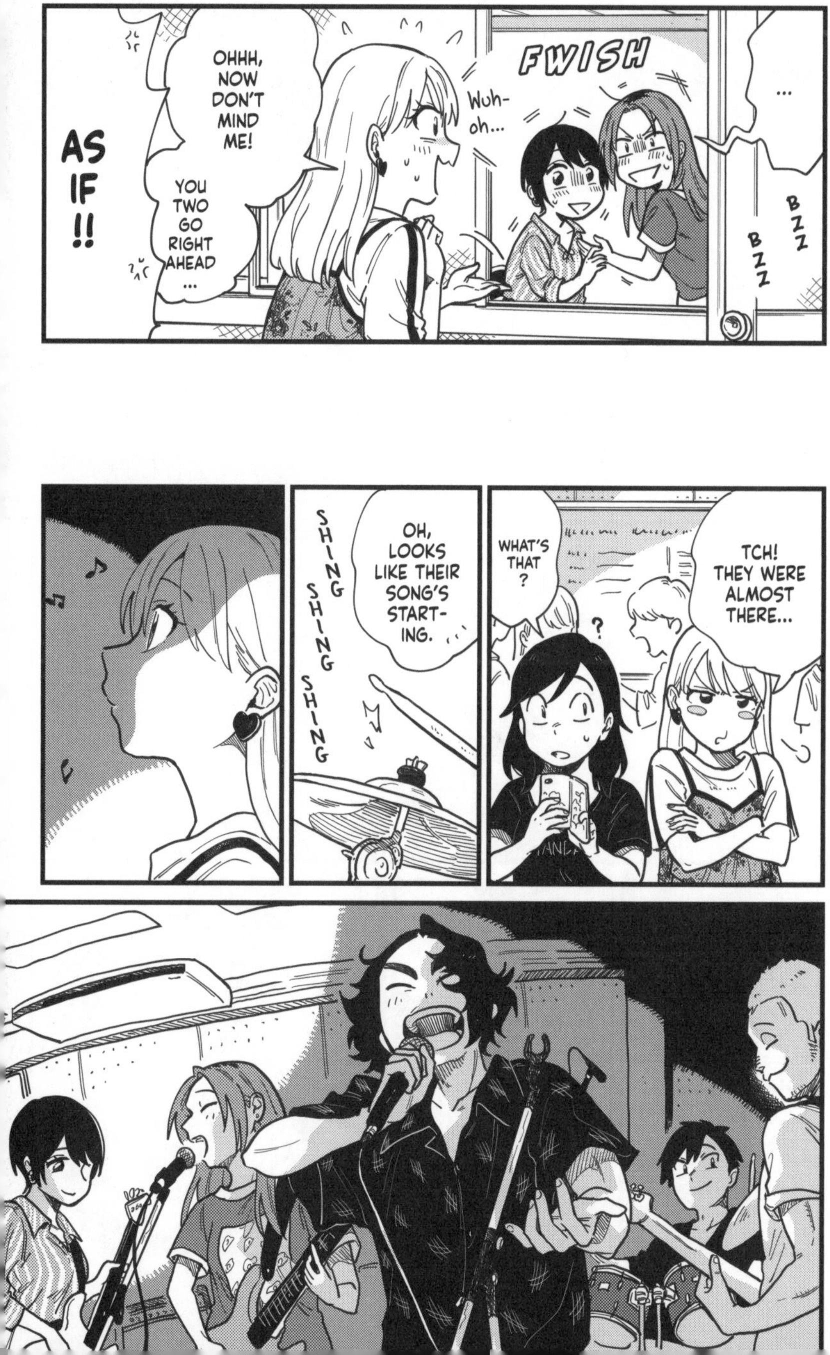
...
BZZ BZZ
FWISH
Wuh-oh...
OHHH, NOW DON'T MIND ME!
YOU TWO GO RIGHT AHEAD...
AS IF!!
TCH! THEY WERE ALMOST THERE...
WHAT'S THAT?
OH, LOOKS LIKE THEIR SONG'S START-ING.
SHING SHING SHING

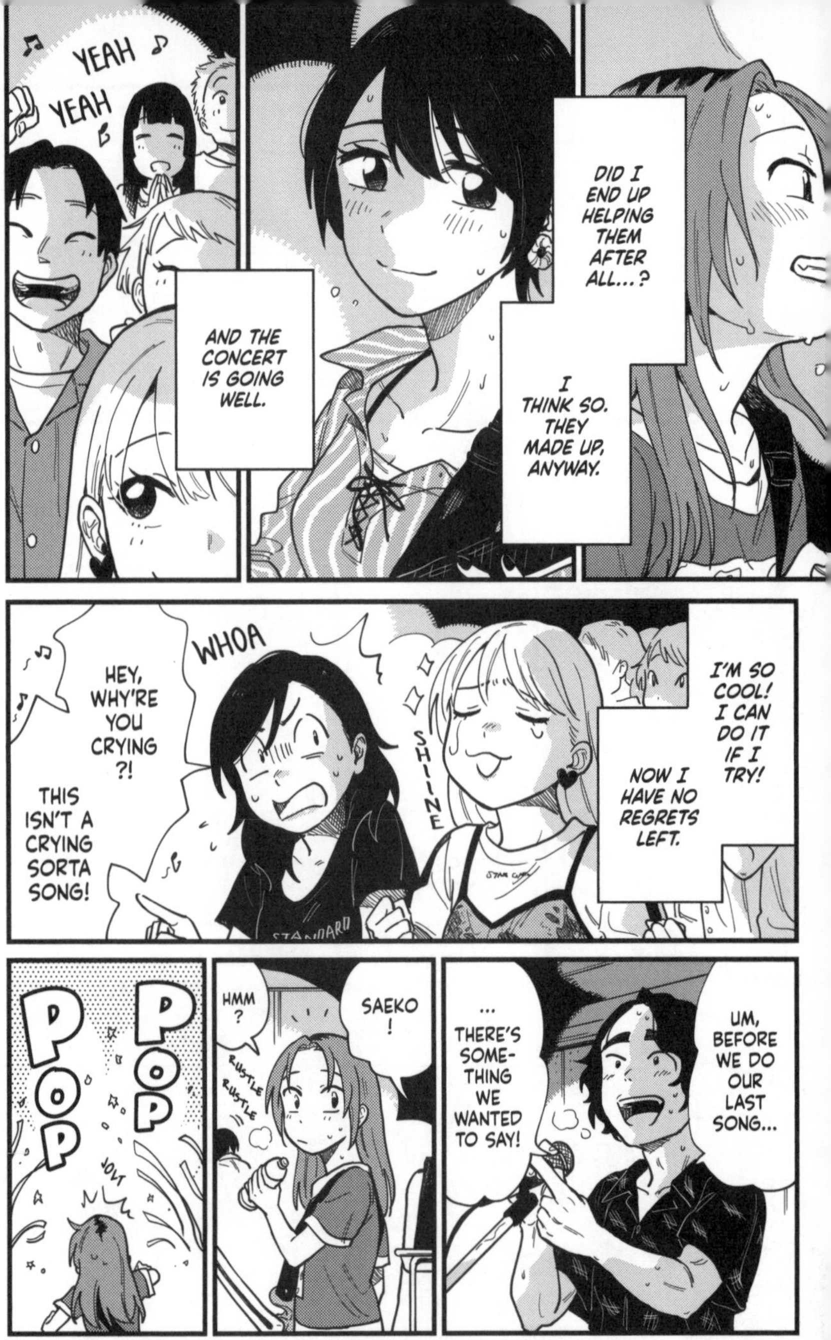
DID I END UP HELPING THEM AFTER ALL...?
I THINK SO. THEY MADE UP, ANYWAY.
AND THE CONCERT IS GOING WELL.
YEAH
YEAH
I'M SO COOL! I CAN DO IT IF I TRY!
NOW I HAVE NO REGRETS LEFT.
SHIINE
WHOA
HEY, WHY'RE YOU CRYING?!
THIS ISN'T A CRYING SORTA SONG!
UM, BEFORE WE DO OUR LAST SONG...
... THERE'S SOME-THING WE WANTED TO SAY!
SAEKO!
HMM?
RUSTLE RUSTLE
POP
POP
POP
JOLT

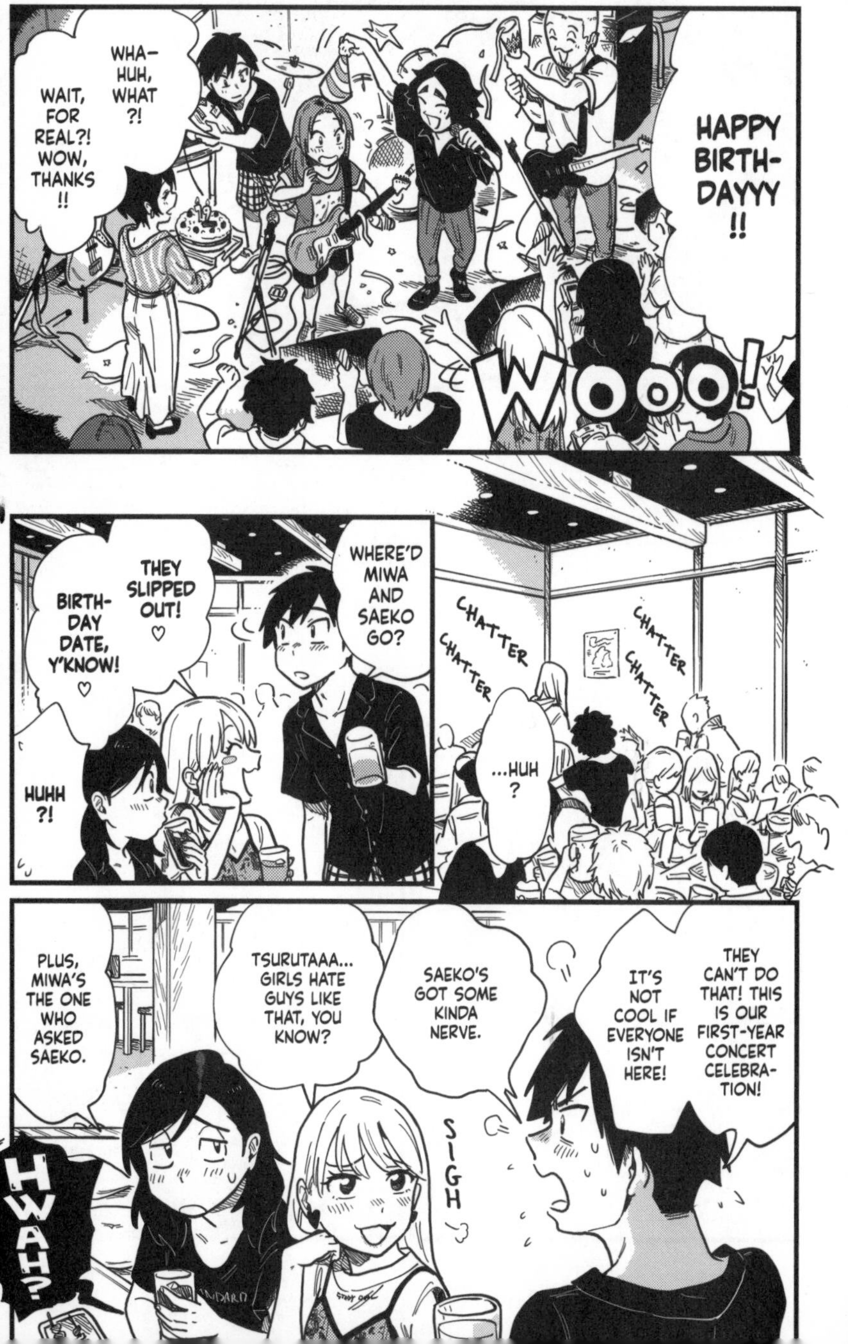
HAPPY BIRTH-DAYYY!!
WHA-HUH, WHAT?!
WAIT, FOR REAL?! WOW, THANKS!!
WOOO!
CHATTER CHATTER
CHATTER CHATTER
...HUH?
WHERE'D MIWA AND SAEKO GO?
THEY SLIPPED OUT! ♡
BIRTH-DAY DATE, Y'KNOW! ♡
HUHH?!
THEY CAN'T DO THAT! THIS IS OUR FIRST-YEAR CONCERT CELEBRA-TION!
IT'S NOT COOL IF EVERYONE ISN'T HERE!
SAEKO'S GOT SOME KINDA NERVE.
SIGH
TSURUTAAA... GIRLS HATE GUYS LIKE THAT, YOU KNOW?
PLUS, MIWA'S THE ONE WHO ASKED SAEKO.
HWAH?

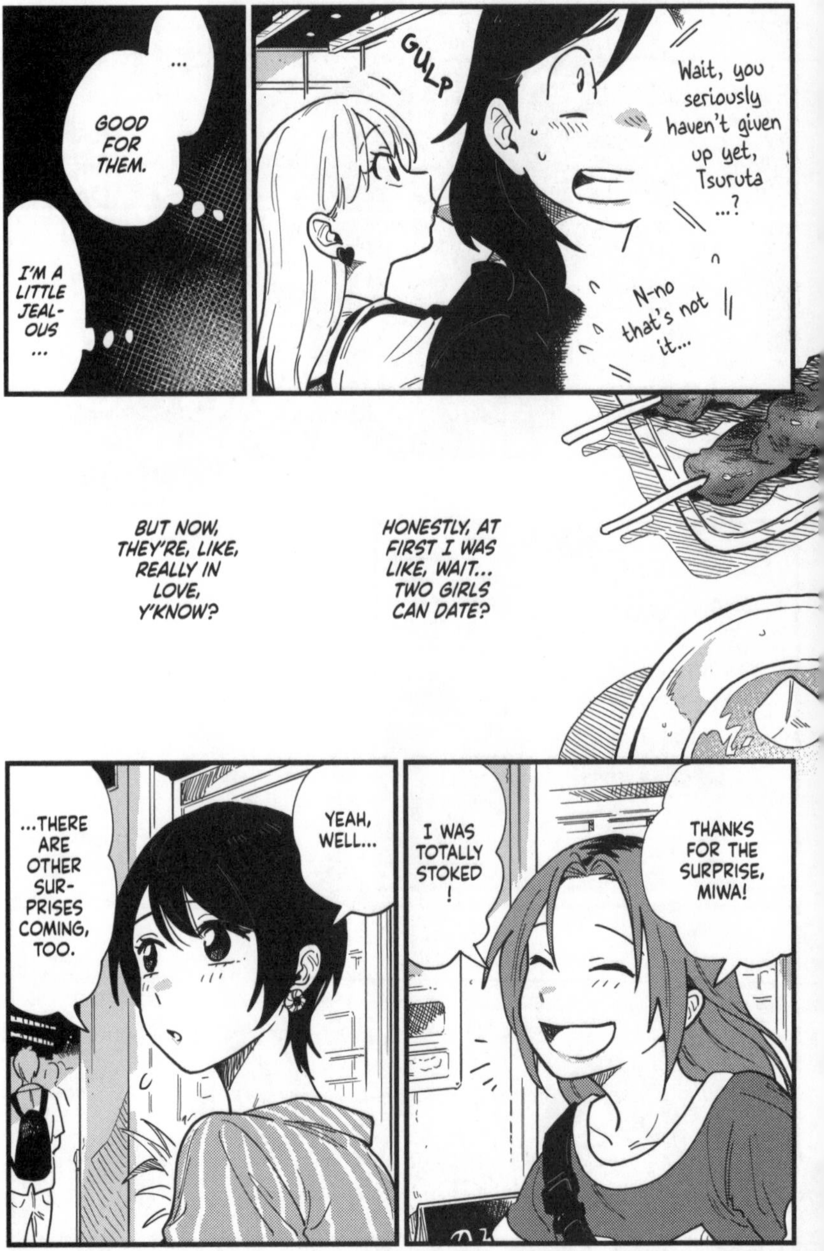
GULP
Wait, you seriously haven't given up yet, Tsuruta ...?
N-no that's not it...
...
GOOD FOR THEM.
I'M A LITTLE JEAL-OUS ...
HONESTLY, AT FIRST I WAS LIKE, WAIT... TWO GIRLS CAN DATE?
BUT NOW, THEY'RE, LIKE, REALLY IN LOVE, Y'KNOW?
THANKS FOR THE SURPRISE, MIWA!
I WAS TOTALLY STOKED !
YEAH, WELL...
...THERE ARE OTHER SUR-PRISES COMING, TOO.

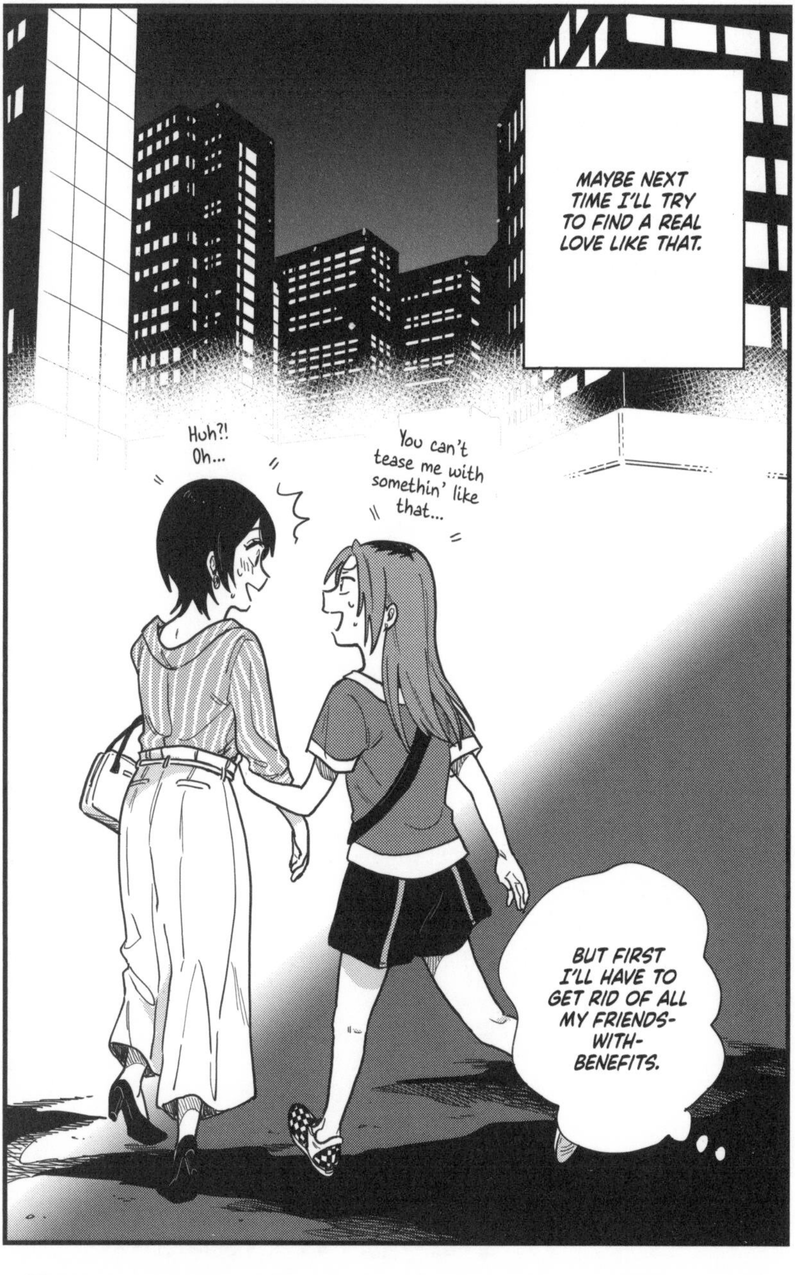
MAYBE NEXT TIME I'LL TRY TO FIND A REAL LOVE LIKE THAT.
You can't tease me with somethin' like that...
Huh?! Oh...
BUT FIRST I'LL HAVE TO GET RID OF ALL MY FRIENDS-WITH-BENEFITS.

How Do We Relationship?

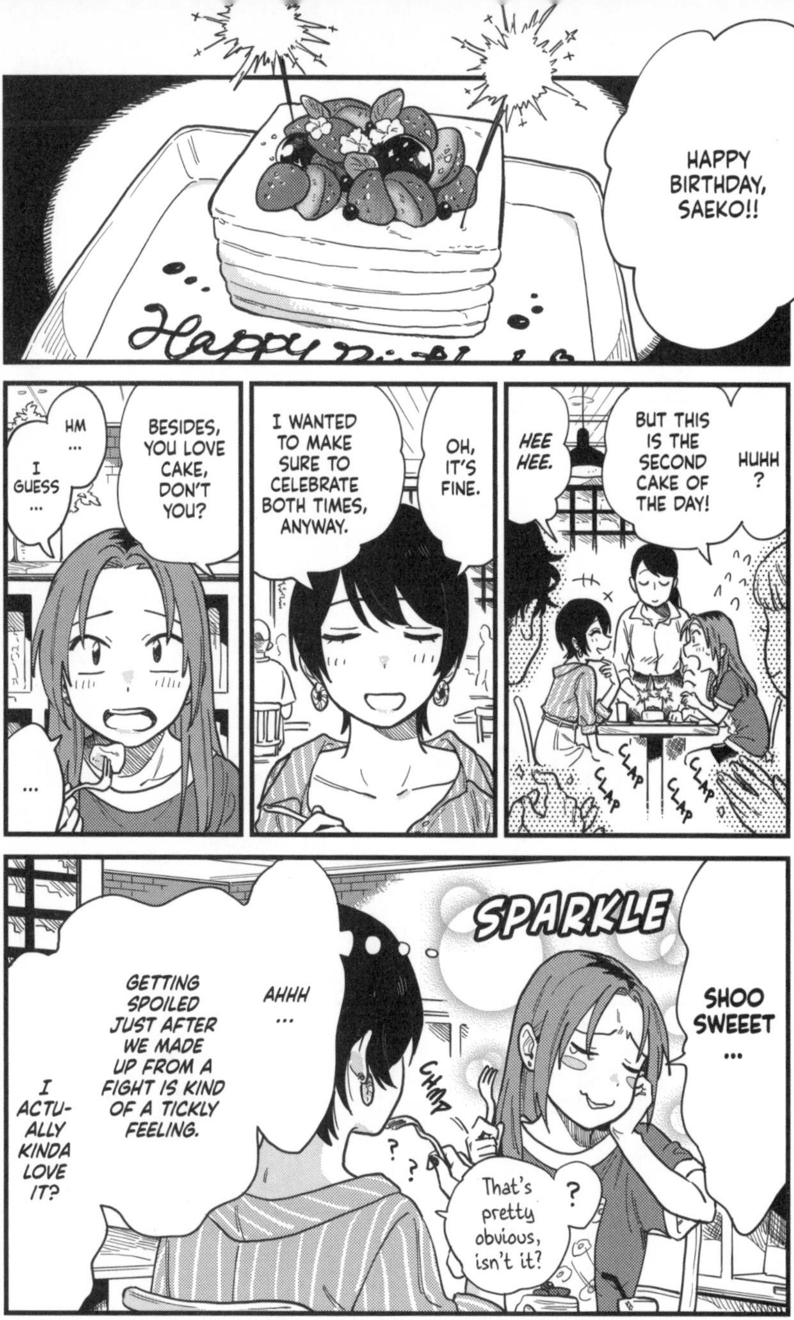
HAPPY BIRTHDAY, SAEKO!!
HUHH ?
BUT THIS IS THE SECOND CAKE OF THE DAY!
HEE HEE.
CLAP CLAP CLAP CLAP
OH, IT'S FINE.
I WANTED TO MAKE SURE TO CELEBRATE BOTH TIMES, ANYWAY.
BESIDES, YOU LOVE CAKE, DON'T YOU?
HM ... I GUESS ...
...
SHOO SWEEET ...
SPARKLE
AHHH ...
GETTING SPOILED JUST AFTER WE MADE UP FROM A FIGHT IS KIND OF A TICKLY FEELING.
I ACTUALLY KINDA LOVE IT?
CHMP
? ? ?
That's pretty obvious, isn't it?
?

Chapter 9: Body and Soul

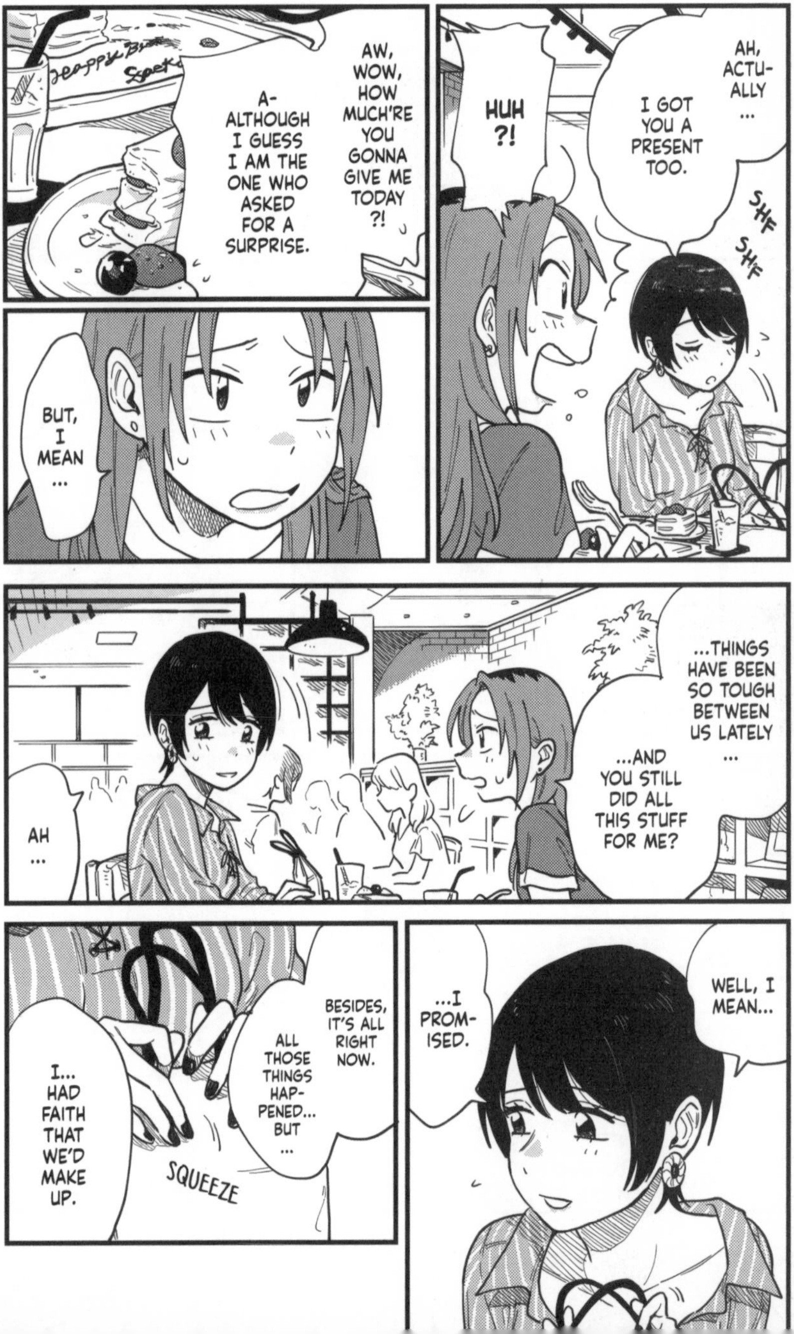
AH, ACTUALLY...
I GOT YOU A PRESENT TOO.
SHF SHF
HUH?!
AW, WOW, HOW MUCH'RE YOU GONNA GIVE ME TODAY?!
A-ALTHOUGH I GUESS I AM THE ONE WHO ASKED FOR A SURPRISE.
BUT, I MEAN...
...THINGS HAVE BEEN SO TOUGH BETWEEN US LATELY...
...AND YOU STILL DID ALL THIS STUFF FOR ME?
AH...
WELL, I MEAN...
...I PROMISED.
BESIDES, IT'S ALL RIGHT NOW.
ALL THOSE THINGS HAPPENED... BUT...
I... HAD FAITH THAT WE'D MAKE UP.
SQUEEZE

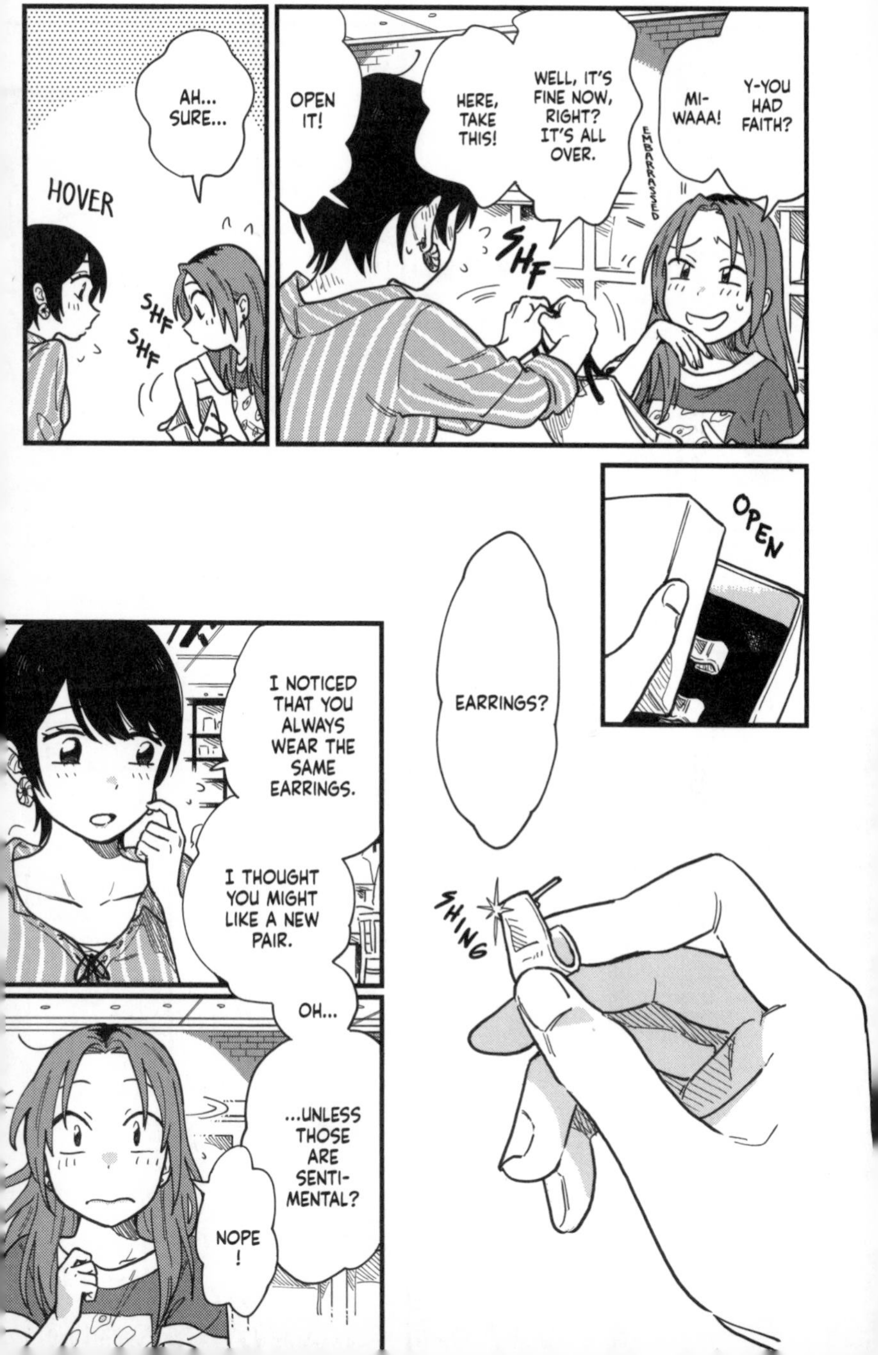
Y-YOU HAD FAITH?
MI-WAAA!
EMBARRASSED
WELL, IT'S FINE NOW, RIGHT? IT'S ALL OVER.
HERE, TAKE THIS!
SHF
OPEN IT!
AH... SURE...
HOVER
SHF
SHF
OPEN
EARRINGS?
SHING
I NOTICED THAT YOU ALWAYS WEAR THE SAME EARRINGS.
I THOUGHT YOU MIGHT LIKE A NEW PAIR.
OH...
...UNLESS THOSE ARE SENTI-MENTAL?
NOPE!

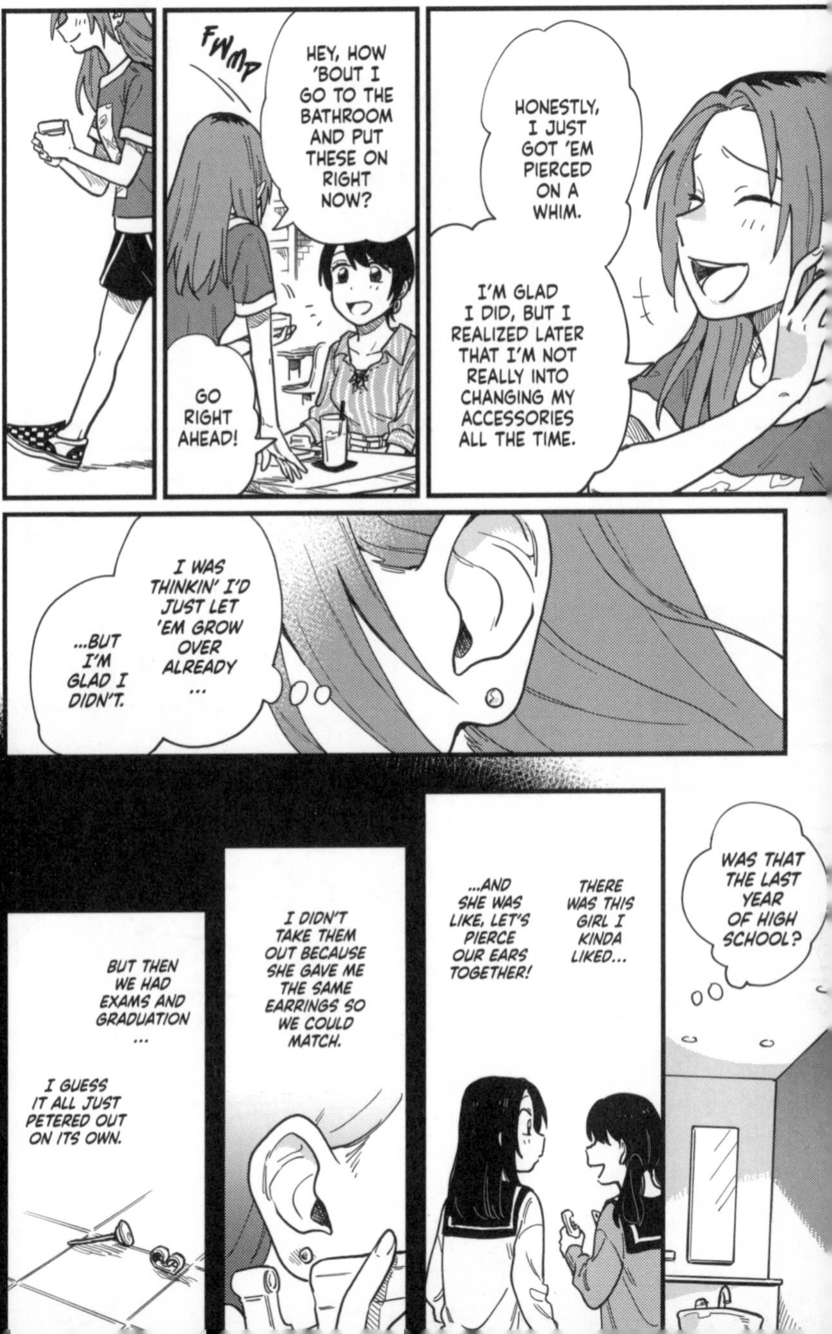
HONESTLY, I JUST GOT 'EM PIERCED ON A WHIM.
I'M GLAD I DID, BUT I REALIZED LATER THAT I'M NOT REALLY INTO CHANGING MY ACCESSORIES ALL THE TIME.
FWMP
HEY, HOW 'BOUT I GO TO THE BATHROOM AND PUT THESE ON RIGHT NOW?
GO RIGHT AHEAD!
I WAS THINKIN' I'D JUST LET 'EM GROW OVER ALREADY...
...BUT I'M GLAD I DIDN'T.
WAS THAT THE LAST YEAR OF HIGH SCHOOL?
THERE WAS THIS GIRL I KINDA LIKED...
...AND SHE WAS LIKE, LET'S PIERCE OUR EARS TOGETHER!
I DIDN'T TAKE THEM OUT BECAUSE SHE GAVE ME THE SAME EARRINGS SO WE COULD MATCH.
BUT THEN WE HAD EXAMS AND GRADUATION...
I GUESS IT ALL JUST PETERED OUT ON ITS OWN.

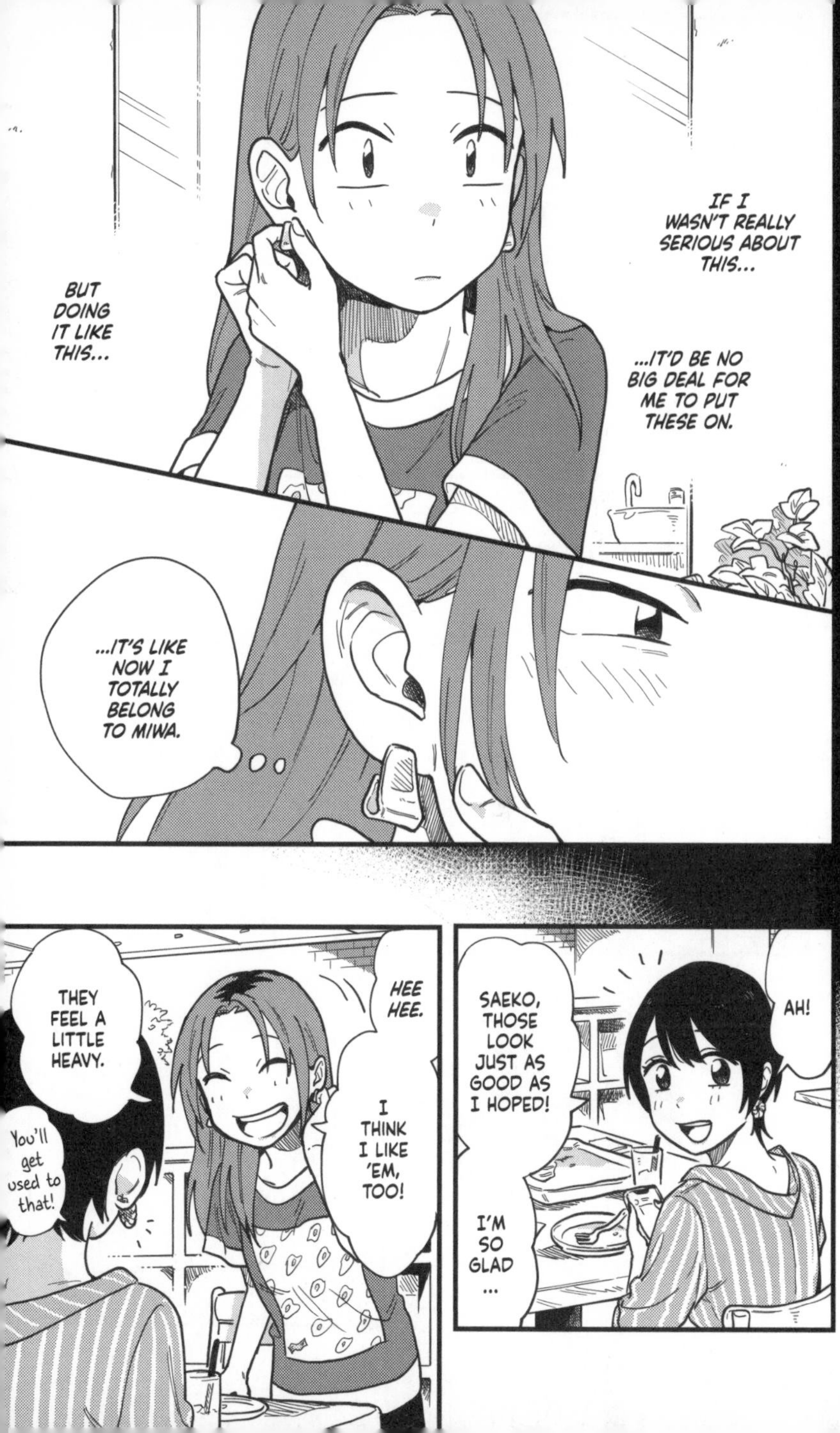
IF I WASN'T REALLY SERIOUS ABOUT THIS...
...IT'D BE NO BIG DEAL FOR ME TO PUT THESE ON.
BUT DOING IT LIKE THIS...
...IT'S LIKE NOW I TOTALLY BELONG TO MIWA.
AH!
SAEKO, THOSE LOOK JUST AS GOOD AS I HOPED!
I'M SO GLAD ...
HEE HEE.
I THINK I LIKE 'EM, TOO!
THEY FEEL A LITTLE HEAVY.
You'll get used to that!

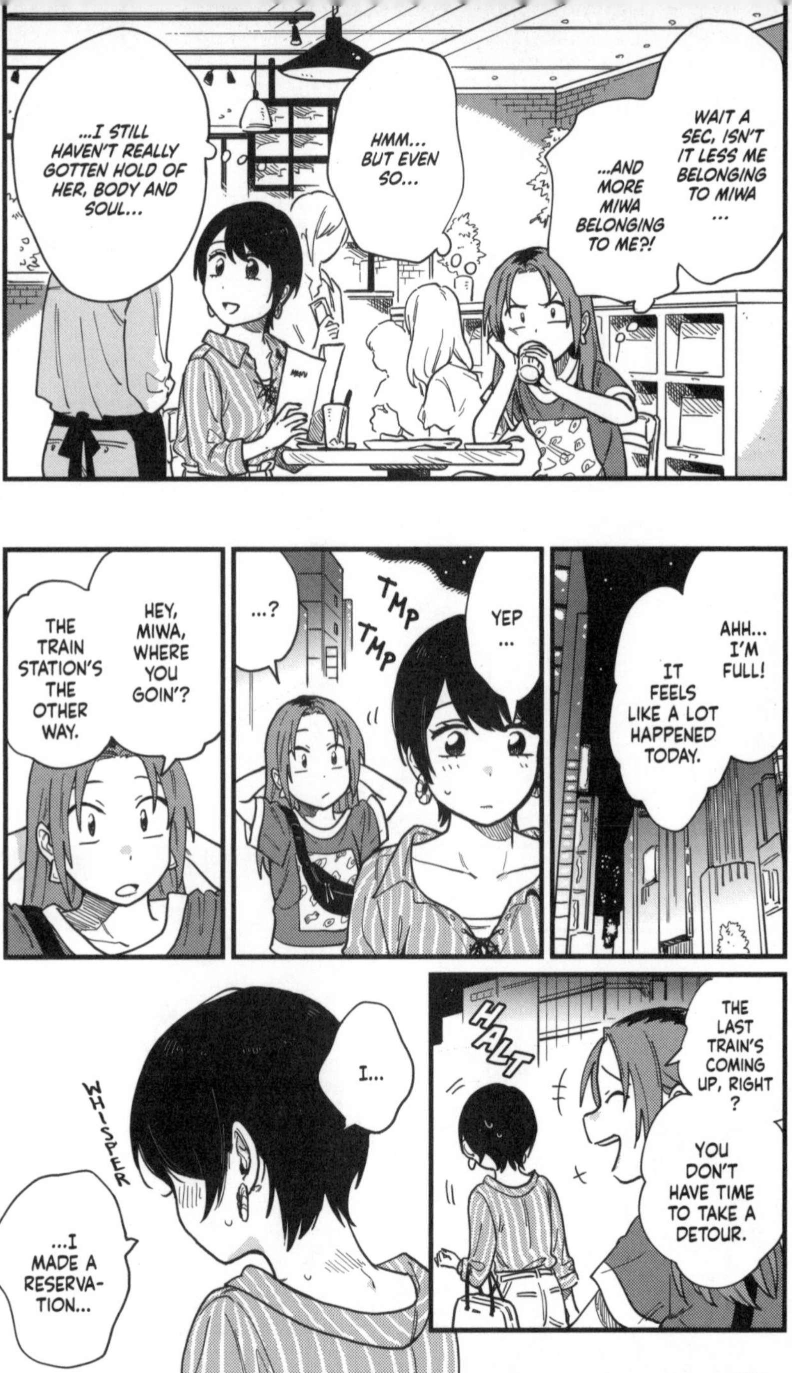
WAIT A SEC, ISN'T IT LESS ME BELONGING TO MIWA...
...AND MORE MIWA BELONGING TO ME?!
HMM... BUT EVEN SO...
...I STILL HAVEN'T REALLY GOTTEN HOLD OF HER, BODY AND SOUL...
AHH... I'M FULL!
IT FEELS LIKE A LOT HAPPENED TODAY.
YEP...
TMP TMP
...?
HEY, MIWA, WHERE YOU GOIN'?
THE TRAIN STATION'S THE OTHER WAY.
THE LAST TRAIN'S COMING UP, RIGHT?
YOU DON'T HAVE TIME TO TAKE A DETOUR.
HALT
I...
WHISPER
...I MADE A RESERVATION...

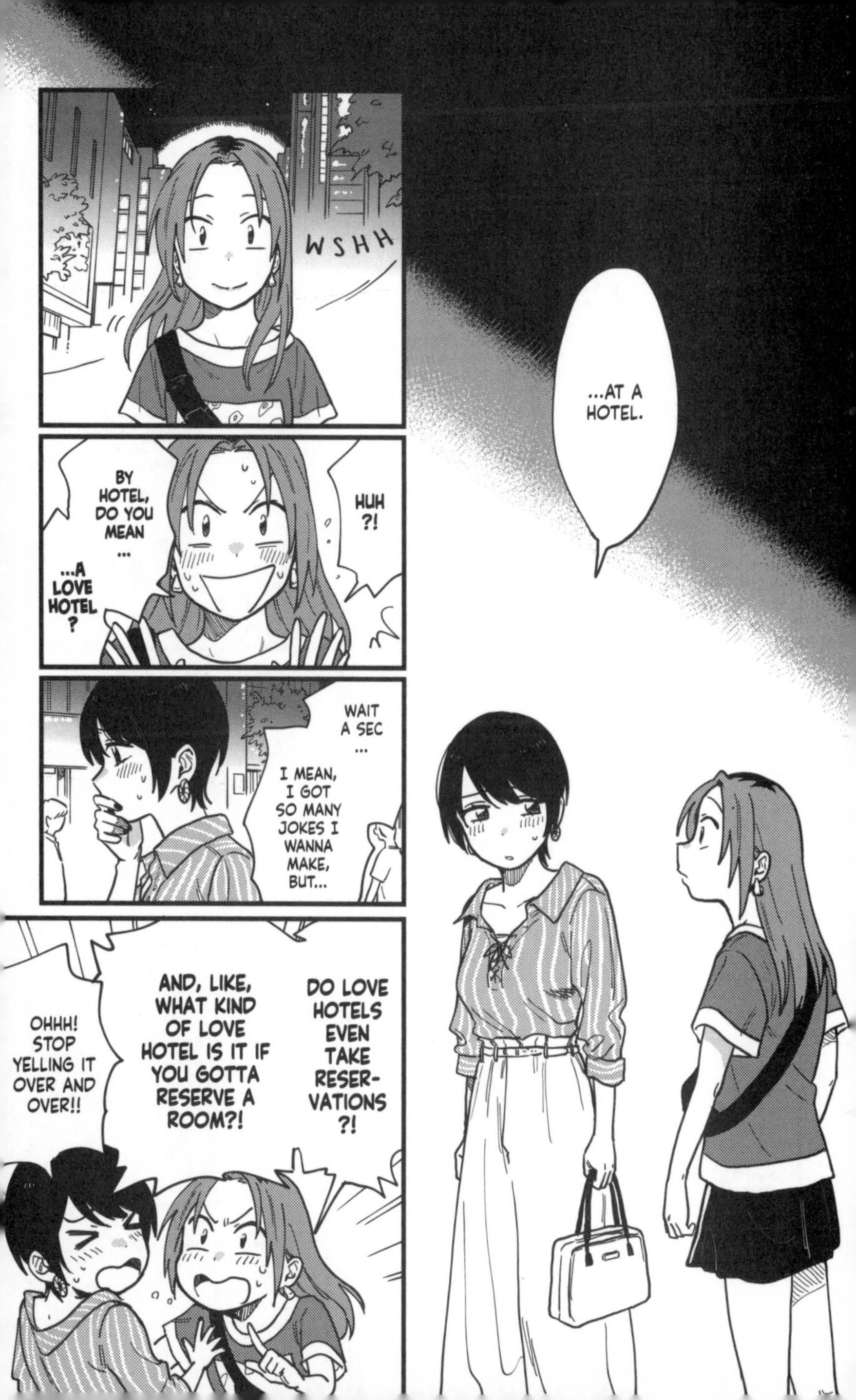
...AT A HOTEL.
WSHH
HUH?!
BY HOTEL, DO YOU MEAN ...
...A LOVE HOTEL?
WAIT A SEC ...
I MEAN, I GOT SO MANY JOKES I WANNA MAKE, BUT...
DO LOVE HOTELS EVEN TAKE RESER-VATIONS?!
AND, LIKE, WHAT KIND OF LOVE HOTEL IS IT IF YOU GOTTA RESERVE A ROOM?!
OHHH! STOP YELLING IT OVER AND OVER!!

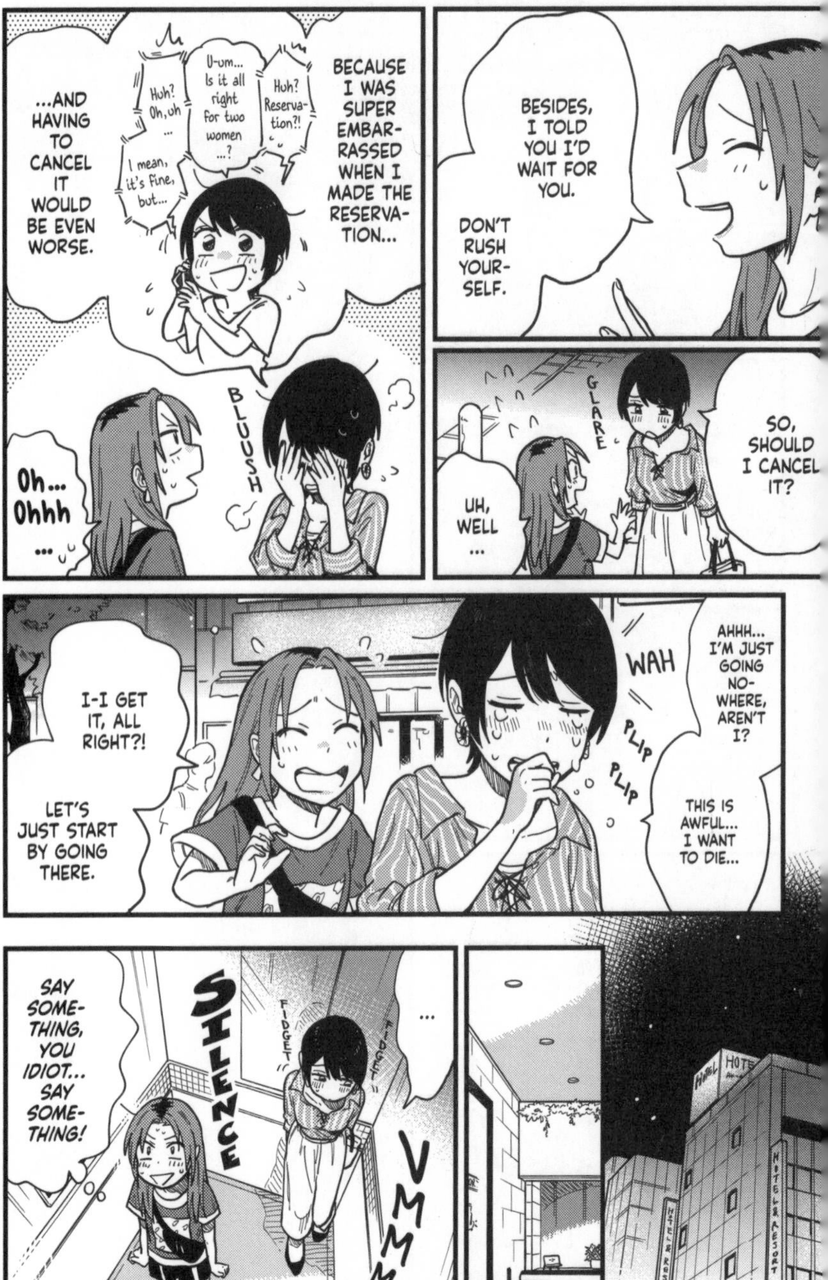
BESIDES, I TOLD YOU I'D WAIT FOR YOU.
DON'T RUSH YOURSELF.
SO, SHOULD I CANCEL IT?
GLARE
UH, WELL ...
BECAUSE I WAS SUPER EMBARRASSED WHEN I MADE THE RESERVATION...
Huh? Reservation?!
U-um... Is it all right for two women ...?
Huh? Oh, uh ...
I mean, it's fine, but...
...AND HAVING TO CANCEL IT WOULD BE EVEN WORSE.
BLUUSH
Oh... Ohhh ...
AHHH... I'M JUST GOING NOWHERE, AREN'T I?
WAH
PLIP
PLIP
THIS IS AWFUL... I WANT TO DIE...
I-I GET IT, ALL RIGHT?!
LET'S JUST START BY GOING THERE.
HOTEL
...
FIDGET
FIDGET
SILENCE
VMMMMM
SAY SOMETHING, YOU IDIOT... SAY SOMETHING!

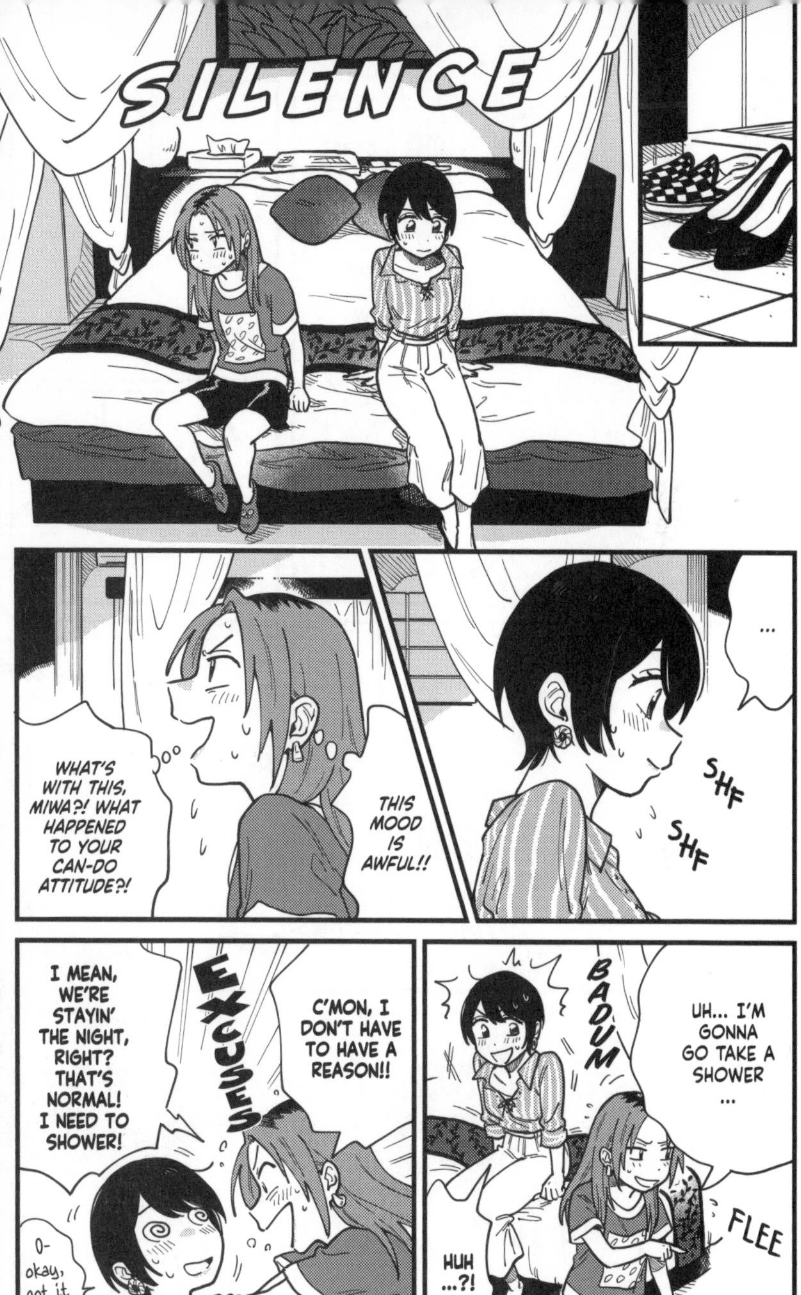
SILENCE
...
SHF
SHF
WHAT'S WITH THIS, MIWA?! WHAT HAPPENED TO YOUR CAN-DO ATTITUDE?!
THIS MOOD IS AWFUL!!
UH... I'M GONNA GO TAKE A SHOWER ...
BADUM
FLEE
HUH ...?!
C'MON, I DON'T HAVE TO HAVE A REASON!!
EXCUSES
I MEAN, WE'RE STAYIN' THE NIGHT, RIGHT? THAT'S NORMAL! I NEED TO SHOWER!
O-okay, got it ...

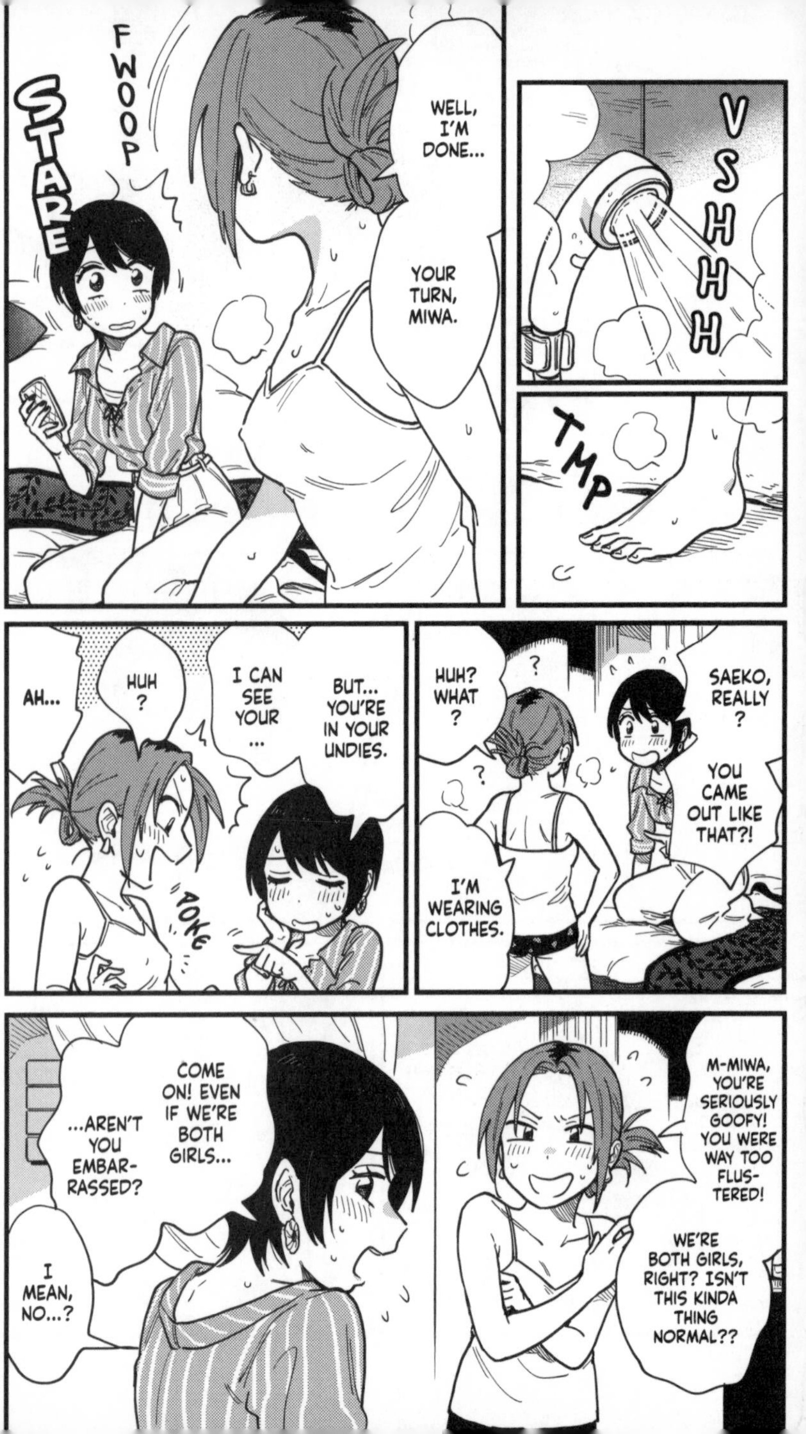
VSHHHH
TMP
WELL, I'M DONE...
YOUR TURN, MIWA.
FWOOP
STARE
SAEKO, REALLY?
YOU CAME OUT LIKE THAT?!
HUH? WHAT?
I'M WEARING CLOTHES.
BUT... YOU'RE IN YOUR UNDIES.
I CAN SEE YOUR ...
HUH?
AH...
POKE
M-MIWA, YOU'RE SERIOUSLY GOOFY! YOU WERE WAY TOO FLUS-TERED!
WE'RE BOTH GIRLS, RIGHT? ISN'T THIS KINDA THING NORMAL??
COME ON! EVEN IF WE'RE BOTH GIRLS...
...AREN'T YOU EMBAR-RASSED?
I MEAN, NO...?

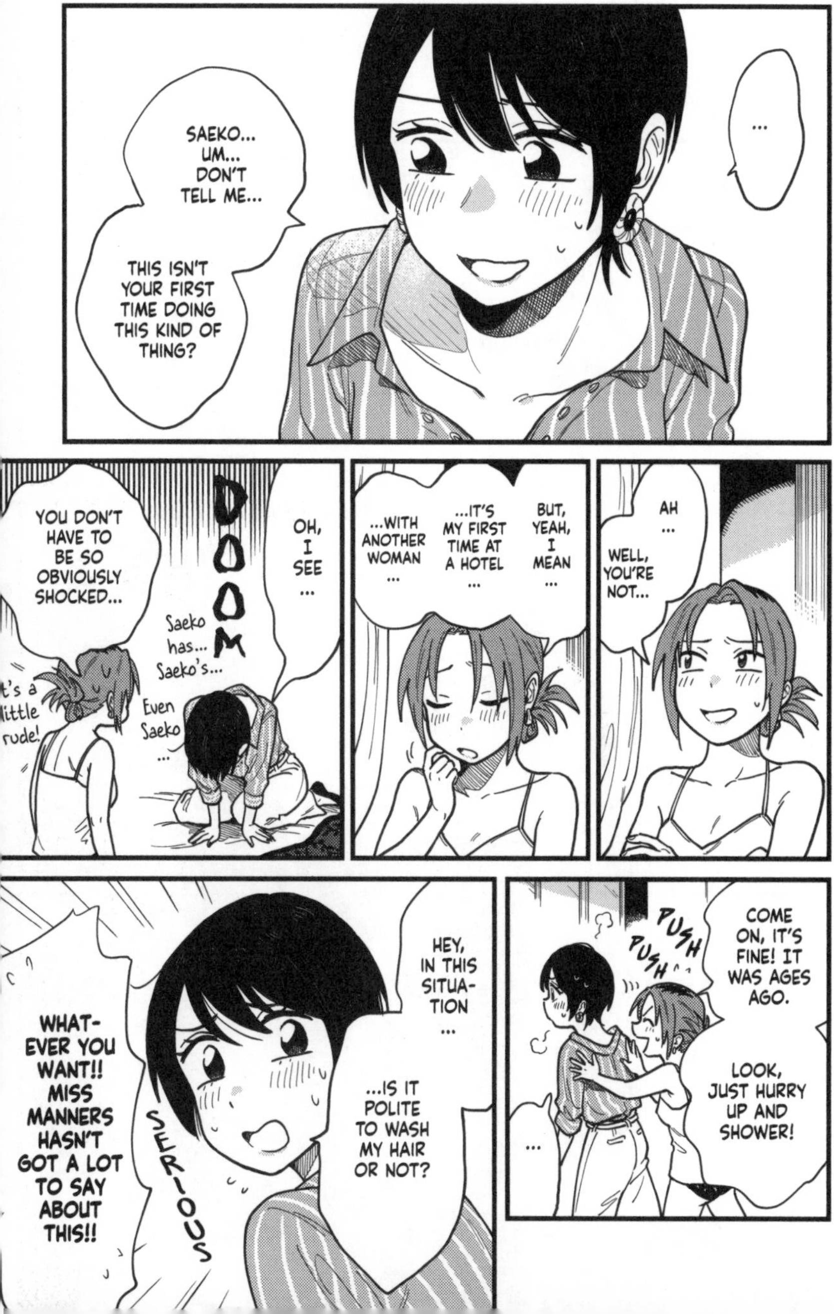
...
SAEKO... UM... DON'T TELL ME...
THIS ISN'T YOUR FIRST TIME DOING THIS KIND OF THING?
AH ...
WELL, YOU'RE NOT...
BUT, YEAH, I MEAN ...
...IT'S MY FIRST TIME AT A HOTEL ...
...WITH ANOTHER WOMAN ...
OH, I SEE ...
DOOOM
Saeko has... Saeko's...
Even Saeko ...
YOU DON'T HAVE TO BE SO OBVIOUSLY SHOCKED...
t's a little rude!
COME ON, IT'S FINE! IT WAS AGES AGO.
PUSH PUSH
LOOK, JUST HURRY UP AND SHOWER!
...
HEY, IN THIS SITUATION ...
...IS IT POLITE TO WASH MY HAIR OR NOT?
SERIOUS
WHATEVER YOU WANT!! MISS MANNERS HASN'T GOT A LOT TO SAY ABOUT THIS!!

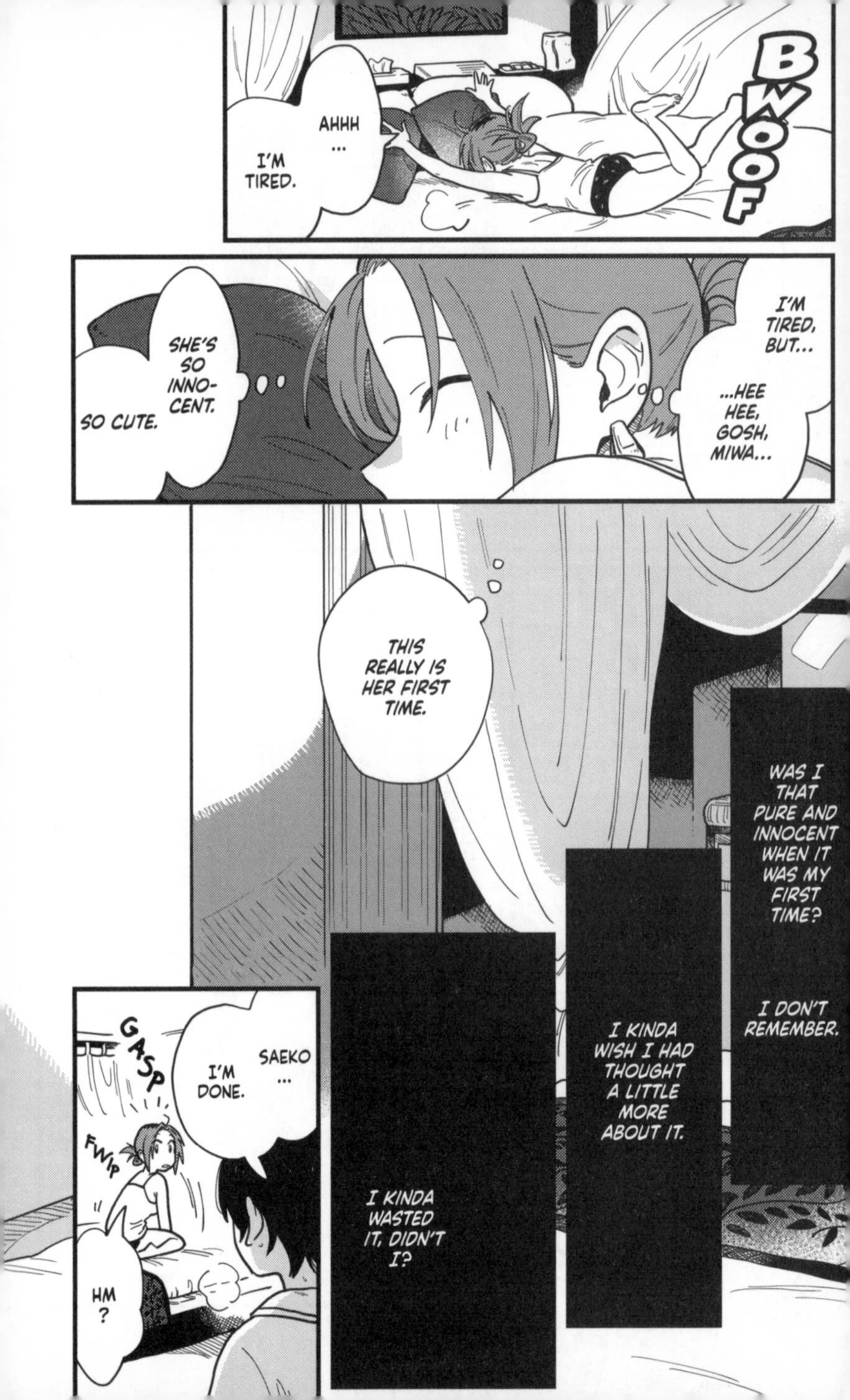
BWOOF
AHHH ... I'M TIRED.
I'M TIRED, BUT... ...HEE HEE, GOSH, MIWA...
SHE'S SO INNOCENT. SO CUTE.
THIS REALLY IS HER FIRST TIME.
WAS I THAT PURE AND INNOCENT WHEN IT WAS MY FIRST TIME?
I DON'T REMEMBER.
I KINDA WISH I HAD THOUGHT A LITTLE MORE ABOUT IT.
I KINDA WASTED IT, DIDN'T I?
SAEKO ... I'M DONE.
GASP
FWIP
HM ?

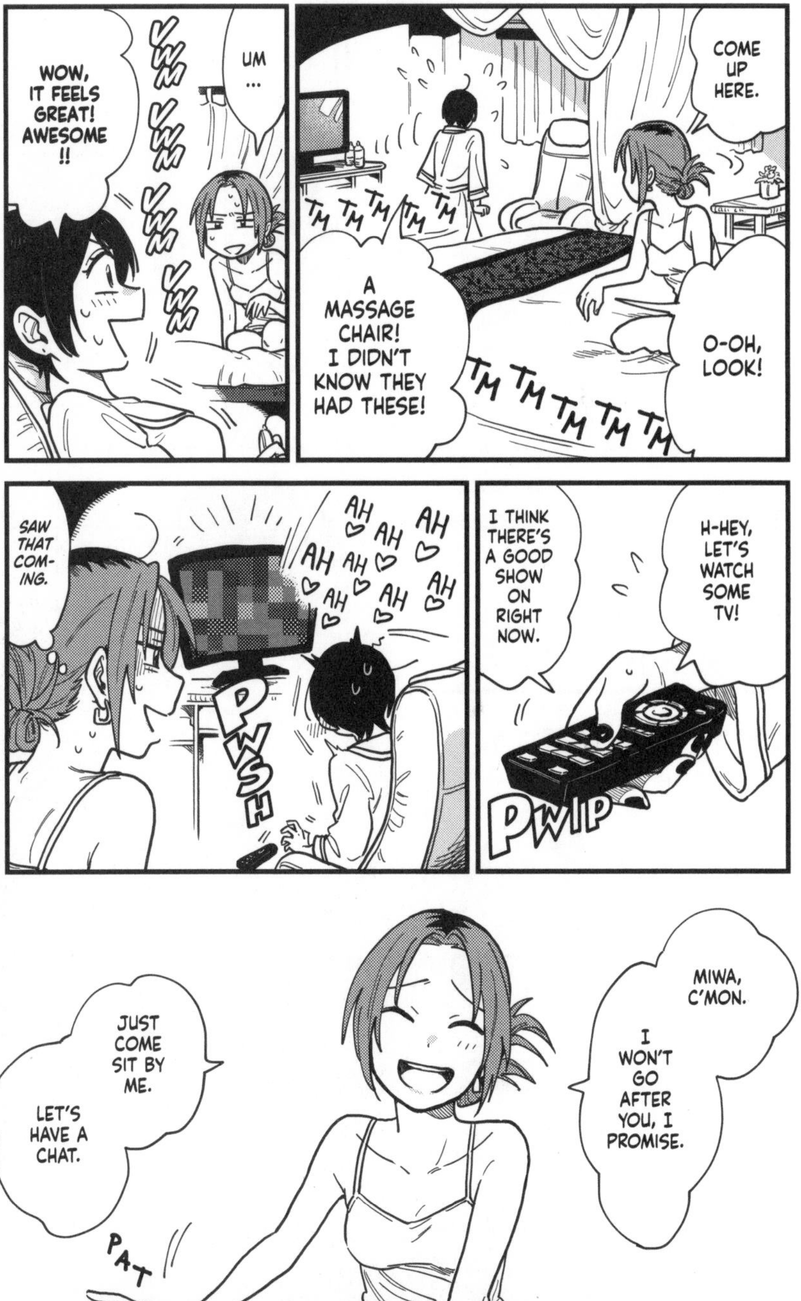
COME UP HERE.
O-OH, LOOK!
TM TM TM TM TM
A MASSAGE CHAIR! I DIDN'T KNOW THEY HAD THESE!
TM TM TM TM TM
UM ...
VWM VWM VWM VWM VWM
WOW, IT FEELS GREAT! AWESOME !!
H-HEY, LET'S WATCH SOME TV!
I THINK THERE'S A GOOD SHOW ON RIGHT NOW.
PWIP
AH AH AH AH AH AH AH AH AH
PWSH
SAW THAT COMING.
MIWA, C'MON.
I WON'T GO AFTER YOU, I PROMISE.
JUST COME SIT BY ME.
LET'S HAVE A CHAT.
PAT

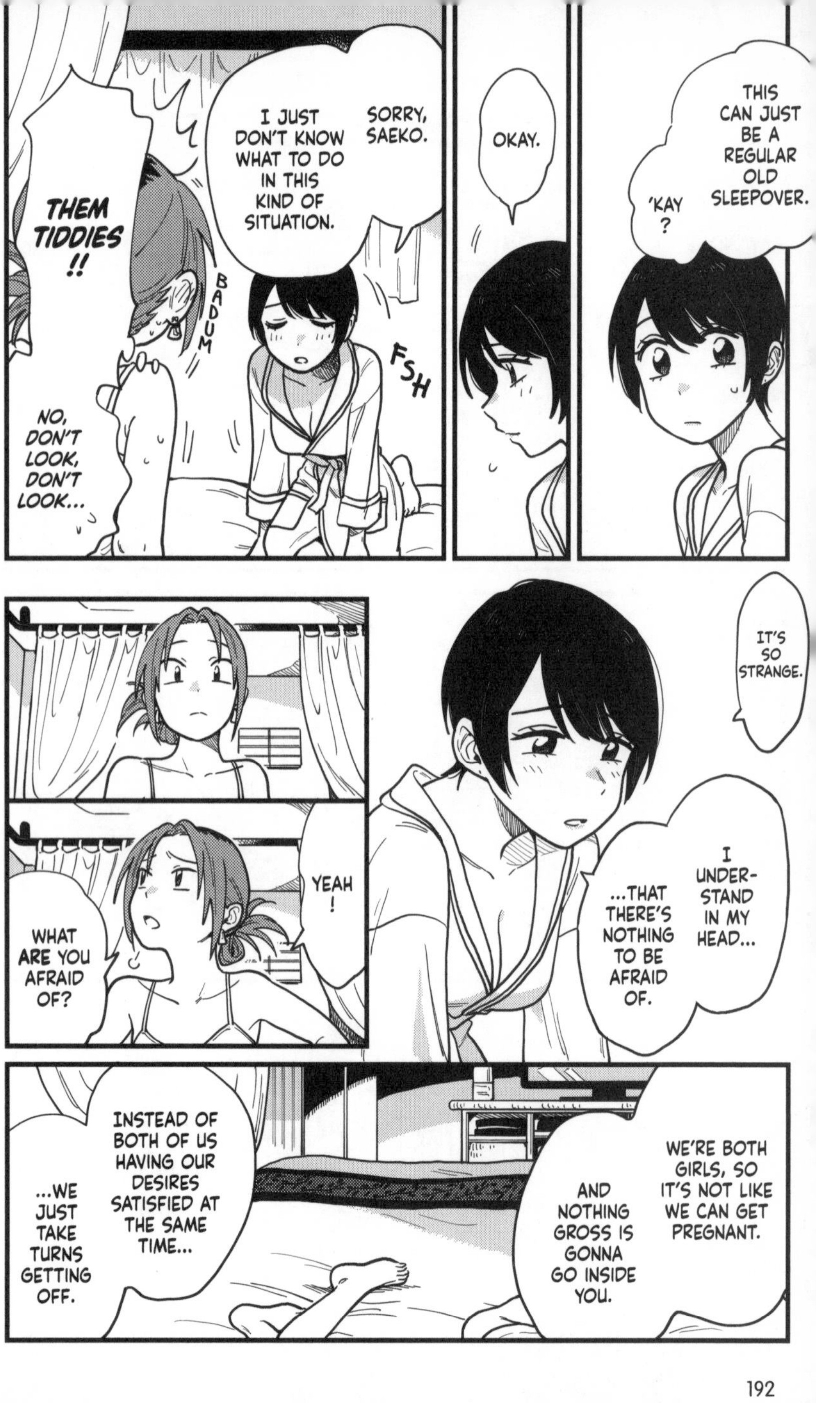

THIS CAN JUST BE A REGULAR OLD SLEEPOVER.
'KAY?
OKAY.
SORRY, SAEKO.
I JUST DON'T KNOW WHAT TO DO IN THIS KIND OF SITUATION.
FSH
BADUM
THEM TIDDIES!!
NO, DON'T LOOK, DON'T LOOK...
IT'S SO STRANGE.
I UNDER-STAND IN MY HEAD...
...THAT THERE'S NOTHING TO BE AFRAID OF.
YEAH!
WHAT ARE YOU AFRAID OF?
WE'RE BOTH GIRLS, SO IT'S NOT LIKE WE CAN GET PREGNANT.
AND NOTHING GROSS IS GONNA GO INSIDE YOU.
INSTEAD OF BOTH OF US HAVING OUR DESIRES SATISFIED AT THE SAME TIME...
...WE JUST TAKE TURNS GETTING OFF.

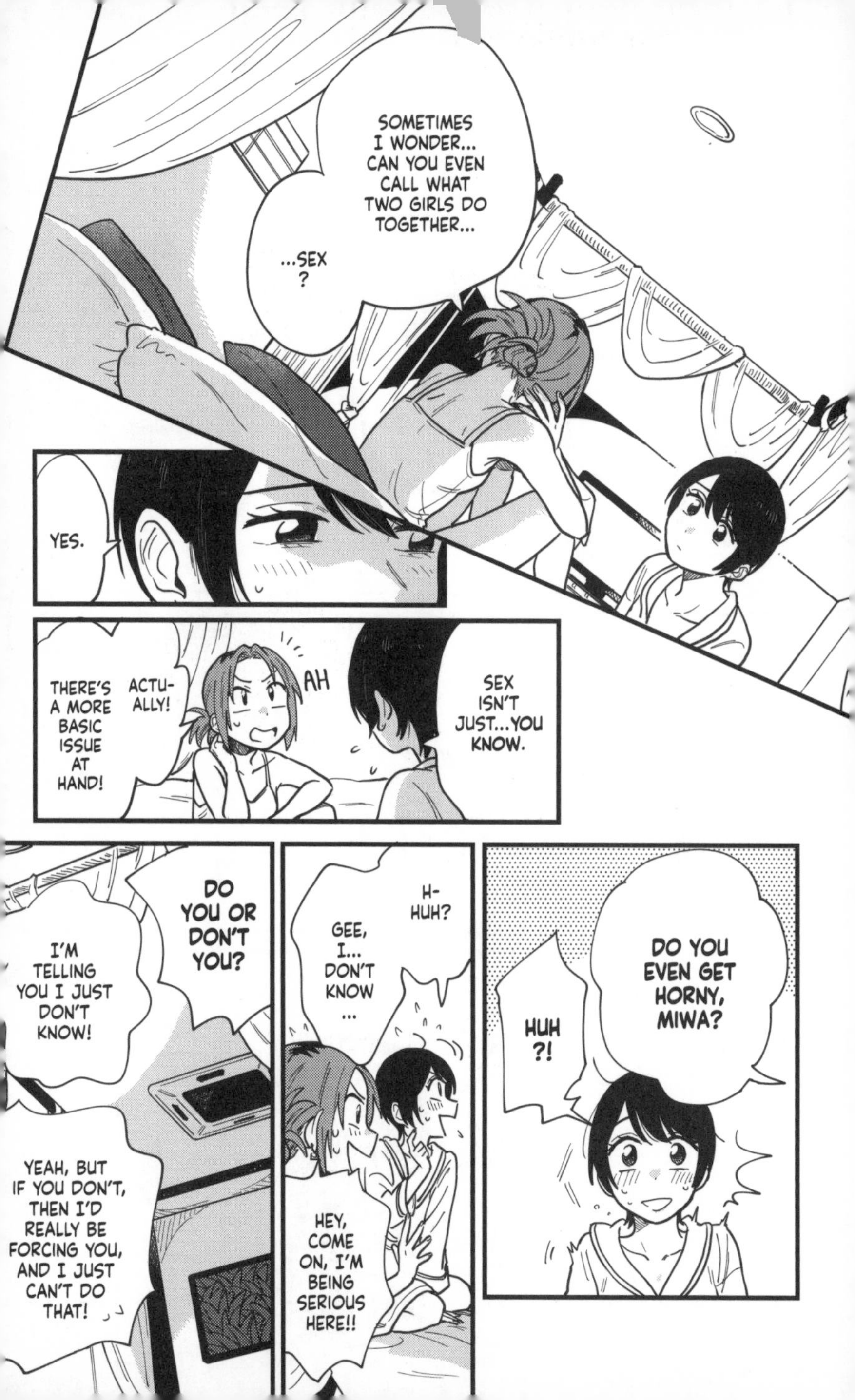
SOMETIMES I WONDER... CAN YOU EVEN CALL WHAT TWO GIRLS DO TOGETHER...
...SEX ?
YES.
SEX ISN'T JUST...YOU KNOW.
AH
ACTU- ALLY!
THERE'S A MORE BASIC ISSUE AT HAND!
DO YOU EVEN GET HORNY, MIWA?
HUH ?!
H- HUH?
GEE, I... DON'T KNOW ...
HEY, COME ON, I'M BEING SERIOUS HERE!!
DO YOU OR DON'T YOU?
I'M TELLING YOU I JUST DON'T KNOW!
YEAH, BUT IF YOU DON'T, THEN I'D REALLY BE FORCING YOU, AND I JUST CAN'T DO THAT!

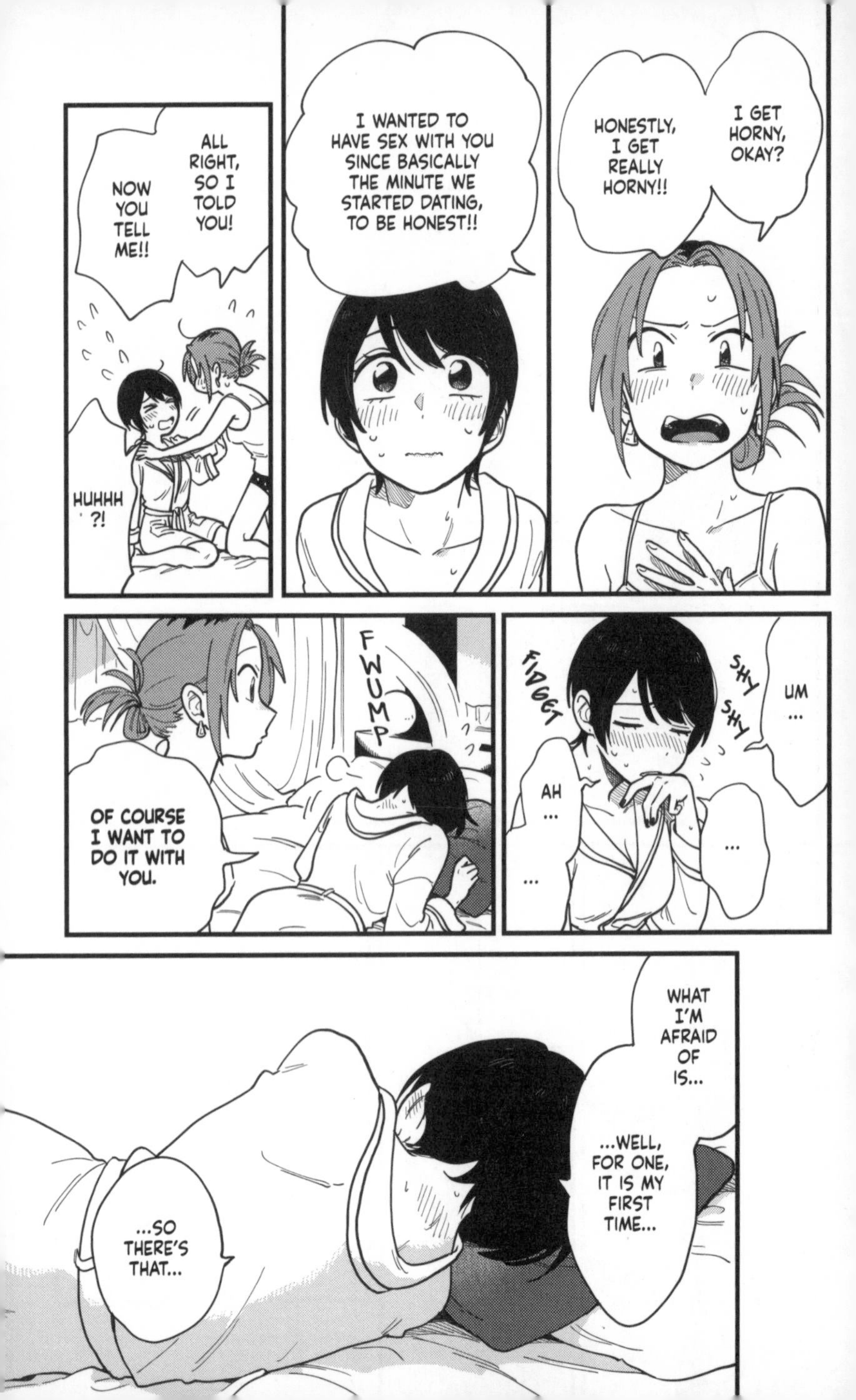
I GET HORNY, OKAY?
HONESTLY, I GET REALLY HORNY!!
I WANTED TO HAVE SEX WITH YOU SINCE BASICALLY THE MINUTE WE STARTED DATING, TO BE HONEST!!
ALL RIGHT, SO I TOLD YOU!
NOW YOU TELL ME!!
HUHHH?!
UM...
SHY SHY
FIDGET
AH...
...
...
FWUMP
OF COURSE I WANT TO DO IT WITH YOU.
WHAT I'M AFRAID OF IS...
...WELL, FOR ONE, IT IS MY FIRST TIME...
...SO THERE'S THAT...

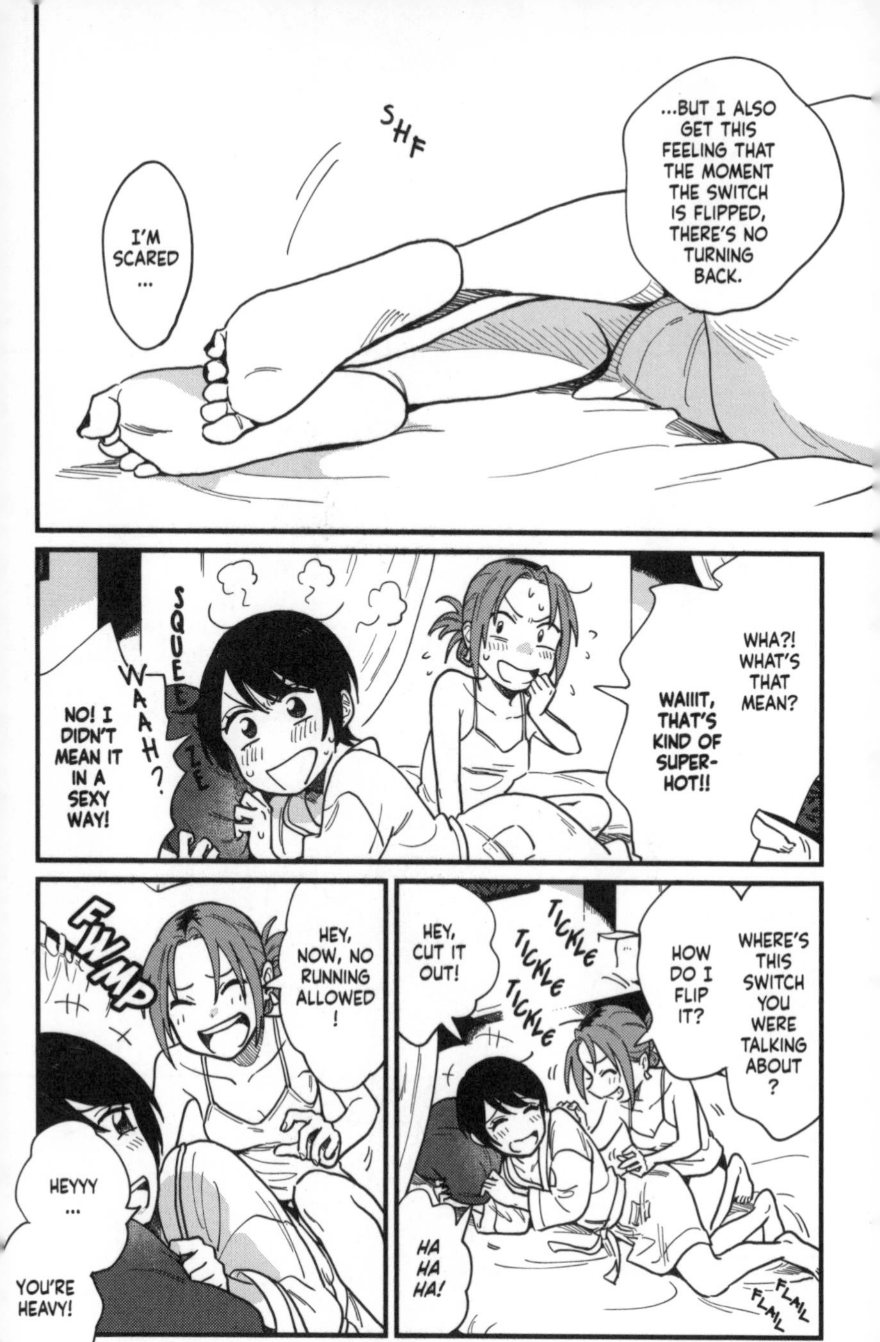
...BUT I ALSO GET THIS FEELING THAT THE MOMENT THE SWITCH IS FLIPPED, THERE'S NO TURNING BACK.
SHF
I'M SCARED...
WHA?! WHAT'S THAT MEAN?
WAIIIT, THAT'S KIND OF SUPER-HOT!!
SQUEEZE
WAAAH?
NO! I DIDN'T MEAN IT IN A SEXY WAY!
WHERE'S THIS SWITCH YOU WERE TALKING ABOUT?
HOW DO I FLIP IT?
TICKLE TICKLE TICKLE
HEY, CUT IT OUT!
HA HA HA!
FLAIL FLAIL
HEY, NOW, NO RUNNING ALLOWED!
FWMP
HEYYY... YOU'RE HEAVY!

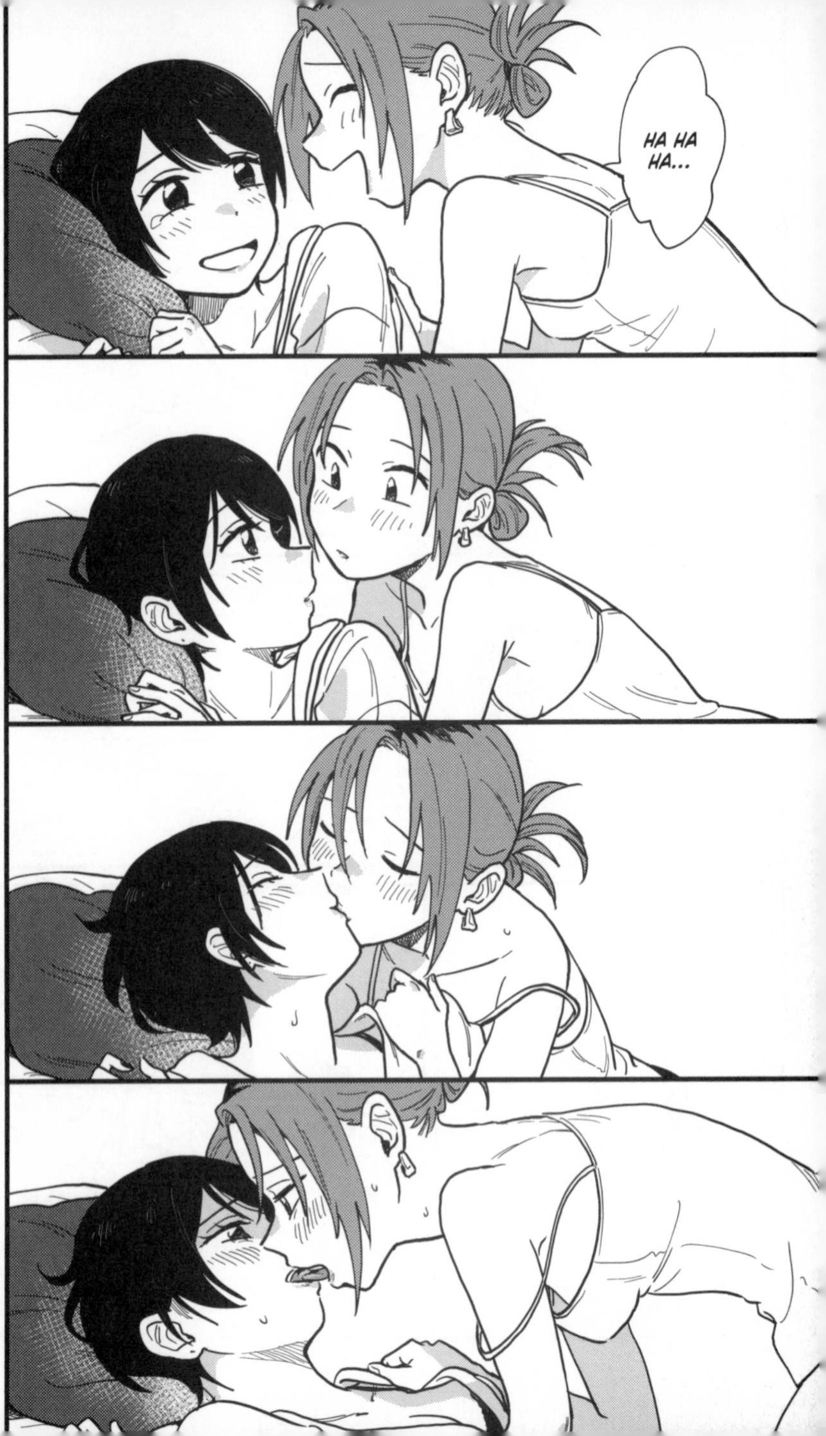
HA HA HA...

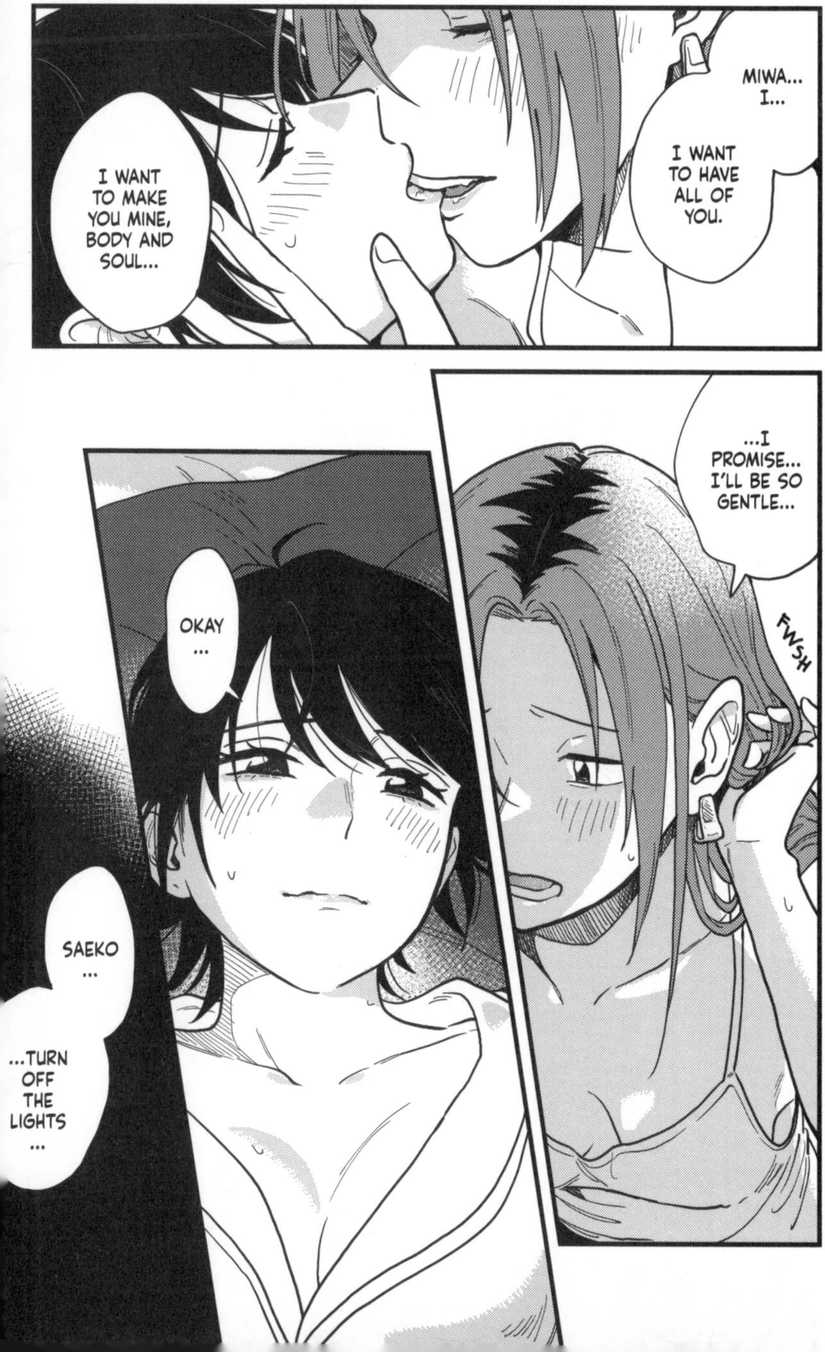
MIWA... I...
I WANT TO HAVE ALL OF YOU.
I WANT TO MAKE YOU MINE, BODY AND SOUL...
...I PROMISE... I'LL BE SO GENTLE...
FWSH
OKAY...
SAEKO...
...TURN OFF THE LIGHTS...

HOW DO WE
RELATIONSHIP?

And That's How It Goes

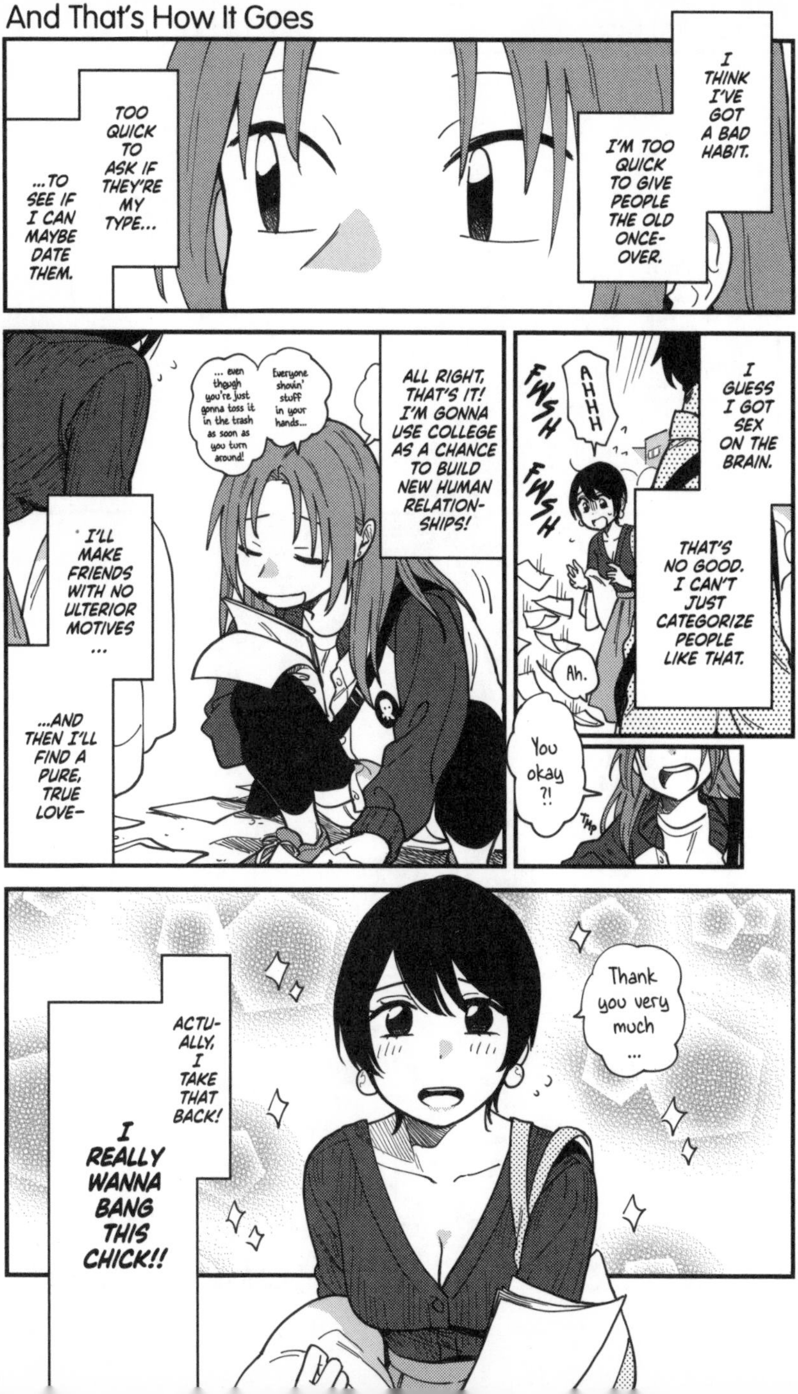
I THINK I'VE GOT A BAD HABIT.
I'M TOO QUICK TO GIVE PEOPLE THE OLD ONCE-OVER.
TOO QUICK TO ASK IF THEY'RE MY TYPE...
...TO SEE IF I CAN MAYBE DATE THEM.
I GUESS I GOT SEX ON THE BRAIN.
FWSH
FWSH
AHHHH
THAT'S NO GOOD. I CAN'T JUST CATEGORIZE PEOPLE LIKE THAT.
Ah.
You okay?!
TMP
ALL RIGHT, THAT'S IT! I'M GONNA USE COLLEGE AS A CHANCE TO BUILD NEW HUMAN RELATIONSHIPS!
Everyone shovin' stuff in your hands...
... even though you're just gonna toss it in the trash as soon as you turn around!
I'LL MAKE FRIENDS WITH NO ULTERIOR MOTIVES...
...AND THEN I'LL FIND A PURE, TRUE LOVE-
Thank you very much...
ACTUALLY, I TAKE THAT BACK!
I REALLY WANNA BANG THIS CHICK!!

Ideal First Kiss

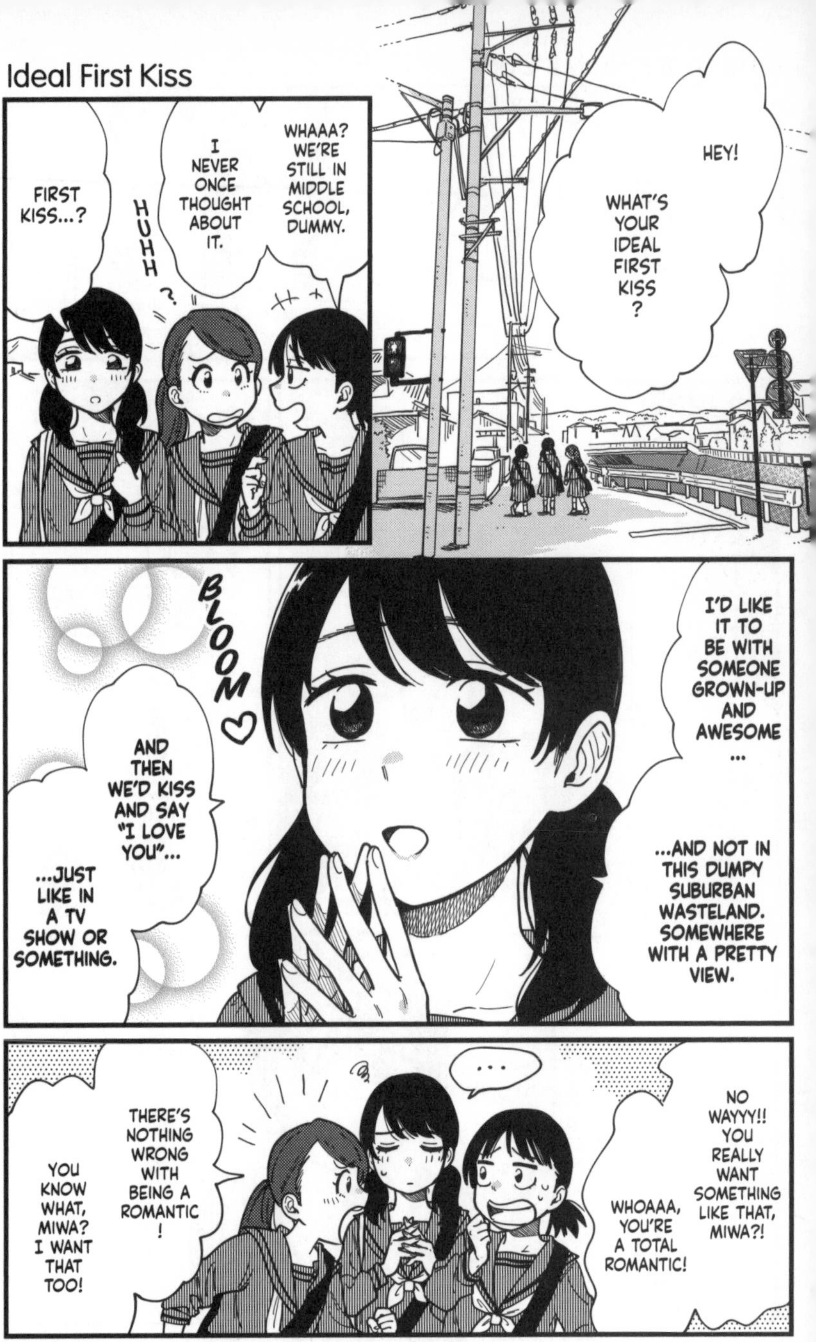
HEY!
WHAT'S YOUR IDEAL FIRST KISS?
WHAAA? WE'RE STILL IN MIDDLE SCHOOL, DUMMY.
I NEVER ONCE THOUGHT ABOUT IT.
HUHH
FIRST KISS...?
BLOOM
I'D LIKE IT TO BE WITH SOMEONE GROWN-UP AND AWESOME...
...AND NOT IN THIS DUMPY SUBURBAN WASTELAND. SOMEWHERE WITH A PRETTY VIEW.
AND THEN WE'D KISS AND SAY "I LOVE YOU"...
...JUST LIKE IN A TV SHOW OR SOMETHING.
NO WAYYY!! YOU REALLY WANT SOMETHING LIKE THAT, MIWA?!
...
WHOAAA, YOU'RE A TOTAL ROMANTIC!
THERE'S NOTHING WRONG WITH BEING A ROMANTIC!
YOU KNOW WHAT, MIWA? I WANT THAT TOO!

Their Reaction

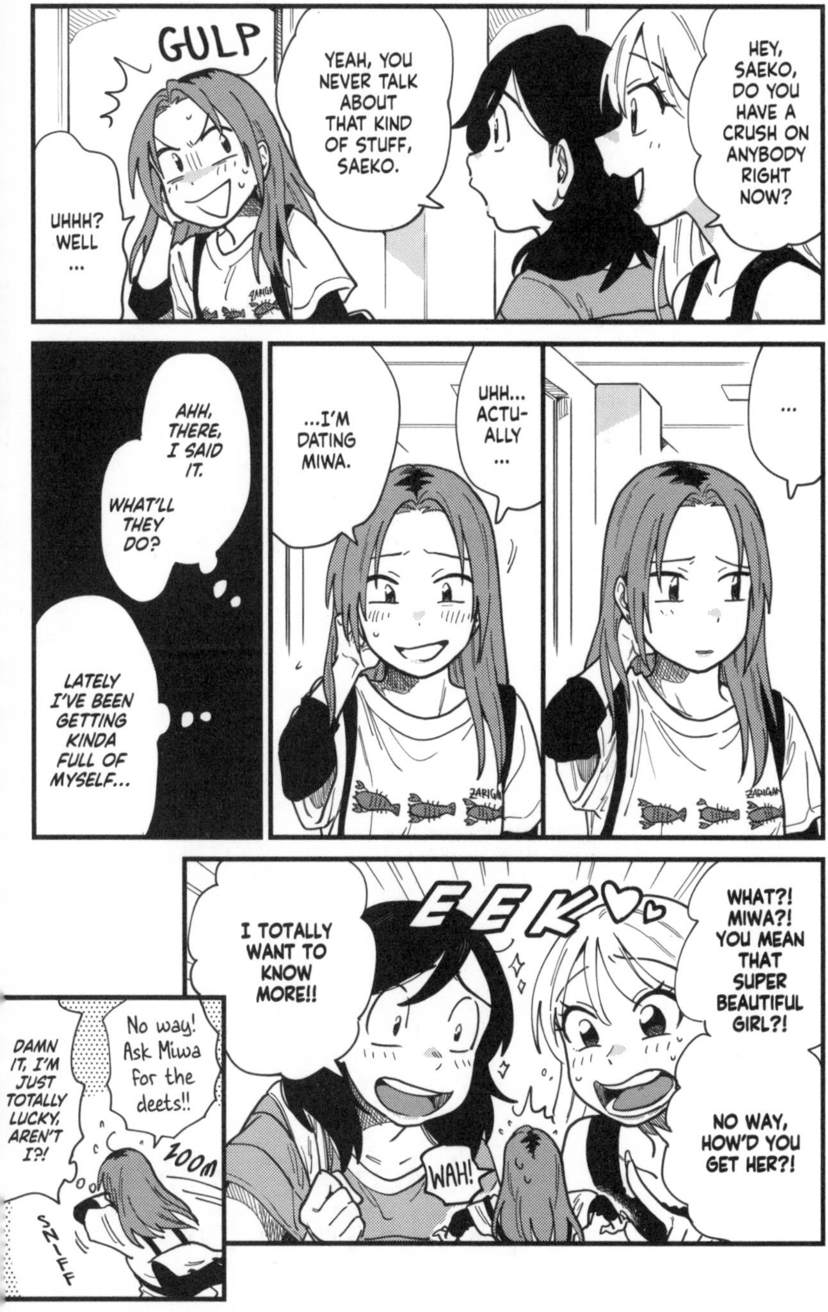
HEY, SAEKO, DO YOU HAVE A CRUSH ON ANYBODY RIGHT NOW?
YEAH, YOU NEVER TALK ABOUT THAT KIND OF STUFF, SAEKO.
GULP
UHHH? WELL ...
...
UHH... ACTU-ALLY ...
...I'M DATING MIWA.
AHH, THERE, I SAID IT.
WHAT'LL THEY DO?
LATELY I'VE BEEN GETTING KINDA FULL OF MYSELF...
WHAT?! MIWA?! YOU MEAN THAT SUPER BEAUTIFUL GIRL?!
EEK
I TOTALLY WANT TO KNOW MORE!!
NO WAY, HOW'D YOU GET HER?!
WAH!
No way! Ask Miwa for the deets!!
ZOOM
DAMN IT, I'M JUST TOTALLY LUCKY, AREN'T I?!
SNIFF

HOW DO WE
RELATIONSHIP?

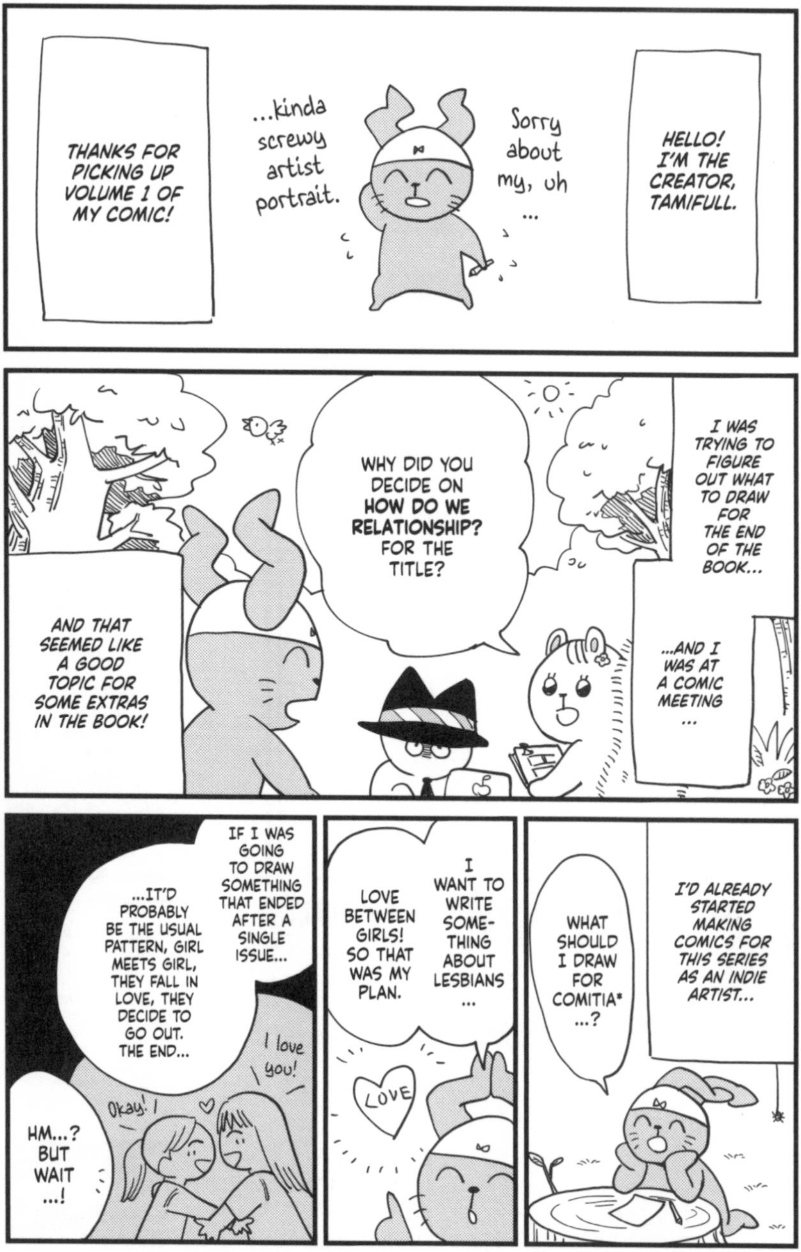
HELLO! I'M THE CREATOR, TAMIFULL.
Sorry about my, uh ...
...kinda screwy artist portrait.
THANKS FOR PICKING UP VOLUME 1 OF MY COMIC!
I WAS TRYING TO FIGURE OUT WHAT TO DRAW FOR THE END OF THE BOOK...
...AND I WAS AT A COMIC MEETING ...
WHY DID YOU DECIDE ON HOW DO WE RELATIONSHIP? FOR THE TITLE?
AND THAT SEEMED LIKE A GOOD TOPIC FOR SOME EXTRAS IN THE BOOK!
I'D ALREADY STARTED MAKING COMICS FOR THIS SERIES AS AN INDIE ARTIST...
WHAT SHOULD I DRAW FOR COMITIA* ...?
I WANT TO WRITE SOME-THING ABOUT LESBIANS ...
LOVE BETWEEN GIRLS! SO THAT WAS MY PLAN.
LOVE
IF I WAS GOING TO DRAW SOMETHING THAT ENDED AFTER A SINGLE ISSUE...
...IT'D PROBABLY BE THE USUAL PATTERN, GIRL MEETS GIRL, THEY FALL IN LOVE, THEY DECIDE TO GO OUT. THE END...
I love you!
Okay!
HM...? BUT WAIT ...!

*Comitia is an indie-comics event.

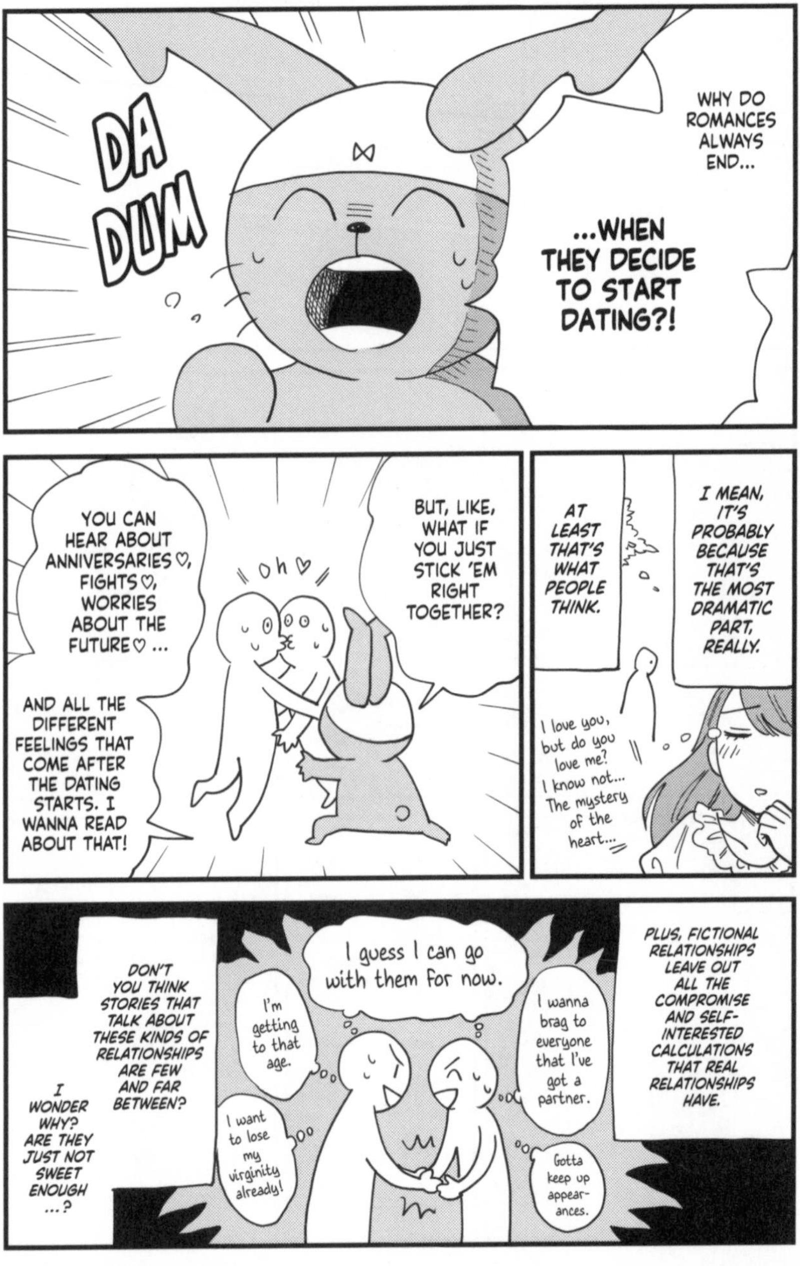
WHY DO ROMANCES ALWAYS END...
...WHEN THEY DECIDE TO START DATING?!
DA DUM
I MEAN, IT'S PROBABLY BECAUSE THAT'S THE MOST DRAMATIC PART, REALLY.
AT LEAST THAT'S WHAT PEOPLE THINK.
I love you, but do you love me? I know not... The mystery of the heart...
BUT, LIKE, WHAT IF YOU JUST STICK 'EM RIGHT TOGETHER?
oh ♡
YOU CAN HEAR ABOUT ANNIVERSARIES ♡, FIGHTS ♡, WORRIES ABOUT THE FUTURE ♡ ...
AND ALL THE DIFFERENT FEELINGS THAT COME AFTER THE DATING STARTS. I WANNA READ ABOUT THAT!
PLUS, FICTIONAL RELATIONSHIPS LEAVE OUT ALL THE COMPROMISE AND SELF-INTERESTED CALCULATIONS THAT REAL RELATIONSHIPS HAVE.
I guess I can go with them for now.
I wanna brag to everyone that I've got a partner.
Gotta keep up appear-ances.
I'm getting to that age.
I want to lose my virginity already!
DON'T YOU THINK STORIES THAT TALK ABOUT THESE KINDS OF RELATIONSHIPS ARE FEW AND FAR BETWEEN?
I WONDER WHY? ARE THEY JUST NOT SWEET ENOUGH ...?

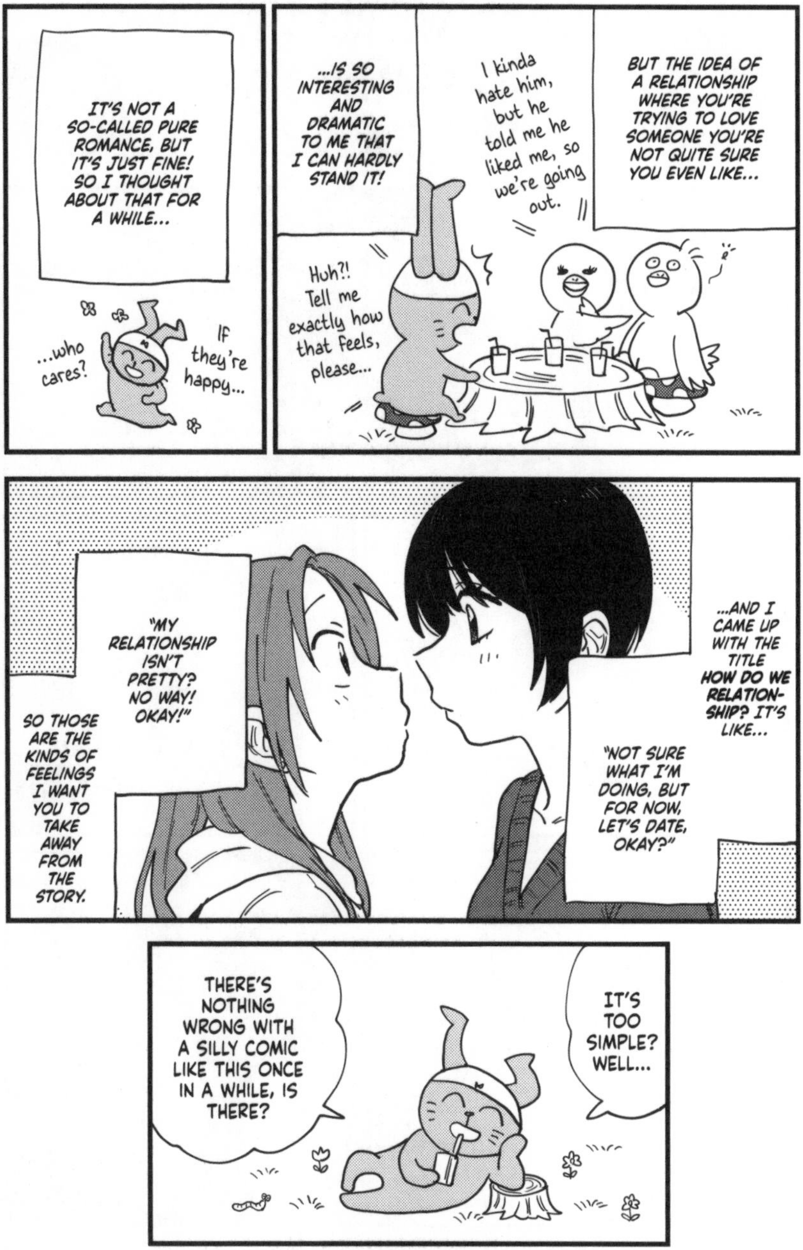
BUT THE IDEA OF A RELATIONSHIP WHERE YOU'RE TRYING TO LOVE SOMEONE YOU'RE NOT QUITE SURE YOU EVEN LIKE...
I kinda hate him, but he told me he liked me, so we're going out.
...IS SO INTERESTING AND DRAMATIC TO ME THAT I CAN HARDLY STAND IT!
Huh?! Tell me exactly how that feels, please...
IT'S NOT A SO-CALLED PURE ROMANCE, BUT IT'S JUST FINE! SO I THOUGHT ABOUT THAT FOR A WHILE...
If they're happy...
...who cares?
...AND I CAME UP WITH THE TITLE HOW DO WE RELATIONSHIP? IT'S LIKE...
"NOT SURE WHAT I'M DOING, BUT FOR NOW, LET'S DATE, OKAY?"
"MY RELATIONSHIP ISN'T PRETTY? NO WAY! OKAY!"
SO THOSE ARE THE KINDS OF FEELINGS I WANT YOU TO TAKE AWAY FROM THE STORY.
IT'S TOO SIMPLE? WELL...
THERE'S NOTHING WRONG WITH A SILLY COMIC LIKE THIS ONCE IN A WHILE, IS THERE?

The End

HOW DO WE RELATIONSHIP? VOLUME 1 COMMENTARY TRACK COMIC

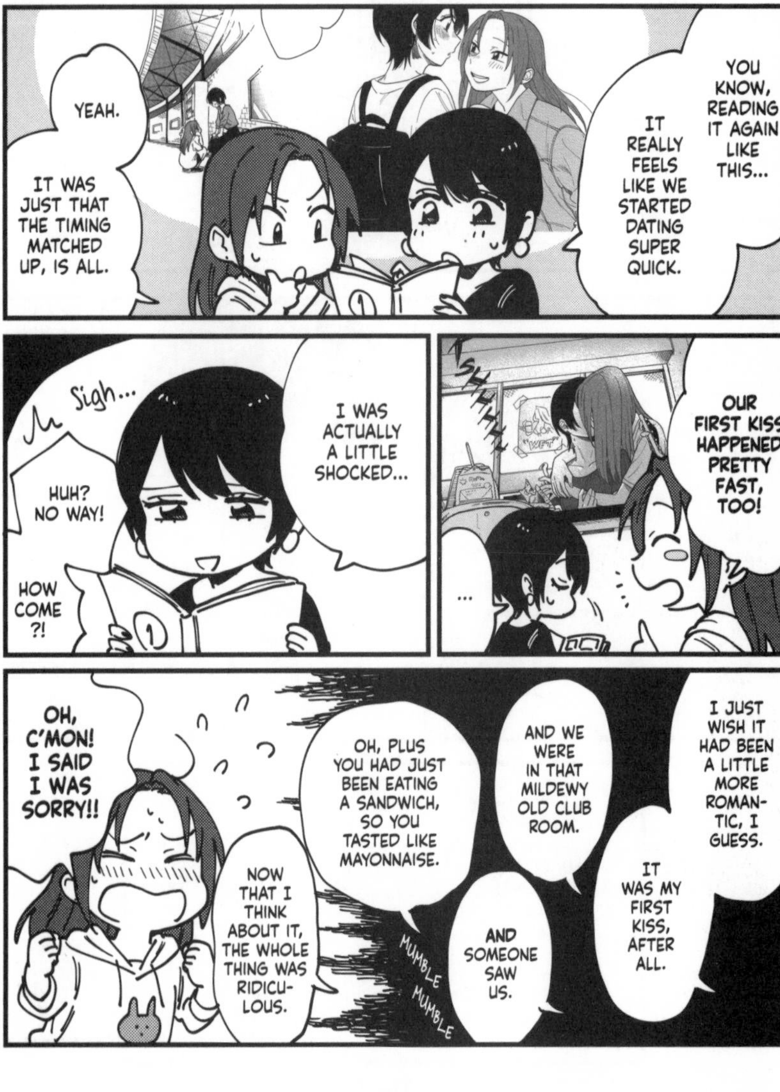
YOU KNOW, READING IT AGAIN LIKE THIS...
IT REALLY FEELS LIKE WE STARTED DATING SUPER QUICK.
YEAH.
IT WAS JUST THAT THE TIMING MATCHED UP, IS ALL.
OUR FIRST KISS HAPPENED PRETTY FAST, TOO!
...
I WAS ACTUALLY A LITTLE SHOCKED...
Sigh...
HUH? NO WAY!
HOW COME?!
I JUST WISH IT HAD BEEN A LITTLE MORE ROMANTIC, I GUESS.
IT WAS MY FIRST KISS, AFTER ALL.
AND WE WERE IN THAT MILDEWY OLD CLUB ROOM.
AND SOMEONE SAW US.
OH, PLUS YOU HAD JUST BEEN EATING A SANDWICH, SO YOU TASTED LIKE MAYONNAISE.
NOW THAT I THINK ABOUT IT, THE WHOLE THING WAS RIDICULOUS.
MUMBLE MUMBLE
OH, C'MON! I SAID I WAS SORRY!!

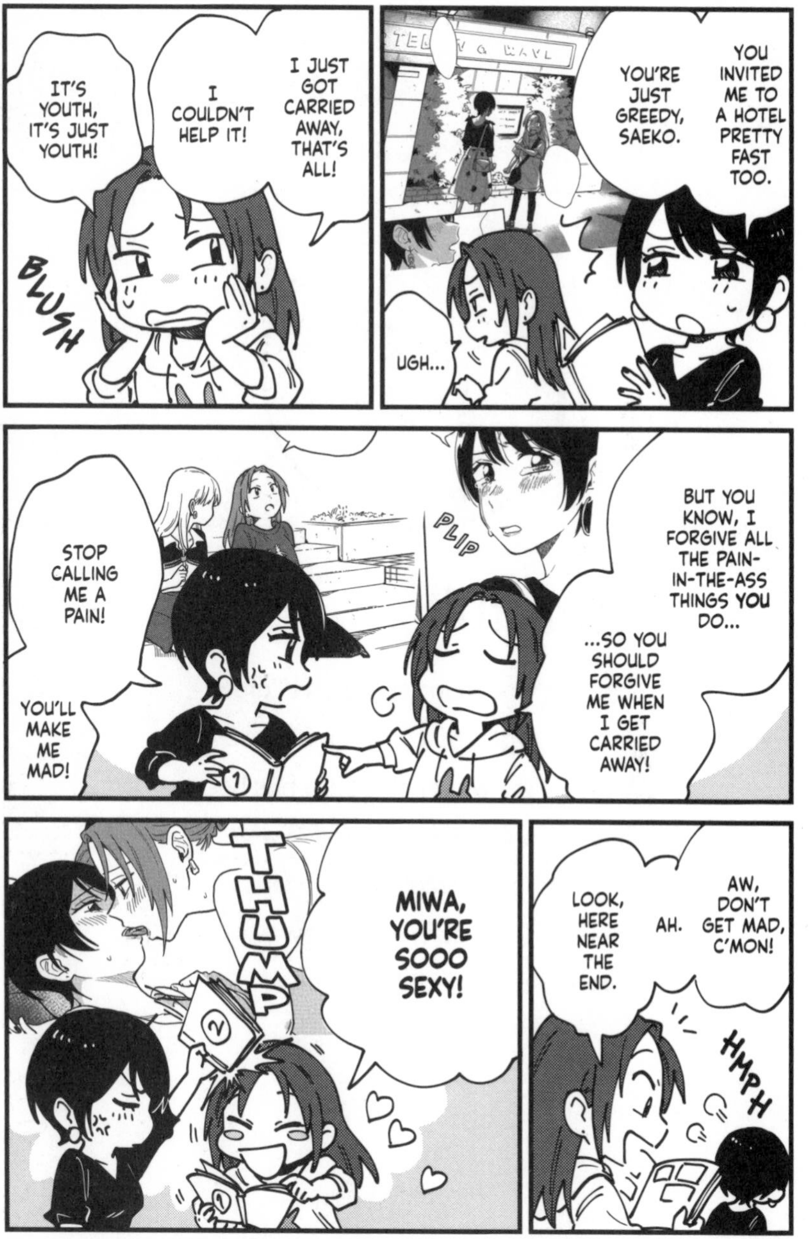
YOU INVITED ME TO A HOTEL PRETTY FAST TOO.
YOU'RE JUST GREEDY, SAEKO.
UGH...
I JUST GOT CARRIED AWAY, THAT'S ALL!
I COULDN'T HELP IT!
IT'S YOUTH, IT'S JUST YOUTH!
BLUSH
BUT YOU KNOW, I FORGIVE ALL THE PAIN-IN-THE-ASS THINGS YOU DO...
...SO YOU SHOULD FORGIVE ME WHEN I GET CARRIED AWAY!
PLIP
STOP CALLING ME A PAIN!
YOU'LL MAKE ME MAD!
AW, DON'T GET MAD, C'MON!
AH.
LOOK, HERE NEAR THE END.
HMPH
MIWA, YOU'RE SOOO SEXY!
THUMP

Continued in volume 2!

Tamifull

I feel as though the characters I drew in the margins of my notebook have come to life. Most of the story has been thought out already. It's as if Miwa and Saeko are creating their stories on their own, so I don't even know what'll happen in the next development.

HOW DO WE RELATIONSHIP?

VOLUME 1
VIZ MEDIA EDITION

STORY AND ART BY
Tamifull

ENGLISH TRANSLATION & ADAPTATION
Abby Lehrke

TOUCH-UP ART & LETTERING
Joanna Estep

DESIGN
Alice Lewis

EDITOR
Pancha Diaz

TSUKIATTE AGETEMO IIKANA Vol. 1
by TAMIFULL
© 2019 TAMIFULL
All rights reserved.
Original Japanese edition published by SHOGAKUKAN.
English translation rights in the United States of America, Canada, the United
Kingdom, Ireland, Australia and New Zealand arranged with SHOGAKUKAN.

Printed in Italy

Published by VIZ Media, LLC.
P.O. Box 77010
San Francisco, CA 94107

10 9 8 7 6 5 4 3
First printing, June 2020
Third printing, August 2022

PARENTAL ADVISORY
HOW DO WE RELATIONSHIP? is rated T+ for Older
Teen and is recommended for ages 16 and up. This
volume contains sexual situations and adult language.

 MEDIA
viz.com

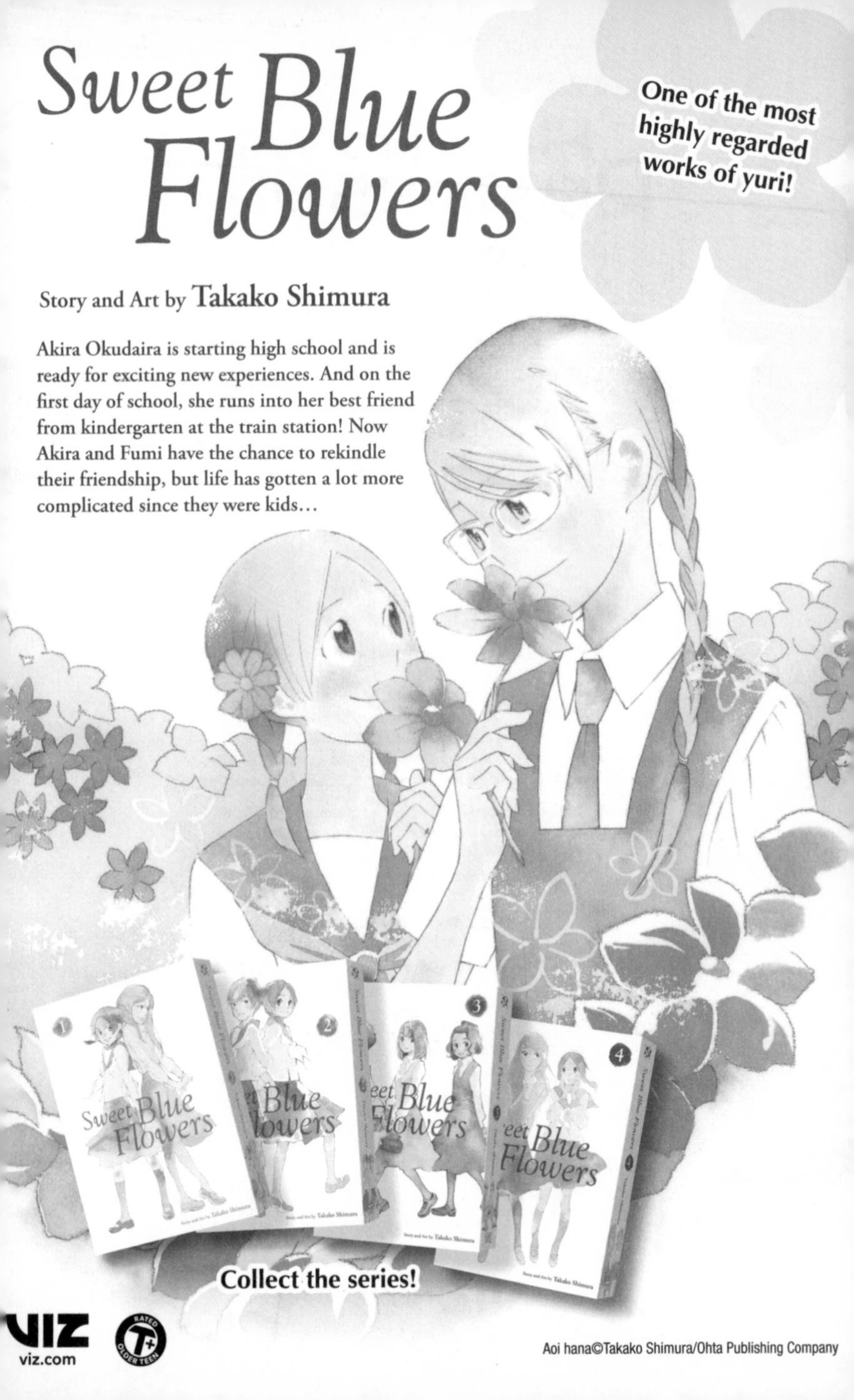
Sweet Blue Flowers
One of the most highly regarded works of yuri!
Story and Art by Takako Shimura
Akira Okudaira is starting high school and is ready for exciting new experiences. And on the first day of school, she runs into her best friend from kindergarten at the train station! Now Akira and Fumi have the chance to rekindle their friendship, but life has gotten a lot more complicated since they were kids…
Collect the series!
VIZ
viz.com
RATED T+ OLDER TEEN
Aoi hana©Takako Shimura/Ohta Publishing Company

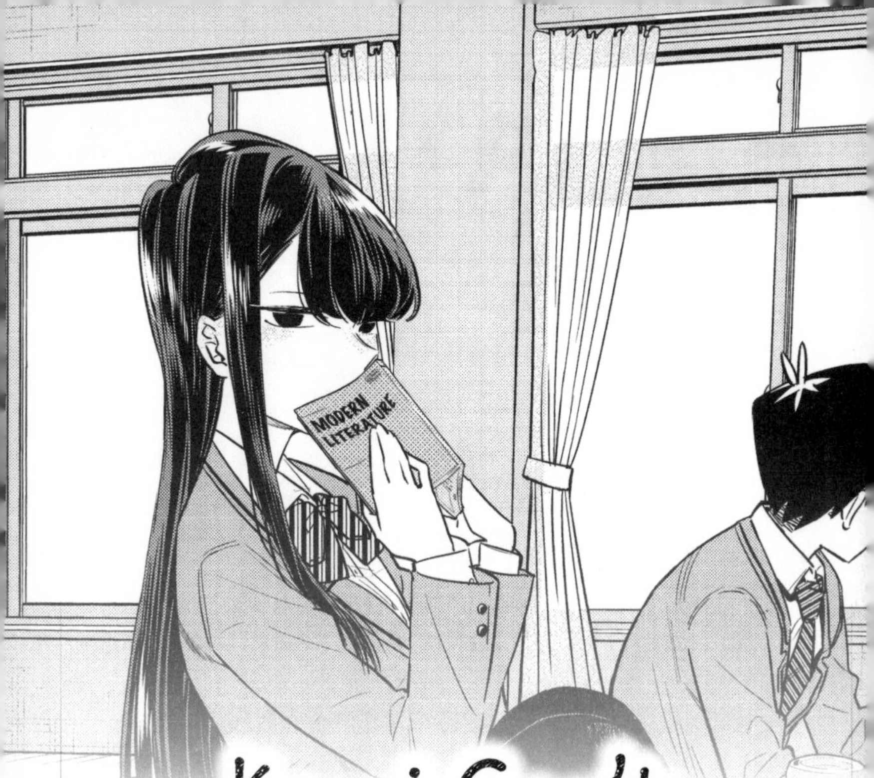
MODERN LITERATURE

Komi Can't Communicate

Story & Art by Tomohito Oda

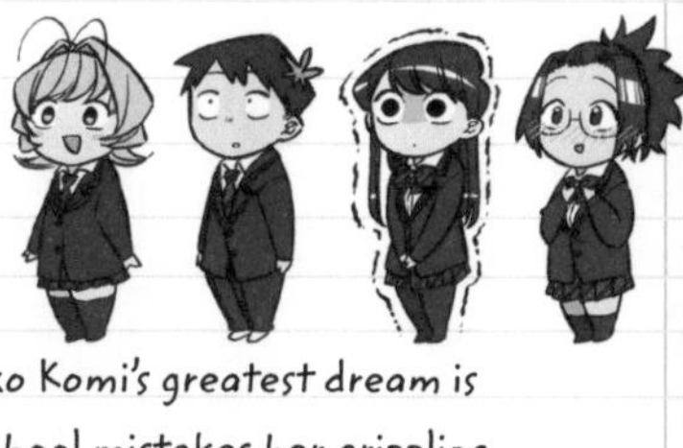

The journey to a hundred friends begins with a single conversation.

Socially anxious high school student Shoko Komi's greatest dream is to make some friends, but everyone at school mistakes her crippling social anxiety for cool reserve. With the whole student body keeping its distance and Komi unable to utter a single word, friendship might be forever beyond her reach.

VIZ

RATED T TEEN

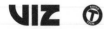

SHORTCAKE CAKE

STORY AND ART BY
suu Morishita

An unflappable girl and a cast of lovable roommates at a boardinghouse create bonds of friendship and romance!

When Ten moves out of her parents' home in the mountains to live in a boardinghouse, she finds herself becoming fast friends with her male roommates. But can love and romance be far behind?

RATED
T
TEEN

VIZ

Written by the creator of **High School Debut!**

MY love STORY!!

KAZUNE KAWAHARA — Story

ARUKO — Art

Takeo Goda is a **GIANT** guy with a **GIANT** *heart*

Too bad the girls don't want him!
(They want his good-looking best friend, Sunakawa.)

Used to being on the sidelines, Takeo simply stands tall and accepts his fate. But one day when he saves a girl named Yamato from a harasser on the train, his (love!) life suddenly takes an incredible turn!

www.viz.com

www.shojobeat.com

RATED T FOR TEEN
ratings.viz.com

ORE MONOGATARI!! © 2011 by Kazune Kawahara, Aruko/SHUEISHA Inc.

Honey So Sweet

Story and Art by Amu Meguro

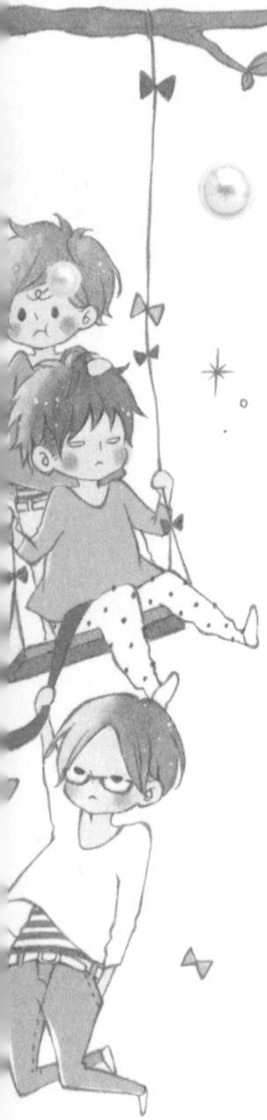

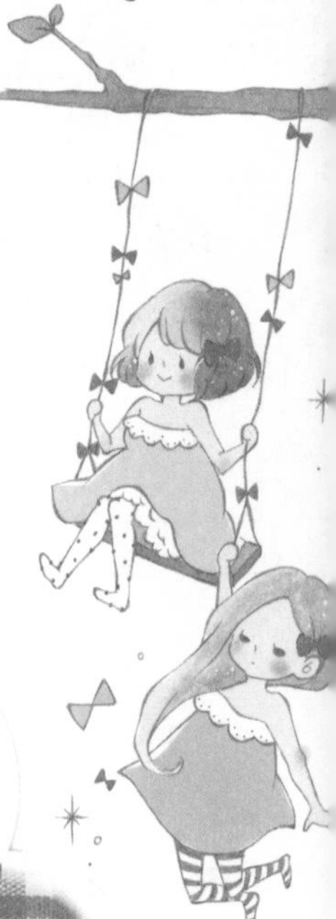

Little did Nao Kogure realize back in middle school that when she left an umbrella and a box of bandages in the rain for injured delinquent Taiga Onise that she would meet him again in high school. Nao wants nothing to do with the gruff and frightening Taiga, but he suddenly presents her with a huge bouquet of flowers and asks her to date him—with marriage in mind! Is Taiga really so scary, or is he a sweetheart in disguise?

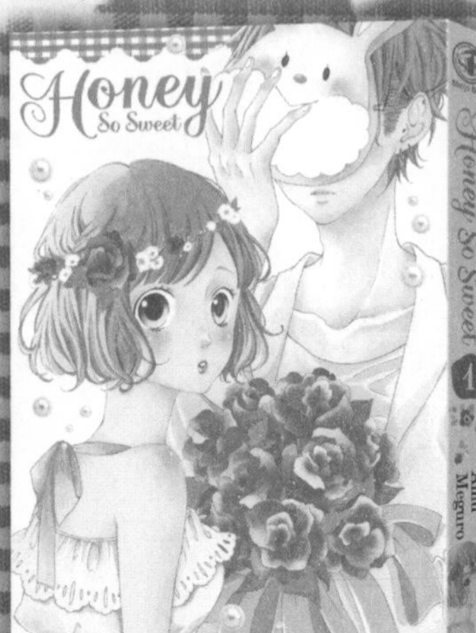
Honey So Sweet
Honey So Sweet 1
Amu Meguro
Story and Art by
Amu Meguro 1

Shojo Beat

RATED T FOR TEEN
ratings.viz.com

viz media
viz.com

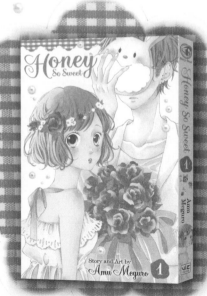